Lecture Notes in Computer Science 12161

More information about this series at http://www.springer.com/series/7410

Shlomi Dolev · Vladimir Kolesnikov ·
Sachin Lodha · Gera Weiss (Eds.)

Cyber Security Cryptography and Machine Learning

Fourth International Symposium, CSCML 2020
Be'er Sheva, Israel, July 2–3, 2020
Proceedings

Springer

Editors
Shlomi Dolev
Department of Computer Science
Ben-Gurion University of the Negev
Be'er Sheva, Israel

Vladimir Kolesnikov
School of Computer Science
Georgia Institute of Technology
Atlanta, GA, USA

Sachin Lodha
Tata Consultancy Services
Chennai, Tamil Nadu, India

Gera Weiss
Department of Computer Science
Ben-Gurion University of the Negev
Be'er Sheva, Israel

ISSN 0302-9743   ISSN 1611-3349   (electronic)
Lecture Notes in Computer Science
ISBN 978-3-030-49784-2   ISBN 978-3-030-49785-9   (eBook)
https://doi.org/10.1007/978-3-030-49785-9

LNCS Sublibrary: SL4 – Security and Cryptology

This Springer imprint is published by the registered company Springer Nature Switzerland AG
The registered company address is: Gewerbestrasse 11, 6330 Cham, Switzerland

Preface

CSCML, the International Symposium on Cyber Security Cryptography and Machine Learning, is an international forum for researchers, entrepreneurs, and practitioners in the theory, design, analysis, implementation, or application of cyber security, cryptography, and machine learning systems and networks, and, in particular, of conceptually innovative topics in these research areas.

Information technology has become crucial to our everyday lives, an indispensable infrastructure of our society and therefore a target for attacks by malicious parties. Cyber security is one of the most important fields of research these days because of these developments. Two of the (sometimes competing) fields of research, cryptography and machine learning, are the most important building blocks of cyber security.

Topics of interest for CSCML include: cyber security design; secure software development methodologies; formal methods, semantics, and verification of secure systems; fault tolerance, reliability, and availability of distributed secure systems; game-theoretic approaches to secure computing; automatic recovery self-stabilizing and self-organizing systems; communication, authentication, and identification security; cyber security for mobile and Internet of Things; cyber security of corporations; security and privacy for cloud, edge, and fog computing; cryptocurrency; blockchain; cryptography; cryptographic implementation analysis and construction; secure multi-party computation; privacy-enhancing technologies and anonymity; post-quantum cryptography and security; machine learning and big data; anomaly detection and malware identification; business intelligence and security; digital forensics, digital rights management; trust management and reputation systems; and information retrieval, risk analysis, and DoS.

The 4th CSCML took place during July 2–3, 2020, in Beer-Sheva, Israel. This year the conference was organized in cooperation with the International Association for Cryptologic Research (IACR) and selected papers will appear in a dedicated special issue in the *Information and Computation Journal*.

This volume contains 12 contributions selected by the Program Committee and 4 short papers. All submitted papers were read and evaluated by Program Committee members, assisted by external reviewers. We are grateful to the EasyChair system in assisting the reviewing process.

The support of Ben-Gurion University (BGU), in particular the BGU-NHSA, BGU Lynne and William Frankel Center for Computer Science, the BGU Cyber Security Research Center, the Department of Computer Science, TATA Consultancy Services, IBM, and Check Point are all gratefully acknowledged.

March 2020

Vladimir Kolesnikov
Gera Weiss
Shlomi Dolev
Sachin Lodha

Organization

CSCML, the International Symposium on Cyber Security Cryptography and Machine Learning, is an international forum for researchers, entrepreneurs, and practitioners in the theory, design, analysis, implementation, or application of cyber security, cryptography, and machine learning systems and networks, and, in particular, of conceptually innovative topics in the scope.

Founding Steering Committee

Orna Berry	DELLEMC, Israel
Shlomi Dolev (Chair)	Ben-Gurion University, Israel
Yuval Elovici	Ben-Gurion University, Israel
Bezalel Gavish	Southern Methodist University, USA
Ehud Gudes	Ben-Gurion University, Israel
Jonathan Katz	University of Maryland, USA
Rafail Ostrovsky	UCLA, USA
Jeffrey D. Ullman	Stanford University, USA
Kalyan Veeramachaneni	MIT, USA
Yaron Wolfsthal	IBM, Israel
Moti Yung	Columbia University and Google, USA

Organizing Committee

General Chairs

Shlomi Dolev	Ben-Gurion University, Israel
Sachin Lodha	Tata Consultancy Services, India

Program Chairs

Vladimir Kolesnikov	Georgia Institute of Technology, USA
Gera Weiss	Ben-Gurion University, Israel

Organizing Chair

Simcha Mahler	Ben-Gurion University, Israel

Program Committee

Adi Akavia	University of Haifa, Israel
Gilad Asharov	Bar-Ilan University, Israel
Manuel Barbosa	University of Porto, Portugal
Carlo Blundo	Università degli Studi di Salerno, Italy
Jacir Luiz Bordim	University of Brasilia, Brazil

Christina Boura	Versailles Saint-Quentin-en-Yvelines University, France
Ronen Brafman	Ben-Gurion University, Israel
Ashish Choudhury	IIIT Bangalore, India
Camil Demetrescu	Sapienza University of Rome, Italy
Orr Dunkelman	University of Haifa, Israel
Klim Efremenko	Ben-Gurion University, Israel
Marc Fischlin	TU Darmstadt, Germany
Dror Fried	The Open University, Israel
Benjamin Fuller	University of Connecticut, USA
Ehud Gudes	Ben-Gurion University, Israel
Shay Gueron	University of Haifa, Israel, and Amazon Web Services, USA
Ofer Hadar	Ben-Gurion University, Israel
David Heath	Georgia Institute of Technology, USA
Ben Kreuter	Google, USA
Miroslaw Kutylowski	Wroclaw University of Science and Technology, Poland
Mark Last	Ben-Gurion University, Israel
Riccardo Lazzeretti	Sapienza University of Rome, Italy
Daniel Masny	VISA Research, USA
Svetla Nikova	KU Leuven, Belgium
Ryo Nishimaki	NTT, Japan
Ariel Nof	Technion - Israel Institute of Technology, Israel
Giuseppe Persiano	Università degli Studi di Salerno, Italy
Thomas Peyrin	Nanyang Technological University, Singapore
Antigoni Polychroniadou	JPMorgan AI Research, USA
Alessandra Scafuro	NC State University, USA
Berry Schoenmakers	Eindhoven University of Technology, The Netherlands
Gil Segev	Hebrew University, Israel
Sandeep Shukla	IIT Kanpur, India
Anatoly Shusterman	Ben Gurion University, Israel
David Starobinski	Boston University, USA
Ni Trieu	Oregon State University, USA
Doug Tygar	UC Berkeley, USA
Daniele Venturi	Sapienza University of Rome, Italy
Ruoyu Wang	Arizona State University, USA
Avishay Yanay	Bar-Ilan University, Israel
Stefano Zanero	Politecnico di Milano, Italy
Vassilis Zikas	University of Edinburgh, UK

External Reviewers

Lilya Kraleva

Sponsors

  אוניברסיטת בן-גוריון בנגב
Ben-Gurion University of the Negev

  BGU NHSA

 ccs

 CBG
Cyber@Ben-Gurion
University of the Negev

TATA
CONSULTANCY
SERVICES

 Check Point
SOFTWARE TECHNOLOGIES LTD.

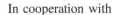 Springer

Lecture Notes in
Computer Science

 Information
and
Computation

 fresh
.fund

In cooperation with

Cyber Week
June 28th – July 2nd, 2020
Tel Aviv University, Israel

Contents

Single Tweakey Cryptanalysis
of Reduced-Round SKINNY-64

Orr Dunkelman, Senyang Huang, Eran Lambooij$^{(\boxtimes)}$, and Stav Perle

University of Haifa, Abba Khoushy Avenue 199, 3498838 Haifa, Israel
eranlambooij@gmail.com

Abstract. SKINNY is a lightweight tweakable block cipher which received a great deal of cryptanalytic attention following its elegant structure and efficiency. Inspired by the SKINNY competitions, multiple attacks on it were reported in different settings (e.g. single vs. related-tweakey) using different techniques (impossible differentials, meet-in-the-middle, etc.). In this paper we revisit some of these attacks, identify issues with several of them, and offer a series of improved attacks which were experimentally verified. Our best attack can attack up to 18 rounds using 2^{60} chosen ciphertexts data, 2^{116} time, and 2^{112} memory.

1 Introduction

Since lightweight cryptography gained academic interest in the early 2000's, many different block ciphers have been proposed. In parallel, the cryptographic community has slowly reached the understanding that "just" block ciphers are not always suitable or offer somewhat inferior solution, e.g., in the context of authenticated encryption. Hence, solutions such as tweakable block ciphers were introduced [9]. Obviously, with the need for lightweight cryptography, the need for lightweight tweakable block ciphers grew. SKINNY [4] is a lightweight tweakable block cipher using the tweakey framework [7]. SKINNY also lies in the basis of three of the submissions to the lightweight cryptography competition held by NIST (US National Institute of Standards and Technology), namely ForkAE [1], Romulus [6], and Skinny-AEAD [5].

This paper contains two main contributions: The paper first looks at extending truncated differential distinguishers of SKINNY by looking at the bias of the differences. Namely, we show that one can extend the probability 1 6-round truncated differential used before in [14] into a longer truncated differential. However, the new truncated differential has a lower probability, and instead of predicting the difference in some specific nibble, we predict its bias from random (in our case, the bias from $1/16$). We show that this bias can be observed after 7-, 8-, and even 9-rounds of SKINNY, where some nibbles are biased towards zero. This results in attacks on up to 15-round SKINNY-64-128 in time 2^{104} and data 2^{33}.

Our second contribution is to revisit previous impossible differential attacks against SKINNY. We show that some of these attacks had subtle flaws in them,

© Springer Nature Switzerland AG 2020
S. Dolev et al. (Eds.): CSCML 2020, LNCS 12161, pp. 1–17, 2020.
https://doi.org/10.1007/978-3-030-49785-9_1

which invalidate the attack. We then set to fix the attacks, which in turn reduce their number of rounds and increases their time and data complexity. The resulting attack is against 18-round SKINNY-64-128 in time 2^{116} and data 2^{60} chosen plaintexts.

1.1 Related Work

Besides being an interesting target of its own accord, the designers of SKINNY organized several cryptanalysis competitions to further inspire its analysis. This effort led to several papers focusing on the cryptanalysis of SKINNY.

Single Tweakey Analysis. For the case of single-tweakey model, a series of impossible differential attacks (against 18-round SKINNY-n-n, 20-round SKINNY-n-$2n$ and 22-round SKINNY-n-$3n$) based on an 11-round impossible differential distinguisher is presented in [14]. As we later show in Sect. 5, these attacks contain some flaw that increases their complexity and reduces the number of affected rounds. An additional impossible differential attack in the single-tweakey setting is presented against 17-round SKINNY-n-n and 19-round SKINNY-n-$2n$ in [16]. In addition to this, [12] presents zero-correlation linear attacks against 14-round SKINNY-64-64 and 18-round SKINNY-64-128 in the single-tweakey model.

Related Tweakey Analysis. An impossible differential attack against 19-round SKINNY-n-n, 23-round SKINNY-n-$2n$ and 27-round SKINNY-n-$3n$ in the related-tweakey model is presented in [10]. In addition, this paper presents several rectangle attacks against 27-round SKINNY-n-$3n$ in the related-tweakey model. Improved impossible differential attacks against these variants in the related-tweakey model are presented in [12]. Zero-correlation attacks in the related-tweakey settings are presented against 20-round SKINNY-64-64 and 23-round SKINNY-64-192 in [3].

Another impossible differential attack in the related-tweakey settings is described in [2] targeting 21-rounds of SKINNY-64-128. Furthermore, this attack is extended to 22-round and 23-round SKINNY-64-128 in the related-tweakey model. These results use the assumption that certain tweakey bits are public. Another related-tweak impossible differential attack is presented in [13]: an 18-round SKINNY-64-64 in the related-tweakey model, which can be transformed to an attack against 18-round SKINNY-64-128 in the related-tweakey model, with 96-bit secret key and 32-bit tweak.

A new automatic search tool for truncated differential characteristics using Mixed Integer Linear Programming is presented in [11]. This paper presents 8-round truncated differential characteristics with bias 2^{-8}, 9-round truncated differential characteristics with bias 2^{-20} and 10-round truncated differential characteristics with bias 2^{-40}.

Table 1 summarizes all previously published attacks against SKINNY-64-64 and SKINNY-64-128.

Table 1. Complexity of single-tweakey attacks against SKINNY-64

Key (bits)	Attack	Complexity				
		Rounds	Time	Data	Memory	Source
64	Zero-correlation	14	2^{62}	$2^{62.58}$	2^{64}	[12]
64	Impossible differential	17	$2^{61.8}$	$2^{59.5}$	$2^{49.6}$	[16]
64	Impossible differential[†]	18	$2^{57.1}$	$2^{47.52}$	$2^{58.52}$	[14]
128	Zero-correlation	18	2^{126}	$2^{62.68}$	2^{64}	[12]
128	Impossible differential	18	2^{116}	2^{60}	2^{112}	Sect. 5.2
128	Impossible differential	19	$2^{119.8}$	2^{62}	2^{110}	[16]
128	Impossible differential[†]	20	$2^{121.08}$	$2^{47.69}$	$2^{74.69}$	[14]

[†] As we show in Sect. 5, the attack is flawed.

1.2 Organization

This paper is organized as follows: In Sect. 2 we briefly reiterate the specification of SKINNY. After that the proposed distinguishers are described, discussing both the construction of the differential distinguisher (Sect. 3) and the extension to biased differential distinguishers (Sect. 4). In Sect. 4.4 we use the previously described distinguishers to construct key recovery attacks. Section 5, contains a discussion of a previous impossible differential analysis of SKINNY, which is fixed in Sect. 5.2, and improved upon in Sect. 5.3. Finally, Sect. 6 summarizes this paper.

2 Specification of SKINNY

SKINNY is a family of lightweight tweakable block ciphers using a substitution-permutation network (SPN) structure. The variants of SKINNY are denoted by SKINNY-n-t, where n represents the block size ($n \in \{64, 128\}$) and t represents the tweakey size ($t \in \{n, 2n, 3n\}$). Namely, the six variants of SKINNY are SKINNY-64-64, SKINNY-64-128, SKINNY-64-192, SKINNY-128-128, SKINNY-128-256, and SKINNY-128-384 with 32, 36, 40, 40, 48 and 56 rounds, respectively. Both the 64-bit and 128-bit internal states are represented as an array of 4×4 cells. The first row contains nibbles 0 to 3 (where 0 is the leftmost nibble, 3 is the rightmost nibble), the second row contains nibbles 4 to 7, etc. The cell is a nibble in case of 64-bit version and a byte in case of 128-bit version. There are 5 operations in each round (depicted in Fig. 1):

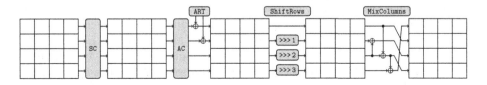

Fig. 1. The SKINNY round function.

1. SubCells (SC): The non-linear layer applies an ℓ-bit S-box on each cell, where $\ell \in \{4, 8\}$.
2. AddConstants (AC): This step XOR's three cells of round constants to the most significant three cells of the internal state.
3. AddRoundTweakey (ART): In this step, the tweakey bits are XORed to the first two lines of the internal state.
4. ShiftRows (SR): The second, third, and fourth rows of the internal state are right-rotated by 1 cell, 2 cells, and 3 cells, respectively.
5. MixColumns (MC): Each column of the internal state is multiplied by the following binary matrix:

$$M = \begin{bmatrix} 1 & 0 & 1 & 0 \\ 1 & 0 & 0 & 0 \\ 0 & 1 & 1 & 0 \\ 1 & 0 & 1 & 0 \end{bmatrix} \tag{1}$$

We omit the tweakey schedule as this is not used in our attacks, and refer the interested reader to [4].

3   Differential Distinguisher

The attacks in this paper are built using extensions of the 6-round truncated differential characteristic used in [14]. The characteristic is depicted in Fig. 2. The colored nibbles depict non-zero differences in the differential characteristic, while the black nibbles signify unknown differences. The distinguisher starts with a single active nibble, nibble 12, which after six rounds leads to four nibbles: 4, 7, 9, and 15, that necessarily have a non-zero difference. The distinguisher can be rotated row-wise, e.g., if we take nibble 13 to be active, after six rounds nibbles: 4, 5, 10, 12, are non-zero, etc.

The six-round characteristic can be extended by one, two, or three rounds by the use of structures at the beginning of the characteristic (see Fig. 3). This technique can also be used in the distinguishers discussed in Sect. 4. Extending by one round does not incur any cost with respect to the data and time complexity since the SC layer is before the key addition. The two and three round extension respectively increase the data complexity by 2^8 and 2^{20} with respect to the non extended distinguisher. The time complexity is increased by 2^4 and 2^{20} due to the added key guessing needed.

3.1   Key Recovery Attack

The first attack that we look at is a 10-round attack using the basic 6-round distinguisher. As can be seen in Fig. 2: if we have an input difference with one active nibble, i.e. nibble 12, the output difference after 6 rounds in nibbles 4, 7, 9, and 15 are necessarily non-zero. This distinguisher can be transformed into an impossible differential attack. We can filter out wrong keys by partially decrypting the ciphertext, such that we recover the difference in one of these

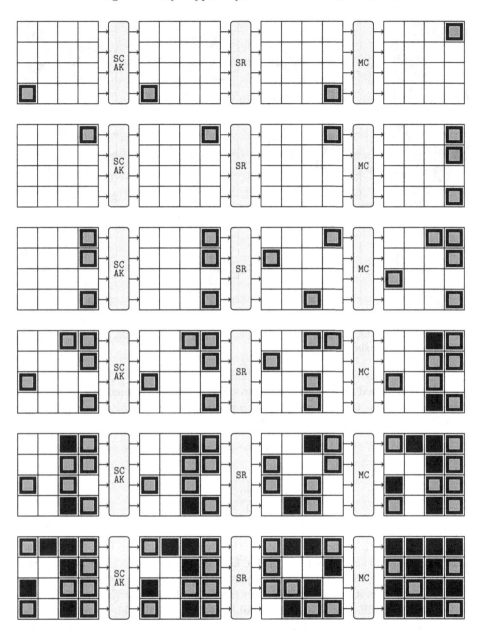

Fig. 2. The basic six round differential. White cells are zero differences, colored cells are non-zero differences and black cells have unknown differences. (Color figure online)

(necessarily non-zero) nibbles, and discard the key if we find a pair for which the difference in one of these nibbles is 0. On average we need to test 2^4 pairs to discard a key. Nevertheless, to filter out all but the correct key, with high

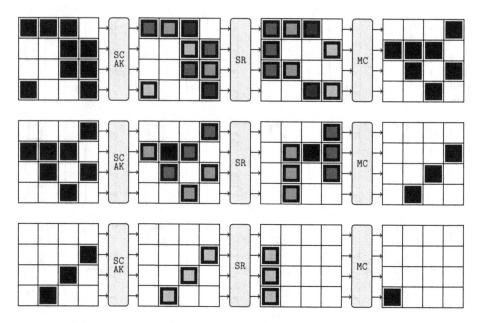

Fig. 3. Extending the characteristics by one, two, or three rounds. Before the main differential distinguisher (Fig. 2).

probability, we need more data. The probability that a wrong key passes the filter is $1 - 2^{-4}$, thus the probability that a wrong key passes x filters is $(1 - 2^{-4})^x$. Given 2^k candidate keys, we get the following equation:

$$(1 - 2^{-4})^x = 2^{-k} \tag{2}$$

Giving,

$$x = \frac{k \log(2)}{\log(1 - 2^{-4})}. \tag{3}$$

For $k = 128$ we get: $x \approx 1374 \approx 2^{10.4}$, which is the maximum amount of data needed to mount this attack. Note that this is an upper bound on the amount of data needed. If the number of possible keys is smaller the amount of data can also be smaller, but to simplify the analysis we chose to keep the amount of data needed constant as it does not affect the time complexities of the attacks.

We denote a difference in the i-th nibble by Δ_i. Using this 6-round distinguisher $\Delta_{12} \rightarrow \Delta_{15}$ we construct a 10-round attack with four rounds of key recovery, for which we need to guess 6 nibbles ($= 6 \cdot 4$ bits) of key material. This results in an attack which uses $2^{6 \cdot 4 + 4} = 2^{28}$ 4-round decryptions and

$$\frac{24 \cdot \log(2)}{\log(1 - 2^{-4})} \approx 258 \approx 2^8$$

data, and 2^8 memory to store the data. Analogous to this we can construct the other attacks using the 6-round distinguisher. Note that in this instance we computed the exact amount of data needed for the attack to succeed, in the summary given in Table 6 we took the maximum amount of data for the attacks of this form, due to the small difference in complexity.

4   A Biased Differential Distinguisher

The attack described in Sect. 4.4 is based on the observation that after seven rounds, in some nibbles of the state, the probability that the nibble difference is 0 is larger or smaller than 2^{-4}, i.e., it is biased with respect to the random case. We first show how to efficiently compute the bias of a difference in a state nibble after r rounds. Then, we list the computed biases after seven and eight rounds in Tables 2 and 3, respectively. Afterwards, we show the results of our experiments that confirm the existence of the bias in the output difference. It is worth noting that in many cases, the observed bias is higher than expected. In other words, the analysis offers evaluation of explainable attacks (and suggests a "worst-case" analysis[1]). Note that although the results discussed here are for the 64-bit version of SKINNY they can easily be extended to SKINNY-128. We expect that the biases of SKINNY-128-128 are squared, i.e., they are expected to exist, but their validation would be infeasible.

4.1   Computing Biases of Differences in Nibbles

To compute the biases in the nibbles after one round we need to compute the biases after each step of SKINNY (AC, ART, MC, SC, SR). The differences are unaffected by the tweakey addition (ART) or the add constant (AC), thus we can ignore these step. The SR operation permutes the nibbles in the state. The other two operations SC and MC change the biases in a more elaborate way and are discussed below. Note that as we do not take the key schedule in consideration we assume independence between the rounds of the cipher.

The bias towards each difference value in a nibble is stored in a vector v, where $v[\Delta]$ contains the bias for the output difference Δ. I.e., v contains 16 different biases, one for each possible difference in the nibble. The state of a cipher is a vector of bias vectors denoted by W, where $W[i]$ denotes the bias vector for state nibble i, with in this case $0 \leq i < 16$. In other words, $W[i][j]$ contains the bias of the i-th nibble of the state with respect to the difference j.

The SC layer applies a non-linear S-box to each nibble in the state. We can compute the biases after the SC layer by using the Difference Distribution Table (DDT) of SKINNY's S-box. Recall that the j-th row of the DDT contains the probability distribution of the output differences given an input difference with value j. We denote the j-th row of the DDT as DDT$[j]$. The equation for computing the biases for a nibble after the SC layer is given in Eq. 4.

$$W'[i] = \sum_{j=0}^{j<16} W[i][j] \cdot \frac{\text{DDT}[i]}{16} \tag{4}$$

---

[1] One can argue that the only way to verify the full attacks is to run then in practice. However, the running time of most of the attacks is far from being feasible.

To compute the bias after the MC layer we multiply each column of the state with the matrix M (Eq. 1) where we define the dot product used in the matrix multiplication between two bias vectors v, w as:

$$w'[i] = \sum_{j=0}^{j<16} w[j] \cdot v[j \oplus i] \tag{5}$$

Obviously, there is a subtle underlying assumption that the differences in different nibbles are independent of each other for the calculation to be accurate (this actually echoes the Markov cipher assumption [8]). As our verification experiments show, this assumption does not always hold, but luckily in our case, on our favor.

We calculated the biases for 7 and 8 rounds of SKINNY and put the results in Tables 2 and 3. From Table 3 we can see that after 8 rounds of SKINNY we have a bias of $\approx 2^{-19.5}$ when inserting a difference of A into nibble C.

One interesting observation, although the effect on the attack is small, is that for some entries the choice of the input difference has an influence on the bias. In some cases this difference is quite significant, but for the biases that we use in the attack the difference is too small to be of any significance. Nevertheless, in other cases, it can be useful to look at different input differences when doing this analysis. To verify the results we ran some experiments, the results of these experiments can be found in Table 4.

We note that the experimental verification suggests that the biases exists, and in some cases it appears the the real bias is larger than we expect. A probable cause for this phenomenon is dependencies between rounds.

4.2 Experimental Verification

We have experimentally verified the computed biases. As listed in Table 4, we can see that in most of the cases, the observed bias either confirms the calculation, or is significantly higher. As our calculation assumes independence it is very likely that the higher biases are the result of dependencies between rounds. The experiments were done using 2^{40} samples under a single key. Hence, reported biases of less than 2^{-19}, are expected to take place at random. We mark in Table 4 the entries which were verified beyond the random case.

4.3 Decreasing the Time and Data Complexity

To distinguish the permutation from random using the bias in the difference, we need to verify the presence of the bias. In this section we discuss the number of samples we need to verify the bias. The cost of verifying the bias directly affects the time and data complexity of the attacks.

Lemma 1 (Number of samples). *Given a differential characteristic with a bias b and block size n we need 2^ℓ samples such that the biased distribution is*

Table 2. The absolute bias ($\log_2$) with respect to zero of each output nibble after 7 full rounds of SKINNY starting with only a difference in nibble 12. The bold values in the table are verified experimentally, while for the underlined values we found higher biases that could be verified experimentally.

Nibble	Input nibble difference value														
	1	2	3	4	5	6	7	8	9	10	11	12	13	14	15
0	−26.7	−27.1	−27.4	−27.2	−27.2	−27.2	−27.4	−27.0	−27.0	−27.0	−26.7	−26.7	−26.7	−27.4	−27.2
1	−61.3	−63.9	−66.1	−64.0	−64.5	−64.2	−66.3	−62.4	−62.4	−63.0	−60.9	−61.4	−61.4	−66.2	−64.6
2	−41.0	−42.1	−42.9	−42.1	−42.2	−42.1	−43.0	−41.6	−41.6	−41.5	−40.8	−41.1	−41.1	−42.9	−42.3
3	−19.6	−19.6	−19.6	−19.6	−19.6	−19.6	−19.6	−19.6	−19.6	−19.5	−19.5	−19.6	−19.6	−19.6	−19.6
4	−7.9	−7.9	−7.9	−7.9	−7.9	−7.9	−7.9	−7.9	−7.9	−7.9	−7.9	−7.9	−7.9	−7.9	−7.9
5	−25.4	−26.4	−27.3	−26.5	−26.7	−26.6	−27.4	−25.9	−25.9	−26.1	−25.2	−25.5	−25.5	−27.3	−26.7
6	−29.4	−30.4	−31.2	−30.4	−30.6	−30.4	−31.3	−29.9	−29.9	−29.9	−29.2	−29.4	−29.4	−31.2	−30.6
7	−7.9	−7.9	−7.9	−7.9	−7.9	−7.9	−7.9	−7.9	−7.9	−7.9	−7.9	−7.9	−7.9	−7.9	−7.9
8	−11.7	−11.8	−11.8	−11.8	−11.8	−11.8	−11.8	−11.8	−11.8	−11.7	−11.7	−11.7	−11.7	−11.8	−11.8
9	−14.5	−15.1	−15.6	−15.2	−15.3	−15.3	−15.7	−14.7	−14.7	−15.0	−14.5	−14.6	−14.6	−15.6	−15.3
10	−15.1	−15.5	−15.7	−15.5	−15.6	−15.5	−15.7	−15.3	−15.3	−15.4	−15.2	−15.2	−15.2	−15.7	−15.6
11	−21.9	−22.7	−23.4	−22.7	−22.9	−22.8	−23.5	−22.2	−22.2	−22.4	−21.7	−21.9	−21.9	−23.4	−22.9
12	−15.6	−15.7	−15.7	−15.7	−15.7	−15.7	−15.7	−15.7	−15.7	−15.6	−15.5	−15.6	−15.6	−15.7	−15.7
13	−35.9	−37.5	−38.9	−37.6	−38.0	−37.8	−39.0	−36.5	−36.5	−37.1	−35.7	−36.0	−36.0	−38.9	−38.1
14	−37.1	−38.2	−39.0	−38.2	−38.3	−38.2	−39.1	−37.7	−37.7	−37.6	−36.9	−37.2	−37.2	−39.0	−38.4
15	−11.8	−11.8	−11.8	−11.8	−11.8	−11.8	−11.8	−11.8	−11.8	−11.8	−11.8	−11.8	−11.8	−11.8	−11.8

Table 3. The absolute bias ($\log_2$) with respect to zero of each output nibble after 8 full rounds of SKINNY starting with only a difference in nibble 12. The bold values in the table are verified experimentally, while for the underlined values we found higher biases that could be verified experimentally.

Nibble	Input nibble difference value														
	1	2	3	4	5	6	7	8	9	10	11	12	13	14	15
0	−77.4	−79.9	−81.8	−80.1	−80.5	−80.3	−82.0	−78.7	−78.7	−79.2	−77.2	−77.7	−77.7	−81.9	−80.6
1	−120	−124	−128	−124	−125	−125	−128	−122	−122	−122	−119	−120	−120	−128	−125
2	−64.3	−65.4	−66.4	−65.5	−65.5	−65.4	−66.4	−64.9	−64.9	−64.8	−64.1	−64.3	−64.3	−66.4	−65.6
3	−49.5	−50.2	−50.8	−50.2	−50.3	−50.3	−50.8	−49.8	−49.8	−49.9	−49.3	−49.5	−49.5	−50.8	−50.4
4	−26.7	−27.1	−27.4	−27.2	−27.2	−27.2	−27.4	−27.0	−27.0	−27.0	−26.7	−26.7	−26.7	−27.4	−27.2
5	−61.3	−63.9	−66.1	−64.0	−64.5	−64.2	−66.3	−62.4	−62.4	−63.0	−60.9	−61.4	−61.4	−66.2	−64.6
6	−41.0	−42.1	−42.9	−42.1	−42.2	−42.1	−43.0	−41.6	−41.6	−41.5	−40.8	−41.1	−41.1	−42.9	−42.3
7	−19.6	−19.6	−19.6	−19.6	−19.6	−19.6	−19.6	−19.6	−19.6	−19.5	−19.5	−19.6	−19.6	−19.6	−19.6
8	−22.9	−21.3	−23.5	−23.3	−23.4	−23.3	−23.5	−23.2	−23.2	−23.2	−22.9	−23.0	−23.0	−23.5	−23.4
9	−29.7	−30.5	−31.2	−30.5	−30.7	−30.6	−31.3	−30.0	−30.0	−30.2	−29.5	−29.7	−29.7	−31.2	−30.7
10	−36.9	−38.1	−39.0	−38.2	−38.4	−38.3	−39.1	−37.5	−37.5	−37.7	−36.8	−37.0	−37.0	−39.0	−38.4
11	−43.8	−45.4	−46.7	−45.4	−45.8	−45.6	−46.9	−44.5	−44.5	−44.8	−43.5	−43.9	−43.9	−46.8	−45.8
12	−41.7	−42.5	−43.0	−42.6	−42.6	−42.6	−43.0	−42.2	−42.2	−42.3	−41.7	−41.8	−41.8	−43.0	−42.7
13	−83.0	−86.5	−89.4	−86.6	−87.3	−86.9	−89.7	−84.5	−84.5	−85.2	−82.5	−83.2	−83.2	−89.5	−87.5
14	−52.6	−53.7	−54.6	−53.7	−53.9	−53.8	−54.7	−53.2	−53.2	−53.1	−52.4	−52.7	−52.7	−54.6	−53.9
15	−34.0	−34.6	−35.2	−34.7	−34.8	−34.8	−35.2	−34.2	−34.2	−34.5	−33.9	−34.0	−34.0	−35.2	−34.8

u *standard deviations away from the distribution of differences for a random permutation. Where:*

$$\ell \geq 2b - n - \log(1 - 2^{-n}) + 2 \cdot \log(u)$$

Table 4. The absolute bias ($\log_2$) with respect to zero for each output nibble after 7 and 8 rounds. The biases are computed using 2^{40} samples. The statistical significant results are marked in bold.

Nibble	Bias after			
	7 rounds		8 rounds	
	Experiment	Theory	Experiment	Theory
0	**−16.986**	−26.7	−22.067	−75.4
1	−19.610	−61.3	−23.053	−120
2	−20.364	−41.0	−21.580	−64.3
3	**−15.505**	−19.6	−22.734	−49.5
4	**−7.535**	−7.9	**−18.696**	−26.7
5	−11.960	−25.4	−20.470	−61.3
6	−15.790	−29.4	−23.493	−41.0
7	**−7.580**	−7.9	**−15.699**	−19.6
8	**−9.884**	−11.7	**−17.772**	−22.9
9	−10.836	−14.5	−19.612	−29.7
10	**−11.756**	−15.5	−20.473	−36.9
11	**−14.620**	−21.9	−20.051	−43.8
12	−10.446	−15.6	−19.454	−41.7
13	−19.297	−35.9	−21.876	−83.0
14	**−18.006**	−37.1	−21.753	−52.6
15	−11.382	−11.8	−24.723	−34.0

Proof. The number of output differences observed after $N = 2^\ell$ samples is binomially distributed with $p_1 = 2^{-n}$ in the random permutation case and $p_2 = 2^{-n} + 2^{-b}$ in the construction case. Due to the high number of samples we are working with we can assume the distributions to be normal. The two distributions are distinguishable with a non-negligible probability when the means are at least u standard deviations apart from each other. Thus we look at the case where:

$$\mu_1 + u \cdot sd_1 \leq \mu_2$$
$$N \cdot p_1 + u \cdot \sqrt{N \cdot p_1 \cdot (1 - p_1)} \leq N \cdot p_2$$
$$u^2 \cdot 2^{-\ell} \cdot 2^{-n}(1 - 2^{-n}) \leq 2^{-2b}$$
$$\ell \geq 2b - n - \log(1 - 2^{-n}) + 2 \cdot \log(u)$$

Following Lemma 1, we obtain that $\ell \geq 2b + 3.450$, for the case that the number of guessed keys, $k' = 128$, and the blocksize $n = 4$.

$$\ell \geq 2b - n - \log(1 - 2^{-n}) + 2 \cdot \log(\text{erf}(\frac{k'}{\sqrt{2}}))$$

$$\ell \geq 2b + 3.451$$

4.4 Key Recovery Attacks

Table 5. For each nibble position the number of key nibbles that have to be guessed to partially decrypt the nibble for the given number of rounds of SKINNY-64-128 is given in the table.

Rounds	Nibble position															
	0	1	2	3	4	5	6	7	8	9	10	11	12	13	14	15
1	1	1	1	1	1	1	1	1	0	0	0	0	0	0	0	0
2	2	2	2	2	2	2	2	2	1	1	1	1	1	1	1	1
3	3	3	3	3	5	5	5	5	3	3	3	3	3	3	3	3
4	6	6	6	6	11	10	11	11	7	8	8	8	6	6	6	6
5	11	11	11	12	20	19	21	22	15	16	16	14	12	11	12	12
6	20	20	21	23	29	29	30	31	26	26	26	22	23	20	22	22
7	29	29	30	31	32	32	32	32	32	32	32	30	31	29	30	30
8	32	32	32	32	32	32	32	32	32	32	32	32	32	32	32	32

In this section we look at several key recovery attacks that can be mounted using the biases in the difference. The attacks are rather straight forward, thus we only discuss in detail some of the attacks and give the complexities for the other attacks in Table 6 (Table 5).

Note that for the attacks in this section we use the theoretical biases (Tables 2 and 3). As is shown in Table 4, the real bias of the distinguishers is significantly higher. Most probably this difference is caused by dependencies between rounds that were not accounted for. In comparison, given that the 8-round distinguisher has an observed bias better by a factor of 16, we expect an attack better by a factor of 256 (data, time, and memory complexities).

Next we construct a 12-round attack using the 7-round distinguisher by prepending one round and appending 4 rounds of key recovery. As can be seen in Table 2 we have four sensible choices for the distinguisher: $\Delta_{12} \rightarrow \Delta_4, \Delta_{12} \rightarrow \Delta_7$, $\Delta_{12} \rightarrow \Delta_8$, and $\Delta_{12} \rightarrow \Delta_{15}$, with biases respectively: $2^{-7.9}, 2^{-7.9}, 2^{-11.7}, 2^{-11.8}$. Recall that as is shown in Lemma 1 to be able to distinguish a bias of b we need at most $2^{-2 \cdot b + 3.451}$ pairs (the exact value depends on the number of candidate keys that need to be filtered and can be computed using Lemma 1). To decrease the number of pairs needed and to optimize the overall time complexity of the key recovery we use the 7-round distinguisher $\Delta_{12} \to \Delta_{15}$. This means that, since we have a set of 2^{24} possible keys, for every key we need to evaluate approximately $2^{2 \cdot 11.8 - 4 + 0.028 + 2 \cdot \log(5.3)} = 2^{24.44}$ plaintext pairs for each of the 2^{24} possible keys. time. This adds up to a time complexity of $2^{24.44+24} = 2^{48.44}$ time, $2^{24.44}$ data complexity and $2^{24.44}$ memory to store the data. We note that due to the SC layer being before the key addition we do not need to guess the first round subkey since we can choose the pairs such that they have the right difference.

Table 6. Summary of the *time (data/memory)* complexities for key recovery attacks on Skinny using the different differential distinguishers described in this paper.

Distinguisher	Rounds					
	10	11	12	13	14	15
6-round	$2^{28.00}(2^{11.00})$	$2^{48.00}(2^{11.00})$	$2^{84.00}(2^{11.00})$	$2^{120.0}(2^{11.00})$	–	–
7-round	$2^{35.12}(2^{23.12})$	$2^{48.43}(2^{24.43})$	$2^{73.55}(2^{25.55})$	$2^{114.49}(2^{26.49})$	–	–
8-round	$2^{46.09}(2^{38.09})$	$2^{59.75}(2^{39.75})$	$2^{74.90}(2^{46.90})$	$2^{108.10}(2^{48.10})$	–	–
1 + 6-round	$2^{16.00}(2^{11.00})$	$2^{28.00}(2^{11.00})$	$2^{48.00}(2^{11.00})$	$2^{84.00}(2^{11.00})$	$2^{120.0}(2^{11.00})$	–
1 + 7-round	–	$2^{35.12}(2^{23.12})$	$2^{48.43}(2^{24.43})$	$2^{73.55}(2^{25.55})$	$2^{114.49}(2^{26.49})$	–
1 + 8-round	–	$2^{46.09}(2^{38.09})$	$2^{59.75}(2^{39.75})$	$2^{74.90}(2^{46.90})$	$2^{108.10}(2^{48.10})$	–
2 + 6-round	$2^{12.00}(2^{19.00})$	$2^{20.00}(2^{19.00})$	$2^{32.00}(2^{19.00})$	$2^{52.00}(2^{19.00})$	$2^{88.00}(2^{19.00})$	$2^{124.0}(2^{19.00})$
2 + 7-round	–	$2^{34.49}(2^{30.49})$	$2^{39.12}(2^{31.12})$	$2^{52.43}(2^{32.43})$	$2^{77.55}(2^{33.55})$	$2^{118.49}(2^{34.49})$
2 + 8-round	–	–	$2^{50.09}(2^{46.09})$	$2^{63.75}(2^{47.75})$	$2^{78.90}(2^{54.90})$	$2^{112.10}(2^{56.10})$
3 + 6-round	–	$2^{28.00}(2^{35.00})$	$2^{36.00}(2^{35.00})$	$2^{48.00}(2^{35.00})$	$2^{68.00}(2^{35.00})$	$2^{104.0}(2^{35.00})$
3 + 7-round	–	–	$2^{55.12}(2^{47.12})$	$2^{68.43}(2^{48.43})$	$2^{93.55}(2^{49.55})$	–
3 + 8-round	–	–	–	–	–	–

5   Revisiting Impossible Differential Attacks on Single-Tweak SKINNY

An impossible differential attack against reduced-round SKINNY in the single-tweakey model is proposed in [14]. The attack uses an 11-round impossible differential, i.e., a single nibble difference in nibble 12 cannot lead to a difference only in nibble 8 after 11 rounds.

5.1   Problems with the Attack of [14]

Given the 11-round impossible differential, a standard impossible differential attack is applied—several structures of plaintexts are taken, such that in each structure there are many pairs which may obtain the input difference needed for the impossible differential. Then, in each structure, all the pairs that may lead to the impossible output difference are located, and each pair is analyzed for the keys it suggests. These keys are of course wrong, and thus discarded.

The attack relies heavily on two parts: first, using a series of elaborate and elegant data structures that allow easy and efficient identification of the proposed key from a given pair, and, that given a pair, it disqualifies a fraction 2^{-72} of the 2^{116} subkeys which are recovered by the attack. Unfortunately,[2] the true ratio is 2^{-84} as can be seen in Fig. 4 in Appendix A: the probability that a pair of plaintexts chosen from the structure reaches the input difference is 2^{-24}, whereas the probability that the corresponding ciphertexts reach the output difference is 2^{-60}.

The result of this issue is that the attack requires more data (and thus time) to succeed—namely, about 2^{12} times the reported time and data (which are $2^{47.5}$ chosen plaintexts for 18-round SKINNY-64-64 and $2^{62.7}$ chosen plaintexts for 20-round SKINNY-64-128). Hence, the corrected attacks either require more data than the entire codebook or take more time than exhaustive search (or both). In Sect. 5.2 we propose a new attack that solves the aforementioned problems.

5.2   Fixing the Impossible Differential Attack

One can fix the attacks by reducing the number of attacked rounds. For example, in the case of SKINNY-64-128, attacking 17-round reduced version (which corresponds to the first 17 rounds of the original attack). Taking 2^m structures of 2^{28} chosen plaintexts, we expect from each structure 2^{55} pairs, out of which $2^{55} \cdot 2^{-36} = 2^{19}$ obtain ciphertext difference that may lead to the output difference of the impossible differential. Even a naïve implementation, of guessing the 60 involved subkey bits (40 in the two rounds before the impossible differential and 20 after), allows checking which subkeys suggest impossible events. The probability of an analyzed (pair, subkey) pair to "succeed" (i.e., that a pair/subkey combination results in a contradiction, thus discarding a wrong subkey guess) is $2^{-24} \cdot 2^{-24} = 2^{-48}$. Hence, we require $2^{60} \cdot (1 - 2^{-48})^{2^{19+m}} \ll 2^{60}$ (as each of the 2^{60} subkeys has probability of $(1 - 2^{-48})$ to be discarded by any of the 2^{19+m} pairs). Picking $m = 32.6$ balances between the complexity of exhaustive search over the remaining key candidates and the naïve partial encryption/decryption of the pairs.

Specifically, $2^{32.7}$ structures offer $2^{19+32.7} = 2^{51.7}$ pairs. Given these pairs, a wrong subkey guess remains with probability $(1 - 2^{-48})^{2^{51.7}} = (1/e)^{2^{3.6}} = (1/e)^{12.1} = 2^{-17.5}$, which implies an exhaustive key search phase of $2^{128} \cdot 2^{-17.5} = 2^{110.5}$, together with $2^{60} \cdot 2^{19+m} \cdot 2 = 2^{112.6}$ partial encryptions/decryptions for each pair. Hence, a naïve implementation takes $2^{112.9}$ time and $2^{60.7}$ chosen plaintexts for attacking 17-round SKINNY-64-128.

We note that there is another small issue with the analysis of the attacks reported in [14] related to the memory complexity. In impossible differential attacks, one needs to store both the data and the list of "discarded" keys (sometimes one can optimize various parts of this complexity). Hence, the memory

---

[2] We have contacted the authors of [14] who confirmed our claim.

complexity reported in [14] should also be considerably higher. Namely, it is more than the data complexity (e.g., for the SKINNY-64-128 attack, it is 2^{116}). In comparison, our 17-round attack has memory complexity of $2^{60.7}$.

5.3 Improving the Fixed Impossible Differential Attack

We note that one can optimize the time complexity of the impossible differential attack using pre-computed tables as in [14]. The simplest (and fastest) one is to construct a table that accepts the two ciphertexts restricted to the 28 bits with difference, and stores the list of all key candidates that lead to an "output difference" of the impossible differential, i.e., a difference only in nibble 8. As for a given 20-bit subkey guessed at the end, the probability that the pair indeed reaches such an output difference is 2^{-24}, we expect for each pair about $2^{20} \cdot 2^{-24} = 2^{-4}$ possible subkey suggestions. There are 2^{56} pairs of two 28-bit values (one from each ciphertext of the pair), and thus we need a hash table of 2^{56} entries (of which only 2^{52} non-empty entries), we can take a ciphertext pair and immediately identify the subkey it proposes (if it proposes one).

This reduces the time complexity of the basic filtering by a factor of 2^{20}, which allows for an improved time complexity, in exchange for some more data.[3] For $m = 24 \cdot 2^{29}$, we obtain an attack with data complexity of $2^{61.6}$ chosen plaintexts and time complexity of $2^{94.6}$ encryptions. The attack can process each structure separately and just store the pre-computed table and a bitmap of the subkeys which are discarded, thus, requiring 2^{60} cells of memory.

The second optimization relies on changing the direction of the attack— from ciphertext to plaintexts, which allows attacking 18-round variant (rather than 17 rounds). We collect $m = 2^{12}$ structures of ciphertexts, each structure with 2^{48} ciphertexts (just before the SC operation of round 18 there are 2^{64} possible values, but they are effectively transformed into 2^{48} possible values when applying the inverse MC operation, so the structures are defined by having 7 active nibbles at the output of round 16). Each such structure suggests 2^{95} pairs, out of which $2^{95} \cdot 2^{-36} = 2^{59}$ satisfy the 0 difference in 9 nibbles when partially encrypting the obtained plaintexts till the first key addition. For each of the 40-bit subkey involved in the plaintext side, there is a chance of 2^{-24} that a pair is partially encrypted to the input difference of the impossible differential. Similarly, such a pair has probability 2^{-44} to partially decrypt (with the 60-bit subkey involved) to the output difference of the impossible differential. Hence, we take each of the 2^{59} pairs of each a structure, and use two pre-computed tables to see which subkeys the pair suggests. On average, we expect a pair to *discard* (through the contradiction) a given subkey guess with probability 2^{-68}. This means that given $m = 2^{12.3}$ structures, the probability of any given key to remain is $(1 - 2^{-68})^{m \cdot 2^{59}} \approx (1/e)^{4.3} = 2^{-12}$. Then, the exhaustive key search part takes time which is $2^{128} \cdot 2^{-12} = 2^{116}$.

---

[3] The extra data is needed to reduce the number of partial keys moving to the exhaustive search phase of the attack, so that the impossible differential phase and the exhaustive search phase are balanced.

We note that the list of proposed subkeys can be pre-computed: From the plaintext side, we take all $(2^{28})^2$ pairs of plaintexts and all 2^{40} subkeys and compute for each pair of plaintexts which keys satisfy the "input difference" (in time 2^{96} and memory of 2^{72}). For the ciphertext side we can either use a straightforward approach of testing all $(2^{48})^2$ pairs of inputs and all 2^{60} bit subkeys, and amortize the pre-computation cost (as is done in many works). The second option is to follow the early abort technique. Namely, we take all $(2^{48})^2$ pairs of input, and by partially encrypting the 8 nibbles which are not involved with the key through the last round, we obtain the output differences needed by the other nibbles to "follow" the differential transitions in the other nibbles. Then, by the standard approach that given an input difference and an output difference one knows the (expected) one solution for the key, we obtain the exact subkey of round 17 that the pair suggests. We then continue for the (pair, subkey value) and try all 2^{20} remaining subkeys to see what options indeed lead to the output difference of the impossible differential. Hence, the pre-computation of the second table takes time $(2^{48})^2 \cdot 2^{20} = 2^{116}$ time (and 2^{112} memory).

To conclude, by using this technique, we can attack 18-round SKINNY-64-128 with a data complexity of 2^{60} chosen ciphertexts, a time complexity of 2^{116} partial encryptions, and using 2^{112} memory.

6   Conclusion

In this paper we analyzed reduced-round versions of the SKINNY-64-128. We made several observations regarding the diffusion offered by 8-round SKINNY, namely showing that even after eight rounds of SKINNY there is a measurable bias in the output difference. This observation shows that 8 rounds of SKINNY does not satisfy the strict avalanche criteria [15]. We then used the bias to offer multiple attacks of which the results are summarized in Table 6.

Finally, we revisited several previous results, showing that [11]'s proposed bias has a lower bias than expected (if at all). We showed that the impossible differential attack of [14] contained a subtle, yet, devastating issue. We followed by fixing the attack (in exchange for a reduced number of attacked rounds). The best attack we could devise is on 18-round SKINNY-64-128 using 2^{60} chosen ciphertexts, with time of 2^{116} encryptions and 2^{112} memory.

Appendices

A   Impossible Differential

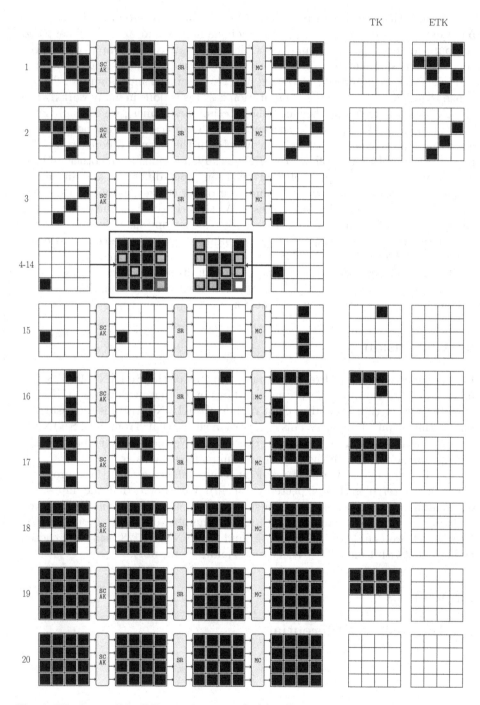

Fig. 4. The impossible differential used in [14] and in our attacks and which nibbles are needed to evaluate its "existence".

References

1. Andreevna, E., Lallemand, V., Purnal, A., Reyhanitabar, R., Roy, A., Vizar, D.: ForkAE (2019)
2. Ankele, R., et al.: Related-key impossible-differential attack on reduced-round SKINNY. In: Gollmann, D., Miyaji, A., Kikuchi, H. (eds.) ACNS 2017. LNCS, vol. 10355, pp. 208–228. Springer, Cham (2017). https://doi.org/10.1007/978-3-319-61204-1_11
3. Ankele, R., Dobraunig, C., Guo, J., Lambooij, E., Leander, G., Todo, Y.: Zero-correlation attacks on tweakable block ciphers with linear tweakey expansion. IACR Trans. Symmetric Cryptol. **2019**(1), 192–235 (2019)
4. Beierle, C., et al.: The SKINNY family of block ciphers and its low-latency variant MANTIS. In: Robshaw, M., Katz, J. (eds.) CRYPTO 2016. LNCS, vol. 9815, pp. 123–153. Springer, Heidelberg (2016). https://doi.org/10.1007/978-3-662-53008-5_5
5. Beierle, C., et al.: Skinny-AEAD (2019)
6. Iwata, T., Khairallah, M., Minematsu, K., Peyrin, T.: Romulus (2019)
7. Jean, J., Nikolić, I., Peyrin, T.: Tweaks and keys for block ciphers: the TWEAKEY framework. In: Sarkar, P., Iwata, T. (eds.) ASIACRYPT 2014. LNCS, vol. 8874, pp. 274–288. Springer, Heidelberg (2014). https://doi.org/10.1007/978-3-662-45608-8_15
8. Lai, X., Massey, J.L., Murphy, S.: Markov ciphers and differential cryptanalysis. In: Davies, D.W. (ed.) EUROCRYPT 1991. LNCS, vol. 547, pp. 17–38. Springer, Heidelberg (1991). https://doi.org/10.1007/3-540-46416-6_2
9. Liskov, M., Rivest, R.L., Wagner, D.A.: Tweakable block ciphers. J. Cryptol. **24**(3), 588–613 (2011)
10. Liu, G., Ghosh, M., Song, L.: Security analysis of SKINNY under related-tweakey settings (long paper). IACR Trans. Symmetric Cryptol. **2017**(3), 37–72 (2017)
11. Moghaddam, A.E., Ahmadian, Z.: New automatic search method for truncated-differential characteristics: application to Midori and SKINNY. IACR Cryptology ePrint Archive 2019, 126 (2019)
12. Sadeghi, S., Mohammadi, T., Bagheri, N.: Cryptanalysis of reduced round SKINNY block cipher. IACR Trans. Symmetric Cryptol. **2018**(3), 124–162 (2018)
13. Sun, S., et al.: Analysis of AES, SKINNY, and others with constraint programming. IACR Trans. Symmetric Cryptol. **2017**(1), 281–306 (2017)
14. Tolba, M., Abdelkhalek, A., Youssef, A.M.: Impossible differential cryptanalysis of reduced-round SKINNY. In: Joye, M., Nitaj, A. (eds.) AFRICACRYPT 2017. LNCS, vol. 10239, pp. 117–134. Springer, Cham (2017). https://doi.org/10.1007/978-3-319-57339-7_7
15. Webster, A.F., Tavares, S.E.: On the design of S-Boxes. In: Williams, H.C. (ed.) CRYPTO 1985. LNCS, vol. 218, pp. 523–534. Springer, Heidelberg (1986). https://doi.org/10.1007/3-540-39799-X_41
16. Yang, D., Qi, W., Chen, H.: Impossible differential attacks on the SKINNY family of block ciphers. IET Inf. Secur. **11**(6), 377–385 (2017)

Zero-Knowledge to the Rescue: Consistent Redundant Backup of Keys Generated for Critical Financial Services

Moti Yung[1]([✉]), Cem Paya[2], and Daniel James[2]

[1] Google and Columbia University, New York, USA
motiyung@gmail.com
[2] Gemini, New York, USA
cemp51d@gmail.com, daniel@gemini.com

Abstract. We present the work on HADKEG: a protocol for Highly Available Distributed Key Generation. The context is a highly sensitive redundant generation for use and redundant recovery of a set of symmetric cryptography keys. These keys need to be trusted (random) and secure against failures of randomness employment and leakages, and be available via a recovery procedure which needs to be redundant (high availability constraints) yet secure and consistent (i.e., the correct recovery has to be assured regardless of recovery server availability). The working environment allows for distributed key generating parties initiating the system, and a set of recovery and operating agents that hold the key and may be at time off-line. These very practical concrete security, redundancy (availability), and integrity requirements, that typify real world highly sensitive services, operate in a special environment where, as we said, not all recovery agents are available at all times, yet where transfers of encrypted information is semi-synchronous and globally available to parties that become on-line. In this architecture, it turned out, that the usually considered theoretical and costly transferable Zero-Knowledge proofs, actually help overcome the operational and integrity constraints. We present a protocol we implemented called HADKEG: Highly Available Distributed Key Generation. It combined distributed key generation, special encryption and transferable zero-knowledge proofs to achieve the practical goal in the working environment.

1 Introduction

Operating online sensitive valuable services like digital assets exchanges or individual wallet hosting service require care. Indeed, every so often in this modern cryptocurrency age, we hear that a currency exchange [1] has lost some stored coins and cannot recover them, or attacks of similar nature [3] or the more recent [2] Canadian exchange incident in 2019. Attacks on such services may grow as the volume and value of transactions increase. Therefore, when one is to operate a reliable exchange or a reliable repository of wallets, or any other service involving

© Springer Nature Switzerland AG 2020
S. Dolev et al. (Eds.): CSCML 2020, LNCS 12161, pp. 18–28, 2020.
https://doi.org/10.1007/978-3-030-49785-9_2

digital assets, one has to assure reliable backup of securely stored assets. These assets may be stored for long time in a cold storage (not available online), and at times, based on client request (that is authenticated and identified) may be moved to operating storage and then a transaction is performed.

In this short paper we review the design of a cryptographic system for reliable secure storage that was implemented in the above context. The emphasize of this report is on the applied side, demonstrating the underlying problems and the solutions taken (rather than delving too much into formalizing the problem, modeling, and proving security). The idea here being that reporting on this in a more accessible fashion may contribute to the state of the art of best practices in an industry which is in formation, and is not yet known to be employing the necessary procedures, in spite of the fact that it is an obvious target to possible attacks and to internal fraud. We note that our solution has been implemented in the context of an operational currency exchange and can serve as an example of such real world concrete implementations (where trust and integrity considerations for real applications may differ then these of many research papers).

In particular, the critical operations like online exchanges need reliability and integrity assurance, based on careful risk analysis based on the concrete setting., which must include the generation and backup of cryptographic keys. A common strategy for such backup is encrypting keys to recovery agents, namely to a sub-set of public-keys which are associated each with a recovery service. This approach provides the following benefits: (1) after encryption, ciphertexts become nonsensitive pieces of information (unlike the plaintext keys); (2) allowing each key generation to choose the subset of recovery keys (based on trust assumptions regarding the owners, geography, operation, etc.); while (3) allowing for easy redundancy, permitting the secret to be recovered using any server (public-key) out of the subset.

The natural and straightforward approach to implementing this runs into two risk analysis problems (and we deal with mission critical systems so we need to mitigate these):

1. The original generation of secrets is done on one system. Therefore, if the hardware/software has been compromised for whatever reason, the resulting secret can be fabricated.
2. There is no way to verify that backups were done correctly, short of something like performing the decryption operation with each of the keys to confirm that the ciphertexts correspond to the identical plaintext (e.g., via Challenge Response protocol). This verification step can be costly and, more importantly, can introduce insecurity if a decryption device is offline and not readily accessible (for instance, because the corresponding private-keys exists on hardware module that is, often, kept offline for security reasons!). Unless backups can be verified, the service runs the added risk of inconsistent future recovery.

This paper presents a new distributed approach centered around transferable zero-knowledge proofs to address both problem. The solution, in fact, demonstrates that sometimes, a cryptographic procedure which is thought to be complicated and unnecessary, given alternatives (e.g., zero-knowledge proofs of possession of a cryptographic key vs. challenge-response protocol to verify possession of a key), actually becomes the elegant method that solves the very practical and sensitive scenario, and its cost can be tolerated as well.

1.1 The Setting

The setting we deal with is quite generic. We assume that the bulk data is encrypted with a symmetric key (collection of symmetric keys) that may be a master key or data key. We need to keep the keys secure and at the same time assure recovery, which means that we may use a number of recovery agents, where availability of one implies the availability of this sensitive key.

For the rest of this paper, we assume that one secret K (obviously, this will be performed for many keys) is to be generated by an online service and be backed-up to n servers at different locations each server is associated with a different public-key. The protocol can be repeated to generate multiple secrets as necessary, and different instances can select a subset of the n public keys, based on trust of the user to deposit its keys with some of the servers but not all (in our example throughout we will assume the entire group is used (w.l.o.g.). The participants will be key generating parties and there are t of them. (We also note that a common approach to importing a new secret into an operational environment involves "wrapping" the secret with a public-key and performing the unwrap operation with the corresponding private key (when holder of the key is available). In particular, hardware security modules (HSM's) compliant with the PKCS #11 interface have functionality for importing a secret that was encrypted using a public-key for which the corresponding private key is present in the HSM.). Further note that each private key corresponding to a public key may be a threshold key held by a few trustees (this may be a software alternative to the hardware modules). The nature of the storage and protection of private keys is left out of the discussion for the rest of this paper, but we assume the holders are well protected by hardware or threshold arrangement, etc.

Given the above scenario, the challenge here is two-fold:

1. Making it possible for multiple t parties to participate in generating the secret such that no subset colluding can influence or recover the final secret generated. (This is a security requirement originating from prevention of a single point of failure; the main concern here is covert tampered random generation).
2. Making it possible to verify backups were done correctly and all n backup servers hold the same key. This reduces to the problem of proving that multiple ciphertexts corresponding to encryptions under different public-keys all correspond to the same plaintext (integrity/consistency assurance).

A somewhat more **formal treatment** of the above setting can define a protocol in which there are n agents each with a public key precomputed and available. For a generated key, let one of these (the first agent) be the key owner and the others be the recovery agents (more generally not every key needs the involvement of all recovery agents as some keys will be handed to only a subset of them). Let a set of t participants (key generators) be the elements generating the key, the key is an element of a group G. The communication is done via a bulletin board where all messages are tagged by their sender and receiver. No synchrony is assumes, a party wakes up and collects all the messages sent to it and can reconstruct its state. The protocol takes place where at the end we want the properties (stated informally):

1. Sound Key Generation: If one of the t key generators is honest, the key is a random element of G.
2. Secure Key Generation: If one of the t key generators is honest and all key recovery agents (or, in general, key recovery agents participating in the key generation) are honest, then the key is secret.
3. Robust Key Generation: any misbehaving key generator that may introduce inconsistency (not following the protocol in communication actions) his contribution is eliminated
4. The key is recoverable: Upon a recovery request, if any of the key recovery agents is available the key is reconstructable (given to the authorized party requesting recovery). Further:
   (a) The recovery is sound: If the authority accepts, the recovered key is the deposited key with very high probability.
   (b) The recovery is consistent: for all recovery agent the result of the recovered key is the same with very high probability.

Approach: In a nutshell, let us review our approach to the solution: First, the second challenge reduces to a problem previously studied under the subject of "ciphertext equality," with solutions in zero-knowledge proofs (ZKP) context. We identified this integrity function as central and use variants of such a protocol (this is a unique case where more traditional integrity methods like "challenge response" checking do not work). Secondly, and perhaps the main conceptual contribution of this paper is showing that the standard approach using ZKP in the context of ElGamal crypto-system [4] also yields an automatic solution to the first problem (using the additive sharing property of the system) so as to assure the secrecy and randomness of the distributively selected key.

Note that our approach is based on proofs by the depositing parties of encrypted data (the key generators which are the input providers), unlike the models describing integrity of cloud data, by clouds giving proofs of properties of data they hold on behalf of users as is given in [12,13], where the issue is integrity (but not secrecy since the data items belong to the verifiers to begin with!).

On Practicality: A few points are worth mentioning:

– First, that typically, distributed processing and redundancy introduce much more work and management in actual systems, yet since our context is a sensitive setting we cannot afford a single point of failure or attack, hence the distribution and employment of various devices or subsystems is feasible and desirable.

- Secondly, note that the multiparty operation is a ceremony at some initial point (or points) in the system life cycle, hence we can afford overhead associated with added procedure, since it does not slow down real time operation, while assuring such future operations will be reliable (this has been verified in our ongoing deployment).
- Thirdly, we note that we have built the system from scratch, hence any valid long standing system can serve as our basic cryptographic cipher (thus, we can choose AES as the standard symmetric key cipher and ElGamal as the public key of choice).

We further note that our system design was implemented and serves for the security of the Gemini crypto assets exchange (https://gemini.com/). In this very practical setting simplicity and complete risk management arguments of the methods of choice are crucial and it is hard to over estimate their importance.

1.2 Recap: ElGamal Cryptosystem

The ElGamal cryptosystem is based on the discrete logarithm problem and can be constructed to operate over any group where DL is considered computationally intractable and it has a proof of semantic security everywhere where the DH exchange produces a randomly looking value in the group (namely, where the Decisional Diffie Hellman problem is hard [7,8]).

Given a plaintext M which is a member of the finite group, the ciphertext is an ordered pair $<R, S>$ of elements in the same group computed as:

$k \in \{1, N - 1\}$ (a random scalar)
$R := k * G$
$S := k * Y + M$

where N is the order of the group, G is a generator, Y is the public-key of the recipient (i.e., the recipient knows a secret key scalar s such that $Y = s * G$ (which enables decryption, which we do not describe above). Note that the asterisk represents the scalar multiplication operation in the group. Also note that the above uses the additive notation typically used over EC groups.

Using the Notation Above, the ElGamal Cryptosystem has a Natural Homomorphism: The encryption of the (component wise) sum of messages is the sum of corresponding ciphertexts for each individual message. This property proves instrumental in combining multiple ciphertexts provided by individual participants.

Comment: Next, we note that we are going to encrypt a value by a number of ElGamal schemes over the same group and the same ciphertext-specific key (random value), and this keeps the semantics security (which is the way the same message is encrypted in our scheme). This is known (based on random self reducibility), yet, for completeness to see why, note that if there is a single ciphertext and a single public-key scheme with public key $<G, Y>$ where $Y = s * G$ and an encryption $<R := k * G, S := k * Y + M>$ encrypted under the scheme, we can generate other cryptosystems and encryption of the same value by choosing an $k2$ and generating a new public key $<G, Y2 = Y + k2 * G>$ and the encryption is generated from known $G, Y, k2$ to be: $<R + k2 * G = (k + k2) * G, k2 * Y + S = (k + k2) * Y + M>$ which is generated without knowing M. The public key is a random public key with the same generator G and the ciphertext distributed randomly (there is a random multiplier unknown to us (since we do not know k) that is used in this second scheme. This shows that if a set of multiple encryption (ciphertext) can break M so is a single ciphertext! With the same random ciphertext key the ciphertext transformation is even simpler. In any event, multiple encryption keeps semantics security under DDH.

2 The System and the Protocol: "Highly Available (Recoverable) Distributed Key Generation" (HADKEG)

In our setting there are redundancies both at the key generating parties (different machines/hardware devices) to assure key is random and secret in spite of possible leaks, and in the key recovery parties, to prevent loss of availability. Namely, we have t participants (key generating parties) which are responsible for jointly generating one secret and assure the backing-up of the key by encrypting it to the public-keys of t different trusted third-parties (trustees). These public keys are ElGamal schemes over the same basic group.

Note again that not all parties have to be online to "get the keys" but based on public record made available, any of these parties is capable of recovery (in fact, some parties being offline adds to security at times). Note, further, that among these trustees' keys, typically one of them will belong to the online service, for use in importing the secret into its operational environment.

What we want is a ceremony of drawing a key (over a semi-synchronized network, but with a record on a bulletin board) and assuring its high availability by any of trustees, with the following specifications as defined above:

1. Sound Key Generation
2. Secure Key Generation
3. Robust Key Generation
4. The key is Recoverable

Some comments:

- Since some trustees recover the key and move it to operation, key availability means that the key used is the key recovered. (Given a publicly available ciphertext it is always possible to demonstrate that the recovered value has been correctly deciphered).
- This procedure of "highly available distributed key generation" may be viewed as a "dual" of verifiable secret sharing over a public channel with multi-sharers into a multiple trustees (secret sharing starts from a single value into many shares, here many shares are collected into a single value (we replicate the process t-wise for reliability).

– Note that the trustee's keys here are assumed to have been pre-generated and belong to a single entity, which is trusted. We may assume that each ElGamal scheme was actually generated by a multi-party key generation [5], and is such that it is random and secure *itself*, as long as one party is honest. In such a configuration full trust in all trustees is reduced to trusting one component of any trustee parties.

– Without loss of generality, we assume the secret is itself an element of the group used for the ElGamal system (obviously, typically a secure key derivation function KDF will apply to this key to get a symmetric key/keys for use).

– The global agreement on operations within the exchange can exploit various consensus methods, in particular using the internal blockchain to resolve operations and get to agree on events (implementing a bulletin board).

– We assume global availability of the protocol transcript so that it is easy to agree on actions of key generation elements, and actions in general (especially if a blockchain is used to manage the protocol).

2.1   The HADKEG Protocol

The protocol is given in three phases (combining distributed replicated key generation with zero knowledge techniques):

1. The public key of the trustees are available (ElGamal schemes over the same group and the same generator). Then, each participant (key generating party) individually generates a share of the secret (a random scalar in the group), encrypts this share with all public-keys of all trustees, and commits to the ciphertexts, and publishes a commitment to the result. (Commitment scheme is binding: can be opened in a unique way and is hiding: until opening it hides the values committed to).

2. Each key generating participant reveals its ciphertexts (for the t trustees). Then: each participant demonstrates, using a zero-knowledge proof, that these ciphertexts correspond to encryptions of the same underlying plaintext under different public-keys.

3. Participants (recovery agents) combine their ciphertexts using the homomorphic property of ElGamal cryptosystem to generate the encryptions of the final secret, which is the "sum" of individual shares according to the group operation. (Use of the key requires its decryption and applying KDF to it and then employing it).

Let us present the protocol in more details and sketch the correctness and security properties achieved.

2.2   Phase 1: Generating Secret Shares

Each key generating participant j independently generates a share of sj of the secret and encrypts it n-ways (this will be our working example, of course a proper subset of the recovery servers may be used, in particular some of the recovery agents are operating agents using the key and they may change for different keys). The encryption is using the ElGamal cryptosystem to the public-key of each trusted third-party, generating a total of n ciphertexts: $Cj, j = 1, ..n$. Then each participant publishes a commitment to their collection of ciphertexts.

Comment: What is achieved here is that if one of the t key generating parties j is honest its share is random. Due to the binding property of the commitment, at the end of this phase all values are determined. A typical implementation shares each value to assure that opening of the commitment will happen, so that the pieces which cannot influence each other (by the security property of commitment as in [5] for example) are all opened and the key is determined after the commitment. There is only one way to open based on the binding property. This is how key generation traditionally is done distributedly, and the proof follows. For our initial implementation setting, we assume a model in which parties open their commitments (or fail benignly only) since these are secure elements (extensions are possible to allow the full malicious parties but for start this works based on the risk analysis of the specific system: distribution is needed since we may not trust all randomness and pseudo-randomness of components, but we trust them to attempt continuation of the protocol with a rare fail stops).

2.3   Phase 2: Proving Plaintext Equality

Each key generating participant then opens its commitment to reveal the set of n ciphertexts, and engages in a zero-knowledge proof to demonstrates that these ciphertexts all represent an encryption of the same plaintext (sj).

This in turn can be implemented as $t - 1$ separate proofs, with the k-th proof showing equivalence between ciphertexts Ck and Ck + 1.

The proof mechanisms is based on existing zero-knowledge proof of knowledge of a ciphertext and knowledge of discrete logarithm equality. In the implementation, such proofs are made transferable non-interactive ones via the Fiat-Shamir compiler [9] (obviously, an interactive version against trusted online available verifiers would also be possible). Also, we did not need to implement any batch verification mechanism.

2.4   The Proofs

The proofs are based on a sigma-round: commitment, binary challenge, and a response (a typical proof like the proof of knowledge of a square root, etc.). Let us view the basic step of a sigma-round in a step; the composition of such steps to an interactive proof system and to a non-interactive system based on the Fiat-Shamir scheme and the fact that they constitute a proof and are simulatable (zero-knowledge) are, by now, standard.

For proof of equality of two messages under two Given ElGamal ciphertexts:

$<P, Q1>$
$<P, Q2>$

That are claimed to be encryptions of same message M with same random ciphertext key (nonce) k, $P = k * G$, which is the same across all ciphertexts. Then, $Q_i = k * Y_i + M$, for public-key Y_i of the i-th recipient.

Then we have:

$$Q2 - Q1 = (k * Y2 + M) - (k * Y1 + M) = k * (Y2 - Y1).$$
$$\text{And}: log_{[baseG]}P = k, log_{[baseY2-Y1]}(Q2 - Q1) = k$$

Now the goal is to use zero-knowledge proof of discrete log (index) equality to prove those logs are equal without revealing k. This is a known procedure that looks like this after the Fiat-Shamir transform:

1. Pick random $w \in (1, order)$ and compute $A1 := w * G$, $A2 := w * (Y2 - Y1)$
2. In place of an interactive challenge, let $c := H(R||Q1||Q2||Y1||Y2||A1||A2)$ mod the group order (and H being a proper cryptographic hash assumed to act as a random oracle) via Fiat-Shamir heuristic to derive this by hashing various inputs.
3. Let $z := w + kc$. Publish $(A1, A2, z)$ as the Schnorr proof [10] of the fact.

The proof is valid if and only if:

1. $z * G = (c * P) + A1$, and
2. $z * (Y2 - Y1) = c * (Q2 - Q1) + A2$

At this point, the ceremony assures publicly that the key pieces drawn and handed to different trustees are the same value. Recall that we have a global agreement mechanism on choosing the proper shares.

2.5 Phase 3: Combining Shares

After all the shares are revealed, participants or an independent third-party can combine the shares by exploiting the additive homomorphism of the ElGamal cryptosystem to create n different encryptions of the combined secret $K = \Sigma_{j=1}^{t}(sj)$.

We note that this final result can not be inferred or fully controlled by any subset of participants other than the entire group of generating parties (which implies security against leaking key generation parties). Since the publicly revealed ciphertexts are by trustees with strong ElGamal keys, the value remain secure unless ElGamal is broken. (We note that, technically, since the ElGamal schemes are over the same group, the proof of security is even tight due to random self reducibility of the schemes, but this is beyond the scope of this short paper). Since one of the pieces s_i is random and independent of all other values, the key s is random as well. The drawing is robust trivially under honest but curious (and fail stop only) behavior of the generating parties.

Next we note that because of the individual zero-knowledge proofs covering each group of ciphertexts output by any key generating participant, the resulting cipher texts are also guaranteed to be encryptions of the same secret under different public-keys, hence the property of key availability holds.

Important Note: One may claim that the system is over using fancy cryptography, and one could have waited till the key is collected at the trustees, and then a challenge-response protocol can be run in parallel on similar challenges to assure the high availability. First, such challenge response parallel scheme needs special care, but more importantly, in our context the trustees are not necessarily available for the protocol (as we said above); namely their ciphertext may be in place but not the holder of the private key which may be hidden in an SHM, or otherwise in cold storage. Thus, we cannot rely on active party at the time of the key generation.

3   Conclusion

Zero knowledge proofs (ZKPs) [6] were originally designed, first, to be proofs that allow showing a property of a public value or statement, while being zero-knowledge, namely, without releasing extra information. It was then extended to proof of possession of a witness (proof of knowledge). Many applications of zero-knowledge exist in the literature (chosen ciphertext security of encryption, signature schemes, assuring anonymity like in group signatures or in a cryptocurrency context, etc.); and also many implications of the existence of zero-knowledge exists like transforming protocols against passive adversary to one against malicious one.

In this work we presented a concrete implemented work that is actually running in a context of a system that requires assurance of integrity (due to the availability need and essentially desire not to rely on a single source of randomness in a system when generating sensitive keys) and is in the context of secure keys. Namely, the assurance has to be performed while not giving extra information, and perhaps when receivers are not present. This is exactly the case that transferable zero-knowledge proofs were designed for (and public key systems are useful at), and it shows that under certain system's needs and settings, variations of ZKPs are the right direct tool, and should be considered in the arsenal of method for assurance and reduced risk in sensitive services (which demand extra integrity and secrecy) such as a digital assets exchange, especially at stages where the cost of the proofs are tolerable. Hence we characterize the situation as "Zero Knowledge to the Rescue." We would like to note that we did not invent any radically novel procedure in this work, but rather started honestly from a set of requirements and reduced them to relatively known procedures that were put together in a way that they achieve the goals, and in a way that it is easy to understand and implement them. While this may look trivial, our goal is to claim that this type of adaptation should be considered in the real world more often since typically solutions avoid more advanced cryptographic techniques: in fact it may be the time to consider variants of Zero-Knowledge proofs to be part of "Applied Cryptography." Let us end with a related comment that such techniques as in our work, due to their applicability and practicality, may require update to modern frameworks of key management like NIST's one [11] which seem to need a revision.

References

1. Digital Currency Exchanges, Wikipedia
2. Quadriga: The cryptocurrency exchange that lost 135 m. https://www.bbc.com/news/world-us-canada-47203706
3. Mt. Gox, Wikipeda
4. ElGamal, T.: A public key cryptosystem and a signature scheme based on discrete logarithms. In: Blakley, G.R., Chaum, D. (eds.) CRYPTO 1984. LNCS, vol. 196, pp. 10–18. Springer, Heidelberg (1985). https://doi.org/10.1007/3-540-39568-7_2
5. Gennaro, R., Jarecki, S., Krawczyk, H., Rabin, T.: Secure distributed key generation for discrete-log based cryptosystems. J. Cryptol. **20**(1), 51–83 (2006)
6. Goldwasser, S., Micali, S., Rackoff, C.: The knowledge complexity of interactive proof systems. SIAM J. Comput. **18**, 186–208 (1989)
7. Tsiounis, Y., Yung, M.: On the security of ElGamal based encryption. In: Imai, H., Zheng, Y. (eds.) PKC 1998. LNCS, vol. 1431, pp. 117–134. Springer, Heidelberg (1998). https://doi.org/10.1007/BFb0054019
8. Boneh, D.: The decision Diffie-Hellman problem. In: Buhler, J.P. (ed.) ANTS 1998. LNCS, vol. 1423, pp. 48–63. Springer, Heidelberg (1998). https://doi.org/10.1007/BFb0054851
9. Fiat, A., Shamir, A.: How to prove yourself: practical solutions to identification and signature problems. In: Odlyzko, A.M. (ed.) CRYPTO 1986. LNCS, vol. 263, pp. 186–194. Springer, Heidelberg (1987). https://doi.org/10.1007/3-540-47721-7_12
10. Schnorr, C.P.: Efficient identification and signatures for smart cards. In: Brassard, G. (ed.) CRYPTO 1989. LNCS, vol. 435, pp. 239–252. Springer, New York (1990). https://doi.org/10.1007/0-387-34805-0_22
11. Barker, E., Smid, M., Branstad, D., Chokhani, S.: NIST Special Publication 800-130: A Framework for Designing Cryptographic Key Management Systems. National Institute of Standards and Technology
12. Ateniese, G., Kamara, S., Katz, J.: Proofs of storage from homomorphic identification protocols. In: Matsui, M. (ed.) ASIACRYPT 2009. LNCS, vol. 5912, pp. 319–333. Springer, Heidelberg (2009). https://doi.org/10.1007/978-3-642-10366-7_19
13. Barsoum, A.F., Hasan, M.A.: Provable multicopy dynamic data possession in cloud computing systems. IEEE Trans. Inf. Forensics Secur. **10**(3), 485–497 (2015)

Security Ranking of IoT Devices Using an AHP Model

Shachar Siboni[1]([✉]), Chanan Glezer[2], Rami Puzis[1], Asaf Shabtai[1], and Yuval Elovici[1]

[1] Department of Software and Information Systems Engineering,
Ben-Gurion University of the Negev, 84105, Beer-Sheva, Israel
{sibonish,puzis,shabtaia,elovici}@bgu.ac.il
[2] Department of Industrial Engineering and Management, Ariel University, 40700 Ariel, Israel
chanang@ariel.ac.il

Abstract. The proliferation of Internet of Things (IoT) technology raises major security and privacy concerns. Specifically, ordinary electrical appliances are being transformed into smart connected devices with the capability to sense, compute, and communicate with their surroundings and the Internet. These smart embedded devices increase the attack surface of the environments in which they are deployed by becoming new points of entry for malicious activities, resulting in severe network security flaws. One of the major challenges lies in examining the influence of IoT devices on the security level of the environment they operate within. In this paper, we propose a security ranking model for IoT devices, based on the analytic hierarchy process (AHP) technique, which can be used for the device risk assessment task. Our implementation of the AHP model is based on a device-centric approach, where both device-specific features and domain-related features are taken into account. We applied the proposed model on several IoT devices in the context of an enterprise network environment, demonstrating its feasibility in analyzing security-related considerations in smart environments.

Keywords: Internet of Things · Security · Device ranking · Risk assessment · Analytic hierarchy process

1 Introduction

The Internet of Things (IoT) defines a new era where physical objects (things), including home appliances, medical equipment, organizational and industrial infrastructure, wearable devices, and more, are transformed into smart connected digital devices with the ability to sense, compute, and communicate with their surroundings, locally and through the Internet [1]. This results in complex information and communication technology, in which most of the data produced by these smart devices is transmitted to, and processed remotely in, the cloud [2].

The proliferation of IoT technology and its applications poses major security and privacy risks due to the range of functionalities and capabilities provided by these IoT systems [3]. Specifically, IoT devices are powered by different operating systems and are therefore exposed to various types of security breaches and attacks. Moreover, most of these smart devices are not developed with security in mind and are designed mainly on the basis of features and cost considerations. As low resource devices, in terms of power source, memory size, bandwidth communication, and computational capabilities, standard security solutions are largely not applicable to such devices [4]. This may result in severe security flaws, as only lightweight encryption mechanisms and authentication algorithms can be applied in order to encrypt the data stored on (data at rest), and transmitted from (data in transit), the device [5].

In addition, as smart connected devices, IoT devices can be continuously connected to the Internet, either directly or indirectly, via dedicated gateways, and therefore they are highly accessible—particularly to attackers [6]. These state-of-the-art devices are equipped with advanced sensing and communication capabilities that permit monitoring their surroundings, as well as tracking individual users' activity, behavior, location, and health condition in real-time. The fact that such devices can operate continuously in order to gather information from their surroundings greatly increases the risk of privacy violations [7]. IoT devices are very diverse and heterogeneous, with numerous types of devices, different vendors and suppliers, a range of operating systems in use, various connectivity capabilities, etc. Moreover, such devices are used in dynamic contexts and states, which significantly complicates the assessment of the security and privacy risks these smart devices pose to the environments they operated on [8].

Recently, IoT technology has been integrated into corporate and industrial environments, in order to ease the workload of employees, and increase business productivity and efficiency levels [9]. However, as IoT devices become more common in the workplace, employers might begin to exploit them, violating privacy by tracking and recording an employee's actions—and even more worrisome—monitoring an employee's health condition [4]. In addition, sensitive corporate information can be exposed and leaked to unauthorized individuals and become more accessible to out-siders via these smart connected devices [10]. The deployment of IoT devices in such environments makes companies much more vulnerable and increases their attack surface, as such smart devices expose new vulnerabilities and infiltration points for attackers [8]. Furthermore, IoT devices can serve as platform for coordinated network attacks (e.g., internal botnet DDoS attacks) by utilizing their computing capabilities, as well physical attacks (lock doors, overheat critical infrastructure, etc.) by misleading their built-in sensors [11]. One of the major problems in such situations is to determine the security risk level the IoT devices pose to the environments in which they are deployed [12].

In this paper, a security ranking model for IoT devices based on the analytic hierarchy process (AHP) technique [13] is proposed. The suggested model employs a device-centric approach and uses both device-specific and domain-related features, in order to derive an individual rank (from a security risk perspective) for IoT devices that operate in different contexts and states. Device-specific features include an IoT device's known vulnerabilities and sensors capabilities elements, with static properties that do not change over time (unless a software/firmware update/upgrade is performed). Domain-related features include the contexts and states in which the IoT device operates, and thus have dynamic properties with respect to the IoT domain use case. Our practical proof of concept implementation and evaluation of the suggested AHP model operation on several IoT devices operated in the context of enterprise environments demonstrate the feasibility of the proposed model as a ranking technique that can be applied for the device risk assessment task.

The rest of the paper is structured as follows. In Sect. 2 we present work related to this study. In Sect. 3, we portray in detail the preliminaries for the suggested AHP ranking model, followed by a model implementation description in Sect. 4. We demonstrate the operation of the AHP model for ranking several IoT devices in the context of enterprise network, and discuss the results obtained in Sect. 5. We conclude and suggest possible future work in Sect. 6.

2 Related Work

Security risk assessment for the IoT domain has been investigated extensively in prior research. IoT security and privacy risk considerations were defined by NIST [14], which helps organizations better characterize IoT devices by their capabilities and used to define their security risks. Nurse et al. [15] presented different methodologies for assessing risks in the context of the IoT by considering the dynamics and changes in IoT systems, in order to provide early warning of emerging risk potential. Scientific-based security risk metrics were defined by Watkins and Hurley [16]; these metrics aim to assess the cyber maturity level of organizations using a modified CVSS base score along with the analytic hierarchy process (AHP) technique.

Hwang and Syamsuddin [17], and Irfan and Junseok [18] examined the application of AHP technique for information security matters by developing a framework that evaluate information security policy performance. Otair and Al-Refaei [19] presented an evaluation to Cybercrimes fighting readiness in organizations using the AHP method; showing how to identify the readiness of an organization to fight cybercrimes and how to determine the critical factors that affect this readiness. Wilamowski et al. [20] compared two decision theory methodologies, the analytical hierarchy and analytical network processes (AHP and ANP respectively), which applied to cyber security-related decisions to derive a measure of effectiveness for risk evaluation. Alexander [21] examined the AHP model for the prioritization of information assurance defense in-depth measures. Mowafi et al. [22], proposed a context-based AHP framework for eliciting context information and adapting it with network access control measures for mobile devices based on real-time assessment of user's context.

Risk analysis for different IoT environments has been discussed in various works. Chang et al. [8] introduced enterprise risk factors for governing the risk of an IoT environment using a Delphi expert questionnaire. Risk analysis for smart homes was proposed by Jacobsson et al. [23], emphasizing the security risks and mitigation mechanisms for such IoT deployments. Abie and Balasingham [24] presented a risk-based adaptive security framework for IoT in the eHealth domain; this framework estimates and predicts risk damage using context awareness and game theory techniques. Mohajerani et al. [25] suggested cyber-related risk assessment within the power grid which is used to detect and improve the vulnerability of power systems against the intrusion and malicious acts of cyber attackers.

3 Preliminaries

In this section, preliminaries for our proposed security ranking model for risk assessment of IoT devices are defined. This consists of two main components, including: (1) the model features and elements description, and (2) the analytic hierarchy process technique definition.

3.1 Features Sets

The ranking of an IoT device under test is derived from the set of features and elements of the device, defined as a device-centric approach. Namely, the device ranking is defined based on: (1) device-specific features, including the set of known vulnerabilities and the set of sensors capabilities (physical sensors and means of communication supported by the device) which have static properties; and (2) domain-related feature, that includes the set of contexts and states in which the IoT device operates, thus have dynamic properties, with respect to the IoT domain use case.

Known Vulnerabilities Feature. The set of known vulnerabilities elements, denoted as V_K, exist in an IoT device, in terms of software, hardware, and firmware vulnerabilities. Using this information, it is possible to exploit the device and utilize it for further malicious activities. The set V_K for IoT device i is defined by $V_K^{(i)} = \left\{ V_{K_{[1]}}^{(i)}, V_{K_{[2]}}^{(i)}, \ldots, V_{K_{[l]}}^{(i)} \right\}$, where $V_{K_{[j]}}^{(i)}$ refers to known vulnerability element j, and l is the number of known vulnerabilities elements exist in the device.

Sensors Capabilities Feature. The set of sensors capabilities elements, denoted as S_C, exist in an IoT device, including the physical sensors and means of communication embedded in the device. Using this set of sensors capabilities, it is possible to collect private and sensitive information from/via the device, change the state of the environment the device is deployed on, and connect to the device via one of its existing means of communication in order to perform further attacks. This feature is based on the device type and functionality, where each IoT device has a different set of sensors such that for IoT device i, the device's set of sensors capabilities elements is defined as $S_C^{(i)} = \left\{ S_{C_{[1]}}^{(i)}, S_{C_{[2]}}^{(i)}, \ldots, S_{C_{[m]}}^{(i)} \right\}$, where $S_{C_{[j]}}^{(i)}$ refers to sensor capability element j built-in/embedded into the device, and m is the number of sensors capabilities elements supported by the device.

Operational Contexts Feature. This feature refers to the set of operational contexts, denoted as C_O, in which the device operates, with respect to the IoT domain use case. Different operational contexts, specifically locations and time of operation, imply different security severity. The set of operational contexts elements for IoT device i is defined by $C_O^{(i)} = \left\{ C_{O_{[1]}}^{(i)}, C_{O_{[2]}}^{(i)}, \ldots, C_{O_{[n]}}^{(i)} \right\}$ where $C_{O_{[j]}}^{(i)}$ refers to operational context element j, and n is the number of contexts the IoT device can be operated in.

3.2 Analytic Hierarchy Process Technique

The analytic hierarchy process (AHP) is a structured technique for decision making problems. It can be used in a variety of decision situations, including conflict resolution, resource allocation, choice and prioritization, ranking, and risk analysis [26]. AHP is a mathematical method based on the solution of eigenvector and eigenvalue tasks, derives ratio scales from paired comparisons and allows some small inconsistency in judgment. The input can be either actual measurement (e.g., price, weight, etc.) or subjective opinion (e.g., satisfaction feeling, preferences, etc.), and the output are ratio scales (results from eigenvector) and consistency index (results from eigenvalue calculations) [27].

The AHP process is done in several steps, as follows. First, it needs to define the objective and elements for the problem at hand. Next, structure the elements of the model in criteria, sub-criteria, and alternatives groups (hierarchy-like structure). Then, in each group separately a pairwise comparison between the elements is conducted, in order to calculate weights (priorities) and consistency ratio. Finally, according to weighting obtained in the model the alternatives are evaluated [26]. A comparison matrix is defined for each group of elements based on the expert decision making. Using this approach, it is possible to rank between the alternatives. Note that, the weights of each group of elements in the model is summed to 1, and consistency ratio less than 10% considered a reasonable inconsistency in the results (otherwise the experts request to modify their selections in order to reduce the bias in the decision making [27]).

In practice, AHP works as follows. For a given group of elements (or criteria), a pairwise comparison is conducted between these elements, such that for n elements there are $\frac{n \times (n-1)}{2}$ comparisons (questions). For each pairwise comparison between two elements i and j, the experts require to select the level of importance between these elements using the relative scores shown in Table 1. For that a comparison matrix A of size of $n \times n$ is established. Each cell a_{ij} in matrix A characterize the importance of the ith element relative to the jth element such that

$$a_{ji} = \frac{1}{a_{ij}} \tag{1}$$

as shown in Table 2 for four elements (criteria). Once matrix A is established, it is possible to compute the weights of the elements and the consistency ratio of that matrix using eigenvector and eigenvalue calculations.

This is obtained by the following. First, the normalized pairwise comparison matrix A_{norm} is defined by normalized each cell a_{ij} in matrix A such that

$$\bar{a}_{ij} = \frac{a_{ij}}{\sum_{l=1}^{n} a_{lj}} \tag{2}$$

result in the sum of each column j equal to 1. Next, the weight for element (criterion) i, denoted as w_i, is defined by averaging the entries on each row of A_{norm}, i.e.,

$$w_i = \frac{\sum_{l=1}^{n} \bar{a}_{il}}{n}. \tag{3}$$

This define the weights vector W (obtained from eigenvector calculations) as shown in Table 2. In order to check the consistency of the results (comparison matrix), a

Table 1. AHP relative scores.

Value	Description
1	i and j are equally important
3	i is slightly more important than j
5	i is more important than j
7	i is strongly more important than j
9	i is absolutely more important than j
2, 4, 6, 8	Values for inverse comparison

Table 2. Example for comparison matrix A and the weights vector W.

A	C1	C2	C3	C4	W
C1	1	a_{12}	a_{13}	a_{14}	w_1
C2	$1/a_{12}$	1	a_{23}	a_{24}	w_2
C3	$1/a_{13}$	$1/a_{23}$	1	a_{34}	w_3
C4	$1/a_{14}$	$1/a_{24}$	$1/a_{34}$	1	w_4

consistency ratio, denoted as CR, is calculated by the following:

$$CR = \frac{CI}{RI} \tag{4}$$

where CI is approximate consistency index defined by:

$$CI = \frac{\lambda_{max} - n}{n - 1} \tag{5}$$

and RI is a random consistency index, which is a constant value for given order of matrix n (as shown in Table 3) with respect to a randomly generated pairwise comparison matrix.

Table 3. Random inconsistency indices for n = 10.

n	1	2	3	4	5	6	7	8	9	10
RI	0.00	0.00	0.58	0.9	1.12	1.24	1.32	1.41	1.45	1.49

Note that λ_{max} is a consistency measure (obtained from eigenvalue calculations) defined by the following:

$$\lambda_{max} = \frac{\sum_{i=1}^{n} \lambda_i}{n} \tag{6}$$

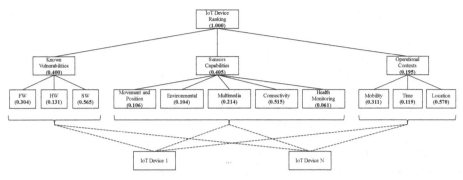

Fig. 1. AHP model (hierarchy-like structure) for IoT devices ranking task.

where

$$\lambda_i = \frac{(Row_i \in A) \times W}{w_i} \qquad (7)$$

namely multiplying row i in matrix A (before normalized) by the weights vector W dividing by the appropriate w_i (weight of criteria i). If $CR > 0.10$ than the results considered not consistent enough and it is required to revise the pairwise comparisons. Otherwise, the results are reasonable consistent, and it is possible to evaluate the alternatives. From the obtained results in the hierarchy, each alternative is evaluated (assigned weight) based on the set of elements (criteria) it contained, with respect to the appropriate weights of the model. The final weight of an alternative defined by the following weighted sum calculation [26]:

$$w^{Alternative} = \sum_{i=1}^{n} w_i \times \left(\sum_{j=1}^{m} w_{ij} \right) \qquad (8)$$

where w_i and n refer to the weight of element i and the number of elements, respectively, in the first level criteria (main criteria) of the AHP hierarchy, and w_{ij} and m refer to the weight of element j and the number of elements, respectively, in the second level criteria under criteria i. Formula (8) represents the calculations for assigning weight for an alternative using AHP hierarchy with only two levels criteria (if the hierarchy contains more levels then the formula should be update appropriately).

4 Model Implementation

In this section, we present the implementation of the proposed AHP ranking model, as hierarchy structure (Fig. 1), for device risk assessment task. The AHP model was established by employing the domain expert questionnaire methodology using a set of pairwise comparisons questions that were defined for each AHP criteria level (group of elements) in the hierarchy. The questionnaire is available in [31].

4.1 Expert Analysis

The following is a descriptive statistics about the panel of experts who participated in the questionnaire, regarding their education, role, and the number of years of experience they have in the areas of cyber security and the IoT domain.

In total, 20 experts answered the questionnaire, 15 of which are from the hi-tech industry, with a variety of expertise (30% SW/HW engineers, 20% IT/QA, and 25% in different areas, such as management and offensive cyber security); the rest of the experts are from academia (25% researchers). Most of the experts have an academic degree (25% BSc, 25% MSc/MBA, and 25% PhD) or are in the process of pursuing a degree. Most also have extensive experience in the cyber security domain (an average of 5 years of experience) and some experience in the IoT domain (approximately 75% have more than one year of IoT experience).

4.2 Model Construction

The obtained AHP model, as hierarchy structure, is presented in Fig. 1. The goal is to rank IoT devices from a security risk perspective. This is obtained based on their features and elements. Accordingly, the first level criteria are the features sets themselves, and the second level criteria are the categories/group of elements of these features respectively. Namely, under known vulnerabilities criterion we defined the Firmware (denoted as FW), Hardware (HW), and Software (SW) vulnerabilities elements (sub-criteria). Under sensors capabilities criterion we defined Connectivity (denoted as Conn, and refer to both wired and wireless communication means exist in IoT devices such as Ethernet, cellular, Wi-Fi, Bluetooth, ZigBee, NFC, etc.), Multimedia (denoted as Mult, and include mic and camera sensors, and printing and scanning capabilities), Environmental (denoted as Env, and include sensors like gas/smoke detector, thermometer, lighting, pressure, barometer, magnetometer, infrared sensor, etc.), Movement and Position (denoted as MP, and refer to GPS, motion detector, accelerometer, proximity, gyroscope sensors and more), and Health Monitoring (denoted as HM, and refer to sensors like hart-rate) capabilities elements (sub-criteria). Under operational contexts criterion we defined the following elements (sub-criteria): Mobility (denoted as Mob, and refer to whether the device is mobile or not), Time (refer to the time of operation), and Location (denoted as Loc, and refer to the physical location the device is operated on with respect to the IoT domain use case). Finally, the alternatives are the IoT devices that we aim to rank, from security risk perspective, using the proposed AHP model.

It should be noted that, we asked the experts to weight/prioritize these elements/criteria in the model (using the pairwise comparison questions) from "Risk" perspective. Meaning, we define risk as a measure for quantifying how an element/criterion in the questionnaire is more risky (from the expert perspective) compared to other elements in the same group. For example, for the first level criteria, we asked the experts which criterion between known vulnerabilities, sensors capabilities, and operational contexts is more risky (pairwise) from its point of view. This process done also for the sub-criteria as well.

The weight for each element in the hierarchy is defined based on the AHP procedure, using the domain expert questionnaire results. We used the multi-criteria AHP calculator

[26] for establishing the comparison matrix for each group of elements in the model, as shown in Tables 4, 5, 6 and 7, consolidate all experts' judgments using the row geometric mean method (RGMM). In addition, Table 8 presents the quality metrics results obtained for all the comparison matrixes, including λ_{max} (Principal Eigenvalue), three consistency indices values: CR (consistency ratio), GCI (geometric consistency index), and Psi (overall dissonance), as well as MRE (mean relative error for eigenvector method) and the level of consensus between the experts [26, 28]. As can be seen in Table 8, all CRs values are less than 10%, the required threshold for AHP, thus the weights of the elements in the model can be used for evaluating alternatives (otherwise, the experts are required to modify their selections iteratively until CR < 0.10 is obtained). Most of the Psi results are zero (as should be), except for S_C which equal to 10.0%; most of the MRE results are quite low, except for S_C which equal to 25.3%; and the consensus levels in most of the criteria are reasonable enough, except for Features criterion which equal to 30.7%. Meaning, the results obtained from the AHP procedure considered relatively good, with a reasonable consistency, low MRE and high consensus levels, therefore the weights in the AHP model can be used for evaluating alternatives. However, as mentioned, both the Psi and the MRE measures are quite high for S_C sub-criterion, and the consensus level is quite low for Features criterion (shown in bold in Table 8). This can be resolved by additional processing, such as adjustment of the selections of these elements by the experts, add additional experts, etc., especially for S_C sub-criterion. Note that, the values presented in the comparison matrices are rounded such that there are minor differences in the weights (e.g., in Table 4 the weights vector should be {0.4, 0.4, 02}), thus we have the MRE metric in Table 8.

5   Model Operation

In this section, we applied our proposed AHP ranking model on several IoT devices in the context of enterprise network environment. Namely, we ranked the list of IoT devices using the suggested model by assigning weights and evaluating alternatives (in terms of AHP). Note that, the possible range for total weights of IoT devices is [0–1], where higher weight refers to higher rank (from a security risk perspective). Meaning, we define which IoT device is more risky and could influence on the security level of the environment it deployed, in our case enterprise network, the most.

5.1   Alternative Evaluation

In this section we illustrate the process of applying our proposed AHP model to evaluate an alternative (an IoT device). For that matter, we choose the IP camera of type of Edimax IC 3116W, containing the following elements. From known vulnerabilities aspect, there is only one vulnerability (obtained by employ Nessus vulnerability scanner [29] on the IP camera), which we define it as Software type vulnerability. This defined by examine the details of CVE-1999-0511 record.

From sensors capabilities aspect, the device has the following elements (obtained from the online specs of that device): Connectivity (the device has Wi-Fi and Ethernet types of connectivity), Multimedia (obviously, the device has camera), Environmental

Table 4. Comparison metrix for model's features (main criteria).

Features	V_K	S_C	C_O	W_i
V_K	1	1	2	0.400
S_C	1	1	2	0.405
C_O	1/2	1/2	1	0.195

Table 5. Comparison metrix for known vulnerabilities feature (sub-criteria).

V_K	FW	HW	SW	W_i
FW	1	2 5/8	1/2	0.304
HW	3/8	1	1/4	0.131
SW	2 1/9	3 5/6	1	0.565

Table 6. Comparison metrix for sensors capabilities feature (sub-criteria).

S_C	Conn	Mult	Env	MP	HM	W_i
Conn	1	3 3/4	4	5 1/2	5 1/2	0.515
Mult	1/4	1	2 1/2	2 1/2	3 2/3	0.214
Env	1/4	2/5	1	8/9	1 8/9	0.104
MP	1/5	2/5	1 1/8	1	2 2/7	0.106
HM	1/5	1/4	1/2	4/9	1	0.061

Table 7. Comparison metrix for operational contexts feature (sub-criteria).

C_O	Mobility	Time	Location	W_i
Mobility	1	3	1/2	0.311
Time	1/3	1	1/4	0.119
Location	2 1/8	4 1/9	1	0.570

(the device has Infrared sensor) and Movement and Position (since the device contains a Motion detector sensor). From operational contexts aspect, the IP camera is stationary device (thus $0.5w_{Mob}$ is used in the calculations), it can be operated at any time, and can be deployed in all locations in the organization (thus w_{Loc} is used in the calculations). According to this definition, we can now evaluate the weight of the IP camera device

Table 8. Quality metrics results for all AHP comparison matrices.

	Features	V_K	S_C	C_O
Lambda	3.000	3.015	5.128	3.023
CR	0.0%	1.6%	2.8%	2.4%
GCI	0.00	0.05	0.11	0.07
Psi	0.0%	0.0%	**10.0%**	0.0%
MRE	0.4%	12.3%	**25.3%**	15.1%
Consensus	**30.7%**	48%	58.9%	63.7%

(the alternative), denoted as w^{IP_Camera}, using the proposed AHP model as follows:

$$w^{IP\_Camera} = w_{Vk} \times w_{SW} + w_{Sc} \times (w_{Conn} + w_{Mult} + w_{Env} + w_{MP}) + w_{Co}$$
$$\times (0.5 w_{Mob} + w_{Time} + w_{Loc}) = 0.400 \times 0.565 + 0.405 \times (0.515 + 0.214 + 0.104$$
$$+0.106) + 0.195 \times (0.5 \times 0.311 + 0.119 + 0.570) = 0.771.$$

5.2   Ranking IoT Devices

In this section we ranked a list of IoT devices that operated in the context of enterprise network environment by applying our proposed AHP model, as shown in Table 9.

For each IoT device in Table 9, we present its type and model, the elements it contains (with respect to the AHP model's features), the device total weight (denoted as DTW), and the final rank (with respect to the given list of devices). Note that, the elements of known vulnerabilities (CVE records obtained by applying the Nessus vulnerability scanner [29] on each IoT device) are considered very sensitive information, as they expose real vulnerabilities that exist in the device. Therefore, we do not present this information in the paper, only their categorization (SW, FW, or HW) from our perspective, as show in Table 9 in column V_K. Moreover, because each device may have several vulnerabilities, in this work we considering only the maximum/highest vulnerability exists, from CVSS severity score [32] perspective, in the device. With respect to the elements of sensors capabilities, for each IoT device we used its technical spec to obtain the set of sensors it contains (due to space constraints, we also omit this information from the paper; for full details see the online specs for each IoT device presented in the table). Based on that information we defined the relevant capabilities, in terms of Connectivity (Conn), Multimedia (Mult), Movement and Position (MP), Health Monitoring (HM), and Environmental (Env), that exists for each device, as show in Table 9 in column S_C. In addition, with respect to operational contexts elements, for each IoT device we referred to its contexts as follows. If the IoT device is mobile device (denoted by M in Table 9 in column C_O), then we considered the full weight of Mobility element (namely 0.311) in the calculations, otherwise we multiplying it by 0.5 (for the case the device is stationary, denoted by S in column C_O, such that we use 0.1555 in the calculations). If the IoT device can be operated at any time at the day (denoted as T:ALL in column C_O), then the weight of the Time element is fully considered in the calculations, otherwise it

Table 9. Ranking of IoT devices using the suggested AHP model. For each device type and specific device model, the device total weight (denoted as DTW) and its final rank (with respect to the other IoT devices in the list) are defined using the proposed model features and elements.

Device type	Model	V_K	Sc	Co	DTW	Rank
IP camera	GeoVision GV-AVD2700	SW	Conn; Mult; MP; Env	S; T:All; L:All	0.771	1
IP camera	Edimax IC 3116W	SW	Conn; Mult; MP; Env	S; T:All; L:All	0.771	1
Smartphone	LG G4	SW	Conn; Mult; MP	M; T:Partical; L:All	0.747	2
Smartwatch	ZGPAX S8	SW	Conn; Mult; MP	M; T:Partical; L:All	0.747	2
Smart TV	Samsung UE40K 6000	SW	Conn; Mult	S; T:ALL; L:Partial	0.630	3
Smartphone	Samsung Galaxy Edge 7	None	Conn; Mult; MP; HM; Env	M; T:Partial; L:All	0.588	4
Smartwatch	Sony 3 SWR50	None	Conn; Mult; MP; Env	M; T:Partial; L:All	0.563	5
Smartphone	HTC One E9 PLUS	None	Conn; Mult; MP	M; T:Partial; L:All	0.521	6
Wireless keyboard	Microsoft 850	FW	Conn; Env	S; T:All; L:Partial	0.481	7
Motion sensor	SimpleHome XHS7-1001	None	Conn; MP; Env	S; T:All; L:All	0.458	8
Wireless MK	Logitech MK 520	HW	Conn; Env	S; T:All; L:Partial	0.412	9
Wi-Fi printer	HP Officejet Pro 6830	None	Conn; Mult	S; T:All; L:Partial	0.404	10
Smart fridge	Samsung RS757LHQESR	None	Conn; Env	S; T:All; L:Partial	0.359	11

considered partially (denoted as T:Partial in the table and the weight is divided by two, such that instead of 0.119 we used 0.0595). The same is applied for Location element, meaning if the IoT device can be operated at any location (denoted as L:ALL in Table 9) then the weight of the Location element is fully considered in the calculations, otherwise it considered partially (denoted as L:Partial in the table and the weight is divided by two, such that instead of 0.570 we used 0.285 in the calculations), as shown in Table 9 in column C_O. For instance, a Smart Fridge is a stationary device that operated at any time (always-on) and located only in the kitchen. Thus, its C_O vector is defined as {S; T:ALL; L:Partial} with the appropriate weights. Note, the Time context refer to morning, afternoon, evening, and night as possible time of operation, and Location context refer to server room, meeting room, CxO offices, IT department, internal locations (such as hallways, kitchen, etc.), and external locations (such as receptionist, parking, etc.) as possible locations of operation for IoT devices in enterprise environment.

As can be seen from the results obtained in Table 9, the IP Cameras are ranked the highest, with respect to the current list of IoT devices. Meaning, based on our proposed ranking model these specific IP cameras (the specific models that were evaluated) are the most risky devices, as their weights are the highest. This is obtained due to the fact that these specific IP cameras contain software vulnerabilities, different sensors capabilities and from different types (Conn, AV, MP, and Env), and although these devices are stationary they operating all the time and can be deployed at any location in the organization (thus are highly accessible to attackers), hence their weights are the highest. The LG G4 smartphone and the ZGPAX S8 smartwatch devices are ranked next, as both are mobile devices that can be operated at any location in the organization and mainly during working hours (thus they defined as T:Partial in the table), both have software vulnerabilities, and contain several sensors capabilities (Conn, Mult, and MP).

Unexpected result was obtained for the Smart TV device which is ranked next (ranked 3 in the table). The device has software vulnerability, two sensors capabilities (Conn and Mult) and it defined as stationary device that can be operated at any time but only in several locations in the organization. It ranked higher than the other smartphone and smartwatch devices, since these devices do not have any vulnerabilities (this element in the model has high weight of 0.4) hence are ranked with moderated risk. Another unexpected result was obtained for the Wi-Fi printer which is ranked 10 (meaning very low risk), lower than the wireless keyboards and the motion sensor devices. This is due to the fact the device has no vulnerabilities, has only two sensors capabilities (by our model) and it is a stationary device that can be operated at any time (namely always-on) but can be deployed only in several locations. Again, since known vulnerabilities criterion has high weight (of 0.4) and the device has no vulnerabilities (from any type), the model ranked it as a low risk device. The device with the lowest rank, hence it is the least risky device, is the Smart Fridge IoT device. The device has no vulnerabilities, has only two sensors capabilities (Conn and Env) and it is a stationary device that always-on which deployed mainly in the kitchen.

6 Summary and Future Work

The Internet of Things domain is evolving everyday with new applications, new IoT devices, and new network deployments. Accordingly, the attack surface of existing systems and environments is increasing, resulting in new security risks that need to be handled. Therefore, a preliminary risk assessment process which quantifies the security level of the new technology in the emerging IoT domain is required. In this paper, a security ranking model for IoT devices is proposed. The suggested model is based on the analytic hierarchy process (AHP) technique, which can be used for the device risk assessment task. Moreover, a device-centric approach is considered by using both device-specific and domain-related features and elements. Device-specific features and elements, with static properties that do not change over time, include the device's set of known vulnerabilities and set of sensors capabilities (physical sensors and means of communication supported by the device). Domain-related features and elements, with dynamic properties that do change over time, include the set of contexts and states in which the IoT devices operate with respect to the IoT domain use case. These features are employed in the model in order to quantify the security level of IoT devices using unique IoT security characterizations.

The AHP model was implemented by employing the domain expert questionnaire methodology, where 20 experts from different domains participated. The model is constructed with a hierarchy structure, where the goal is to rank IoT devices from a security risk perspective. Therefore, the main criteria of the model are the features themselves (V_K, S_C, C_O), and the subcriteria are the elements used as the unique characterizations in the IoT security domain. The alternatives are the IoT devices that we would like to rank. We applied the suggested model on several IoT devices in the context of a typical enterprise network, demonstrating the feasibility of the proposed model to analyze security-related considerations in smart environments. The proposed model could be used to prioritize (based on the device ranking assignment) which IoT devices should be updated or patched first, as well as which devices require additional security analysis using a security testbed for the IoT domain [30]. Moreover, the proposed model could also be used as part of a context-based network access control solution for IoT environments, providing decision-making functionality, in order to determine whether and in what context(s) (e.g., specific location, time of operation) to connect a specific IoT device to the network. Therefore, our suggested security ranking model can be used as a benchmark for the device risk assessment task.

In future work, additional device-specific and domain-related features and elements will be used in order to generate a more accurate ranking for the IoT devices, as well as to adjust the model with respect to different IoT application domains. Moreover, currently the model considers only the family types of elements (defined as subcriteria in the AHP model). The specific type and number of elements that exist in each feature must also be considered, since each element (e.g., specific CVE or specific sensor) is an attack vector by itself. In addition, regarding the domain expert questionnaire, questions will address different contexts (e.g., specific attacks, etc.), and additional experts will be included in order to improve the quality metrics results shown in Table 8. Furthermore, additional devices and device types will be evaluated in order to test and verify the model's assignment in different contexts and states (from both the device and IoT domain level perspectives). Finally, one of the main disadvantages of using a domain expert questionnaire is that the model is static (i.e., in order to add a new element to the model, all of the experts must answer another set of questions or complete the questionnaire again). Thus, we would like to consider other approaches for the problem at hand.

References

1. Atzori, L., Iera, A., Morabito, G.: The Internet of Things: a survey. Comput. Netw. **54**(15), 2787–2805 (2010)
2. Gubbi, J., Buyya, R., Marusic, S., Palaniswami, M.: Internet of Things (IoT): a vision, architectural elements, and future directions. Future Gener. Comput. Syst. **29**(7), 1645–1660 (2013)

3. Sicari, S., Rizzardi, A., Grieco, L.A., Coen-Porisini, A.: Security, privacy and trust in Internet of Things: the road ahead. Comput. Netw. **76**, 146–164 (2015)
4. Weber, R.H.: Internet of Things – new security and privacy challenges. Comput. Law Secur. Rev. **26**(1), 23–30 (2010)
5. Yan, Z., Zhang, P., Vasilakos, A.V.: A survey on trust management for Internet of Things. J. Netw. Comput. Appl. **42**, 120–134 (2014)
6. Roman, R., Zhou, J., Lopez, J.: On the features and challenges of security and privacy in distributed Internet of Things. Comput. Netw. **57**(10), 2266–2279 (2013)
7. Ukil, A., Sen, J., Koilakonda, S.: Embedded security for Internet of Things. In: 2011 2nd National Conference on Emerging Trends and Applications in Computer Science (NCETACS), pp. 1–6. IEEE (2011)
8. Chang, S.I., Huang, A., Chang, L.M., Liao, J.C.: Risk factors of enterprise internal control: governance refers to Internet of Things (IoT) environment. In: Pacific Asia Conference on Information Systems (PACIS) (2016)
9. Bi, Z., Da Xu, L., Wang, C.: Internet of Things for enterprise systems of modern manufacturing. IEEE Trans. Ind. Inf. **10**(2), 1537–1546 (2014)
10. Abomhara, M., Køien, G.M.: Security and privacy in the Internet of Things: current status and open issues. In: 2014 International Conference on Privacy and Security in Mobile Systems (PRISMS), pp. 1–8. IEEE (2014)
11. Sikder, A.K., Petracca, G., Aksu, H., Jaeger, T., Uluagac, A.S.: A survey on sensor-based threats to Internet-of-Things (IoT) devices and applications. arXiv preprint: arXiv:1802.02041 (2018)
12. Siboni, S., Glezer, C., Shabtai, A., Elovici, Y.: A weighted risk score model for IoT devices. In: Wang, G., Feng, J., Bhuiyan, M.Z.A., Lu, R. (eds.) SpaCCS 2019. LNCS, vol. 11637, pp. 20–34. Springer, Cham (2019). https://doi.org/10.1007/978-3-030-24900-7_2
13. Saaty, T.L.: Risk—its priority and probability: the analytic hierarchy process. Risk Anal. **7**(2), 159–172 (1987)
14. NIST: IoT Security and Privacy Risk Considerations (2017). https://www.nist.gov/sites/def ault/files/documents/2017/12/20/nist_iot_security_and_pri-vacy_risk_considerations_dis cussion_draft.pdf. Accessed 10 Mar 2019
15. Nurse, J.R., Creese, S., De Roure, D.: Security risk assessment in Internet of Things systems. IT Prof. **19**(5), 20–26 (2017)
16. Watkins, L.A., Hurley, J.S.: Cyber maturity as measured by scientific-based risk metrics. J. Inf. Warfare **14**(3), 57–65 (2015)
17. Hwang, J., Syamsuddin, I.: Information security policy decision making: an analytic hierarchy process approach. In: 2009 Third Asia International Conference on Modelling and Simulation, pp. 158–163. IEEE (2009)
18. Irfan, S., Junseok, H.: The use of AHP in security policy decision making: an open office calc application. J. Softw. **5**(2), 1162–1169 (2010)
19. Otair, M., Al-Refaei, A.: Cybercrime fighting readiness evaluation using analytic hierarchy process. In: Proceedings of 48th the IIER International Conference, Spain, Barcelona (2015)
20. Wilamowski, G.C., Dever, J.R., Stuban, S.M.: Using analytical hierarchy and analytical network processes to create cyber security metrics. Def. Acquis. Res. J. **24**(2), 186–221 (2017)
21. Alexander, R.: Using the analytical hierarchy process model in the prioritization of information assurance defense in-depth measures?—A quantitative study. J. Inf. Secur. **8**(03), 166 (2017)
22. Mowafi, Y., Dhiah el Diehn, I., Zmily, A., Al-Aqarbeh, T., Abilov, M., Dmitriyevr, V.: Exploring a context-based network access control for mobile devices. Procedia Comput. Sci. **62**, 547–554 (2015)

23. Jacobsson, A., Boldt, M., Carlsson, B.: A risk analysis of a smart home automation system. Future Gener. Comput. Syst. **56**, 719–733 (2016)
24. Abie, H., Balasingham, I.: Risk-based adaptive security for smart IoT in eHealth. In: Proceedings of the 7th International Conference on Body Area Networks, pp. 269–275. Institute for Computer Sciences, Social-Informatics and Telecommunications Engineering (2012)
25. Mohajerani, Z., et al.: Cyber-related risk assessment and critical asset identification within the power grid. In: IEEE PES on Transmission and Distribution Conference and Exposition (2010)
26. Goepel, K.D.: Implementing the analytic hierarchy process as a standard method for multi-criteria decision making in corporate enterprises – a new AHP excel template with multiple inputs. In: Proceedings of the International Symposium on the Analytic Hierarchy Process, pp. 1–10. Creative Decisions Foundation Kuala Lumpur (2013)
27. Alonso, J.A., Lamata, M.T.: Consistency in the analytic hierarchy process: a new approach. Int. J. Uncertain. Fuzziness Knowl. Based Syst. **14**(04), 445–459 (2006)
28. Aguarón, J., Moreno-Jiménez, J.M.: The geometric consistency index: approximated thresholds. Eur. J. Oper. Res. **147**(1), 137–145 (2003)
29. Tenable: Nessus vulnerability scanner tool for network security (2018). https://www.tenable.com/products/nessus-home. Accessed 16 Feb 2020
30. Siboni, S., et al.: Security testbed for Internet-of-Things devices. IEEE Trans. Reliab. **68**(1), 23–44 (2018)
31. Siboni, S.: An AHP questionnaire for device ranking task (2020). https://drive.google.com/file/d/1Bx7YMZdTcRMyIwWt5HVIzsExW5U72OgT/view?usp=sharing. Accessed 24 Mar 2020
32. NIST: NVD Vulnerability Metrics and Severity Ratings for CVSS v3.0. https://nvd.nist.gov/vuln-metrics/cvss. Accessed 28 Mar 2020

Robust Malicious Domain Detection

Nitay Hason[1,3], Amit Dvir[1,3(✉)] (iD), and Chen Hajaj[2,3,4] (iD)

[1] Department of Computer Science, Ariel University, Ariel, Israel
nitay.has@gmail.com
[2] Department of Industrial Engineering and Management,
Ariel University, Ariel, Israel
[3] Ariel Cyber Innovation Center, Ariel University, Ariel, Israel
{amitdv,chenha}@ariel.ac.il
[4] Data Science and Artificial Intelligence Research Center,
Ariel University, Ariel, Israel
https://www.ariel.ac.il/wp/amitd/,
https://www.ariel.ac.il/wp/chen-hajaj/

Abstract. Malicious domains are increasingly common and pose a severe cybersecurity threat. Specifically, many types of current cyber attacks use URLs for attack communications (e.g., C&C, phishing, and spear-phishing). Despite the continuous progress in detecting these attacks, many alarming problems remain open, such as the weak spots of the defense mechanisms. Because ML has become one of the most prominent methods of malware detection, we propose a robust feature selection mechanism that results in malicious domain detection models that are resistant to black-box evasion attacks. This paper makes two main contributions. Our mechanism exhibits high performance based on data collected from ~5000 benign active URLs and ~1350 malicious active (attacks) URLs. We also provide an analysis of robust feature selection based on widely used features in the literature. Note that even though we cut the feature set dimensional space in half (from nine to four features), we still improve the performance of the classifier (an increase in the model's F1-score from 92.92% to 95.81%). The fact that our models are robust to malicious perturbations but are also useful for clean data demonstrates the effectiveness of constructing a model that is solely trained on robust features.

Keywords: Malware detection · Robust features · Domain

1 Introduction

In the past two decades, cybersecurity attacks have become a major issue for governments and civilians [43]. Many of these attacks are based on malicious web domains or URLs (See Fig. 1 for the structure of a URL). These domains are used for phishing [13, 23, 25, 36, 41] (e.g. spear phishing), Command and Control (C&C) [40] and a vast set of virus and malware [15] attacks.

This is a regular submission to CSCML 2020.

© Springer Nature Switzerland AG 2020
S. Dolev et al. (Eds.): CSCML 2020, LNCS 12161, pp. 45–61, 2020.
https://doi.org/10.1007/978-3-030-49785-9_4

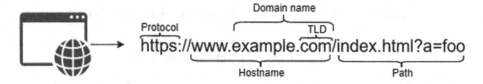

Fig. 1. The URL structure

The Domain Name System (DNS) maps human-readable domain names to their associated IP addresses (e.g., google.com to 172.217.16.174). However, DNS services are abused in different ways to conduct various attacks. In such attacks, the adversary can utilize a set of domains and IP addresses to orchestrate sophisticated attacks [9,42]. Therefore, the ability to identify a malicious domain in advance is a massive game-changer [8–12,14,16,18–21,30,34,35,37,42,44,46,48,49]. In this context, one of the main questions is how to identify malicious/compromised domains in the presence of an intelligent adversary that can manipulate domain properties.

A common way of identifying malicious/compromised domains is to collect information about the domain names (alphanumeric characters) and network information (such as DNS and passive DNS data[1]). This information is then used for extracting a set of features, according to which machine learning (ML) algorithms are trained based on a desirably massive amount of data [9–12,14,16,19–21,27,30,34,35,37,44,48]. A mathematical approach can also be used in a variety of ways [18,48], such as measuring the distance between a known malicious domain name and the analyzed domain (benign or malicious) [48]. Still, while ML-based solutions are widely used, many of them are not robust; an attacker can easily bypass these models with minimal feature perturbations (e.g., change the length of the domain or modify network parameters such as Time To Live, TTL) [32,45].

For these reasons, we tackle the problem of identifying malicious domains using a feature selection mechanism which is robust to adversarial manipulation. Thus, even if the attacker has black-box access to our model, tampering with the domain properties or network parameters will have a negligible effect on the model's accuracy. In order to achieve this goal, we collected a broad set of both malicious and benign URLs and surveyed for them commonly used features. Then, we manipulated these features to show that some of them, although widely used, are only slightly robust or not robust at all.

The rest of the paper is organized as follows: Sect. 2 summarizes related works, Sect. 3 describes our methodology. In Sect. 4, we present our empirical analysis and evaluation. Finally, Sect. 5 concludes and summarizes our work.

---

[1] Most works dealing with malicious domain detection are based on DNS features, and only some take the passive DNS features into account as well.

2   Related Work

The issue of identifying malicious domains is a fundamental problem in cybersecurity. In this section, we survey recent results in identifying malicious domains. We focus on three significant methodologies: Mathematical Theory approaches, ML-based techniques, and Big Data approaches.

The use of graph theory to identify malicious domains was more pervasive in the past [18,22,28,31,48]. Yadav et al. [48] presented a method for recognizing malicious domain names based on fast flux. Fast flux is a DNS technique used by botnets to hide phishing and malware delivery sites behind an ever-changing network of compromised hosts acting as proxies. Their methodology analyzed the DNS queries and responses to detect if and when domain names are being generated by a Domain Generation Algorithm (DGA). Their solution was based on computing the distribution of alphanumeric characters for groups of domains and by statistical metrics with the KL (Kullback-Leibler) distance, Edit distance and Jaccard measure to identify these domains. Their results for a fast-flux attack using the Jaccard Index achieved impressive results, with 100% detection and 0% false positives. However, for smaller numbers of generated domains for each TLD, their false-positive results were much higher, at 15% when 50 domains were generated for the TLD using the KL-divergence over unigrams and 8% when 200 domains were generated for each TLD using Edit distance.

Dolberg et al. [18] described a system called *Multi-dimensional Aggregation Monitoring (MAM)* that detects anomalies in DNS data by measuring and comparing a "steadiness" metric over time for domain names and IP addresses using a tree-based mechanism. The steadiness metric is based on a similar domain to IP resolution patterns when comparing DNS data over a sequence of consecutive time frames. The domain name to IP mappings were based on an aggregation scheme and measured steadiness. In terms of detecting malicious domains, the results showed that an average steadiness value of 0.45 could be used as a reasonable threshold value, with a 73% true positive rate and only 0.3% false positives. The steadiness values might not be considered a good indicator when fewer malicious activities were present (e.g., <10%).

However, the most common approach to identifying malicious domains is using machine learning (ML) [9,10,14,17,30,35,39,42,44]. Using a set of extracted features, researchers can train ML algorithms to label URLs as malicious or benign. Shi et al. [42] proposed a machine learning methodology to detect malicious domain names using the Extreme Learning Machine (ELM) [21] which is closest to the one employed here. ELM is a new neural network with high accuracy and fast learning speed. The authors divided their features into four categories: construction-based, IP-based, TTL-based, and WHOIS-based. Their evaluation resulted in a high detection rate, an accuracy exceeding 95%, and a fast learning speed. However, as we show below, a significant fraction of the features used in this work emerged as non-robust and ineffective in the presence of an intelligent adversary.

Sun et al. [44] presented a system called *HinDom*, that generate a heterogeneous graph (in contrast to a homogeneous graphs created by [37,48]) in order to robustly identify malicious attacks (e.g. spams, phishing, malware and bot-nets). Even though, HinDom collected DNS and pDNS data, it also has the ability to collect information from various of clients inside networks (e.g. CER-NET2 and TUNET) and by that the perspective of it is different than ours (i.e. client perspective). Nevertheless, HinDom has achieved remarkable results, using transductive classifier it managed to achieve high accuracy and F1-score with 99% and 97.5% respectively.

Bilge et al. [12] created a system called *Exposure*, designed to detect malicious domain names. Their system uses passive DNS data collected over some period of time to extract features related to known malicious and benign domains. Exposure is designed to detect malware- and spam-related domains. It can also detect malicious fast-flux and DGA related domains based on their unique features. The system computes the following four sets of features from anonymized DNS records: (a) Time-based features related to the periods and frequencies that a specific domain name was queried in; (b) DNS-answer-based features calculated based on the number of distinctive resolved IP addresses and domain names, the countries that the IP addresses reside in, and the ratio of the resolved IP addresses that can be matched with valid domain names and other services; (c) TTL-based features that are calculated based on statistical analysis of the TTL over a given time series; (d) Domain-name-based features are extracted by computing the ratio of the numerical characters to the domain name string, and the ratio of the size of the longest meaningful substring in the domain name. Using a Decision Tree model, Exposure reported a total of 100,261 distinct domains as being malicious, which resolved to 19,742 unique IP addresses. The combination of features that were used to identify malicious domains led to the successful identification of several domains that were related to botnets, flux networks, and DGAs, with low false-positive and high detection rates. It may not be possible to generalize the detection rate results reported by the authors (98%) since they were highly dependent on comparisons with biased datasets. Despite the positive results, once an identification scheme is published, it is always possible for an attacker to evade detection by mimicking the behaviors of benign domains.

Rahbarinia et al. [37] presented a system called *Segugio*, an anomaly detection system based on passive DNS traffic to identify malware-controlled domain names based on their relationship to known malicious domains. The system detects malware-controlled domains by creating a machine-domain bipartite graph that represents the underlying relations between new domains and known benign/malicious domains. The system operates by calculating the following features: (a) Machine Behavior based on the ratio of "known malicious" and "unknown" domains that query a given domain d over the total number of machines that query d. The larger the total number of queries and the fraction of malicious related queries, the higher the probability that d is a malware controlled domain; (b) Domain Activity where given a time period, domain activity is computed by counting the total number of days in which a domain was actively queried; (c) IP Abuse where given a set of IP addresses that the domain resolves to, this feature represents the fraction of those IP addresses that were previously targeted by known malware controlled domains. Using a Random Forest model,

Segugio was shown to produce high true positive and very low false positive rates (94% and 0.1% respectively). It was also able to detect malicious domains earlier than commercial blacklisting websites. However, Segugio is a system that can only detect malware-related domains based on their relationship to previously known domains and therefore cannot detect new (unrelated to previous malicious domains) malicious domains. More information about malicious domain filtering and malicious URL detection can be found in [17, 39].

Big Data is an evolving term that describes any voluminous amount of structured, semi-structured and unstructured data that can be mined for information. Big data is often characterized by 3Vs: the extreme Volume of data, the wide Variety of data types and the Velocity at which the data must be processed. To implement Big Data, high volumes of low-density, unstructured data need to be processed. This can be data of unknown value, such as Twitter data feeds, click streams on a web page or a mobile app, or sensor-enabled equipment. For some organizations, this might be tens of terabytes of data. For others, it may be hundreds of petabytes. Velocity is the fast rate at which data are received and (perhaps) acted on. Normally, the highest velocity of data streams directly into memory rather than written to disk.

Torabi et al. [46] surveyed state of the art systems that utilize passive DNS traffic for the purpose of detecting malicious behaviors on the Internet. They highlighted the main strengths and weaknesses of these systems in an in-depth analysis of the detection approach, collected data, and detection outcomes. They showed that almost all systems have implemented supervised machine learning. In addition, while all these systems require several hours or even days before detecting threats, they can achieve enhanced performance by implementing a system prototype that utilizes big data analytic frameworks to detect threats in near real-time. This overview contributed in four ways to the literature. (1) They surveyed implemented systems that used passive DNS analysis to detect DNS abuse/misuse; (2) They performed an in-depth analysis of the systems and highlighted their strengths and limitations; (3) They implemented a system prototype for near real-time threat detection using a big data analytic framework and passive DNS traffic; (4) they presented real-life cases of DNS misuse/abuse to demonstrate the feasibility of a near real-time threat detection system prototype. However, the use cases that were presented were too specific. In order to understand the real abilities of their system, the system must be analyzed with a much larger test dataset.

3   Methodology

Much effort needs to be devoted to collecting an extensive amount of (preferably) heterogeneous information and a considerable thought needs to be devolved to choosing the right model to implement and the set of features for its training phase. In this section, we adhere to these criteria: we first outline the way we collected the dataset and its characteristics (Sect. 3.1). Next, in Sect. 3.2, we define each of the features we evaluate, followed by the evaluation of their robustness in Sect. 3.3.

3.1   Data Collection

The main ingredient of ML models is the data on which the models are trained. As discussed above, data collection should be as heterogeneous as possible to model reality. The data we collected for this work include both malicious and benign URLs: the benign URLs are based on the Alexa top 1 million [1], and the malicious domains were crawled from multiple sources [3, 4, 6] due to the fact they are quite rare. These resources yielded 1,356 malicious active unique URLs and 5,345 benign active unique URLs (75% benign, 25% malicious). For each instance, as presented in Fig. 2, we crawled the URL and domain information properties from Whois, and DNS records.

Whois is a widely used Internet record listing that identifies who owns a domain, how to get in contact with them, the creation date, update dates, and expiration date of the domain. Whois records have proven to be extremely useful and have developed into an essential resource for maintaining the integrity of the domain name registration and website ownership process. Note that according to a study by ICANN[2] [5], many malicious attackers abuse the Whois system. Hence we only used the information that could not be manipulated.

Finally, based on these resources (Whois and DNS records), we generated the following features: the length of the domain, the number of consecutive characters, and the entropy of the domain from the URLs' datasets. Next, we calculated the lifetime of the domain and the active time of domain from the Whois data. Based on the DNS response dataset (a total of 263,223 DNS records), we extracted the number of IP addresses, distinct geolocations of the IP addresses, average Time to Live (TTL) value, and the Standard deviation of the TTL.

3.2   Feature Engineering

Based on previous works surveyed, we extracted a set of features which are commonly used for malicious domain classification [9, 10, 12, 35, 37–39, 42, 47]. Specifically, we used the following nine features as our baseline:

– **Length of domain:**

$$\text{Length of domain} = length(Domain_{(i)}) \tag{1}$$

The length of domain is calculated by the domain name followed by the TLD (gTLD or ccTLD). Hence, the minimum length of a domain is four since the domain name needs to be at least one character (most domain names have at least three characters) and the TLD (gTLD or ccTLD) is composed of at least three characters (including the dot character) as well. For example, for the URL http://www.ariel-cyber.co.il, the length of the domain is 17 (the number of characters for the domain name - "ariel-cyber.co.il").

---

[2] Internet Corporation for Assigned Names and Numbers.

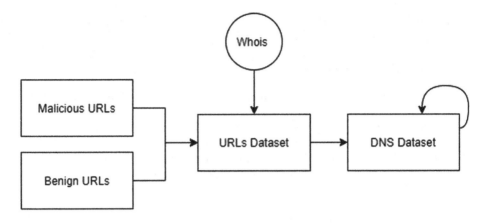

Fig. 2. Data collection framework

– **Number of consecutive characters:**

$$\text{Number of consecutive characters} = \max\{\text{consecutive repeated characters in } Domain_{(i)}\} \tag{2}$$

The maximum number of consecutive repeated characters in the domain. This includes the domain name and the TLD (gTLD or ccTLD). For example for the domain "aabbbcccc.com" the maximum number of consecutive repeated characters value is 4.

– **Entropy of the domain:**

$$\text{Entropy of the domain} = -\sum_{j=1}^{n_i} \frac{count(c_j^i)}{length(Domain_{(i)})} \cdot \log \frac{count(c_j^i)}{length(Domain_{(i)})} \tag{3}$$

The calculation of the entropy (i.e., Feature 3) for a given domain $Domain_{(i)}$ consists of n_i distinct characters $\{c_1^i, c_2^i, \ldots, c_{n_i}^i\}$. For example, for the domain "google.com" the entropy is

$$-(5 \cdot (\frac{1}{10} \cdot \log \frac{1}{10}) + 2 \cdot (\frac{2}{10} \cdot \log \frac{2}{10}) + 3(\cdot \frac{3}{10} \cdot \log \frac{3}{10})) = 1.25$$

The domain has 5 characters that appear once ('l', 'e', '.', 'c', 'm'), one character that appears twice ('g') and one character that appears three times ('o').

– **Number of IP addresses:**

$$\text{Number of IP addresses} = \|\text{distinct IP addresses}\| \tag{4}$$

The number of distinct IP addresses in the domain's DNS record. For example for the list ["1.1.1.1", "1.1.1.1", "2.2.2.2"] the number of distinct IP addresses is 2.

– **Distinct Geo-locations of the IP addresses:**

$$\text{Distinct Geo-locations of the IP addresses} = \|\text{distinct countries}\| \qquad (5)$$

For each IP address in the DNS record, we listed the countries for each IP and counted the number of countries. For example for the list of IP addresses ["1.1.1.1", "1.1.1.1", "2.2.2.2"] the list of countries is ["Australia", "Australia", "France"] and the number of distinct countries is 2.

– **Mean TTL value:**

$$\text{Mean TTL value} = \mu\{\text{TTL in DNS records of } Domain_{(i)}\} \qquad (6)$$

For all the DNS records of the domain in the DNS dataset, we averaged the TTL values. For example, if we conducted 30 checks of some domain's DNS records, and in 20 of these checks the TTL value was "60" and in 10 checks the TTL value was "1200", the mean is $\frac{20 \cdot 60 + 10 \cdot 1200}{30} = 440$.

– **Standard deviation of the TTL:**

$$\text{Standard deviation of TTL} = \sigma\{\text{TTL in DNS records of } Domain_{(i)}\} \qquad (7)$$

For all the DNS records of the domain in the DNS dataset, we calculated the standard deviation of the TTL values. For the "Mean TTL value" example above, the standard deviation of the TTL values is 537.401.

– **Lifetime of domain:**

$$\text{Lifetime of domain} = Date_{Expiration} - Date_{Created} \qquad (8)$$

The interval between a domain's expiration date and creation date in years. For example for the domain "ariel-cyber.co.il", according to Whois information, the dates are: Created on 2015-05-14, Expires in 2020-05-14, Updated on 2015-05-14. Therefore the lifetime of the domain is the number of years from 2015-05-14 to 2020-05-14; i.e. 5.

– **Active time of domain:**

$$\text{Active time of domain} = Date_{Updated} - Date_{Created} \qquad (9)$$

Similar to the lifetime of a domain, the active time of a domain is calculated as the interval between a domain's update date and creation date in years. Using the same example as for the "Lifetime of domain", the active time of the domain "ariel-cyber.co.il" is the number of years from 2015-05-14 to 2018-06-04; i.e., 3.

3.3 Robust Feature Selection

We then turned to evaluating the robustness of the set of features described above to filter those that could significantly harm the classification process given basic manipulations. In the following analyse, we assess these features' robustness (i.e., the complexity of manipulating the feature's values to result in a false classification). Table 1 lists the common features along with the mean value and standard deviation for malicious and benign URLs based on our dataset. Strikingly, the table shows that some of the features have similar mean values for both benign and malicious instances. For example, whereas "Distinct geolocations of the IP addresses" is quite similar for both types of instances (i.e., not effective in malicious domain classification), it is widely used [10,12,42]. Furthermore, whereas "Standard deviation of the TTL" has distinct values for benign and malicious domains, we show that an intelligent adversary can easily manipulate this feature, leading to a benign classification of malicious domains.

Table 1. Feature distributions

Feature	Benign mean (std)	Malicious mean (std)
Length of domain	14.38 (4.06)	15.54 (4.09)
Number of consecutive characters	1.29 (0.46)	1.46 (0.5)
Entropy of the domain	4.85 (1.18)	5.16 (1.34)
Number of IP addresses	2.09 (1.25)	1.94 (0.94)
Distinct geolocations of the IP addresses	1.00 (0.17)	1.02 (0.31)
Mean TTL value	7,578.13 (17,781.47)	8,039.92 (15,466.29)
Standard deviation of the TTL	2,971.65 (8,777.26)	2,531.38 (7,456.62)
Lifetime of domain	10.98 (7.46)	6.75 (5.77)
Active time of domain	8.40 (6.79)	4.64 (5.66)

In order to understand the malicious abilities of an adversary, we manipulated the base features over a wide range of possible values, one feature at a time.[3] For each feature we took into account only the range of possible values. Our analysis considers an intelligent adversary with black-box access to the model (i.e., a set of features or output for a given input). Our robustness analysis is based on an ANN model that classifies the manipulated samples, where the train set is our empirically crawled data, and the test set includes the manipulated malicious samples. Figure 3 depicts the possible adversary manipulations over any of the features. Our evaluation metric, the prediction percentage, was defined as the average detection rate after our modification.

---

[3] Each feature was evaluated over all possible values for that feature.

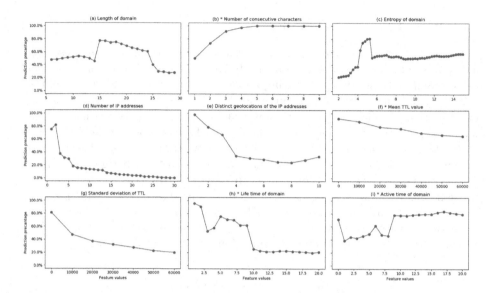

Fig. 3. Base feature manipulation graphs (* robust or semi-robust features)

We divided the well-known features into three groups: robust features, robust features that seemed non-robust (defined as semi-robust), and non-robust features. Next, we show how an attacker can manipulate the classifier for each feature and define its robustness:

1. **"Length of domain"**: an adversary can easily purchase a short or long domain to result in a benign classification for a malicious domain; hence this feature was classified as non-robust.

2. **"Number of consecutive characters"**: surprisingly, as depicted in Fig. 3, manipulating the "Number of consecutive characters" feature can significantly lower the prediction percentage (e.g., move from three consecutive characters to one or two). Nevertheless, as depicted in Table 1, on average, there were 1.46 consecutive characters in malicious domains. Therefore, manipulating this feature is not enough to break the model, and we considered it a robust feature.

3. **"Entropy of the domain"**: in order to manipulate the "Entropy of the domain" feature as benign domain entropy, the adversary can create a domain name with entropy <4. For example, let us take the domain "ddcd.cc" which is available for purchase. The entropy for this domain is 3.54. This value falls precisely in the entropy area of the benign domains defined by the trained model. This example breaks the model and causes a malicious domain to look like a benign URL. Hence, we classified this feature as non-robust.

4. **"Number of IP addresses"**: note that an adversary can dd many A records to the DNS zone file of its domain to imitate a benign domain. Thus, to manipulate the number of IP addresses, an intelligent adversary

only needs to have several different IP addresses and add them to the zone file. This fact classifies this feature as non-robust.

5. **"Distinct Geolocations of the IP addresses"**: in order to be able to break the model with the "Distinct Geolocations of the IP addresses" feature, the adversary needs to use several IP addresses from different geolocations. If the adversary can determine how many different countries are sufficient to mimic the number of distinct countries of benign domains, he will be able to append this number of IP addresses (a different IP address from each geo-location) to the DNS zone file. Thus, this feature was also classified as non-robust.

6–7. **"Mean TTL value"** and **"Standard deviation of the TTL"**: there is a clear correlation between the "Mean TTL value" and the "Standard deviation of the TTL" features since the value manipulated by the adversary is the TTL itself. Thus, it makes no difference if the adversary cannot manipulate the "Mean TTL value" feature if the model uses both. In order to robustify the more, it is better to use the "Mean TTL value" feature without the "Standard deviation of the TTL" one. Solely in terms of the "Mean TTL value" feature, Fig. 3 shows that manipulation will not result in a false classification since the prediction percentage does not drop dramatically, even when this feature is drastically manipulated. Therefore we considered this feature to be robust.

An adversary can set the DNS TTL values to [0,120000] (according to the RFC 2181 [2] the TTL value range is from 0 to $2^{31} - 1$). Figure 3 shows that even manipulating the value of this feature to 60000 will break the model and cause a malicious domain to be wrongly classified as a benign URL. Therefore the "Standard deviation of the TTL" cannot be considered a robust feature.

8. **"Lifetime of domain"**: as for the lifetime of domains, based on [42] we know that a benign domain's lifetime is typically much longer than a malicious domain's lifetime. In order to break the model by manipulating the "Lifetime of domain" feature, the adversary must buy an old domain that is available on the market. Even though it is possible to buy an appropriate domain, it will take time to find one, and it will be expensive. Hence we considered this to be a semi-robust feature.

9. **"Active time of domain"**: similar to the previous feature, in order to break "Active time of domain", an adversary must find a domain with a particular active time (Fig. 3), which is much more tricky. It is hard, expensive, and possibly unfeasible. Therefore we considered this to be a semi-robust feature.

4   Empirical Analysis and Evaluation

4.1   Experimental Design

Before turning to the training phase, we needed to verify that our dataset accurately represented the real-world distribution of URL malware. Hence, we constructed our dataset such that 75% were benign URLs, and the remaining 25%

were malicious domains (~5,000 benign URLs and ~1,350 malicious domains respectively) [7].

The evaluation step measured the efficiency of our different models while varying the robustness of the features included in the model. Specifically, we trained the different models using the following feature sets:

– Base (B) - the base feature set defined as the ones commonly used in previous works (see Table 1 for more details).
– Base Robust (BR) - the subset of base features that were found to be robust (marked with a * in Fig. 3).

There are many ways to define the efficiency of a model. To account for most of them, we looked at a broad set of metrics including Accuracy, Recall, the F1-score, and training time. Note that for each model, we split the dataset into train and test using the above proportion of 75/25, which is different from the 75/25 (benign/malicious) division used to construct the dataset.

4.2 Models and Parameters

We decided to analyze four commonly used classification models: Logistic Regression (LR), Support Vector Machines (SVM), Extreme Learning Machine (ELM), and Artificial Neural Networks (ANN). All the models were trained and evaluated on a Dell XPS 8920 computer, Windows 10 64Bit OS with 3.60 GHz Intel Core i7-7700 CPU, 16 GB of RAM, and NVIDIA GeForce GTX 1060 6 GB.

In the following paragraphs, for each model, we first describe the hyperparameters used for the evaluation, followed by the empirical, experimental results (which summed several tests results using different random train-test sets), and a short discussion of our findings and their implications.

Logistic Regression. As a baseline for the experiments, and before using the nonlinear models, we used the LR classification model. We trained the LR model with the two feature sets and tuned the hyperparameters to maximize the model's performance. For the model hyperparameters, the polynomial feature degree was 3, K-Fold CV, where K = 10 and L-BFGS [26] as the solver.

Table 2. Summary of the results for the LR model

Feature set	Accuracy	Recall	F1-Score	Training time
Base	89.99%	38.82%	53.21%	13.41 min
Robust Base	88.33%	38.87%	49.42%	1.77 min

Table 2 shows that the Accuracy rates for the feature sets were very similar. However, the Accuracy rate measures how well the model predicts (i.e., TP+TN) with respect to all the predictions (i.e., TP+TN+FP+FN). Thus given the unbalanced dataset, ˜90% Accuracy is not a necessarily a sufficient result. This can be proven to be correct when looking at the Recall that focuses solely on the malicious domains that the model identified (i.e., TP) with respect to all the malicious domains samples that were tested (i.e., TP + FN). These findings suggest that the Accuracy rate was not a good measure in our domain; therefore, we decided to focus on the F1-score measure, which is a harmonic mean formula of the Precision and the Recall measures. Finally, based on the resulting F1-scores, we concluded that LR was not strong enough to learn the right patterns. Next, we decided to use the SVM model with an RBF kernel as a nonlinear model.

SVM. For the model hyperparameters, the polynomial feature degree was 3, K-Fold where k = 10, gamma = 2 and the RBF [33] as the kernel. Compared to Table 2, Table 3 shows a significant improvement in the Recall and F1-score measures; e.g., for *Base*, the Recall and the F1-score measures were both above 90%. By comparison to the similar analysis provided by [42], our SVM model resulted in a higher Accuracy rate.[4] One could be concerned by the fact that the model trained on the *Base* feature set resulted in a higher recall (and F1-score) than the one trained on the *Robust Base* feature set. However, it should be recalled that the *Robust Base* feature set is composed of fewer than half of the *Base* features, and may perform worse. We note that our results are based on analyzing a non-manipulated dataset. As stated above, the *Base* feature set includes some non-robust features. Hence, an intelligent adversary can manipulate the values of these features, resulting in a wrong classification of malicious instances (up to the extreme of a 0% recall). This would be significantly harder for a model that was trained using the *Robust Base* features, since each of them was specifically chosen to avoid such manipulations. In order to find models that were also efficient on the non-manipulated dataset, we examined the two sophisticated models in our analysis, the ELM model as presented in [42] and the ANN model.

Table 3. Summary of the results for the SVM model

Feature set	Accuracy	Recall	F1-Score	Training time
Base	96.49%	91.20%	91.36%	6.06 min
Robust Base	90.14%	56.51%	69.93%	4.7 min

ELM. Model hyperparameters: We generated this model with one input layer, one hidden layer (that contained 50 or 100 nodes, depending on the ability of the model to converge), and one output layer. The activation function for the first layer was ReLU [29], and for the hidden layer was Sigmoid. As with the former algorithms, in this case as well, we used K-Fold, where k = 10.

---

[4] Because the dataset used by [42] is not publicly available, we could not directly compare the two models.

Table 4. Summary of the results for the ELM model

Feature set	Accuracy	Recall	F1-Score	Training time
Base	98.17%	88.81%	92.92%	0.01 min
Robust Base	98.83%	92.24%	95.81%	0.006 min

The ELM model resulted in high accuracy, and higher Recall rates compared to Table 2. When compared to the SVM models, the *Base* model resulted in lower recall, while the *Robust Base* resulted in a higher one. Even though the *Robust Base* feature set had a low dimensional space, the three rates (i.e., Accuracy, Recall, and F1-score) were high enough. Next, we compared the ELM model to an ANN model.

ANN. Model hyperparameters: We generated this model with one input layer, three hidden layers, and one output layer. For the input layer and the first hidden layer, we used ReLU; for the second hidden layer, we used LeakyReLU, and for the third hidden layer, we used Sigmoid as the activation functions. The batch size was 150, with a learning rate of 0.01 and the Adam [24] optimizer with $\beta_1 = 0.9$ and $\beta_2 = 0.999$. As for the K-Fold Cross-Validation, k was set to 10 (Table 5).

Table 5. Summary of the results for the ANN model

Feature set	Accuracy	Recall	F1-Score	Training time
Base	97.20%	88.03%	90.23%	2.63 min
Robust Base	95.71%	83.63%	88.78%	2.68 min

As shown in the table, the *Robust Base* feature set returned almost 90% F1-score and around a 83% Recall rate, such that given the low dimensional space of *Robust Base*, these results were very good. However, in comparison to Table 4, the above results were less good even though our goal was met.

Note that all the results provided in this section are based on clean data (i.e., with no adversarial manipulation). Naturally, given an adversarial model where the attacker can manipulate the values of features, models which are based on the *Robust Base* feature set will dominate models that are trained using the *Base* dataset. Thus, by showing the the *Roubst Base* feature set does not dramatically decrease the performance of the defender model using clean data, and based on the fact that it will be not fail in adversarial settings, we conclude that the defender should use this feature set of its robust malicious domain detection.

5   Conclusion

Numerous attempts have been made to tackle the problem of identifying malicious domains. However, many of them fail to successfully classify malware in realistic environments where an adversary can manipulate the URLs and/or other extracted features. Specifically, we tackled the case where an attacker has black-box access to the model (i.e., a set of features or output for a given input), and tampers with the domain properties (or network parameters). This tampering has a catastrophic effect on the model's efficiency.

As a countermeasure, we used a novel intelligent feature selection procedure which is robust to adversarial manipulation. We evaluate feature robustness and model effectiveness based on well-known machine and deep learning models over a sizeable realistic dataset (composed of 5,345 benign URLs and 1,356 malicious ones). Our evaluation showed that models that are trained using our robust features are more precise in terms of manipulated data while maintaining good results on clean data as well. Clearly, further research is needed to create models that can also classify malicious domains into malicious attack types. Another promising direction would be clustering a set of malicious domains into one cyber campaign.

Acknowledgement. This work was supported by the Ariel Cyber Innovation Center in conjunction with the Israel National Cyber directorate in the Prime Minister's Office. This work was supported by the Data Science and Artificial Intelligence Research Center at Ariel University.

References

1. Alexa. https://www.alexa.com
2. Clarifications to the DNS specification. https://tools.ietf.org/html/rfc2181
3. Phishtank. https://www.phishtank.com
4. Scumware. https://www.scumware.org
5. A study of whois privacy and proxy service abuse. https://gnso.icann.org/sites/default/files/filefield_41831/pp-abuse-study-20sep13-en.pdf
6. URL hause by abuse. https://urlhaus.abuse.ch
7. Webroot. https://www.webroot.com
8. Ahmed, M., Khan, A., Saleem, O., Haris, M.: A fault tolerant approach for malicious URL filtering. In: 2018 International Symposium on Networks, Computers and Communications (ISNCC), pp. 1–6. IEEE (2018)
9. Antonakakis, M., Perdisci, R., Dagon, D., Lee, W., Feamster, N.: Building a dynamic reputation system for DNS. In: USENIX Security Symposium, pp. 273–290 (2010)
10. Antonakakis, M., Perdisci, R., Lee, W., Vasiloglou, N., Dagon, D.: Detecting malware domains at the upper DNS hierarchy. In: USENIX Security Symposium, vol. 11, pp. 1–16 (2011)
11. Berger, H., Dvir, A.Z., Geva, M.: A wrinkle in time: a case study in DNS poisoning. CoRR abs/1906.10928 (2019). http://arxiv.org/abs/1906.10928
12. Bilge, L., Sen, S., Balzarotti, D., Kirda, E., Kruegel, C.: Exposure: a passive DNS analysis service to detect and report malicious domains. ACM Trans. Inf. Syst. Secur. **16**(4), 14:1–14:28 (2014). http://doi.acm.org/10.1145/2584679

13. Blum, A., Wardman, B., Solorio, T., Warner, G.: Lexical feature based phishing URL detection using online learning. In: Proceedings of the 3rd ACM Workshop on Artificial Intelligence and Security, pp. 54–60. ACM (2010)

14. Caglayan, A., Toothaker, M., Drapeau, D., Burke, D., Eaton, G.: Real-time detection of fast flux service networks. In: Conference For Homeland Security, CATCH 2009. Cybersecurity Applications & Technology, pp. 285–292. IEEE (2009)

15. Canali, D., Cova, M., Vigna, G., Kruegel, C.: Prophiler: a fast filter for the large-scale detection of malicious web pages. In: Proceedings of the 20th International Conference on World Wide Web, pp. 197–206. ACM (2011)

16. Choi, H., Zhu, B.B., Lee, H.: Detecting malicious web links and identifying their attack types. WebApps 11(11), 218 (2011)

17. Das, A., Data, G., Platform, A., Jain, E., Dey, S.: Machine learning features for malicious URL filtering-the survey (2019)

18. Dolberg, L., François, J., Engel, T.: Efficient multidimensional aggregation for large scale monitoring. In: LISA, pp. 163–180 (2012)

19. Harel, N., Dvir, A., Dubin, R., Barkan, R., Shalala, R., Hadar, O.: Misal-a minimal quality representation switch logic for adaptive streaming. Multimed. Tools Appl. 78, 26483–26508 (2019)

20. Hu, Z., Chiong, R., Pranata, I., Susilo, W., Bao, Y.: Identifying malicious web domains using machine learning techniques with online credibility and performance data. In: 2016 IEEE Congress on Evolutionary Computation (CEC), pp. 5186–5194. IEEE (2016)

21. Huang, G.B., Zhu, Q.Y., Siew, C.K.: Extreme learning machine: theory and applications. Neurocomputing 70(1–3), 489–501 (2006)

22. Jung, J., Sit, E.: An empirical study of spam traffic and the use of DNS black lists. In: Proceedings of the 4th ACM SIGCOMM Conference on Internet Measurement, pp. 370–375. ACM (2004)

23. Khonji, M., Iraqi, Y., Jones, A.: Phishing detection: a literature survey. IEEE Commun. Surv. Tutor. 15(4), 2091–2121 (2013)

24. Kingma, D.P., Ba, J.: Adam: a method for stochastic optimization. arXiv preprint arXiv:1412.6980 (2014)

25. Le, A., Markopoulou, A., Faloutsos, M.: PhishDef: URL names say it all. In: 2011 Proceedings IEEE INFOCOM, pp. 191–195. IEEE (2011)

26. Liu, D.C., Nocedal, J.: On the limited memory BFGS method for large scale optimization. Math. Program. 45, 503–528 (1989)

27. Ma, J., Saul, L.K., Savage, S., Voelker, G.M.: Beyond blacklists: learning to detect malicious web sites from suspicious URLs. In: Proceedings of the 15th ACM SIGKDD International Conference on Knowledge Discovery and Data Mining, pp. 1245–1254. ACM (2009)

28. Mishsky, I., Gal-Oz, N., Gudes, E.: A topology based flow model for computing domain reputation. In: Samarati, P. (ed.) DBSec 2015. LNCS, vol. 9149, pp. 277–292. Springer, Cham (2015). https://doi.org/10.1007/978-3-319-20810-7_20

29. Nair, V., Hinton, G.E.: Rectified linear units improve restricted Boltzmann machines. In: Proceedings of the 27th International Conference on Machine Learning (ICML 2010), pp. 807–814 (2010)

30. Nelms, T., Perdisci, R., Ahamad, M.: ExecScent: mining for new C&C domains in live networks with adaptive control protocol templates. In: USENIX Security Symposium, pp. 589–604 (2013)

31. Othman, H., Gudes, E., Gal-Oz, N.: Advanced flow models for computing the reputation of internet domains. In: Steghöfer, J.-P., Esfandiari, B. (eds.) IFIPTM

2017. IAICT, vol. 505, pp. 119–134. Springer, Cham (2017). https://doi.org/10.1007/978-3-319-59171-1_10

32. Papernot, N., McDaniel, P., Wu, X., Jha, S.: Distillation as a defense to adversarial perturbations against deep neural networks. In: IEEE Symposium on Security and Privacy (2016)

33. Park, J., Sandberg, I.W.: Universal approximation using radial-basis-function networks. Neural Comput. **3**(2), 246–257 (1991)

34. Peng, T., Harris, I., Sawa, Y.: Detecting phishing attacks using natural language processing and machine learning. In: 2018 IEEE 12th International Conference on Semantic Computing (ICSC), pp. 300–301. IEEE (2018)

35. Perdisci, R., Corona, I., Giacinto, G.: Early detection of malicious flux networks via large-scale passive dns traffic analysis. IEEE Trans. Dependable Secure Comput. **9**(5), 714–726 (2012)

36. Prakash, P., Kumar, M., Kompella, R.R., Gupta, M.: PhishNet: predictive blacklisting to detect phishing attacks. In: 2010 Proceedings IEEE INFOCOM, pp. 1–5. IEEE (2010)

37. Rahbarinia, B., Perdisci, R., Antonakakis, M.: Efficient and accurate behavior-based tracking of malware-control domains in large ISP networks. ACM Trans. Priv. Secur. (TOPS) **19**(2), 4 (2016)

38. Ranganayakulu, D., Chellappan, C.: Detecting malicious urls in e-mail-an implementation. AASRI Procedia **4**, 125–131 (2013)

39. Sahoo, D., Liu, C., Hoi, S.C.: Malicious URL detection using machine learning: a survey. arXiv preprint arXiv:1701.07179 (2017)

40. Sandell, N., Varaiya, P., Athans, M., Safonov, M.: Survey of decentralized control methods for large scale systems. IEEE Trans. Autom. Control **23**(2), 108–128 (1978)

41. Sheng, S., Wardman, B., Warner, G., Cranor, L.F., Hong, J., Zhang, C.: An empirical analysis of phishing blacklists. In: Sixth Conference on Email and Anti-Spam (CEAS), California, USA (2009)

42. Shi, Y., Chen, G., Li, J.: Malicious domain name detection based on extreme machine learning. Neural Process. Lett. **48**, 1–11 (2017)

43. Shu, X., Tian, K., Ciambrone, A., Yao, D.: Breaking the target: an analysis of target data breach and lessons learned. arXiv preprint arXiv:1701.04940 (2017)

44. Sun, X., Tong, M., Yang, J., Xinran, L., Heng, L.: HinDom: a robust malicious domain detection system based on heterogeneous information network with transductive classification. In: 22nd International Symposium on Research in Attacks, Intrusions and Defenses (RAID 2019), pp. 399–412 (2019)

45. Tong, L., Li, B., Hajaj, C., Xiao, C., Zhang, N., Vorobeychik, Y.: Improving robustness of ML classifiers against realizable evasion attacks using conserved features. In: The 28th USENIX Security Symposium, USENIX Security 2019 (2019)

46. Torabi, S., Boukhtouta, A., Assi, C., Debbabi, M.: Detecting internet abuse by analyzing passive DNS traffic: a survey of implemented systems. IEEE Commun. Surv. Tutor. **20**, 3389–3415 (2018)

47. Xiang, G., Hong, J., Rose, C.P., Cranor, L.: Cantina+: a feature-rich machine learning framework for detecting phishing web sites. ACM Trans. Inf. Syst. Secur. (TISSEC) **14**(2), 21 (2011)

48. Yadav, S., Reddy, A.K.K., Reddy, A.L.N., Ranjan, S.: Detecting algorithmically generated domain-flux attacks with DNS traffic analysis. IEEE/ACM Trans. Netw. **20**(5), 1663–1677 (2012). https://doi.org/10.1109/TNET.2012.2184552

49. Zwaan, A.: Malicious domain name detection system (2016)

NeuroGIFT: Using a Machine Learning Based Sat Solver for Cryptanalysis

Ling Sun[1], David Gerault[2(✉)], Adrien Benamira[2], and Thomas Peyrin[2]

[1] Key Laboratory of Cryptologic Technology and Information Security,
Ministry of Education, Shandong University, Jinan 250100, China
[2] Temasek Laboratories, Nanyang Technological University, Singapore, Singapore
`david@gerault.net`

Abstract. A recent trend in machine learning is the implementation of machine learning based solvers, such as the sat solver NeuroSat. The main limitation of NeuroSat is its scaling to large problems. We conjecture that this lack of scaling is due to learning an all-purpose SAT solver, and that learning to solve specialized SAT problems instead should yield better results. In this article, we evaluate our hypothesis by training and testing NeuroSat on SAT problems for differential cryptanalysis on the block cipher GIFT, and present the resulting classifier NeuroGift. We show that on these highly structured problems, our models are able to perform orders of magnitude better than the original NeuroSat, potentially paving the way for the use of specialized solvers for cryptanalysis problems.

Keywords: Machine learning · Neural network · SAT · GIFT · Cryptanalysis

1 Introduction

In recent years, machine learning techniques have become prominent for solving a wide range of problems. Recently, a promising method to solve combinatorial problems using machine learning was proposed. In NeuroSat [SLB+18], the authors propose to train a machine learning to solve combinatorial problems expressed in the SAT formalism. Since its publication in 2018, the article gained a lot of traction, and started a very active (over 80 citations to this day) research area on how to develop solvers based on machine learning.

In the field of cryptanalysis, SAT solvers, as well as other paradigms, such as MILP and constraint programming, are frequently used to evaluate the security of a primitive [MWGP11,GMS16]. In particular, one of the most prominent forms of cryptanalysis, differential cryptanalysis, requires solving a heavily combinatorial problem as a starting point to a key recovery attack. Namely, this preliminary phase requires finding good *differential paths*, *i.e.*, propagation patterns from a difference between two plaintexts to a difference between two ciphertexts, that occur with a good probability. Among other optimisation tools,

© Springer Nature Switzerland AG 2020
S. Dolev et al. (Eds.): CSCML 2020, LNCS 12161, pp. 62–84, 2020.
https://doi.org/10.1007/978-3-030-49785-9_5

SAT solvers have been successfully used for this task [KLT15, MP13]. However, the SAT problems studied for cryptanalysis typically have way more variables and clauses than those solvable by NeuroSat (for instance, the problems studied in this article have thousands of variables). In addition, the main limitation of NeuroSat is its training regime: the generation of the training set requires to repeatedly call an external solver, and becomes impractical when the number of variables goes over a few hundreds [AMW19]. Therefore, it is not possible to directly apply the original NeuroSat to cryptanalysis problems. On the other hand, our cryptanalysis problems are very structured, as opposed to the random problems for which NeuroSat is trained. Therefore, our hypothesis is that the neural network can learn from the structure of these problems, yielding a cryptanalysis-oriented specialised solver, rather than a general purpose SAT solver. Hence, the research question we are interested in answering is

Can NeuroSat learn to solve highly specialized cryptanalysis problems more efficiently than generic random problems?

In this article, we present the experiments we led to solve that question. Training a neural network requires a training set composed of positive samples and negative samples. In our case, the positive samples are the SAT problems where the fixed input and output difference correspond to optimal differential characteristics (i.e., characteristics that have the minimal number of active S-boxes given a number of rounds), and the negative samples are SAT problems with fixed input and output differences that do no not correspond to optimal characteristic (i.e., for which the best possible characteristic has more active S-boxes than the overall optimal characteristic). We therefore need to be able to determine rapidly, for a large number of samples, the best possible characteristic given an input and output difference. We chose to perform our experiments on the block cipher GIFT, for which this task can be solved rapidly using Crypto-MiniSat [SNC09] (less than 3 s per problem for 10 rounds).

On the problems we studied, our classifier, NeuroGift, showed remarkable performance. It was able to solve instances with significantly more variables than the original NeuroSat, obtain better accuracies, and generalise to bigger instances much better. Table 1 shows a comparison between the results obtained in the NeuroSat article and our best classifiers.

Table 1. Comparison of NeuroSat and NeuroGift

	NeuroSat	NeuroGift
Variables	$10 \leq n \leq 40$	$699 \leq n \leq 1494$
Training set	"Millions of pairs"	600 pairs
Best test accuracy	85%	100%

In this article, we present our experimental results, which can be summarised by the following contributions:

- We introduce NeuroGift, an adaptation of NeuroSat to the problem of determining whether there exists an optimal differential path for GIFT-64-128, satisfying a given input difference, output difference, and number of rounds.
- We present experiments aiming at validating that NeuroGift is actually able to learn to solve the corresponding SAT problem, rather than exploiting side information to do its classification.

2   Preliminaries

Since we aim to apply NeuroSAT to a specific kind of SAT problems in cryptanalysis, we first introduce the related SAT problems. Following that, some relevant information in the field of machine learning is provided. Finally, we recall NeuroSAT, which is the network we use in this paper.

2.1   GIFT-64-128

GIFT [BPP+17] is a family of lightweight block ciphers proposed at CHES 2017. As an improved version of PRESENT [BKL+07], it provides much-increased efficiency in all domains. At the same time, the well-known weakness of PRESENT regarding linear hull effect is overcome. There are two versions of GIFT - GIFT-64-128 and GIFT-128-128. We only focus on GIFT-64-128 in this paper and sometimes denote it as GIFT for short.

GIFT-64-128 is a 28-round Substitution Permutation Network (SPN) block cipher with 64-bit block size that supports 128-bit key. The round function, which is depicted in Fig. 1, consists of standard operations such as substitution, permutation and subkey XOR. At the beginning of each round, 16 identical 4-bit S-boxes are applied in parallel as a non-linear substitution layer. Just after the substitution, a linear permutation is performed to provide diffusion, and finally, the state is XORed with the round key and the round constant. For more information, please find [BPP+17].

2.2   Differential Cryptanalysis

Differential cryptanalysis was first introduced by Biham and Shamir in [BS90]. It is one of the most widely used and efficient forms of cryptanalysis. Consider a function $f : \mathbb{F}_2^b \to \mathbb{F}_2^b$. Let x and x' be two different inputs for the function f with a difference $\Delta x := x \oplus x'$, and let $y = f(x)$ and $y' = f(x')$, such that $\Delta y = y \oplus y'$. Now, we are interested in the probability p such that $\Delta x \xrightarrow{f} \Delta y$. This can be calculated as such:

$$\mathbb{P}(\Delta x \xrightarrow{f} \Delta y) := \frac{\#\{x | f(x) \oplus f(x \oplus \Delta x) = \Delta y\}}{2^b} \tag{1}$$

If f is linear, then $\mathbb{P}(\Delta x \xrightarrow{f} \Delta y)$ can only be 0 or 1. Thus, the interest lies in when f is non-linear. In particular, for GIFT, the non-linear component is the

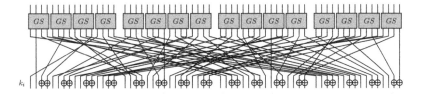

Fig. 1. Round function of `GIFT-64-128`.

S-box, which operates on consecutive nibbles (4-bit words) of the state. In order to study the propagation of a given difference through the S-box, the classical method is to build a Difference Distribution Table (DDT). Each entry of the DDT is of the form $(\Delta_{in}, \Delta_{out}, p)$, where p is the probability that the difference Δ_{in} results in the difference Δ_{out} after an S-Box.

The first step of differential cryptanalysis is to build *differential characteristics*, *i.e.*, difference propagation paths through the cipher. In particular, we are interested in maximizing the probability, over all plaintexts and differences,

$$\mathbb{P}^{opt}_{P,\delta_{in},\delta_{out}\in\mathbb{P}^3}(E(P) \oplus E(P') = \delta_{out}|P \oplus P' = \delta_{in})$$

Finding such an optimal path is a highly combinatorial problem. One of the common approaches to tackle it is to use SAT solvers.

2.3 SAT Problem

The boolean satisfiability problem (SAT) focuses on the satisfiability of a given Boolean formula. The SAT problem is *satisfiable* if the variables can be replaced with the values `True` or `False` so that the formula is evaluated to be `True`. It was shown that the problem is NP-complete [Coo71]. However, modern SAT solvers based on backtracking search can solve problems of practical interest with millions of variables and clauses [VHLP08].

For every Boolean formula, there is an equi-satisfiable formula in Conjunctive Normal Form (CNF), expressed as the conjunction ($\wedge$) of the disjunction ($\vee$) of (possibly negated) variables. Every conjunct of the Boolean formula in CNF is called a *clause*, and each (possibly negated) variable within a clause is called a *literal*. Since most SAT solvers regard problems in CNF as standard input, we are required to transform the question into an equivalent one in CNF when we plan to exploit SAT solver to solve it.

2.4 SAT Problems for `GIFT-64-128`

The problem we are interested in is about the optimal differential characteristic of `GIFT` with the minimum number of active S-boxes. An S-box is said to be active if it has a non-zero input difference. In practice, the number of active S-boxes provide a bound on the probability $\mathbb{P}^{opt}$, and is easier to obtain than the exact probability of a characteristic. We adopt the method in [SWW18] to construct the corresponding SAT problems.

Basically, the clauses in the SAT problem can be divided into two groups. One group is used to propagate the input difference through the internal components of the cipher, and the other one depicts the objective function.

To trace the difference propagation of GIFT, the critical point lies in the manipulation of the S-box, since it is the unique non-linear operation inside the cipher. Denote $x_0\|x_1\|x_2\|x_3$ and $y_0\|y_1\|y_2\|y_3$ the input and output differences of the S-box, respectively. An auxiliary boolean variable w is introduced for each S-box to indicate whether the S-box is active or not. We aim to generate a group of clauses about x_i, y_i and w, and all the solutions of these clauses have a one-to-one correspondence with the elements in the following set

$$S = \left\{ \boldsymbol{x}\|\boldsymbol{y}\|w \;\middle|\; \begin{array}{l} \boldsymbol{x} \rightarrow \boldsymbol{y} \text{ is a possible propagation,} \\ w = x_0 \vee x_1 \vee x_2 \vee x_3 \end{array} \right\},$$

where $\boldsymbol{x} = x_0\|x_1\|x_2\|x_3$, $\boldsymbol{y} = y_0\|y_1\|y_2\|y_3$. The idea is to add clauses, which delete the vectors not belonging to the set S. To realise this goal, we first define a 9-bit boolean function

$$f(\boldsymbol{x}\|\boldsymbol{y}\|w) = \begin{cases} 1, \text{ if } \boldsymbol{x}\|\boldsymbol{y}\|w \in S \\ 0, \text{ else} \end{cases}.$$

According to the difference distribution table (DDT) of the S-box, we can generate the product-of-sum representation of f. Each term of the representation stands for a clause that deletes an impossible case in $\mathbb{F}_2^9 \setminus S$. This representation can be simplified by invoking Logic Friday[1] software. After that, from the simplified representation of f, the clauses tracing the differential propagation of the S-box are decoded. In total, we obtain 36 clauses, which can be found in Appendix A.

Note that the active S-boxes satisfy $w = 1$. The sum of w_i's $\sum_i w_i$ equals the number of active S-boxes of the characteristic. Since we target characteristics with the minimum number of S-boxes, the objective function is set as $\sum_i w_i \leqslant \tau$, where τ is a predetermined threshold. This kind of constraint is called cardinality constraint which can be transformed into a SAT problem in CNF with the sequential encoding method [Sin05]. Specifically, for the constraint $\sum_{i=0}^{n} w_i \leqslant \tau$, new dummy variables $u_{i,j}$ $(0 \leqslant i \leqslant n-2, 0 \leqslant j \leqslant \tau-1)$ are introduced, and the following clauses will return unsatisfiable when $\sum_{i=0}^{n} w_i$ is larger than τ,

$$\begin{cases} \overline{w_0} \vee u_{0,0} = 1 \\ \overline{u_{0,j}} = 1 \\ \overline{w_i} \vee u_{i,0} = 1 \\ \overline{u_{i-1,0}} \vee u_{i,0} = 1 \\ \overline{w_i} \vee \overline{u_{i-1,j-1}} \vee u_{i,j} = 1 \\ \overline{u_{i-1,j}} \vee u_{i,j} = 1 \\ \overline{w_i} \vee \overline{u_{i-1,\tau-1}} = 1 \\ \overline{w_{n-1}} \vee \overline{u_{n-2,\tau-1}} = 1 \end{cases} \tag{2}$$

where $1 \leqslant i \leqslant n-2$, $1 \leqslant j \leqslant \tau-1$.

---

[1] http://sontrak.com/.

Denote u_i's the partial sums $u_i = \sum_{j=1}^{i} w_j$ for increasing the value of i up to the final $i = n$. The dummy variable $u_{i,j}$ denotes the j-th digit of the i-th partial sum u_i. With sequential encoding method, the constraint $\sum_{i=0}^{n} w_i \leqslant \tau$ is converted into Eq. (2), and it is satisfiable only when the inequality constraint holds.

For the constraint $\sum_{i=0}^{n} w_i = \tau$, we only need to notice

$$\sum_{i=0}^{n} w_i = \tau \Leftrightarrow \sum_{i=0}^{n} w_i \leqslant \tau \text{ and } \sum_{i=0}^{n} \overline{w_i} \leqslant n - \tau.$$

That is, the equality constraint can be replaced with two sets of clauses, which are obtained by slightly adjusting the parameters in (2).

2.5 NeuroSAT

NeuroSAT [SLB+18] is designed as a neural classifier to predict the satisfiability of a SAT problem. In this section, we give an overview of NeuroSAT. For a more complete explanation and examples, please refer to [SLB+18]. The SAT problems are encoded as undirected graphs, and NeuroSAT operates on graphs as a Message Passing Neural Network (MPNN) [GSR+17]. Denote P a SAT problem with n literals composed of m clauses. The graph G_P of P consists of $2n + m$ nodes. Each element of the n pairs of complementary literals (x_i and $\overline{x_i}$) is represented as a node. Besides, one node is distributed for each of the m clauses. The edge between the literal x_i and the clause c_j exists if and only if c_j is related to x_i. To clarify the relationship between x_i and $\overline{x_i}$, a different type of line is allocated between the corresponding nodes. We define the characteristic function $\phi(P)$ of P as

$$\phi(P) = \begin{cases} 1, \text{ if } P \text{ is satisfiable,} \\ 0, \text{ otherwise.} \end{cases}$$

NeuroSAT acts as an approximation of the function $\phi(P)$.

In the message passing phase, the graph is embedded in a d-dimensional space. Each node has an embedding at each time step, and NeuroSAT iteratively updates this vector space embedding by passing messages back and forth along the edges of the graph. Denote $L^{(t)}$ a $2n \times d$ matrix where the i-th row stands for the embedding of the i-th literal l_i at the time step t. Let $C^{(t)}$ be an $m \times d$ matrix, and its j-th row represents the embedding of the j-th clause c_j at the time step t. The elements of $L^{(0)}$ and $C^{(0)}$ are initialised with a normal distribution. Let M be a $2n \times m$ matrix, which maintains the messages about the edges in the graph. $M(i, j) = 1$ if the literal l_i occurs in the clause c_j, otherwise, $M(i, j) = 0$. For encompassing the negation invariance of the SAT problem into the model, an operation F is introduced. F is parameterised by a matrix $L \in \mathbb{R}^{2n \times d}$, which contains the embeddings of all literals. The function of F is to swap the row corresponding to the embedding of x_i with the row of $\overline{x_i}$. An iteration consists of two stages:

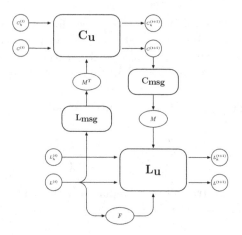

Fig. 2. An iteration of NeuroSAT.

1. each clause receives messages from all its neighbour literals and updates its embedding, accordingly;
2. each literal refines its embedding according to the messages from its neighbour clauses as well as its complementary literal.

These operations are implemented by two vanilla neural networks ($\mathbf{L_{msg}}$, $\mathbf{C_{msg}}$) and two LSTMs ?? ($\mathbf{L_u}$, $\mathbf{C_u}$). Formally, a single iteration can be expressed as

$$\left(C^{(t+1)}, C_h^{(t+1)}\right) \leftarrow \mathbf{C_u}\left(C^{(t)} \| M^T \cdot \mathbf{L_{msg}}\left(L^{(t)}\right), C_h^{(t)}\right),$$

$$\left(L^{(t+1)}, L_h^{(t+1)}\right) \leftarrow \mathbf{L_u}\left(L^{(t)} \| F(L^{(t)}) \| M \cdot \mathbf{C_{msg}}\left(C^{(t+1)}\right), L_h^{(t)}\right),$$

where $L_h^{(t)} \in \mathbb{R}^{2n \times d}$ and $C_h^{(t)} \in \mathbb{R}^{m \times d}$ are the hidden states of $\mathbf{L_u}$ and $\mathbf{C_u}$, respectively. Please refer to Fig. 2 for the framework of the iteration.

After T iterations, in the readout phase, a real number $y^{(T)}$ is computed as

$$L_*^{(T)} \leftarrow \mathbf{L_{vote}}\left(L^{(T)}\right),$$

$$y^{(T)} \leftarrow mean\left(L_*^{(T)}\right),$$

where $\mathbf{L_{vote}}$ is a 3-layer neural network, $L_*^{(T)}$ is a $2n$-dimensional vector. Denote the prediction of NeuroSAT for the problem P as $\mathtt{NeuroSAT}(P)$. $\mathtt{NeuroSAT}(P)$ depends on the value of $y^{(T)}$,

$$\mathtt{NeuroSAT}(P) = \begin{cases} 1, \text{ if } y^{(T)} > 0, \\ 0, \text{ otherwise.} \end{cases}$$

NeuroSAT is trained to minimise the sigmoid cross entropy between $y^{(T)}$ and the correct label $\phi(P)$.

Table 2. Parameters of SAT problems for `GIFT`.

Round	1	2	3	4	5	6	7	8	9	10
#{Variables}	159	286	445	699	1017	1494	2067	2736	3358	4044
#{Clauses}	748	1433	2182	3120	4186	5569	7144	8911	10585	12387
#{Nodes}	1066	2005	3072	4518	6220	8557	11278	14383	17301	20475

The training set of NeuroSAT is composed of pairs of random SAT problems on n variables. One problem in the pair is satisfiable, and the other one is unsatisfiable. The two samples differ by negating only a single literal occurring in one clause. All the pairs satisfying these properties constitute the set $\mathbf{SR}(n)$. In [SLB+18], the authors trained NeuroSAT with samples randomly drawn from $\mathbf{SR}(\mathbf{U}(10, 40)) = \bigcup_{n=10}^{40} \mathbf{SR}(n)$ and tested it on $\mathbf{SR}(40)$. On average, the accuracy of NeuroSAT reaches 85%. When the network is generalised to $\mathbf{SR}(200)$, NeuroSAT can solve about 25% of them by running for more iterations of message passing [SLB+18].

3 NeuroGIFT

It was pointed in the paper [SLB+18] that the performance of the network on problems with more variables (e.g., $\mathbf{SR}(200)$) is not very good. However, in cryptanalysis, we are faced with problems with more than 200 variables. Table 2 lists the parameters of SAT problems for `GIFT` regarding different lengths. Our SAT problems for GIFT, from 2 rounds onwards, already have more than 200 variables. Therefore, in this section, we analyse the feasibility of training NeuroSAT on GIFT-related SAT problems. Then, the construction of the training set is introduced.

3.1 Motivations

Constricted Domain of Definition. If there is no limitation on the system memory, the training set of NeuroSAT can be randomly drawn from $\mathbf{SR}(\mathbf{U}(1, \infty))$, which contains all possible SAT problems in theory. The ultimate goal of NeuroSAT is to approximate $\phi(P)$ by transforming P into graphs. Note that there is a one-to-one correspondence between $\mathbf{SR}(\mathbf{U}(1, \infty))$ and the set $\mathcal{G}$ of all graphs. NeuroSAT is trained to identify various features of all graphs. However, when we invoke SAT solvers to realise the automatic search of characteristics used in cryptanalysis, the SAT problems we are interested in constitute only a small subclass of all possible SAT problems. That is to say, we do not require a powerful classifier as NeuroSAT. What we need in this case is a relatively weaker classifier, which only works well on a small sub-class of $\mathbf{SR}(\mathbf{U}(1, \infty))$. It is easier to train a customised classifier on a restricted domain, intuitively, since the features of the graphs in the sub-class are not as versatile as those in $\mathcal{G}$. Enlightened by this observation, we manage to apply NeuroSAT to identify the optimal differential characteristic of GIFT. We name this customised classifier as NeuroGIFT.

Similar Structures in Graphs. Although NeuroSAT is trained with small-scale SAT problems, the authors attempt to extend its scope of application and employ it to solve bigger problems in the test phase. The performance of the network in the generalised case is not very good. A possible explanation is that the diversity of graphs is affected by the number of nodes in the graphs. Thus, in the generalised case, there may exist some features that NeuroSAT never saw during the training phase, and NeuroSAT does not know how to make decisions with these novel features. In cryptanalysis, when we consider the search of differential characteristics for iterative ciphers, the clauses for one round of difference propagation are iterated several times. Thus, the graphs of SAT problems regarding different lengths may share a similar structure. We illustrate the graphs of SAT problems from 5 rounds to 8 rounds of GIFT in Fig. 3. From Fig. 3, we can identify an apparent iterative property. The outer layers of these figures are similar, and the graphs corresponding to the long characteristics contain more internal layers than those related to short characteristics. This figure is to be compared with Fig. 5, which shows that the graphs for lower number of rounds appear to be disconnected. In contrast, for 5 to 8 rounds, the graph is connected. We consider the possibility to apply a network trained with SAT problems no more than r rounds to predict the satisfiability of SAT problems longer than r rounds. The intuition is that if NeuroGIFT could learn the rule of iteration in the graphs, the generalisation would be more accessible than the case in NeuroSAT.

3.2   Construction of Training Set

In NeuroSAT, the information on the graph is involved in the matrix M. Thus, for NeuroSAT, identifying the graph is equivalent to recognising the matrix. The construction of $\mathbf{SR}(\mathbf{U}(1, \infty))$ ensures that M may take any pattern in theory. Nevertheless, since we restrict ourselves to the specific kind of SAT problems in NeuroGIFT, the pattern of M is almost fixed. In the case of GIFT, only the input/output differences and the number of rounds constitute the variations of M. To guarantee the generality of the model, we must generate the samples, carefully.

Similarly to the case of NeuroSAT, the training set of NeuroGIFT is composed of pairs of SAT problems - one is SAT sample, and the other one is UNSAT sample. Let k_r denote the number of active S-boxes in the optimal differential characteristic for r rounds. In all our SAT formulations, we add a constraint stating that the number of active s-boxes must be k_r. In our SAT samples, the variables of the SAT problem corresponding to the input and output difference are fixed to values $\delta_{in}, \delta_{out}$ such that there exists a differential characteristic with k_r active S-boxes starting with δ_{in} and ending with δ_{out}. In our UNSAT samples, the corresponding variables are set to $\delta_{in}, \delta_{out}$, such that there exists no differential trail with k_r active s-boxes starting with δ_{in} and ending with δ_{out}.

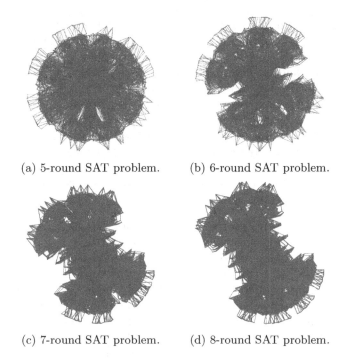

(a) 5-round SAT problem.   (b) 6-round SAT problem.

(c) 7-round SAT problem.   (d) 8-round SAT problem.

Fig. 3. Graphs of our SAT problems with different numbers of rounds.

To generate the SAT samples in the training set, we first generate the input and output differences of all optimal characteristics for the corresponding number of rounds with the SAT solver Cryptominisat5[2]. Then, we randomly pick one pair of input and output differences and set them as the input and output differences of one SAT sample. In this manner, the SAT samples are created one by one.

The selection of the UNSAT sample is technical and will affect the quality of the final classifier. First, note that the complementary set of the set $\mathcal{O}$ consisting all optimal characteristics contains all possible characteristics overriding the condition of the minimum number of active S-boxes as well as all impossible characteristics, i.e., we have

$$\mathcal{U} \backslash \mathcal{O} = \mathcal{P} \cup \mathcal{I},$$

where $\mathcal{U}$ is the set of all characteristics, $\mathcal{P}$ denotes the set of all possible characteristics overriding the condition of the minimum number of active S-boxes and $\mathcal{I}$ stands for the set composed of all impossible characteristics. A natural way to draw the input and output differences of the UNSAT samples is to set them as random numbers. Because every bit of a random number has an equal chance of being a zero or a one, the Hamming weight of the random number in nibble is usually high[3]. However, the input and output differences of an optimal

---

[2] https://github.com/msoos/cryptominisat.

[3] The probability that any nibble of a random number equals 0x0 is 1/16.

characteristic usually have relatively low Hamming weights. This distinction on the Hamming weight results in that the characteristics with random input and output differences only cover the cases in $\mathcal{I}$ and a subset of $\mathcal{P}$. A shortcoming of employing this kind of UNSAT samples is that NeuroSAT cannot learn comprehensive information in the underlying space of the training set. Just deciding by observing the Hamming weights of the input/output differences enables it to acquire high success probability in the training phase. Whereas it barely makes right predictions when we feed it with UNSAT samples having low Hamming weights in the input/output differences during the test phase.

To overcome this shortage, we should make sure that the UNSAT samples will adequately cover all cases in the set $\mathcal{U} \setminus \mathcal{O}$. We utilise the following procedures to generate the r-round UNSAT samples.

1. Suppose that the optimal r-round characteristic has k_r active S-boxes. We call Cryptominisat5 to output characteristics with $k_r + 1$, $k_r + 2$, ..., $16 \cdot r$ active S-boxes as many as possible[4] and store these solutions into File_{k_r+1}, File_{k_r+2}, ..., $\text{File}_{16 \cdot r}$, respectively.
2. Every time we are required to generate a UNSAT sample, we randomly select an integer seed s at random and compute the value $c = s \mod (16r + 1)$. If $k_r < c \leqslant 16r$, we sample a pair of input and output differences from the File_c and set them as the input and output differences of the UNSAT sample. Otherwise, the UNSAT sample is given with random input and output differences.

In this way, we guarantee that the UNSAT samples are almost uniformly distributed over the set $\mathcal{U} \setminus \mathcal{O}$. In the training phase, the network may 'see' different kinds of counterexamples, which include not only the characteristics with contradictions but also characteristics with a different number of active S-boxes. It tries to learn the features in these graphs, and evaluate its learning outcome in the test phase.

Note that we do not take into account the differential effect: there may exist differentials for which the best differential characteristic has a relatively low probability, but that over all possible differential characteristics, have a high probability. However, we verify (using CryptoMiniSat), for each of our UNSAT samples, that the best corresponding differential characteristic is not optimal.

We present the three versions of the corresponding classifier, NeuroGift.

3.3   Three Versions of NeuroGIFT

Our experiments resulted in three versions of NeuroGift:

– NeuroGift-V1 is the baseline model. The samples are generated as described in Sect. 3.2.

---

[4] Since the solver has limited computation power, we cannot obtain all solutions. However, with the observation on the outputs, we think these solutions are enough to ensure the versatile of the sample space.

- NeuroGift-trunc is designed to verify whether NeuroGift-V1 actually learns the resolution of the SAT problems. Hence, the variables corresponding to the objective function are removed from the SAT problems.
- NeuroGift-V2 is our best classifier. We keep the input and output differences in the SAT and UNSAT samples of one pair have same number of non-zero 4-bit nibbles. By forcing the SAT and UNSAT samples to be more similar, we hope to force NeuroSat to learn the actual resolution of the formula.

3.4 Parameter Setting

After each epoch of training, we evaluate the performance of the classifier on the training set. Let T denote a classification as positive, F denote a classification as negative, and let $X \in \{T, F\}, Y \in \{T, F\}$ respectively represent the prediction made by the classifier, and the ground truth. For instance, TT denotes number of samples the classifier correctly classified as positive, whereas TF denotes the number of samples classified as positive while actually being negative. The success probability (or accuracy) P_S of the classifier is

$$P_S = \frac{TT + FF}{TT + TF + FT + FF}.$$

This quantity expresses the fraction of the samples that are correctly classified. There are many tunable parameters for NeuroSat, which affect the performance of the network. It is observed that different parameters have different levels of influence on the model. We list those with non-negligible influences.

- The type of learning rate decay - There are three ways to modify the learning rate during the training phase, which are no_decay, polynomial_decay and exponential_decay. Usually, we are suggested to anneal the learning rate over time in training deep networks, since it may help us avoid wasting computation bouncing around chaotically with little improvement for a long time. However, when to decay the learning rate and how to decay it are somewhat difficult to determine because NeuroSAT is a very complicated network. So, we take a no_decay style in all experiments.
- Learning rate α - Adjusting the learning rate is a little technical. A high learning rate will make the system unstable, while it takes the model quite a long time to converge under a low learning rate.
- ℓ_2 weight - This term, which enables us to implement ℓ_2 regularisation, is used in the objective function. The intention of exploiting ℓ_2 regularisation is to escape overfitting and enhance the generalisation ability of the model.
- Clip value - It is used to clip the gradient, and this countermeasure allows us to ensure the gradient within a reasonable scale. With this method, we can effectively prevent the occurrence of gradient explosion, which is often encountered in training a deep network.

The memory complexity of NeuroSAT is related to the number of iterations T and the number of nodes in one batch. Increasing the number of iteration

T, which is the depth of the deep network, improves the performance of NeuroSAT, potentially. Increasing the number of nodes in the batch will accelerate the training phase. In NeuroGIFT, we must allocate more nodes in the batch since the problems under consideration involve much more variables and clauses than those in NeuroSAT. Thus, the value of T remains unchanged in our case, that is, $T = 26$.

4   Experimental Results

All our experiments are performed with classifiers trained on problems between 1 and 6 rounds. In additional experiments, we evaluate the generalisation ability of these classifiers on problems from 7 to 9 rounds. We give the final accuracy of our classifiers with the following setting: The training and test set composed of 4 to 6 rounds samples. More specifically, we train the networks on 600 pairs of problems, composed of 200 4-round problems, 200 5-round problems, and 200 6-round problems. The test set is composed of 100 4-round problems, 100 5-round problems, and 100 6-round problems. We use a learning rate of 2×10^{-5}, ℓ_2 weight of 10^{-7} and clip value: 0.5.

4.1   NeuroGift-V1

Our first set of experiments directly applies the training method described in the previous section, and correspond to the classifier NeuroGift-V1.

In preliminary experiments, we use SAT problems varying from 1-round to 6-round to train and evaluate the model. We observe that, while the test results are good for problems from 1 to 3 rounds, they become heavily biased for the 4 to 6-rounds samples. For the 6-round samples, the network almost regards all SAT samples as UNSAT samples (Fig. 4).

Our hypothesis is that the low-round samples have a negative effect on the accuracy of the resulting classifier. Indeed, the structure of the NeuroSat graph for these samples is different from the general structure for more rounds. This different structure is illustrated by Fig. 5 (1- and 2-round graphs) and Fig. 3 (5- to 8-round graphs). In particular, the graphs for shorter problems appear to be disconnected, as opposed to the graphs for larger problems (4 and more rounds). We conjecture that these disconnected graphs may lead the network to learn biased solving strategies.

To verify our conjecture, we use a training set composed of problems varying from 4-round to 6-round to train the network. We evaluate the classifier on a test set with 60 pairs varying from 4-round problems to 6-round problems, and the levels of confidence of the network for these problems are shown in Fig. 6. Note that this training set and the one used to train the classifier in Fig. 6 have the same amount of samples, but the scale of the vertical axis is enlarged.

It therefore appears that, for the basic classifier NeuroGift-V1, the training set with problems on 4 to 6 rounds grants better results.

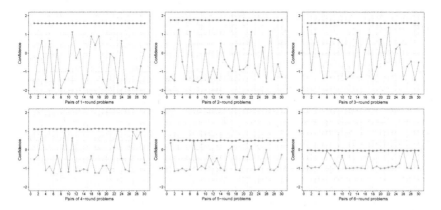

Fig. 4. Confidence of the NeuroGift-V1 trained with pairs from 1 to 6 rounds, in blue for the SAT samples, and in red for the UNSAT samples. (Color figure online)

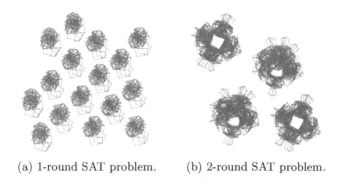

(a) 1-round SAT problem.   (b) 2-round SAT problem.

Fig. 5. Graphs corresponding to SAT problems with short lengths.

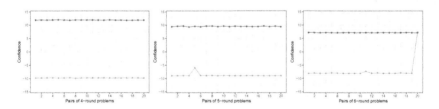

Fig. 6. Confidence of the model on the shrunken test set.

The final test accuracy, in the setting described at the beginning of the section, of the NeuroGift-V1 classifier, is 97%. From this classifier, we attempt to extract a satisfiable assignment from the SAT samples, following the methodology presented in the NeuroSat article. However, we were not able to extract a solution, leading us to wonder whether our model actually learns to solve the SAT problem. The corresponding experiments are presented in the next section.

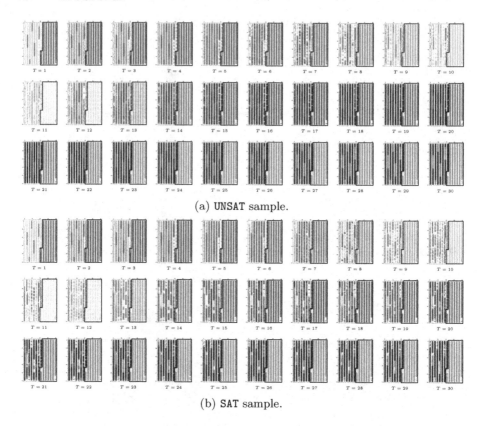

(a) UNSAT sample.

(b) SAT sample.

Fig. 7. Propagation of the vector $L_*^{(T)}$.

4.2 NeuroGift-trunc

One of our attempts at extracting a solution is illustrated on Fig. 7, through the vectors $L_*^{(T)}$'s related to different T's ($1 \leqslant T \leqslant 30$). The positive values are represented in red while the negative values are displayed in blue. The darker the colour, the larger the absolute value of the number.

An unexpected phenomenon can be observed: the variables within the black frame, which are exactly the set of variables used to count the number of active SBoxes, seems to be irrelevant to the decision of the classifier. The same pattern can be observed for SAT and UNSAT samples.

Thus, we design NeuroGift-trunc to test whether NeuroGift-V1 really needs this part from the SAT problems. This version is different from NeuroGift-V1 in the construction of the samples. The setting of input and output differences for the SAT and UNSAT samples is the same as the case of NeuroGIFT-V1. However, for all samples, we delete the auxiliary variables and clauses corresponding to the objective function. Thus, SAT problem now encodes the question of whether the characteristic with the input and output differences is possible or not, whereas the labels are still related to the objective function.

The final accuracy of this model is 99%: NeuroGift-trunc performs even better than NeuroGift-V1. This is very counter-intuitive, as the UNSAT samples are not strictly unsatisfiable: the model does not really describe what a satisfiable sample is anymore. However, NeuroGift-trunc is able to predict the corresponding artificial labels. We conjecture that the very structure of the input and output difference may give enough information for the classifier to succeed solely based on the corresponding litterals. We therefore design a new model, NeuroGift-trunc, where the training set is more carefully designed to eliminate this structure.

NeuroGift-V2. In general, differential characteristics with an optimal number of active SBoxes are such that their input and output difference have a given structure. Typically, the number of non-zero nibbles in these differences is low. While our experiments, described in Appendix B, did not provide definitive evidence that NeuroGift-V1 makes decisions by counting the number of non-zero nibbles of the input/output differences, we still wonder its performance after removing this feature from the training set. In particular, making the number of non-zero nibbles similar for the SAT and UNSAT samples may force the classifier to learn more specialized resolution features. The resulting classifier is called NeuroGift-V2. The innovation lies in the construction of the UNSAT samples. In one pair of samples, we ensure that the Hamming weights of the input/output differences of the UNSAT and SAT sample are equal, which is accomplished by the following steps.

1. We randomly sample a pair of input and output differences corresponding to an r-round optimal characteristic. Then, the Hamming weight h_{in} of the input difference and the Hamming weight h_{out} of the output difference are computed, respectively.
2. Two sets of integers $\{p_0^{in}, p_1^{in}, \ldots, p_{h_{in}-1}^{in}\}$ and $\{p_0^{out}, p_1^{out}, \ldots, p_{h_{out}-1}^{out}\}$ satisfying the following conditions are generated:
   - p_i^{in} and p_j^{out} are random positive integers no more than 16;
   - $p_i^{in} \neq p_j^{in}$ for all $0 \leqslant i < j \leqslant h_{in} - 1$;
   - $p_i^{out} \neq p_j^{out}$ for all $0 \leqslant i < j \leqslant h_{out} - 1$.

   p_i^{in}'s and p_j^{out}'s point out the non-zero nibble positions in the input and output differences of the UNSAT sample.
3. The positions of the input (resp. output) difference lie in the set $\{p_0^{in}, p_1^{in}, \ldots, p_{h_{in}-1}^{in}\}$ (resp. $\{p_0^{out}, p_1^{out}, \ldots, p_{h_{out}-1}^{out}\}$) are set with random non-zero 4-bit values. Moreover, the remaining positions are fixed as 0x0.

With this method, we eliminate the effect of the Hamming weight on the training set.

On the same test set as the other 2 variants, NeuroGift-V2 achieves 100% accuracy. However, we were still not able to extract a solution from the variable embeddings.

4.3 Generalisation to More Rounds

The results of the three models are consistent, and the best test accuracies we obtained are respectively 97%, 100% and 99%. For comparison, the results of the original NeuroSat article are given in Table 1. These results are encouraging, and seem to give a positive answer to our main question, which was to determine whether NeuroSat could perform better on sets of problems sharing similar structures, rather than random problems.

In essence, with only 600 pairs, our models were able to reach as much as 100% accuracy, whereas the best NeuroSat instance presented in the original article only reached 85% accuracy, despite being trained on millions of pairs, and studying problems with over 15 times less variables. For applications in cryptography, the ability of a neural network to make predictions for more rounds than it was trained for is very important. In particular, while solving the problem for a few rounds might be easy, it generally becomes exponentially harder as the number of rounds increases. Therefore, when applying the techniques of NeuroGift to other ciphers, we will not necessarily be able to generate an appropriate training set for a high number of rounds efficiently.

In order to evaluate the generalisation abilities of NeuroGift, we pick our best model (NeuroGift-V2), and tune its parameters for better results. After performing control experiments, the setting that resulted in the best generalisation was the following. We train the model on 500 pairs of problems from 1 to 5 rounds (100 of each), with learning rate 10^{-5}, l2 weight: 10^{-9}, and clip value: 0.5. Under this setting, we evaluated the generalisation of NeuroGift-V2 on a different test set for each number of rounds, from 6 to 10. The resulting test accuracies are given in Table 3.

Table 3. Generalisation ability of NeuroGIFT-V2.

Rounds	6	7	8	9	10
Accuracy	100%	100%	99%	99%	98%

The generalisation accuracy remains very close to 100%, even for 10 rounds problems, even though 10-rounds problems have 4 times more variables (4044) compared to the 5-rounds samples seen in training. As a comparison, in the original NeuroSat article, the accuracy dropped to approximately 40% in a similar setting (going from at most 40 variables to 160), even though the number of message passing iterations was increased from 26 to 1000. In contrast, we restricted ourselves to 26 iterations. In additional experiments, we observed that NeuroGift-V1 and NeuroGift-trunc did not generalise as well as NeuroGift-V2. In particular, the accuracy of NeuroGift-trunc drops to below 90% for 9 rounds. This could be an indication that NeuroGift-V2 actually learns something closer to the actual resolution of the SAT problem, even though we were not able to completely confirm it.

5   Conclusion

Related Work and Extentions. Following the publication of NeuroSat, a wide range of articles proposing extentions were published. We believe the most promising one for our application is the PDP framework. The PDP framework [AMW19], which is an extension of the CircuitSAT framework [AMW18], belongs to the deep learning SAT solver family as NeuroSAT [SLB+18]. But whereas NeuroSAT is a supervised framework, the work of Amizadeh et al. takes the advantage of the probabilistic inference formulation in order to propose an unsupervised setting. In fact, they introduce a differential expression of the energy function that they want to minimize. With this formulation of the problem, the work in [AMW19] outperforms the NeuroSAT model. Moreover, the work allows three different times for learning (Propagation Decimation and Prediction) which leads to an hybrid model. In fact, the three stages are modular: they can be a fully a neural embedding block or they can be replace by a traditional non trainable block (like the Survey-propagation guided decimation algorithm [MMM09] as propagator block for example). However, despite a highly parallelizable model, the training and the inference is quite long (in comparison to NeuroSAT) when the number of variable of the SAT problem growth. This is certainly due to the combination of the fact that the model has twice more embedding than NeuroSAT and the unsupervised setting. Finally, the second shortcoming of the model is that it is not clear how the model can label an UNSAT problem.

Discussion of our Results. The use of specialized solvers based on machine learning, rather than classical solvers, seems to be a promising research direction. The reason why boils down to the distinction between genericity and speciality: a solver that only aims at solving cryptanalysis problem does not need to be good at unrelated problems, and may therefore perform better on very specific problems. The main limitation to the use of such solvers, if the scaling issues are solved, will be their approximate nature. A solver such as NeuroGift gives a likelihood for the presence of a characteristic with k active S-boxes, as opposed to a traditional solver that would give an exact answer. While an approximation is, in itself, useful (after all, using the best differential characteristic is, in itself, an approximation to the resistance of a cipher against differential attacks), we believe further research should consider integrating machine learning solvers as heuristics to drive the search of classical solvers. This approach has proven efficient for generic SAT solving [SB19]. We believe combining machine learning based approaches with state-of-the-art solvers will enable progress on problems that are still difficult for classical solvers, such as cryptanalysis problems on hash functions.

Conclusion. In this article, we present models for the resolution of differential cryptanalysis problems with NeuroSat. We show that, when trained on a restricted set of problems, rather than the set of all SAT problems, the resulting classifier NeuroGift scales to significantly more variables than the original NeuroSat. However, more experiments are required to confirm that NeuroGift is able to determine the values of the variables, rather than just classifying based on some hidden structure in the input and output differences. In particular, future works includes the design of a model where the structure of the UNSAT samples is even closer to that of the SAT sample, in order to force NeuroGift to learn the actual resolution. For instance, we could set the input and output differences of the UNSAT samples to those of two different SAT samples.

While the results presented in this paper are encouraging, they do not address a fundamental limitation of NeuroSat: the size of the generated graph. For 10 rounds, the graph already has over 20000 nodes. As a comparison, on our original benchmarking GPU (GTX 970), we were not able to generate the graph for more than 7 rounds (11278 nodes) without exhausting the graphic card's memory. Therefore, for a broader application of these methods on harder cryptanalysis problems, a solution must be found to restrict the size of the graph. The experiments performed with NeuroGift-trunc seem to be a promising option: for 10 rounds, the size of the graph is only 7616 nodes. On the other hand, the generalisation capabilities of NeuroGift-trunc are not on par with NeuroGift-V2, so further improvements are needed. A potentially promising alternative left for future work would be to merge NeuroGift-V2 and NeuroGift-trunc into a single model, with the training set constraints of NeuroGift-V2, and the truncation of the objective function from NeuroGift-trunc. Our hope is that the results presented in this paper lay the groundwork for a larger scale application of machine learning based solvers to cryptanalysis problems. From these first experimental results, future research directions include studying primitives and number of rounds which are more challenging to for classical dedicated solvers.

Appendix

A   Clauses for the S-Box of GIFT

The 36 clauses are provided as follows

$$
\begin{cases}
\overline{x_0} \lor \overline{x_1} \lor \overline{x_2} \lor x_3 \lor \overline{y_2} = 1 \\
x_0 \lor \overline{x_1} \lor \overline{x_2} \lor \overline{x_3} \lor \overline{y_1} \lor \overline{y_2} = 1 \\
x_0 \lor \overline{x_1} \lor x_2 \lor \overline{y_0} \lor y_1 \lor \overline{y_2} = 1 \\
x_1 \lor x_2 \lor \overline{y_0} \lor \overline{y_1} \lor \overline{y_2} \lor y_3 = 1 \\
x_1 \lor \overline{x_2} \lor \overline{x_3} \lor y_1 \lor \overline{y_2} \lor y_3 = 1 \\
x_0 \lor x_1 \lor x_2 \lor \overline{y_0} \lor \overline{y_1} \lor y_2 \lor \overline{y_3} = 1 \\
x_0 \lor x_1 \lor \overline{x_2} \lor \overline{x_3} \lor y_1 \lor y_2 \lor \overline{y_3} = 1 \\
\overline{y_0} \lor w = 1 \\
\overline{y_1} \lor w = 1 \\
\overline{y_2} \lor w = 1 \\
\overline{y_3} \lor w = 1 \\
x_0 \lor \overline{x_1} \lor \overline{x_2} \lor x_3 \lor y_2 = 1 \\
x_1 \lor \overline{x_2} \lor x_3 \lor \overline{y_2} \lor \overline{y_3} = 1 \\
\overline{x_1} \lor x_3 \lor \overline{y_0} \lor \overline{y_2} \lor \overline{y_3} = 1 \\
\overline{x_0} \lor \overline{x_1} \lor y_0 \lor \overline{y_2} \lor \overline{y_3} = 1 \\
x_0 \lor \overline{x_3} \lor y_0 \lor \overline{y_2} \lor \overline{y_3} = 1 \\
\overline{x_0} \lor x_2 \lor x_3 \lor y_2 \lor \overline{y_3} = 1 \\
\overline{x_0} \lor y_0 \lor \overline{y_1} \lor y_2 \lor \overline{y_3} = 1 \\
x_0 \lor \overline{x_1} \lor x_2 \lor x_3 \lor y_3 = 1 \\
\overline{x_0} \lor x_1 \lor x_2 \lor x_3 \lor y_3 = 1 \\
\overline{x_1} \lor y_0 \lor \overline{y_1} \lor \overline{y_2} \lor y_3 = 1 \\
x_1 \lor \overline{x_2} \lor x_3 \lor y_2 \lor y_3 = 1 \\
x_1 \lor \overline{x_3} \lor y_0 \lor y_2 \lor y_3 = 1 \\
x_0 \lor y_0 \lor \overline{y_1} \lor y_2 \lor y_3 = 1 \\
\overline{x_1} \lor y_0 \lor y_1 \lor y_2 \lor y_3 = 1 \\
x_0 \lor x_1 \lor x_2 \lor x_3 \lor \overline{w} = 1 \\
x_0 \lor y_0 \lor y_1 \lor y_2 \lor \overline{w} = 1 \\
x_1 \lor y_0 \lor y_1 \lor y_3 \lor \overline{w} = 1 \\
x_0 \lor \overline{x_1} \lor x_2 \lor \overline{x_3} \lor y_1 \lor \overline{y_3} = 1 \\
\overline{x_0} \lor x_1 \lor \overline{x_3} \lor \overline{y_0} \lor \overline{y_2} \lor \overline{y_3} = 1 \\
\overline{x_0} \lor x_2 \lor \overline{y_0} \lor y_1 \lor y_2 \lor \overline{y_3} = 1 \\
\overline{x_0} \lor \overline{x_1} \lor \overline{x_3} \lor \overline{y_0} \lor y_2 \lor y_3 = 1 \\
\overline{x_0} \lor x_1 \lor \overline{x_2} \lor \overline{x_3} \lor \overline{y_0} \lor \overline{y_1} \lor \overline{y_3} = 1 \\
\overline{x_1} \lor \overline{x_2} \lor \overline{x_3} \lor \overline{y_0} \lor \overline{y_1} \lor y_2 \lor \overline{y_3} = 1 \\
\overline{x_0} \lor \overline{x_1} \lor x_2 \lor \overline{x_3} \lor \overline{y_0} \lor \overline{y_1} \lor y_3 = 1 \\
\overline{x_0} \lor \overline{x_1} \lor \overline{x_2} \lor \overline{x_3} \lor \overline{y_0} \lor y_1 \lor y_3 = 1
\end{cases}
$$

B   Impact of the Samples with Low Hamming Weight

In order to evaluate the impact of samples where the difference has low hamming weight, we plot the confidence of the network after each message passing iteration

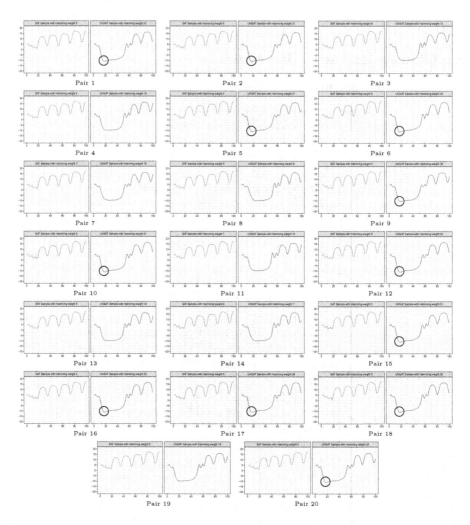

Fig. 8. Confidence for 6-round Samples. The horizontal axis corresponds to the number of iterations, and the vertical axis is the value of $y^{(T)}$. The circles show a characteristic feature of the UNSAT samples.

during the test phase of NeuroGift-V1, while keeping track of the structure of the input and output difference. Figure 8 illustrates the confidence of the network for 6-rounds samples. We can observe that the curves for all SAT samples of the same length are similar. But the curves of the UNSAT samples are different. We think that two parameters result in the difference. One reason is the Hamming weight of the input/output differences. Another one is the differential effect. We analyse the 60 pairs of samples in the test set. The Hamming weight of the UNSAT samples are provided in the figures. The samples with the same Hamming weight are illustrated with same color. It can be found that the curves with same color are similar. An interesting example is the UNSAT sample of the 20-th pair of 6-round samples, this is the unique sample that is wrongfully classified by the network. Firstly, the Hamming weight of the input/output differences of this sample is 4, which is even smaller than the value of the optimal trail. Another fact is that the corresponding differential only have one trail with 16 active S-boxes. Since NeuroGift-V1 is designed to identify the topology structure of the figure, the dominant trail property causes the network to make the wrong decision.

References

[AMW18] Amizadeh, S., Matusevych, S., Weimer, M.: Learning to solve circuit-SAT: an unsupervised differentiable approach (2018)

[AMW19] Amizadeh, S., Matusevych, S., Weimer, M.: PDP: a general neural framework for learning constraint satisfaction solvers. arXiv preprint arXiv:1903.01969 (2019)

[BKL+07] Bogdanov, A., et al.: PRESENT: an ultra-lightweight block cipher. In: Paillier, P., Verbauwhede, I. (eds.) CHES 2007. LNCS, vol. 4727, pp. 450–466. Springer, Heidelberg (2007). https://doi.org/10.1007/978-3-540-74735-2_31

[BPP+17] Banik, S., Pandey, S.K., Peyrin, T., Sasaki, Y., Sim, S.M., Todo, Y.: GIFT: a small present. In: Fischer, W., Homma, N. (eds.) CHES 2017. LNCS, vol. 10529, pp. 321–345. Springer, Cham (2017). https://doi.org/10.1007/978-3-319-66787-4_16

[BS90] Biham, E., Shamir, A.: Differential cryptanalysis of DES-like cryptosystems. In: Menezes, A.J., Vanstone, S.A. (eds.) CRYPTO 1990. LNCS, vol. 537, pp. 2–21. Springer, Heidelberg (1991). https://doi.org/10.1007/3-540-38424-3_1

[Coo71] Cook, S.A.: The complexity of theorem-proving procedures. In: Proceedings of the Third Annual ACM Symposium on Theory of Computing, pp. 151–158. ACM (1971)

[GMS16] Gerault, D., Minier, M., Solnon, C.: Constraint programming models for chosen key differential cryptanalysis. In: Rueher, M. (ed.) CP 2016. LNCS, vol. 9892, pp. 584–601. Springer, Cham (2016). https://doi.org/10.1007/978-3-319-44953-1_37

[GSR+17] Gilmer, J., Schoenholz, S.S., Riley, P.F., Vinyals, O., Dahl, G.E.: Neural message passing for quantum chemistry. arXiv preprint arXiv:1704.01212 (2017)

[KLT15] Kölbl, S., Leander, G., Tiessen, T.: Observations on the SIMON block cipher family. In: Gennaro, R., Robshaw, M. (eds.) CRYPTO 2015. LNCS, vol. 9215, pp. 161–185. Springer, Heidelberg (2015). https://doi.org/10.1007/978-3-662-47989-6_8

[MMM09] Mezard, M., Mezard, M., Montanari, A.: Information, Physics, and Computation. Oxford University Press, Oxford (2009)

[MP13] Mouha, N., Preneel, B.: Towards finding optimal differential characteristics for ARX: application to Salsa20. Cryptology ePrint Archive, Report 2013/328 (2013)

[MWGP11] Mouha, N., Wang, Q., Gu, D., Preneel, B.: Differential and linear crypt-analysis using mixed-integer linear programming. In: Wu, C.-K., Yung, M., Lin, D. (eds.) Inscrypt 2011. LNCS, vol. 7537, pp. 57–76. Springer, Heidelberg (2012). https://doi.org/10.1007/978-3-642-34704-7_5

[SB19]   Selsam, D., Bjørner, N.: Neurocore: guiding high-performance SAT solvers with unsat-core predictions. CoRR, abs/1903.04671 (2019)

[Sin05] Sinz, C.: Towards an optimal CNF encoding of boolean cardinality con-straints. In: van Beek, P. (ed.) CP 2005. LNCS, vol. 3709, pp. 827–831. Springer, Heidelberg (2005). https://doi.org/10.1007/11564751_73

[SLB+18] Selsam, D., Lamm, M., Bunz, B., Liang, P., de Moura, L., Dill, D.L.: Learning a sat solver from single-bit supervision. arXiv preprint arXiv:1802.03685 (2018)

[SNC09] Soos, M., Nohl, K., Castelluccia, C.: Extending SAT solvers to crypto-graphic problems. In: Kullmann, O. (ed.) SAT 2009. LNCS, vol. 5584, pp. 244–257. Springer, Heidelberg (2009). https://doi.org/10.1007/978-3-642-02777-2_24

[SWW18] Sun, L., Wang, W., Wang, M.: More accurate differential properties of LED64 and Midori64. IACR Trans. Symmetric Cryptol. 2018(3), 93–123 (2018)

[VHLP08] Van Harmelen, F., Lifschitz, V., Porter, B.: Handbook of Knowledge Rep-resentation. Elsevier, Amsterdam (2008)

Can the Operator of a Drone Be Located by Following the Drone's Path?

Eliyahu Mashhadi[(⊠)], Yossi Oren, and Gera Weiss

Ben Gurion University of The Negev, Beersheba, Israel
`mashhadi@post.bgu.ac.il`

Abstract. Small commercial Unmanned Aerial Systems (UASs), called drones in common language, pose significant security risks due to their agility, high availability and low price. There is, therefor, a growing need to develop methods for detection, localization and mitigation of malicious and other harmful operation of these drones. This paper presents our work towards autonomously localizing drone operators based only on following their path in the sky. We use a realistic simulation environment and collect the path of the drone when flown from different points of view. A deep neural network was trained to be able to predict the location of drone operators, given the path of the drones. The model is able to achieve prediction of the location of the location of the operator with 73% accuracy.

Keywords: Drone · UAS · Surveillance · Security · Deep learning · Deep neural network

1 Introduction

The massive use of drones for civilian and military applications raises many concerns for airports and other organizations [4]. In December 2018, for example, drones infamously caused the shutdown of the Gatwick airport in the United Kingdom. This also happened in Germany, where a drone caused the suspension of flights in Frankfurt. As the threats that drones incur include also surveillance and active attacks, defense agencies are looking for ways to mitigate the risks by locating and tracking operators of drones [3].

A number of different sensor types are available for the detection and localisation of drones and their operators. The most common sensor types studied by the research community used commercially are: Radio Frequency (RF) [6,10], Electro-Optical (EO), acoustic and radar. All the approaches that we are aware of for locating operators, not just the drones, use RF sensors. There are automatic and semi-automatic methods for locating the operators based on the radio communication between the drone and its operator. There are a number of problems with this approach. Firstly, such methods are usually tailored to a specific brand of drones. Furthermore, the radio signal can only be recorded near the

© Springer Nature Switzerland AG 2020
S. Dolev et al. (Eds.): CSCML 2020, LNCS 12161, pp. 85–93, 2020.
https://doi.org/10.1007/978-3-030-49785-9_6

drone. Finally, there are ways for malicious drone designers to apply cryptography and electronic warfare techniques to make localization by analysis of radio signals very difficult.

In this work we propose a novel method for the localisation of UAS operators using only the path of the drone in the sky. The approach is based on the observation that the behaviour of a drone in the air is visibly different depending on where the pilot is. An experienced external viewer can usually tell if the pilots uses First-Person-View (FPV) machinery or if they look at the drone from east or if they look at it from a distance. We assume that the defenders are capable of tracking the path of the drone in the sky, and show that this information is enough to gain valuable information on the location of the operator. While the path can be measured from a relatively large distance [1], it contains information because the operators usually react to environmental conditions such as sun dazzle, obstructions, etc. Our experiments show that the reactions of the operators to these conditions gives away enough information for obtaining substantial information about the location of the operator by analyzing the path of the drone in the sky. Note that we are not necessarily aiming for full localization in all setting, even the ability of distinguish between three different operators, looking from three different points of view, carrying the same known task (which is what we demonstrate in this paper) can be useful for defenders. For example, the defenders of an airport cad use such knowledge to block the line of sight of the pilot of an infiltrating drone. To the best of our knowledge, we are the first to provide a data-set of flight-paths labeled with the point-of-view of the operator and to train neural networks on such data.

2 Methodology

To allow for a controlled environment, we conducted all our experiments with a flight simulator that provides a realistic flight experience for the operator that includes sun gazes, obstructions, and other visual effects that produce the reactions of the operators that allow us to identify their location. Specifically, we used AirSim (Aerial Informatics and Robotics Simulation), which is an open-source, cross platform simulator for drones, ground vehicles such as cars and various other objects, built on Epic Games' Unreal Engine 4 [5]. AirSim provides more than 10 km of roads with many city blocks. We used it via its API that allowed us to retrieve data and control drones in a safe environment. AirSim supports hardware-in-the-loop with driving wheels and flight controllers physically and visually realistic simulations. This allowed us to provide drone pilots with a real remote control and a simulation of the full piloting experience, including the artifacts that cause pilots to perform maneuvers that unintentionally disclose their position to the defenders that watch the path of the drone.

Fig. 1. The setting of our experiments.

As shown in Fig. 1, we collected the path of the drone when flown from three different viewpoints. Two points, marked with 1 and 2, on two opposite sides of the intersection and a third point, marked by 3, from First Person View (FPV) where the operator gets the perspective of a real pilot that seats aboard the drone. In all the experiments the pilots were instructed to fly the drone from point A, in the middle of the intersection, to point B, at the bottom left.

	TimeStamp	POS_X	POS_Y	POS_Z	Q_W	Q_X	Q_Y	Q_Z
2	1557313139904	0.020689	0.025806	-1.014527	0.995622	0.001442	-0.001119	0.093454
3	1557313140027	0.024383	0.030536	-1.035369	0.991322	0.001469	-0.001079	0.131444
4	1557313140150	0.028316	0.035702	-1.044194	0.985579	0.001503	-0.001028	0.169208
5	1557313140276	0.032581	0.041509	-1.054980	0.979984	0.001545	-0.000964	0.199066
6	1557313140411	0.037385	0.048357	-1.077708	0.975740	0.001586	-0.000898	0.218925
7	1557313140537	0.047059	0.055367	-1.114959	0.973107	0.001614	-0.000851	0.230346

Fig. 2. A log of a flight produced by AirSim.

The results of the experiments were files, such as the one presented in Fig. 2, containing the log of the flight produced by AirSim. This simulates the data that we expect that the defenders can collect. It contains the full path information including the position, the orientation, and the picture of the drone in each time step. As elaborated below, we did not always use all this information with full accuracy, because it is not necessarily available.

```
!head -n7 {TRAIN_DATASET_FILE_PATH}

57,360,FPV,north_west_tree,south_east_sewer
1.8e-06,2.5333333333333334e-06,-0.004928333333333334,3.626666666666667e-05,4.4733333333333334e-05,-0.0053670666666666
1.000000000000001e-07,1.3333333333333334e-07,-0.004885833333333334,1.8333333333333335e-06,2.3666666666666667e-06,-
2.3333333333333333e-06,1.0333333333333333e-06,-0.004908133333333334,1.3366666666666667e-05,5.666666666666667e-06,-6
6.666666666666667e-08,-2.6666666666666667e-07,-0.004909966666666667,1.8333333333333335e-06,-5.666666666666667e-06,-
2.3333333333333333e-07,3.3333333333333335e-07,-0.0051110999999999995,4.666666666666666e-06,6e-06,-0.00664216666666666
0.0007380333333333334,0.0481248333333333,-0.0107641333333333,0.00275249000000000007,0.0561876666666666,-0.02101
```

Fig. 3. A comma separated file ready to be used for machine learning.

We then parsed these text files and translated them to the format shown in Fig. 3 that is more amenable for efficient machine learning tasks. The data-set that we have created is publicly available and is considered one of the contributions of this paper. The data-set contains 81 flights, 27 from each operator location (A, B, or C). Each flight is represented by a file with 360 features consisting of 120 (X, Y, Z) triplets, each representing the position of the drone at a specific time along the flight. The location of the drone was captured in 8 Hz, i.e., we recorded an (X, Y, Z) triplet every 125 ms.

3   Results

In this section we report on the main results we obtained with our experiments.

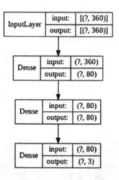

Fig. 4. A dense neural network we used for identification of the location of the drone's operator.

3.1   The Path of the Drone Gives Away Information on the Location of the Pilot

We used the data-set described in Sect. 2 to train neural networks with different parameters and typologies, as shown in Fig. 5. The topology that yielded the best results is built of two dense layers as shown in Fig. 4. It allowed us to demonstrate that it is possible to infer significant information about the location of the operator form by analyzing the path of the drone.

We repeated the training and quality measurement process many times with an automatic script that created a variety of similar models by varying the parameters of the model shown above. We chose the variation of the model that produced the best results, and tested its accuracy with respect to records in the data set that were not used for training. This model was able to guess the viewpoint of the operator with 73% accuracy.

3.2   The Orientation of the Drone Is Not Needed

Beyond location, the defender that observes the drone can also measure its Euler angles. Because such measurements may require more expensive equipment mounted closer to the drone, we ran experiments to measure how much

batch size.	number of neurons	epochs	activation function	Accuracy
10	80	13	relu	73.99
20	80	13	sigmoid	73.99
20	80	10	relu	73.64
10	20	10	elu	73.64
20	80	13	relu	73.28
10	20	8	relu	73.28
20	20	13	sigmoid	72.92
10	80	10	relu	72.92
10	20	13	elu	72.57
10	80	8	sigmoid	72.57
⋮	⋮	⋮	⋮	⋮

Fig. 5. The variations of the neural networks produced by our script.

this information can contribute to the accuracy of identification of the pilot's point-of-view.

To this end, we extended our data-set with information about the orientation of the drone along its flight. When trained and tested with both location and orientation data, our neural networks achieved accuracy of 74%, which is a one percent improvement over the accuracy we obtained with location information only. When trained with orientation data only, the performance degraded a little to 71% precision. Our conclusion is that it seems that there is no need for measuring the orientation of the drone, if this entails costs and limitations.

Our explanation to the fact that the orientation information did not contribute much to the accuracy of the inference is that the location and the orientation variables are coupled. Specifically, the speed of the drone in each direction is a direct function of the thrust of the rotors and the Euler angle that corresponds to that direction. Thus, the location of the drone can be inferred within some error margins by integrating its rotations on all axes. Evidently, the neural network that we have designed was able to take advantage of these relations when we asked it to use only position or only rotation information.

3.3 Recurrent Networks Are Not Better for the Task

Since our motivation was to identify temporal patterns in the data, we thought that it may be possible to improve the accuracy of the network in performing the required task by applying a recurrent neural network (RNN). Such networks have a temporal dimension so they can handle time and sequences.

We tried the recurrent topologies depicted in Fig. 6. As shown in Fig. 7, these networks yielded only 55% accuracy. We do not know how to explain this performance degradation.

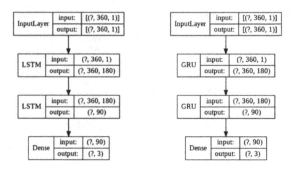

Fig. 6. Recurrent neural networks that we applied.

3.4   The Effect of Measurement Disturbances, Measurement Accuracy and and Sampling Rate

While we ideally want to measure the a time-varying position of the drone so we can accurately reconstruction of the signal from collected discrete data points, the sampling speed and precision of the measurement instruments can directly affect the ability to reconstruct the signal [7]. Ideally, the measurement infrastructure captures the signal continuously with perfect accuracy (precision and trueness). But in reality, many devices sample signals discretely. And they are affected by noise. Systematic noise affects trueness, while random noise compromises precision. Clearly, the more information about the signal we can capture with the data points, the better accuracy. Where necessary, the amount of signal data can be increased by collecting more samples per unit of time, and by improving the signal-to-noise ratio of each sample.

LSTM:
average_result:55.00000059604645, number_of_neurons:130, activation_func:<function softplus at 0x7f7ad3034c80>,
average_result:52.85714417695999, number_of_neurons:150, activation_func:<function sigmoid at 0x7f7ad304d950>,
average_result:50.000001192092896, number_of_neurons:130, activation_func:<function sigmoid at 0x7f7ad304d950>,
average_result:48.571429550647736, number_of_neurons:180, activation_func:<function softplus at 0x7f7ad3034c80>
average_result:48.571429550647736, number_of_neurons:100, activation_func:<function softplus at 0x7f7ad3034c80>
average_result:47.857143580013544, number_of_neurons:80, activation_func:<function softplus at 0x7f7ad3034c80>

GRU:
average_result:57.85714417695999, number_of_neurons:130, activation_func:<function sigmoid at 0x7f7ad304d
average_result:55.71428745985031, number_of_neurons:180, activation_func:<function sigmoid at 0x7f7ad304d
average_result:53.5714298486709 6, number_of_neurons:150, activation_func:<function softplus at 0x7f7ad303
average_result:50.00000089406967, number_of_neurons:180, activation_func:<function softplus at 0x7f7ad303
average_result:49.285715222358704, number_of_neurons:80, activation_func:<function softplus at 0x7f7ad303
average_result:48.571429550647736, number_of_neurons:100, activation_func:<function sigmoid at 0x7f7ad304
average_result:47.1428582072258, number_of_neurons:80, activation_func:<function sigmoid at 0x7f7ad304d95
average_result:47.14285790920257 6, number_of_neurons:150, activation_func:<function sigmoid at 0x7f7ad304

Fig. 7. Recurrent neural networks that we applied.

Figure 8 shows the trade-off between sampling rate and precision. The table shows that, as expected, reducing the sampling frequency reduces the accuracy rather dramatically. This shows that the identification of the position of the operator of the drone relies on relatively high frequency properties of the signal, i.e., on variation of the path that can only be detected when the position of the drone is sampled at high frequency.

Rate	Time diff.	Accuracy
Hz.	seconds	
8	0.125	73.57
4	0.25	67.5
3	0.375	60.35
2	0.5	56.07
4/3	0.75	47.28
8/7	0.875	44.64
1	1	40.71

Fig. 8. The effect of the sampling rate on accuracy.

Figure 9 shows the trade-off between the sampling precision and the accuracy of the estimation. This data shows that our ability to estimate where the operator of a drone is does not drop very dramatically when the location of the drone is measured with lower precision. This indicates that the maneuvers that the network bases its estimation upon are relatively wide, i.e., we see that the network is able to detect the differences even with a precision level of one decimeter.

Figure 10 shows the effect of sampling disturbances on the accuracy of the estimation. This data shows that event with noise that add up to 5 m to the measurement, the neural network is able to maintain high estimation accuracy. This data indicates that the network is capable to ignore the distur

Sampling precision	Estimation
meters	Accuracy
10^{-4}	73.57
10^{-3}	72.85
10^{-2}	72.85
10^{-1}	68.21
1	37.85

Sampling Disturbance	Estimation
$Uniform[0, x]$ meters	Accuracy
0	73.57
1	67.14
5	62.14
10	48.57
15	46.43

Fig. 9. The effect of the sampling precision on estimation accuracy.

Fig. 10. The effect of the sampling precision on estimation accuracy.

4 Related Work

The usual way for locating drone operators is via RF techniques. Locating drone signals can be a challenge due to the amount of other WiFi, Bluetooth and IoT signals in the air. Drone operation radio signal have short duration, their frequency usually hops over most of the band and they have relatively low power. To effectively collect these signals, network-enabled sensors must be distributed around the flight area so the defenders can detect and locate the needed signals. For successful pinpointing of the operator, the signals should be isolated in frequency and time. After detecting the RC, the geolocation system must triangulate the signal using data it collects from the sensors. Since broad scanning of all the traffic is expensive due to sensor allocation and computational complexity, our work may complement RF based system by narrowing the search to more probable areas based on the drone path, which is easier to follow.

Another way that our work can complement RF based technique is by the observation that there is a strong association between the maneuvers of the drone and the command patterns sent via RF. This may allow to solve a crucial issue with RF based techniques that have trouble identifying the signal related to a specific drone in an urban environment where many similar signals (possible, even, from other drones of the same brand). We can train our neural networks to identify command patterns of the signal transmitted from the operator when the drone is turning, rotating, accelerating, and decelerating and use it to connect a signal to a specific drone in the air.

Lastly, RF based techniques can only detect the antenna from which the signal is sent. This may allow to intercept that antenna, but malicious operators can easily redirect their signal to another antenna without interrupting their mission. Our technique allows to get direct information about the viewpoint of the operators which allows more effective interception. Even identifying that the operator uses the FPV viewpoint can be useful, because the defenders can distract this view by clouding the area of the drone.

In the technical level, our work is also related to driver identification [2, 8, 9]. Models of driving behaviors is an active field of research since the 1950s. Because driving consists complex actions and reactions, different driver express different driving behaviors in different traffic situations. These differences can be detected by observing how drivers use the pedals, the way they use the steering wheel, how they keep their eyes on the road, how much distance they keep from the other cars, and many other factors. There is much work on using neural networks for translating sensory data that is easily collected while driving to an educated guess of who is currently driving the car. This work is related to ours in that it also tries to use machine learning for inference of hidden information from human behaviour. It is interesting to note that while recurrent networks are the state of the art in the domain of driver identification, we obtained better performance with dense networks.

5   Conclusions and Future Work

Our initial results indicate that observing the path of a drone can indeed serve to identify the location of the drone's operator. It would be interesting to explore what additional data can be extracted from this information. Possible insights would include the technical experience level of the drone operator, where was the drone operator trained in flying, and possibly even the precise identity of the operator. Another direction would be in improving the machine learning pipeline. It would be interesting to compare different deep learning architectures, especially those tailored for the treatment of time-series data. The data-set used for training and evaluating our models is naturally smaller than machine-generated corpora used for other tasks such as malware classification. As such, it would be interesting to look for a feature set which can be used as input to a classical machine learning algorithm such as KNN or SVM, which traditionally requires less data than deep learning models.

References

1. Drozdowicz, J., et al.: 35 GHz FMCW drone detection system. In: IRS 2016
2. Ezzini, S., Berrada, I., Ghogho, M.: Who is behind the wheel? Driver identification and fingerprinting. J. Big Data **5**, 9 (2018)
3. García, M., Viguria, A., Heredia, G., Ollero, A.: Minimal-time trajectories for interception of malicious drones in constrained environments. In: Tzovaras, D., Giakoumis, D., Vincze, M., Argyros, A. (eds.) ICVS 2019. LNCS, vol. 11754, pp. 734–743. Springer, Cham (2019). https://doi.org/10.1007/978-3-030-34995-0_67
4. Russo, J., Woods, D., Shaffer, J.S., Jackson, B.A.: Countering threats to correctional institution security: identifying innovation needs to address current and emerging concerns. RAND Corp. (2019)
5. Shah, S., Dey, D., Lovett, C., Kapoor, A.: AirSim: high-fidelity visual and physical simulation for autonomous vehicles. In: Hutter, M., Siegwart, R. (eds.) Field and Service Robotics. SPAR, vol. 5, pp. 621–635. Springer, Cham (2018). https://doi.org/10.1007/978-3-319-67361-5_40
6. Solomitckii, D., Gapeyenko, M., Semkin, V., Andreev, S., Koucheryavy, Y.: Technologies for efficient amateur drone detection in 5g millimeter-wave cellular infrastructure. IEEE Commun. Mag. **56**(1), 43–50 (2018)
7. Wang, C.-C., Tomizuka, M.: Iterative learning control of mechanical systems with slow sampling rate position measurements. In: ASME 2008
8. Zhang, J., et al.: Attention-based convolutional and recurrent neural networks for driving behavior recognition using smartphone sensor data. IEEE Access **7**, 148031–148046 (2019)
9. Zhang, J., et al.: A deep learning framework for driving behavior identification on in-vehicle CAN-BUS sensor data. Sensors **19**(6), 1356 (2019)
10. Zhen, J.: Localization of unmanned aerial vehicle operators based on reconnaissance plane with multiple array sensors. IEEE Access **7**, 105354–105362 (2019)

Detecting Malicious Accounts
on the Ethereum Blockchain
with Supervised Learning

Nitesh Kumar, Ajay Singh, Anand Handa$^{(\boxtimes)}$, and Sandeep Kumar Shukla

C3i Center, Department of CSE, Indian Institute of Technology, Kanpur, India
{niteshkr,ajay,ahanda,sandeeps}@cse.iitk.ac.in

Abstract. Ethereum is a blockchain platform where users can transact cryptocurrency as well as build and deploy decentralized applications using smart contracts. The participants in the Ethereum platform are 'pseudo-anonymous' and same user can have multiple accounts under multiple cryptographic identities. As a result, detecting malicious users engaged in fraudulent activities as well as attribution are quite difficult. In the recent past, multiple such activities came to light. In the famous Ethereum DAO attack, hackers exploited bug in smart contracts stole large amount of cryptocurrency using fraudulent transactions. However, activities such as ponzi-scheme, tax evasion by transacting in cryptocurrency, using pseudo-anonymous accounts for receiving ransom payment, consolidation of funds accumulated under multiple identities etc. should be monitored and detected in order to keep legitimate users safe on the platform. In this work, we detect malicious nodes by using supervised machine learning based anomaly detection in the transactional behavior of the accounts. Depending on the two prevalent account types – Externally Owned Account (EOA) and smart contract accounts, we apply two distinct machine learning models. Our models achieve a detection accuracy of 96.54% with 0.92% false-positive ratio and 96.82% with 0.78% false-positive ratio for EOA and smart contract account analysis, respectively. We also find the listing of 85 new malicious EOA and 1 smart contract addresses between 20 January 2020 and 24 February 2020. We evaluate our model on these, and the accuracy of that evaluation is 96.21% with 3% false positive.

Keywords: Ethereum blockchain · Malicious accounts · Machine learning · Anomaly detection · Feature extraction

1 Introduction

In the last decade, blockchain has emerged as an innovative technology platform for a variety of cryptocurrency as well as other applications. The Bitcoin

This research is partially funded by the Office of the National Cyber Security Coordinator, Government of India.

cryptocurrency ecosystem [12] is built on the blockchain technology. Transactions between participants of a blockchain platform are verified and agreed on through a distributed consensus mechanism which obviates the need for a centralized authority. While cryptocurrency was the first demonstrated application of blockchain technology, due to the fact that blockchain enables tamper resistant property to the history of transactions using cryptographic hashing, and it enables authentication of transactions through public key cryptography, it has proven itself to be a potential technology for building trusted interaction platform between multiple participants involved in mutual transactions without having to trust any individual participant. Bitcoin, Ethereum, Monero etc., are blockchain based cryptocurrency platforms for financial transactions and also offers pseudo-anonymity to users. This has also given rise to a lot of malicious activities on these platforms which makes it unsafe for legitimate users on these platforms. Therefore, automated detection of users who might be engaging in malicious activities is of utmost importance.

The pseudo-anonymity of participants led the hackers and money launderers to be part of the network without any fear attribution. However, since pseudo-anonymity does not provide guaranteed anonymity, researchers have been engaged in deducing pattern of transactions that could then be matched against fraudulent transaction patterns. It is worth noting cryptocurrencies are still illegal in some countries as the cryptocurrencies are generated in these platforms without any connection to the central banking system in the countries, leading to tax evasion, illegal transactions, ransom payments etc. Soon after the inception of the bitcoin, Online underworld marketplaces like Silk Road emerged for selling contraband drugs and other illegitimate items. A vulnerability in the Parity multi-signature wallet on the Ethereum network resulted in a loss of 31 million US Dollars in a few minutes. If some benevolent hackers had not stopped the ongoing exploitation, it might have resulted in a loss of 180 million US Dollars [1].

It is therefore, our focus in this work to find irregularities and the fraudulent transactional behaviors in the Ethereum network. We investigate the past Ethereum transaction data from its genesis till a certain date (Ethereum being a public blockchain, one can download the entire data) in search of abnormal activities. We extract relevant information to train machine learning models for anomaly detection. The main contributions of this work are as follows:

- We collect the malicous Ethereum addresses of various attack types like phish-hack, cryptopia-hack, etc. from multiple sources and filter them to obtain relevant addresses. We also label non-malicious addresses after data preprocessing.
- We extract features from the transactions and use feature engineering to find the relevant features for classification.
- We detect the malicious nodes in the Ethereum network with a good accuracy.
- We evaluate our model on newly collected 85 malicious EOA and 1 smart contract addresses between 20 January 2020 and 24 February 2020. The model achieves a good evaluation accuracy.

The rest of the paper is organized as follows: Sect. 2 briefly describes the Ethereum blockchain. Section 3 describes relevant related work. Section 4 discusses the proposed methodology. Section 5 describes evaluation results. Section 7 concludes the work.

2   Background

Vitalik Buterin developed Ethereum [6] in 2013. It is a step forward in the blockchain technology which brought advances over the Bitcoin blockchain technology by introducing a programming language which is Turing-complete, and providing a program execution platform in the blockchain. The programs that run on Ethereum are called smart contracts. One can build complex decentralized applications using smart contracts. The cryptocurrency of Ethereum is called Ether, which fuels the Ethereum network. Ethereum Virtual Machine (EVM) is the computing infrastructure for Ethereum nodes. Currently the main consensus mechanism used by Ethereum blockchain is Proof of Work (POW), but Ethereum announced that it will switch to Proof of Stake (POS). The reason is that that Proof of work is a computationally-intensive process and consumes an enormous amount of energy.

2.1   Ethereum Accounts

Ethereum has two types of accounts which participate in transactions on the platform. Figure 1 shows how these accounts interact with each other.

1. **Externally Owned Account (EOA):** The end-users create EOAs to become participants in the Ethereum network. Participants generate private key for each account to digital sign transactions. An externally controlled account may have a non-zero Ether balance, and can perform transactions with other EOAs and contracts.
2. **Contract/Smart Contracts:** These are the self-executing code which can be invoked by EOAs or by another contract as an internal transaction. A contract also may have an Ether balance and an associated code which performs arbitrary complex operations on execution.

2.2   Ethereum Transactions

There are three types of transactions in the Ethreum network and they are as follows:

– **Fund Transfer Between EOAs:** In this type of transaction, one EOA transfers funds to another EOA as shown in Fig. 2.

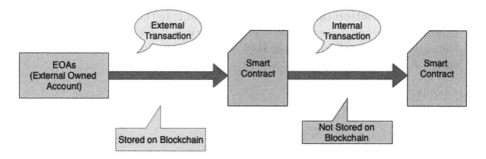

Fig. 1. Account interaction

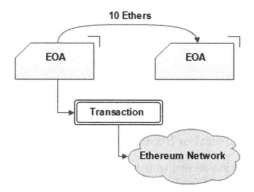

Fig. 2. Fund transfer between EOA

– **Deploy a Contract on the Ethereum Platform:** In this type of transaction, EOA deploys a contract using a transaction on the Ethereum network, as shown in Fig. 3.

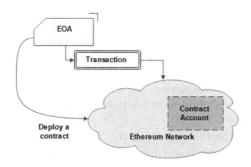

Fig. 3. Deploy a contract on ethereum network

– **Execute a Function on a Deployed Contract:** In this type of transaction,
  Ethereum sends a transaction to execute functions defined in a contract. The
  transaction gets performed after the contract deployment, and Fig. 4 shows
  such a transaction.

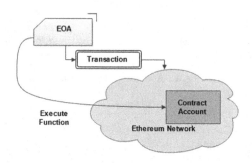

Fig. 4. Execute a function on a deployed contract

2.3 Ethereum Transaction Structure

An Ethereum Transaction record as it is formed and eventually persisted on the
blockchain has a number of fields.

1. **From:** This field contains the transaction sender's address. The length of
   this field is 20 bytes. An address is a hash of a public key associated with the
   account.
2. **To:** This field has the address of the receiver of the transaction. The length
   of this field is 20 bytes. This field can be the address of either an EOA or a
   contract account or empty, depending on the type of transaction.
3. **Value:** This field has the amount in terms of wei (1 ether $= 10^{18}$ weis)
   transferred in the transaction.
4. **Data/Input:** In case of contract deployment, this field contains the bytecode
   and the encoded arguments and is empty when there is a fund transfer.
5. **Gas Price and Gas Limit:** Gas price is the amount (in terms of wei) for
   each gas unit related to the processing cost of any transaction which a sender
   is willing to pay. In a transaction, the maximum gas units that can be spent
   is the gas limit. The gas limit ensures that there is no infinite loop in a smart
   contract execution.
6. **Timestamp:** It is the time at which the block is published or mined. Below
   is an example of an Ethereum transaction structure.

```
 1  {"status":"1",
 2  "message":"OK",
 3  "result":
 4  {"blockNumber":"6026742",
 5  "timeStamp":"1532511199",
 6  "hash":"0x94917b89296051b066db2ac572987d...",
 7  "nonce":"2560067",
 8  "blockHash":"0xad77b360c7a8401ea81e875a8fbc9...",
 9  "transactionIndex":"8",
10  "from":"0x3f5ce5fbfe3e9af3971dd833d26ba9b5c936f0be",
11  "to":"0x0a0ba956038d4a66002d612648332b9c4ab7646c",
12  "value":"500000000000000000",
13  "gas":"21000",
14  "gasPrice":"60000000000",
15  "isError":"0",
16  "txreceipt_status":"1",
17  "input":"0x",
18  "contractAddress":"",
19  "cumulativeGasUsed":"227318",
20  "gasUsed":"21000",
21  "confirmations":"3212860"
22  }
23  }
```

3   Related Work

In this section, we discuss some existing work related to the anomaly detection in blockchain, more specifically to Bitcoin and Ethereum blockchain. BitIodine is a framework to deanonymize the users [16] and is used to extract intelligence from the Bitcoin network. It labels the addresses automatically or semi-automatically using the information fetched from web scrapping. The labels used for addresses are gambling, exchanges, wallets, donations, scammer, disposable, miner, malware, FBI, killer, Silk Road, shareholder, etc. BitIodine first parses the transaction data from the Bitcoin blockchain. Then it performs clustering based on user interaction and labels the clusters and users. Their objective is to label every address in the network into one of the mentioned categories. Also, they detect some of the anomalous addresses in the network by tracing their transactions. The authors verify their system performance on some of the known theft and frauds in the Bitcoin platform. BitIodine detects addresses that belong to Silk Road cold wallet, CryptoLocker ransomware. The proposed modular structure is also applicable to other blockchains. However, BitIodine does not use any machine learning techniques.

In [17], the authors propose a Graph-based forensic investigation of Bitcoin transactions and perform analysis on Bitcoin transaction data and evaluate the network data. They use 34,839,029 Bitcoin transactions and 35,770,360 distinct addresses. The objective is to detect money theft, fraudulent transactions, and illegal payments made to the black market. The proposed framework retrieves all the transaction details of a given address. The proposed framework does not attempt to detect the anomalous addresses in the network, but it provides detailed information on addresses. They use clustering to group users together and multiple graph-based techniques to analyze the money flow within the network. They analyze the flow of money using algorithms like Breadth-First Search (BFS) algorithm, edge-convergent pattern, and the existence of cycles in the network to detect any money laundering activity.

Thai T. Pham et al. [13,14] propose an anomaly detection method in the Bitcoin network using the unsupervised learning classifiers like K-means clustering, Mahalanobis distance, and Support Vector Machine (SVM). The aim is to detect the suspicious transactions that take place within the network and mark the users based on these transactions. They use user graph and transaction graph as the underlying space on which clustering are performed based on a 6 features of each node in the user graph, and 3 features in the transaction graphs. They also ran into computational difficulty and had to limit their study to a limited number of nodes.

Xiapu Luo et al. [11] perform a graph-analysis of the Ethereum network. They claim to be the first to perform a graph-based analysis of Ethereum blockchain. The model constructs three different graphs to analyze money transfer, smart contract creation, and smart contract invocation. The size of the dataset is – 28,502,131 external transactions and 19,759,821 internal transactions. After analyzing the graph, they have given the following preliminary insights – the participants use the Ethereum network more than smart contracts for money transfer. The insights made by them is pretty obvious as the number of transactions done by a regular user is not comparable to a huge number of transactions performed in exchanges. Every user does not know the Solidity or Golang to deploy their contracts. Hence, only a few of them can deploy the contract and use it. All participants have different requirements for which they interact with the Ethereum network, so they have the same behavior.

Although some of the above approaches try to find an anomaly in the Bitcoin network, but none of them has a sophisticated method for anomaly detection. Like BitIodine [16], the authors attempt to detect paths by searching the network manually, but the proposed method does not have an automated mechanism to detect malicious addresses. Although in [13], the authors use machine learning techniques for anomaly detection, the reported accuracy is not very good. Therefore there is a need for an automated and efficient mechanism for anomalous addresses detection in any blockchain network with high accuracy.

4   Proposed Methodology

In the Ethereum network, addresses which try to carry out tasks for which they are not authorized or addresses that attempt to execute the fraudulent transactions are suspicious addresses. We call their behavior as anomalous. In this work, we focus on the past Ethereum transactions to detect the anomaly in behavior/actions by addresses. We train supervised machine learning models using features we extract from the transactions performed by the addresses on the Ethereum network. We mark the addresses as malicious and non-malicious after the classification by the trained model. We train two models for a different account types of the Ethereum platform – EOA and smart contract accounts because both accounts have distinct characteristics and behavior. Our anomaly detection method performs the following steps:

1. Collection of already publicly available malicious and non-malicious addresses from various repositories.
2. Collection of transactions executed by all such addresses in the past.
3. Data preprocessing, feature extraction, training and evaluation for:
   – EOA Analysis
   – Smart contract account analysis.

4.1 Collection of Malicious and Non-malicious Addresses

We use supervised machine learning classification methods to detect malicious and non-malicious addresses in the Ethereum network. Therefore, we collect the labeled malicious and non-malicious addresses from various sources. We collect malicious addresses from the sources, namely etherscan [7], cryptoscamdb [5], and few addresses from a GitHub repository [9]. Malicious addresses are publicly listed based on different kinds of attack such as a heist, cryptopia-hack, Upbit-hack, phish-hack, etc., that these addresses have carried out in the past. These attack types are the same as the ones used by etherscan label word cloud [8]. We fetch non-malicious addresses from the same sources cryptoscamdb and etherscan [4]. Initially, we collect a total of 6,154 malicious addresses and 0.1 million non-malicious addresses.

4.2 Collection of Transactions for a Given Address

In this step, we extract all the transactions performed by all malicious and non-malicious addresses from the Ethereum Blockchain data that we had previously collected. Transactions contain various fields such as address of the sender, address of the receiver, timestamp, gas value used for the transaction, the gas limit for the transaction, transaction hash, block number, etc. Algorithm 1 shows an approach to extract the transactions from a given address. We collect all the transactions using the etherscan API and save the transactions in a JSON file for further processing.

Algorithm 1. Algorithm for Extraction of Transactions for a given address

---

Input: *Address*   // List of Ethereum account addresses
                                              (Malicious/Non-Malicious)
Output: *Txns*   // List of transactions for a given address

foreach *address* ∈ *Address* **do**
 | *Txns* ⟵ ExtractTxn(*address*)
end

Function ExtractTxn(*address*):
 | *F* ⟵ 'curl -X GET http://api.etherscan.io/api?module=account&
 | action=txlist&address=*address*&sort=asc&apikey=*ApiKeyToken*'
 | **return** *F*;
End Function

4.3 Data Preprocessing

In data preprocessing, out of the collected 6,154 malicious addresses, we find
that there are a few duplicate addresses, so we filter them using string comparison because the addresses contains the alphanumeric values and we are left
with 5,000 unique malicious addresses. After the string comparison, we find
that few addresses are left, which have the same transactions. This problem
occurs because some addresses are present in two different formats. For example, an address is present as 0xfea28ca175a80f5a348016583961f63be8605f80
and 0xFeA28ca175A80F5A348016583961f63bE8605f80, but when we compare
them as a string both are different. Therefore, we first convert all the addresses
to lowercase and then we remove all the duplicate addresses. There are a few
addresses in our dataset which have the null transaction. Hence, we remove all
of them too, and finally, we are left with **4,375** malicious address. We apply
the same technique to select the unique non-malicious address. After the unique
address collection, we perform data preprocessing in two steps – filter contract
account & EOA addresses and select verified non-malicious Ethereum account
addresses.

Select Verified Non-malicious Ethereum Account Addresses. Figure 5
shows the process of selection of verified non-malicious addresses for further analysis. We filter all the non-malicious addresses by checking the "to" and "from"
fields from all transactions performed by a given address. These fields provide
the addresses with which the non-malicious addresses perform the transactions.
If the non-malicious address performs a transaction with any malicious address,
then we drop that address. The assumption is that such an address engaging
in business with a known malicious address could itself be suspicious and hence
we do not want it to represent non-malicious addresses. Finally, we select only
those addresses which do not perform any transaction with any of the malicious
addresses present in our dataset.

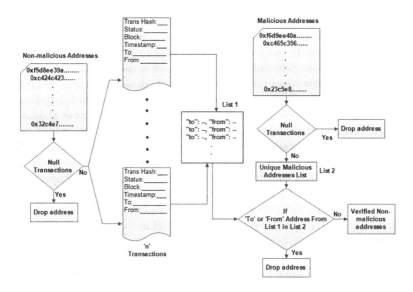

Fig. 5. Verification of non-malicious addresses

Filter Contract Account and EOA Addresses. We filter the EOAs and contract account addresses because both the account have different transaction behavioral features and they need to be analyzed separately. To filter the EOA and contract account addresses, we check the input data field from the collected transactions and find that in the case of EOA addresses, the input data field contains the "0x" value. However, in the case of contract account addresses, this field contains the bytecode of smart contract source code. Also, in the first transaction of the contract account addresses the "to" field is null, and the "contractAddress" field includes the address, which is opposite in case of EOA addresses. At last, after filtering the contract account and EOA addresses, we are left with 4,124 EOA and 251 contract account addresses out of 4,375 unique malicious addresses. Similarly, we randomly choose 5,000 non-malicious EOA addresses and 450 contract addresses for EOA and contract account address analysis, respectively.

4.4   EOA Analysis

In this section, we discuss the features extracted from the transactions performed by EOA addresses. All the transactions are stored in JSON file format. We use Python's JSON library to load, parse the file, and extract the pieces of information from the stored transactions. We extract the information from various fields of the transaction structure such as "to", "from", "timestamp", "gas", "gasPrice", "gasUsed", "value", "txreceipt_status". The features such as Value_out, Value_in, Value_difference, Last_Txn_Value, Avg_value_in, Avg_value_out, and other features related to ether values sent and received are extracted from the `value` field. We extract features from the `timestamp` field such as first, last, and mean transaction time among all the transactions performed by an address. The `txreceipt_status` field from the transaction structure provides information about success and failed transactions. If the `txreceipt_status` field returns 1 then the transaction is successful or vice versa. We extract features like the number of failed and successful transactions in the incoming and outgoing transactions with the help of `txreceipt_status` field. The percentage of gas used for the transaction is calculated using `gasUsed` field value divided by the `gas` field value, which is set for the transaction. We get the percentage of gas used for all the incoming and outgoing transactions and the average value is taken to calculate the `AP_gasUsed_in` and `AP_gasUsed_out` features. All the features related to gas price, which is set in the transaction by the user who is willing to pay per gas used are extracted from the `gasPrice` field. All the extracted features from the transactions are shown in Table 1.

We extract 44 features for EOA addresses analysis in our feature extraction phase. Though we understand that all the extracted features are not essential to train the classifiers, and some may make the results of classification models worse because they do not participate in improving the performance of classification models. Therefore, we use the Information gain algorithm as a feature reduction method for dimensionality reduction of the feature vector. We select the top-10, top-20, top-30, top-40, and top-44 features with the highest info-gain score, as shown in Table 2. To do this selection process, we apply Random Forest [10], XGBoost [3], Decision Tree [15], and k-nearest neighbour (k-NN) [2] machine learning classifiers on top-10, top-20, top-30, top-40, and top-44 features. The final feature vector for EOA addresses consists of the selected top-30 features because we obtain the maximum ten-fold cross-validation accuracy for the top-30 features using the XGBoost classifier as shown in Table 5.

4.5 Smart Contract Account Analysis

There are two kinds of transactions present in the contract account addresses – contract creation and contract invocation by an EOA address as described in Subsect. 2.2. We first remove all the contract addresses before starting the analysis for a smart contract that contains a similar bytecode that is present in the input data field of the transaction structure. Finally, we have 250 malicious and 300 non-malicious smart contract account address for the analysis. The information we extract from the transactions performed by the contract account addresses. It is based on the interaction of the EOA account with the contract account. The various fields of the transaction structure such as `"to"`, `"from"`, `"contractAddress"`, `"timestamp"`, `"gas"`, `"gasPrice"`, `"gasUsed"`, `"value"` are used to extract the features. Table 3 shows the extracted features for the smart contract analysis in the Ethereum network. From Table 3, one can observe that we extract the features from both creation and invocation transactions present in contract addresses. Features from feature id `F_1` to `F_4` are derived from the contract creation

Table 1. Extracted features for EOA analysis

F_ID	Feature	Description
F_1	TxnSent	The total number of transactions sent
F_2	TxnReceived	The total number of transactions received
F_3	Value_out	The total ether value sent
F_4	Value_in	The total ether value received
F_5	Value_difference	Absolute difference between value sent and received [(Value_out) - (Value_in)]
F_6	distinct_address	Number of distinct Address contacted
F_7	Total_Txn	Total Number of Transactions sent and received
F_8	Unique_TxnSent	The total number of transactions sent to unique addresses
F_9	Unique_TxnReceived	The total number of transactions received from unique addresses
F_10	First_Txn_time	The timestamp of the block in which the first ever transaction is made
F_11	Last_Txn_time	The timestamp of the block in which the last transaction is made so far
F_12	Active_duration	Active duration in second [(Last_Txn_time) - (First_Txn_time)]
F_13	Last_Txn_Bit	0/1 (0 if last transaction is incoming transaction else 1)
F_14	Last_Txn_Value	The ether value transferred in the last transaction
F_15	Avg_value_in	Average ether value received in incoming transaction
F_16	Avg_value_out	Average ether value sent in outgoing transaction
F_17	AP_gasUsed_in	The Average percentage of gas used in incoming transactions
F_18	AP_gasUsed_out	The Average percentage of gas used in outgoing transactions
F_19	gasPrice_out	The total number of gasPrice used in outgoing transactions
F_20	gasPrice_in	The total number of gasPrice used in incoming transactions
F_21	Avg_gasPrice_in	The Average gasPrice used in incoming transactions
F_22	Avg_gasPrice_out	Average gasPrice_out used in outgoing transaction
F_23	Failed_Txn_in	Total number of failed incoming transactions
F_24	Failed_Txn_out	Total number of failed outgoing transactions
F_25	Total_Failed_Txn	Total number of failed transactions (Failed_Txn_in + Failed_Txn_out)
F_26	Success_Txn_in	Total number of Success incoiming transactions
F_27	Success_Txn_out	Total number of Success outgoing transactions
F_28	Total_Success_Txn	Total number of Success transactions (Success_Txn_in + Success_Txn_out)
F_29	gasUsed_in	Total gasUsed in incoming transaction
F_30	gasUsed_out	total gasUsed in outgoing transaction
F_31	Per_TxnSent	Percentage of transactions sent from all the transactions
F_32	Per_TxnReceived	Percentage of transactions received from all the transactions
F_33	Std_value_in	Standard deviation of ether value received in incoming transaction
F_34	Std_value_out	Standard deviation of ether value sent in outgoing transaction
F_35	Std_gasPrice_in	Standard deviation of gasPrice used in incoming transactions
F_36	Std_gasPrice_out	Standard deviation of gasPrice used in outgoing transactions
F_37	First_Txn_Bit	0/1 (0 if last transaction is incoming transaction else 1)
F_38	First_Txn_Value	The ether value transferred in the first transaction
F_39	mean_in_time	Average time difference between incoming transaction
F_40	mean_out_time	Average time difference between outgoing transaction
F_41	mean_time	Average time difference between all transactions
F_42	Txn_fee_in	Total Transaction fee spent in incoming transaction
F_43	Txn_fee_out	Total Transaction fee spent in outgoing transaction
F_44	Total_Txn_fee	Total Transaction fee spent in all transaction (incoming + outgoing)

Table 2. Infogain results for EOA analysis

Rank	F_ID	Feature	Rank score	F_ID	Feature	Rank score	F_ID	Feature
0.46029	F_11	Last_Txn_time	0.19721	F_21	Avg_gasPrice_in	0.10026	F_44	Total_Txn_fee
0.42853	F_39	mean_in_time	0.19601	F_35	Std_gasPrice_in	0.10004	F_12	Active_duration
0.37441	F_10	First_Txn_time	0.19324	F_3	Value_out	0.07407	F_28	Total_Success_Txn
0.34817	F_40	mean_out_time	0.19112	F_16	Avg_Value_out	0.07407	F_7	Total_Txn
0.25935	F_17	AP_gasUsed_in	0.15878	F_19	gasPrice_out	0.05612	F_34	Std_value_out
0.24183	F_22	Avg_gasPrice_out	0.15177	F_29	gasUsed_in	0.02647	F_36	Std_gasPrice_out
0.23784	F_9	Unique_TxnReceived	0.14819	F_26	Success_Txn_in	0.01895	F_8	Unique_TxnSent
0.23590	F_33	Std_value_in	0.14819	F_2	TxnReceived	0.01500	F_13	Last_Txn_Bit
0.23146	F_15	Avg_Value_in	0.14327	F_5	Value_difference	0.01096	F_1	TxnSent
0.23082	F_4	Value_in	0.14327	F_6	distinct_address	0.01096	F_27	Success_Txn_out
0.22359	F_38	First_Txn_Value	0.13781	F_18	AP_gasUsed_out	0.00797	F_37	First_Txn_Bit
0.22202	F_32	Per_TxnReceived	0.13506	F_41	mean_time	0	F_25	Total_Failed_Txn
0.22202	F_31	Per_TxnSent	0.13322	F_14	Last_Txn_Value	0	F_23	Failed_Txn_in
0.21338	F_20	gasPrice_in	0.12016	F_43	Txn_fee_out	0	F_24	Failed_Txn_out
0.19777	F_42	Txn_fee_in	0.11065	F_30	gasUsed_out			

Table 3. Extracted features for smart contract account analysis

F_ID	Feature	Description
F_1	Contract_Create	Contract creation time
F_2	Txn_fee_contract_create	Transaction fee spent in contract creation
F_3	Per_gasUsed_contract_create	The percentage of gas used during contract creation
F_4	gasPrice_contract_create	Gas price used to create a contract
F_5	First_contract_invoke_time	Timestamp for first contract invocation
F_6	Last_contract_invoke_time	Timestamp for last contract invocation
F_7	Active_duration	Active duration (seconds) of contract address
F_8	Total_invoke	Total number of contract invocations
F_9	unique_invoke	Total number of contract invocations using unique address
F_10	Avg_Per_gasUsed_contract_invoke	The average percentage of gas used during contract invocations
F_11	gasPrice_contract_invoke	Total gas price used for contract invocations
F_12	Avg_gasPrice_contract_invoke	Average gas price used for contract invocations
F_13	Txn_fee_contract_invoke	Total transaction fee spent in contract invocations
F_14	Avg_Txn_fee_contract_invoke	Average transaction fee spent in contract invocations
F_15	Value_contract_invoke	Total ether value used in contract invocations
F_16	Avg_Value_contract_invoke	Average ether value used in contract invocations
F_17	gasUsed_contract_invoke	Total gas used for contract invocations
F_18	Avg_gasUsed_contract_invoke	Average gas used for contract invocations

transactions and features from feature id F_5 to F_18 are taken from the contract invocation transactions.

For smart contract address analysis, we extract 18 features. Similar to EOA address analysis, we use infogain as a feature selection algorithm to reduce the dimensionality of the feature vector. We select top-5, top-10, top-15, and top-18 features with the highest infogain score as shown in Table 4 and then apply the same set of classifiers to train and test the model. Finally, we select the top-10 features to train the final model. The reason for selecting the top-10 features is that these set of features provide the highest ten-fold cross-validation accuracy using XGBoost classifier as shown in Table 5.

4.6 Classification

We use different machine learning classifiers using Python's Sckit-learn library, namely k-NN, Decision Tree, Random Forest, and XGBoost for the classification of malicious addresses in the Ethereum network. The experiments are carried out using the Intel i7 octa-core processor having Ubuntu 18.04 LTS with 32 GB RAM. We split the dataset into 70%-30% for the training and testing of our model. To check the performance of our model, we apply ten-fold stratified cross-validation. Also, we tune parameters to minimize the misclassification error.

Table 4. Infogain results for smart contract analysis

Rank score	F_ID	Feature	Rank score	F_ID	Feature
0.5732	F_6	Last_contract_invoke_time	0.2498	F_13	Txn_fee_contract_invoke
0.5389	F_17	gasUsed_contract_invoke	0.2498	F_4	gasPrice_contract_create
0.5387	F_5	First_contract_invoke_time	0.2006	F_12	Avg_gasPrice_contract_invoke
0.3442	F_18	Avg_gasUsed_contract_invoke	0.1418	F_10	Avg_Per_gasUsed_contract_invoke
0.3442	F_8	Total_invoke	0.141	F_7	Active_duration
0.3047	F_9	unique_invoke	0.1091	F_14	Avg_Txn_fee_contract_invoke
0.3047	F_3	Per_gasUsed_contract_create	0.1064	F_16	Avg_Value_contract_invoke
0.2498	F_11	gasPrice_contract_invoke	0.0459	F_15	Value_contract_invoke
0.2498	F_2	Txn_fee_contract_create	0.0459	F_1	Contract_Create

5   Experimental Results

This section describes the results achieved from the EOA analysis and smart contract account analysis. We perform the analysis for both the account types separately and extract the features from the behavior of the transactions present. We apply ten-fold cross-validation for both the analysis to evaluate our machine learning models' performance. Table 5 presents the 10-fold cross-validation results for separate machine learning classifiers on various numbers of selected features. First, we do the experiments for EOA addresses and examine the results presented in Table 5. We achieve the highest accuracy that is 96.54% with a False Positive Rate (FPR) of 0.92% for EOA analysis using XGBoost classifier with top-30 features. Secondly, we perform the analysis of smart contracts and examine the results presented in Table 5. For smart contracts analysis, we achieve the highest accuracy of 96.82% with an FPR 0.78% using the XGBoost classifier and top-10 features.

Table 5. Experimental results for EOA and smart contract analysis

Experimental results for EOA analysis				
No. of features	Random Forest(%)	XGBoost(%)	Decision Tree(%)	k-NN(%)
top-10	95.28	95.74	92.75	92.75
top-20	95.28	96.08	91.93	91.93
top-30	95.62	**96.54**	92.63	92.63
top-40	95.97	96.31	93.78	93.78
top-44	95.74	96.43	92.86	92.86
Experimental results for smart contract analysis				
top-5	94.73	94.73	94.73	94.73
top-10	94.73	**96.82**	94.73	94.73
top-15	94.73	96.49	96.49	96.49
top-18	94.82	96.49	96.49	96.49

6   Evaluation

Since 20th January, when we last collected our experimental data – 85 new EOA addresses and only 1 new contract address are flagged as malicious. To further validate our models, we do the ensemble of all the machine learning classifiers used earlier to improve the detection accuracy. We test them on the data collected after 20th January. Out of 85 malicious EOA addresses, our EOA address analysis model detects 81 as malicious. We also randomly choose 100 non-malicious addresses that are not part of our earlier dataset. Out of 100 non-malicious EOA addresses, our EOA address analysis model detects 97 as non-malicious, i.e., the overall accuracy of our model is 96.21% with FPR of 3% and FNR 4.71%. Similarly, our contract address analysis model detects the one newly collected contract address as malicious. This validates that our model works to a reasonable extent.

7   Conclusion

In this work, we train two classifiers using transactions performed by the Ethereum addresses on the Ethereum network for EOA analysis and smart contract account analysis. We collect malicious and non-malicious addresses from various sources. Still, the most important challenge is to label the non-malicious addresses because this work aims to detect malicious and non-malicious address with the help of supervised learning. We perform data preprocessing to select the verified non-malicious addresses and to filter the contract account and EOA addresses. We extract and select the features from the transactions of addresses and train different machine learning models, namely Random Forest, Decision tree, XGBoost, and k-NN for EOA and smart contract account analysis. Finally, we achieve the highest accuracy of 96.54% and 96.82% for EOA and smart contract account analysis respectively. In the future, we will investigate how to reduce the false positives and false negatives.

References

1. FreeCodeCamp (2017). https://www.freecodecamp.org/news/a-hacker-stole-31m-of-ether-how-it-happened-and-what-it-means-for-ethereum-9e5dc29e33ce/
2. Nearest neighbors (2018). http://scikit-learn.org/stable/modules/neighbors.html
3. Xgboost (2018). http://xgboost.readthedocs.io/en/latest/python/python_api.html
4. Contracts with verified source codes only (2019). https://etherscan.io/contractsVerified?filter=opensourcelicense
5. Cryptoscamdb (2019). https://documenter.getpostman.com/view/4298426/RzZ7nKcM?version=latest
6. Ethereum (2019). https://www.ethereum.org/
7. Ethereum blockchain explorer (2019). https://etherscan.io/
8. Etherscan label word cloud (2019). https://etherscan.io/labelcloud
9. MyEtherWallet Ethereum Darklist (2019). https://github.com/MyEtherWallet/ethereum-lists/blob/master/src/addresses/addresses-darklist.json
10. Breiman, L.: Random forests. Mach. Learn. **45**(1), 5–32 (2001)
11. Chen, T., et al.: Understanding ethereum via graph analysis. In: IEEE INFOCOM 2018 - IEEE Conference on Computer Communications, pp. 1484–1492, April 2018. https://doi.org/10.1109/INFOCOM.2018.8486401
12. Nakamoto, S.: Bitcoin: a peer-to-peer electronic cash system (2008). http://bitcoin.org/bitcoin.pdf
13. Pham, T., Lee, S.: Anomaly detection in bitcoin network using unsupervised learning methods. arXiv preprint arXiv:1611.03941 (2016)
14. Pham, T., Lee, S.: Anomaly detection in the bitcoin system-a network perspective. arXiv preprint arXiv:1611.03942 (2016)
15. Quinlan, R.: C4.5: Programs for Machine Learning. Morgan Kaufmann Publishers, San Mateo (1993)
16. Spagnuolo, M., Maggi, F., Zanero, S.: BitIodine: extracting intelligence from the bitcoin network. In: Christin, N., Safavi-Naini, R. (eds.) FC 2014. LNCS, vol. 8437, pp. 457–468. Springer, Heidelberg (2014). https://doi.org/10.1007/978-3-662-45472-5_29
17. Zhao, C.: Graph-based forensic investigation of bitcoin transactions (2014)

Fast Polynomial Inversion for Post Quantum QC-MDPC Cryptography

Nir Drucker[1,2(✉)] ⓘ, Shay Gueron[1,2] ⓘ, and Dusan Kostic[3] ⓘ

[1] University of Haifa, Haifa, Israel
drucker.nir@gmail.com
[2] Amazon, Seattle, USA
[3] EPFL Switzerland, Lausanne, Switzerland

Abstract. The NIST PQC standardization project evaluates multiple new designs for post-quantum Key Encapsulation Mechanisms (KEMs). Some of them present challenging tradeoffs between communication bandwidth and computational overheads. An interesting case is the set of QC-MDPC based KEMs. Here, schemes that use the Niederreiter framework require only half the communication bandwidth compared to schemes that use the McEliece framework. However, this requires costly polynomial inversion during the key generation, which is prohibitive when ephemeral keys are used. One example is BIKE, where the BIKE-1 variant uses McEliece and the BIKE-2 variant uses Niederreiter. This paper shows an optimized constant-time polynomial inversion method that makes the computation costs of BIKE-2 key generation tolerable. We report a speedup of 11.8× over the commonly used NTL library, and 55.5× over OpenSSL. We achieve additional speedups by leveraging the latest Intel's Vector-PCLMULQDQ instructions on a laptop machine, 14.3× over NTL and 96.8× over OpenSSL. With this, BIKE-2 becomes a competitive variant of BIKE.

Keywords: Polynomial inversion · BIKE · QC-MDPC codes · Constant-time algorithm · Constant-time implementation

1 Introduction

Bit Flipping Key Encapsulation (BIKE) [3] is a code-based KEM that uses Quasi-Cyclic Moderate-Density Parity-Check (QC-MDPC) codes. It is one of the Round-2 candidates of the NIST PQC Standardization Project [20]. BIKE submission includes three variants: BIKE-1 and BIKE-3 that follow the McEliece [17] framework and BIKE-2 that follows the Niederreiter [19] framework. The main advantage of BIKE-2 is communication bandwidth (in both directions) that is half the size compared to BIKE-1 and BIKE-3. Another advantage is that BIKE-2 IND-CCA has a tighter security reduction compared to the other variants. However, it is currently not the popular BIKE variant (e. g., only BIKE-1 is integrated into LibOQS [21] and s2n [2]). The reason is that BIKE-2 key

© Springer Nature Switzerland AG 2020
S. Dolev et al. (Eds.): CSCML 2020, LNCS 12161, pp. 110–127, 2020.
https://doi.org/10.1007/978-3-030-49785-9_8

generation involves polynomial inversion (over $\mathbb{F}_2$) with computational cost that shadows the cost of decapsulation (see [18]). This is especially prominent when protocols are designed to achieve forward-secrecy through using ephemeral keys.

Polynomial inversion over a finite field is a time-consuming operation in several post-quantum cryptosystems (e. g., BIKE [3], HQC [1], ntruhrss701 [15], LEDAcrypt [4]). The literature includes different approaches for inversions, depending on the polynomial degree and the field/ring over which the polynomials are defined. For example, the Itoh-Tsuji inversion (ITI) algorithm [16] is efficient when the underlying field is $\mathbb{F}_{2^k}$ for some k. Safegcd [5] implements inversion through a fast and constant-time Extended GCD algorithm. It is demonstrated in [5] as a means for speeding up ntruhrss701 [15] and for ECC with Curve25519. It is also used in the latest implementation of LEDAcrypt [4]. Algorithms for inversion of sparse polynomials over binary fields are discussed in [13,14]. These algorithms are based on the division algorithm of [7].

There are (at least) two popular open-source libraries that provide polynomial inversion over $\mathbb{F}_2$: a) NTL [24], compiled with the GF2X library [22]; b) OpenSSL [25]. We note that the Additional code of BIKE (BIKE-2) [9] can be compiled to use either NTL or OpenSSL. We use this as our comparison baseline. For this research, we implemented a variant of the ITI algorithm (see also [6]) for polynomial inversion that leverages the special algebraic structure in our context, and runs in constant-time.

The paper is organized as follows. Section 2 offers some background and notation. In Sect. 3 we briefly explain our polynomial inversion method. Section 5 provides our performance results and Sect. 6 concludes this paper with several concrete proposals.

2   Preliminaries and Notation

In this paper, we indicate hexadecimal notation with a $\texttt{0x}$ prefix, and place the LSB on the right-most position. Let Y be a string of bits. We use $Y[j]$ to refer to the jth bit of Y. Let $\mathbb{F}_2$ be the finite field of characteristic 2. Let $\mathcal{R}$ be the polynomial ring $\mathbb{F}_2[x]/\langle x^r - 1\rangle$ for some *block size* r and let $\mathcal{R}^*$ denote the set of invertible elements in $\mathcal{R}$. We treat polynomials, interchangeably, as vectors of bits. For every element $v \in \mathcal{R}$ its Hamming weight is denoted by $wt(v)$, its bit length by $|v|$, and its support (i.e., the positions of the non-zero bits) by $supp(v)$. In other words, if an element $a \in \mathcal{R}$ is defined by $a = \sum_{i=0}^{r-1} \alpha_i x^i$ then $supp(a)$ is the set of positions of the non-zero bits, $supp(a) = \{i : \alpha_i = 1\}$. Uniform random sampling from a set U is denoted by $u \xleftarrow{\$} U$. Uniform random sampling of an element with fixed Hamming weight w from a set U is denoted by $u \xleftarrow{w} U$.

2.1   BIKE

Table 1 shows the key generation of the variants of BIKE. The computations are executed over $\mathcal{R}$, and the block size r is a parameter. The weight of the secret key (sk) is w and we denote the public key by pk. For example, the parameters of BIKE-1-CCA for NIST Level-1 as defined in the specification [3] are: $r = 11779$, $|pk| = 23558$, $w = 142$. Table 1 shows that the key generation for BIKE-2 requires polynomial inversion. This is a heavy operation that can be a barrier for adoption when targeting forward-secrecy via ephemeral keys. On the other hand, BIKE-2 has half the communication cost compared to BIKE-1 (and $\sim 2/3$ the communication cost compared to the bandwidth-optimized version of BIKE-3). Specifically, the initiator in BIKE KEM sends pk to the responder, i.e., f_0 for BIKE-2 versus (f_1, f_0) for BIKE-1. In the other direction, the responder sends a ciphertext to the initiator (not shown in Table 1). The length of BIKE-2's ciphertext is half the length of BIKE-1's ciphertext (see [3]). Therefore, reducing the computational cost of polynomial inversion can place BIKE-2 in an advantageous position.

Table 1. BIKE key generation. Polynomial inversion is required with BIKE-2.

	BIKE-1-CPA CPA	BIKE-1 CCA	BIKE-2 CPA	BIKE-2 CCA	BIKE-3 CPA	BIKE-3 CCA
	$h_0, h_1 \xleftarrow{w/2} \mathcal{R}$					
	$g \xleftarrow{\approx r/2,\ \text{odd}} \mathcal{R}$ $(f_0, f_1) = (gh_1, gh_0)$		$f_0 = h_1 h_0^{-1}$		$g \xleftarrow{\approx r/2,\ \text{odd}} \mathcal{R}$ $(f_0, f_1) = (h_1 + gh_0, g)$	
	$\sigma_0, \sigma_1 \xleftarrow{\$} \mathcal{R}$		$\sigma_0, \sigma_1 \xleftarrow{\$} \mathcal{R}$		$\sigma_0, \sigma_1, \sigma_2 \xleftarrow{\$} \mathcal{R}$	
$sk =$	(h_0, h_1)	$(h_0, h_1, \sigma_0, \sigma_1)$	(h_0, h_1)	$(h_0, h_1, \sigma_0, \sigma_1)$	(h_0, h_1)	$(h_0, h_1, \sigma_0, \sigma_1, \sigma_2)$
$pk =$	(f_0, f_1)		f_0		(f_0, f_1)	

3 Optimized Polynomial Inversion in $\mathbb{F}_2[x]/\langle(x-1)h\rangle$ with Irreducible h

In this paper, we propose to use an algorithm that is similar to the ITI algorithm [16]. In both cases, the essence is that raising an element a to the power 2^k (referred to as k-squaring hereafter), can be done efficiently. The ITI algorithm inverts an element of $\mathbb{F}_{2^k}$, where the field elements are represented in normal basis where computing a^{2^k} consists of k cyclic shifts of a's vector representation. This results in fast k-squaring. However, we note that the ITI algorithm can be generalized to other cases where k-squaring is efficient. One example is the set of polynomial rings that are used in BIKE and in other QC-MDPC based schemes.

Our inversion algorithm is Algorithm 2. It applies Algorithm 1 that computes a^{2^k-1} for some $k = 2^t$. Algorithm 1 is analogous to [16][Algorithm 2] that computes $a^{-1} \in \mathbb{F}_{2^\ell}$ for $\ell = 2^t + 1$ through Fermat's Little Theorem as

$$a^{-1} = a^{2^\ell - 2} = (a^{2^{\ell-1}-1})^2 = (a^{2^{2^t}-1})^2$$

BIKE, on the other hand, operates in the polynomial ring $\mathcal{R}$ with a value r for which

$$\mathcal{R} = \mathbb{F}_2[x]/\langle x^r - 1\rangle = \mathbb{F}_2[x]/\langle(x-1)h\rangle$$

Algorithm 1. Computing a^{2^k-1} where $k = 2^t$

    Input: a
    Output: a^{2^k-1}
1: **procedure** CUSTOM_EXPONENTIATION(a)
2:     $f = a$
3:     **for** $i = 0$ to $t - 1$ **do**
4:         $g = f^{2^{2^i}}$
5:         $f = f \cdot g$
6:     **return** f

---

and h is an irreducible polynomial of degree $r - 1$. In this ring, $ord(a) \mid 2^{r-1} - 1$ for every $a \in \mathcal{R}^*$, and therefore

$$a^{-1} = a^{2^{r-1}-2} \tag{1}$$

Here, Algorithm [16][Algorithm 2] cannot be used directly because $a^{2^{r-1}-2} = (a^{2^{r-2}-1})^2$ and $r - 2$ is not a power of 2. Therefore, we use the following decomposition.

Decomposition of $2^{r-1} - 2$. In order to apply Algorithm 1, we write $s = supp(r - 2)$ and rewrite $z = 2^{r-1} - 2$ in a convenient way:

$$z = 2 \cdot (2^{r-2} - 1) = 2 \cdot \sum_{i \in s} \left((2^{2^i} - 1) \cdot \left(2^{(r-2) \bmod 2^i} \right) \right) \tag{2}$$

Algorithm 2 uses Algorithm 1 and the decomposition (2) as follows.

Algorithm 2. Inversion in $\mathcal{R} = \mathbb{F}_2[x]/\langle(x-1)h\rangle$ with an irreducible h

---

    Input: $a \in \mathcal{R}^*$
    Output: a^{-1}
1: **procedure** INVERT(a)
2:     $f = a$
3:     $res = a$
4:     **for** $i = 1$ to $\lfloor \log(r-2) \rfloor$ **do**
5:         $g = f^{2^{2^{(i-1)}}}$ ▷ As in Alg. 1
6:         $f = f \cdot g$
7:         **if** $((r-2)[i] = 1)$ **then**   ▷ i^{th} bit of $r-2$
8:             $res = res \cdot f^{2^{(r-2) \bmod 2^i}}$
9:     $res = res^2$
10:    **return** res

Algorithm 2 requires $\lfloor \log(r-2) \rfloor + wt(r-2) - 1$ multiplications plus $\lfloor \log(r-2) \rfloor + wt(r-2) - 1$ k-squarings and 1 squaring (in $\mathcal{R}$). The performance depends on $|r - 2|$ and on $wt(r-2)$ and choices of r with smaller $|r - 2|$ and $wt(r - 2)$ lead to better performance.

Remark 1. The last square in line 9 of Algorithm 2 can be saved by changing line 6 therein to the following line

$$res = res \cdot f^{2^{1+(r-2) \bmod 2^i}}$$

This optimization is omitted from the algorithm's description for clarity.

Example 1. The recommended block size (r) for BIKE-1-CCA/BIKE-2-CCA, Level-1, is $r = 11779$. Here, $2^{r-1} - 2$ can be written as:

$$2^{11778} - 2 = 2 \cdot (1 + 2(2^{512} - 1) + 2^{513}(2^{1024} - 1) + 2^{1537}(2^{2048} - 1) + 2^{3585}(2^{8192} - 1))$$

With this decomposition, Algorithm 2 requires 17 polynomial multiplications, 17 k-squarings and 1 squaring.

For implementation efficiency, our method leverages the following observation.

Observation 1. *Let $a = \sum_{j \in supp(a)} x^j \in \mathcal{R}^*$. Then,*

$$a^{2^k} = \left(\sum_{j \in supp(a)} x^j \right)^{2^k} = \sum_{j \in supp(a)} (x^j)^{2^k} \tag{3}$$

$$= \sum_{j \in supp(a)} x^{j \cdot 2^k} = \sum_{j \in supp(a)} x^{j \cdot 2^k \bmod r}$$

The first step in (3) is an identity in a ring with characteristic 2. The last step uses the fact that $ord(x) = r$ in $\mathcal{R}$. Using Observation 1, we can compute the k-square of $a \in \mathcal{R}^*$ as a permutation of the bits of a.

4   Our Implementation

This section discusses our implementation and further optimizations for Algorithm 2. Some explanatory code snippets are provided in Appendices A, B and C.

Speeding Up the Implementation with Precomputed Tables. The actual values of k in all the k-squarings of Algorithm 2 depend on r but not on a. Therefore, if r is fixed, the permutation $p_0 : j \to j \cdot 2^k \bmod r$ can be pre-computed for all the relevant values of k (which depends only on r). This speeds up the implementation. The required storage is $\lfloor \log(r - 2) \rfloor + 1 + wt(r - 2)$ tables where each one holds $|r|$ values.

Inverted Permutation. The BIKE implementation stores the polynomials in a *dense* representation, i.e., an array of $\lceil r/word\_size \rceil$ words where each word holds *word_size* bits of the polynomial. The straightforward way to permute is to go over all the words of the data, extract all the *word_size* bits, and store every one of them in the required position of the output polynomial (as defined by the permutation map). This approach requires one memory read and *word_size* writes to random locations in the output data, per word of the input. However, when we apply the inverted permutation map, the k-square requires *word_size* random memory reads from the input data and only one memory write to the output array, per word of the input array. This speeds up the k-squaring in a noticeable way.

Using Regular Polynomial Square. Squaring a polynomial in $\mathcal{R}$ is very efficient (significantly faster than a k-squaring. See Appendix A). This leads to the following optimization for small values of k: execute a chain of k single squarings instead of executing a k-square routine. The k value for preferring a k-square over a chain of squares depends on the implementation. We provide Table 6 in Appendix A to this end. Consequently, in addition to $r - 2$ and $wt(r - 2)$, the efficiency of inversion depends on the number of k-squares that can be replaced with regular squares. For example, consider $r_1 = 11779$ and $r_2 = 12347$. Here, inverting a polynomial of degree r_1 is expected to be faster than for r_2, because $wt(r_1 - 2) = 5 < 6 = wt(r_2 - 2)$. However, from the binary representations $r_1 - 2 = $ 0b10111000000001 and $r_2 - 2 = $ 0b11000000111001, we see that the set bits in $r_2 - 2$ are positioned close to the LSB, and the set bits in $r_1 - 2$ are positioned close to the MSB. If the k-square threshold is 64, then for r_1 we can replace (only) one k-square with a chain of (regular) squares, and for r_2 we can replace 4 such k-squares.

Constant-Time Considerations. Algorithm 2 involves a constant number of steps for every given (fixed) r because the number and the order of multiplications and k-squarings are independent of the input. However, to achieve a constant-time implementation, the multiplication and k-squaring have to be constant-time routines. The Additional code of BIKE [9] already implements multiplication in constant-time. Since the k-squaring operation is merely a permutation of bits, it is straightforward to implement it in constant-time as follows: scan every bit of the input and update the appropriate bit in the output polynomial. This approach enjoys also constant memory access because the permutation is determined only by the (fixed) value of r.

Using Vector-PCLMULQDQ. Modern CPUs offer a fast carry-less multiplication instruction (PCLMULQDQ) that can be used for multiplication in binary fields. We note that PCLMULQDQ can be a bottleneck when algorithms that involve polynomial multiplication run on modern architectures: while AVX512 architectures can use wider 512-bit registers (zmm), PCLMULQDQ operates only on 128-bit registers (xmm). In the recent 10th generation CPUs (codename "Ice Lake") Intel® introduced a vector PCLMULQDQ instruction, and we leverage this feature to our advantage. We replaced the 4×4 64-bit words schoolbook implementation that is used in the Additional code of BIKE, with the 8×8 64-bit words schoolbook algorithm of [11]. This yields some improvements. We further optimized the code to use a 16×16 64-bit words Karatsuba multiplication and observed a total speedup by a factor of 1.08 with this architecture. The details are explained in Appendix B.

Using Binary-Recursive-Karatsuba. In [8] we recommended to use the binary recursive-Karatsuba for multiplication for polynomials whose degree is slightly smaller than a power of two (e.g., $r = 32749$ for BIKE-1-CPA Level-5). This allows some optimizations and simpler code because implementation of a 4×4 schoolbook suffices (in addition to the binary recursive Karatsuba code). However, the values of r for the IND-CCA variants of BIKE and for IND-CPA BIKE in Level-1 and Level-3 are not close to a power of two. Here, padding every multiplicand to the closest power of 2 can be costly. For example, padding $r = 11779$ (as in BIKE-2-CCA Level-1) to the 16384 increases the multiplicands size by $\sim40\%$. To this end, we replaced the lower 8×8 multiplication (using Vector-PCLMULQDQ) with $\beta \times \beta$ ($9 \leq \beta \leq 16$) multiplication. This yields multiplications of sizes $2^\alpha \cdot \beta$, for some integer $\alpha > 1$. Table 2 shows the exact values. For example, for $r = 11779$, with $\beta = 12$, the closest value of the form $2^\alpha \cdot \beta$ is 12288 ($\alpha = 10$) with only $\sim5\%$ increase in the overall multiplicands size. Our experiments for BIKE-2-CCA Level-1 show that the fastest implementation is as in [8] with $\beta = 16$ and $\alpha = 10$.

In this case, we can make the implementation faster by avoiding multiplications of the higher parts of the multiplicands, which are zero. This optimization depends on the values of r and β.

Table 2. The sizes of the multiplicands ($2^\alpha \cdot \beta$) for different choices of α and β. Boldface values are the closest from above to $r = 11779$ (BIKE-2-CCA Level-1). Italic values are the closest from above to $r = 24821$ (BIKE-2-CCA Level-3).

α	$\beta = 9$	10	11	12	13	14	15	16
10	9216	10240	11264	**12288**	13312	**14336**	**15360**	**16384**
11	**18432**	**20480**	**22558**	24576	*26624*	*28672*	*30720*	*32768*
12	*36864*	*40960*	*45056*	*49152*	53248	57344	61440	65536
13	73728	81920	90112	98304	106496	114688	122880	131072

5 Results

This section provides performance results and compares them to the specified baseline.

The Platforms. We carried out performance measurements on two different platforms, which we call "laptop" and "server" platforms:

- The laptop platform is a Dell XPS 13 7390 2-in-1 laptop. It has a 10th generation Intel®Core^{TM} processor (microarchitecture codename "Ice Lake"[ICL]). The specifics are Intel®Core^{TM} i7-1065G7 CPU 1.30 GHz. This platform has 16 GB RAM, 48 K L1d cache, 32 K L1i cache, 512 K L2 cache, and 8 MiB L3 cache and it supports AVX512 and Vector-PCLMULQDQ instructions. For the experiments, we turned off the Intel® Turbo Boost Technology (in order to work with a fixed frequency and measure performance in cycles).
- The server platform is an AWS EC2 m5.24xlarge instance with the 6th Intel®Core^{TM} Generation (Micro architecture Codename "Sky Lake" [SKL]) Xeon®Platinum 8175 M CPU 2.50 GHz. This platform has 384 GB RAM, 32 K L1d and L1i cache, 1 MiB L2 cache, and 32 MiB L3 cache that only have AVX512 capabilities.

Measurements Methodology. The performance reported hereafter is measured in processor cycles (per single core), where lower count is better. We obtain the results using the following methodology. Every measured function was isolated, run 25 times (warm-up), followed by 100 iterations that were clocked (using the RDTSC instruction) and averaged. To minimize the effect of background tasks running on the system, every experiment was repeated 10 times, and the minimum result was recorded.

The Code. Our code is written mainly in C with some x86-64 assembly routines. Some versions use the Vector-PCLMULQDQ and other AVX512 instructions. On the Ice Lake machine we compiled the code with gcc (version 9.2.1), using the "-O3 -march=native" optimization flags and ran it on a Linux OS (Ubuntu 19.04). On the server platform the code is compiled with gcc (version 7.4.0) in 64-bit mode, using the "-O3 -march=native" optimization flags and ran on Ubuntu 18.04.2 LTS.

The Comparison Baseline. Our comparison baseline are the implementations of the popular open-source libraries NTL (compiled with GF2X) [22,24] and OpenSSL [25]. We do not compare to [7,13,14,16] because they are all slower than NTL: a) the inversion algorithm of [13] is reported to be 2× faster than [7], 12× faster than [16], but 1.7× slower than NTL; b) the implementation in [14] is reported to be 3× slower than NTL. We also measured the inversion function of the LEDAcrypt optimized code [4] that implements safegcd [5]. This code uses AVX2, and our implementation uses AVX512. For fair comparison, we compiled our code with AVX2 instructions only. The performance of the LEDAcrypt inversion (on "laptop") is: a) using gcc: 4.05/12.43/27.32 million cycles for Level-1/3/5, respectively; b) using clang: 3.29/10.30/22.94 million cycles for Level-1/3/5, respectively. The performance of our inversion on the same platform is: 0.65/2.36/5.37 million cycles for Level-1/3/5, respectively. The code of [4] runs in constant time and is faster than NTL. On the other hand, it is slower than our implementation even when we use only the AVX2 code.

Blinding a Non-constant Time Inversion. Binary polynomial inversion does not operate in constant-time for either OpenSSL [25] or NTL [24] because these libraries use the extended GCD based algorithms to compute the inverse. To address this issue, a recent change in OpenSSL, (between version 1.0.2 to version 1.1.0) protects the implementation by *blinding* the inversion as follows. The function BN_GF2m_mod_inv(a, s) computes a^{-1} mod s by the following sequence: 1) choose a random b; 2) compute $c = ab$; 3) invert c); 4) multiply by b. Unfortunately, this does not work in the general case, where s is not necessarily an irreducible polynomial (see discussion in [12]). If s is reducible, $c = ab$ may be non-invertible modulo s. This is exactly the case of BIKE-2 where $x^r - 1$ is reducible. Although the OpenSSL function BN_GF2m_mod_inv(a, $x^r - 1$) is called with invertible a, the blinding may select a random non-invertible polynomial b and then inverting $c = ab$ would fail. In the polynomial ring $\mathcal{R}$ a randomly selected b has probability $\frac{1}{2}$ to be non-invertible. For a fair comparison (of constant-time implementations), we use the same blinding technique for NTL as well. For correctness, we always choose b such that $wt(b)$ is odd, and therefore b is invertible in $\mathcal{R}$.

The results are summarized in Table 3 (for "laptop"), and Table 4 (for "server"). In all cases, our implementation outperforms the baseline. The relative speedups for BIKE-2 are higher for Level-1 than for Level-5. This is quite fortunate because our focus is anyway on Level-1. Note that NIST has announced that Level-5 is not critical for standardization (we provide Level 5 performance for the sake of comparison with other works).

We observe that the relative speedup on "laptop" is only slightly better than on "server" despite the fact that the laptop has a newer (10th generation) CPU with Vector-PCLMULQDQ. In fact, we expect to see additional speedup as soon as Intel releases servers with the 10th generation processor.

Table 3. BIKE-2 key generation when the inversion uses NTL with GF2X [22,24], OpenSSL [25], and our method. The platform is "laptop" (see text). Columns 2–5 count cycles in millions, and lower is better. The r values correspond to the IND-CCA variants of BIKE for Level-1/3/5.

r	NTL [22, 24]	OpenSSL [25]	This work	This work (w/tables)	Speedup NTL/Our	Speedup NTL/T (w/tables)	Speedup OpenSSL/T (w/tables)
11779	6.28	42.51	0.47	0.44	13.46	14.31	96.86
24821	9.29	164.95	1.71	1.65	5.44	5.62	99.86
40597	16.37	515.21	4.08	3.85	4.02	4.25	133.91

The use of precomputed permutation tables (see Sect. 3) provides an interesting tradeoff. It improves the overall performance at a cost of occupying some memory space. The tables that we need to store hold $r \cdot (\lfloor \log(r-2) \rfloor + 1 + wt(r-2))$ entries of size r bits (for all security levels of BIKE the entries can be stored

Table 4. BIKE-2 key generation when the inversion uses NTL with GF2X [22,24], OpenSSL [25], and our method. The platform is "server" (see text). Columns 2–5 count cycles in millions, and lower is better. The r values correspond to the IND-CCA variants of BIKE for Level-1/3/5.

r	NTL [22,24]	OpenSSL [25]	This work	This work (w/tables)	Speedup NTL/Our	Speedup NTL/T (w/tables)	Speedup OpenSSL/T (w/tables)
11779	4.93	23.22	0.43	0.42	11.51	11.79	55.53
24821	7.64	121.86	1.61	1.59	4.75	4.82	76.78
40597	15.24	342.61	3.89	3.80	3.92	4.01	90.13

in 2 bytes of memory). For example, for BIKE-2-CCA the required memory is 450 KB for Level-1, 1.1 MB for Level-3, and 2 MB for Level-5.

Table 5 shows relative speedups in the BIKE-2 key generation for different values of r and illustrates the effect of $wt(r-2)$ on the performance of the key generation. All the values of r are legitimate choices for BIKE (i.e., $x^r - 1 = (x-1)h$, where h is irreducible). We chose one representative for every value of $wt(r-2)$ and the table includes the recommended parameters from the [3] specification.

6   Discussion

The Effect of Different Choices of r on BIKE-2 Performance. In general, the parameter r determines the sizes of the public key, the ciphertext and thus the overall latency and bandwidth. So far, r was chosen as the minimum value that satisfies the security target [3] and the target Decoding Failure Rate (DFR)Decoding Failure Rate (DFR) of the decoder [10,23]. We propose an additional consideration, namely $wt(r-2)$ (recall how the inversion Algorithm 2 depends on $wt(r-2)$). The currently recommended r for Level-1 is $r = 11779$ for which $wt(r-2) = 5$. Interestingly, a considerably larger $r = 12323$ has $wt(r-2) = 4$. Note that [10] shows that $\sim r = 12323$ is needed and sufficient in order to achieve a DFR of 2^{-128}.

Two considerations are pointed out in [8]: a) rejection sampling is faster for values of r that are close (from below) to a power of 2 (e. g., $r = 32749$ is close to $2^{15} = 32768$ and the rejection rate is $32749/32768 \approx 1$); b) it is useful to pad multiplicands to the nearest power of two. It follows that the three considerations should be taken into account together. For example, $wt(32749-2) = 13$ is quite large and the slightly larger r=32771 has $wt(32771-2) = 2$ and seems to be preferable. However, key generation with $r = 32749$ takes 4.2M compared to 5.3M cycles with $r = 32771$.

BIKE-2 Versus BIKE-1. Until now, BIKE-1 seemed to be a more appealing option than BIKE-2. This is the result of the prohibitive cost of BIKE-2 key generation that seemed to be an obstacle for adoption, especially when ephemeral

Table 5. Relative speedups in the BIKE-2 key generation for different values of r. The table shows how the performance depends on $wt(r-2)$. The values in boldface corresponds to the recommended parameters in [3].

r	$wt(r-2)$	Speedup over NTL		Speedup over NTL (with tables)		Speedup over OpenSSL (with tables)	
		Server	Laptop	Server	Laptop	Server	Laptop
12323	4	11.60	13.89	11.81	14.27	62.08	99.13
11779	**5**	**11.51**	**13.46**	**11.79**	14.31	**55.53**	**96.86**
12347	6	10.46	12.62	10.63	12.96	59.64	87.97
11789	7	10.85	12.91	11.09	13.30	70.09	79.63
11821	8	10.37	12.43	10.46	12.72	62.04	68.48
11933	9	9.89	11.96	10.09	12.45	52.86	72.74
12149	10	9.56	11.20	9.76	11.56	52.71	63.69
12157	11	9.23	10.91	9.43	11.39	42.76	64.20
25603	4	5.87	6.70	5.97	7.08	92.06	142.05
24659	5	5.40	6.12	5.49	6.34	87.44	122.43
24677	6	5.18	5.96	5.25	6.17	65.65	107.28
24733	7	5.00	5.89	5.08	6.09	83.44	91.20
24821	**8**	**4.75**	**5.44**	**4.82**	**5.62**	**76.78**	**99.86**
25453	9	4.65	5.31	4.71	5.54	81.13	101.41
24547	10	4.01	4.59	4.08	4.74	70.83	79.28
24533	11	3.90	4.49	3.97	4.63	58.92	82.64
24509	12	4.49	5.18	4.58	5.45	72.75	93.95
40973	5	4.51	5.18	4.59	5.37	103.48	133.27
41051	6	4.28	4.82	4.33	5.07	107.19	128.89
41077	7	4.06	4.61	4.12	4.77	84.17	132.74
40709	8	3.71	4.23	3.81	4.50	80.66	117.54
40597	**9**	**3.92**	**4.02**	**4.01**	**4.25**	**90.13**	**133.91**
40763	10	3.41	3.91	3.48	4.13	86.89	105.37
40637	11	3.33	3.71	3.39	3.96	84.55	111.01
40829	12	3.19	3.61	3.27	3.84	83.73	107.99

keys are desired. This left out BIKE-2's bandwidth advantage. BIKE specification [3] addresses this difficulty by using a "batch inversion" approach that requires pre-computation of a batch of key pairs. Such solutions require that other protocols are adapted to using batched key pairs, and this raises additional complications.

Our improved inversion and hence faster key generation avoids the difficulty. For Level-1 ($r = 11779$) BIKE-2 has key generation/encapsulation/decapsulation at $440\,\mathrm{K}/180\,\mathrm{K}/1.2\,\mathrm{M}$ cycles, and communication bandwidth of $1.4\,\mathrm{KB}$ in each direction. By comparison, BIKE-1 (after using our latest multiplication implementation) has key generation/encapsulation/decapsulation at

$67\,\mathrm{K}/230\,\mathrm{K}/1.3\,\mathrm{M}$ cycles, and communication bandwidth of $2.8\,\mathrm{KB}$ in each direction. We believe that our results position BIKE-2 as an appealing design choice among the BIKE variants.

Acknowledgements. This research was partly supported by: NSF-BSF Grant 2018640; The BIU Center for Research in Applied Cryptography and Cyber Security, and the Center for Cyber Law and Policy at the University of Haifa, both in conjunction with the Israel National Cyber Bureau in the Prime Minister's Office.

We would also like to thank Thorsten Kleinjung for his valuable comments on this work.

A   Squaring Using **PCLMULQDQ** and **VPCLMULQDQ**

This appendix describes our C implementation for squaring in $\mathcal{R}$, using PCLMULQDQ. For brevity, we replace the long names of the C intrinsics with shorter macros as follows.

```
#define PERM64(a, mask)          _mm512_permutex_epi64(a, mask)            1
#define PERM64X2(a, mask, b)     _mm512_permutex2var_epi64(a, mask, b)     2
#define PERM64VAR(mask, a)       _mm512_permutexvar_epi64(mask, a)         3
#define MUL(a, b, imm8)          _mm512_clmulepi64_epi128(a, b, imm8)      4
#define MXOR(src, mask, a, b)    _mm512_mask_xor_epi64(src, mask, a, b)    5
#define ALIGN(a, b, count)       _mm512_alignr_epi64(a, b, count)          6
#define STORE(mem, reg)          _mm512_storeu_si512(mem, reg)             7
#define LOAD(mem)                _mm512_loadu_si512(mem)                   8
#define EXPANDLOAD(mask, mem)    _mm512_maskz_expandloadu_epi64(mask, mem) 9
                                                                          10
#define LOAD128(mem)             _mm_loadu_si128(mem)                      11
#define STORE128(mem, reg)       _mm_storeu_si128(mem, reg)                12
#define MUL128(a, b, imm8)       _mm_clmulepi64_si128(a, b, imm8)          13
```

When PCLMULQDQ (and not vector-PCLMULQDQ) is available, the square function is

```
void gf2x_sqr(uint64_t *res, const uint64_t *a)                           1
{                                                                         2
  for (size_t i = 0; i < ceil(R/128); i++)                               3
  {                                                                       4
    __m128i va = LOAD128((__m128i*)(a+i*2));                             5
    STORE128((__m128i*)(&res[i*4]), MUL128(va, va, 0x00););              6
    STORE128((__m128i*)(&res[i*4+2]), MUL128(va, va, 0x11););            7
  }                                                                       8
}                                                                         9
```

When vector-PCLMULQDQ is available, four multiplications can be executed in parallel and the code is

```
void gf2x_sqr_vpclmulqdq(uint64_t *res, const uint64_t *a)          1
{                                                                   2
    __m512i vm = _mm512_set_epi64(7, 3, 6, 2, 5, 1, 4, 0);          3
    for (int i = 0; i < ceil(R/512); i++)                          4
    {                                                               5
        __m512i va  = LOAD(&a[i*8]);                                6
        va  = PERM64VAR(vm, va);                                    7
                                                                    8
        STORE(&res[i*16], MUL(va, va, 0x00));                       9
        STORE(&res[i*16+8], MUL(va, va, 0x11));                     10
    }                                                               11
}                                                                   12
```

The permutation and thus some of the flow's serialization can be removed by using the _mm512_maskz_expandloadu_epi64 instruction.

```
void gf2x_sqr_vpclmulq(uint64_t *res, const uint64_t *a)            1
{                                                                   2
    for (int i = 0; i < ceil(R/512); i++)                          3
    {                                                               4
        __m512i va1  = EXPANDLOAD(0x55, &a[i*8]);                   5
        __m512i va2  = EXPANDLOAD(0x55, &a[i*8+1]);                 6
                                                                    7
        STORE(&res[i*16], MUL(va1, va1, 0x00));                     8
        STORE(&res[i*16+8], MUL(va2, va2, 0x00));                   9
    }                                                               10
}                                                                   11
```

However, our experiments show slower results with this instruction.

Table 6 compares squaring and k-squaring in $\mathcal{R}$ using our code. Our implementation starts with squaring up to the described threshold and then continues with k-squaring. The threshold depends on the platform.

Table 6. Squaring and k-squaring in $\mathcal{R}$ using our code. Columns 2 and 3 count cycles, where lower is better (threshold = floor(k-square/square)). The r values correspond to the IND-CCA variants of BIKE for Level-1/3/5.

<table>
<tr><td colspan="4">(a) Laptop</td><td colspan="4">(b) Server</td></tr>
<tr><td>r</td><td>k-square</td><td>square</td><td>threshold</td><td>r</td><td>k-square</td><td>square</td><td>threshold</td></tr>
<tr><td>11779</td><td>16000</td><td>230</td><td>69</td><td>11779</td><td>20000</td><td>350</td><td>57</td></tr>
<tr><td>24821</td><td>35000</td><td>510</td><td>68</td><td>24821</td><td>42000</td><td>680</td><td>61</td></tr>
<tr><td>40597</td><td>65000</td><td>790</td><td>82</td><td>40597</td><td>68000</td><td>1100</td><td>61</td></tr>
</table>

B   A 16 × 16 Quad-Words Multiplication Using VPCLMULQDQ

This appendix describes the C code of our recursive Karatsuba multiplication.

The `mul128x4` function performs four 128-bit Karatsuba multiplications in parallel.

```
static inline void mul128x4(__m512i *h, __m512i *l, __m512i a, __m512i b)   1
{                                                                            2
    const __m512i mask_abq = _mm512_set_epi64(6, 7, 4, 5, 2, 3, 0, 1);       3
    __m512i      s1 = a ^ PERM64(a, _MM_SHUFFLE(2, 3, 0, 1));                 4
    __m512i      s2 = b ^ PERM64(b, _MM_SHUFFLE(2, 3, 0, 1));                 5
                                                                             6
    __m512i lq  = MUL(a, b, 0x00);                                           7
    __m512i hq  = MUL(a, b, 0x11);                                           8
    __m512i abq = lq ^ hq ^ MUL(s1, s2, 0x00);                               9
    abq         = PERM64VAR(mask_abq, abq);                                  10
    *l          = MXOR(lq, 0xaa, lq, abq);                                   11
    *h          = MXOR(hq, 0x55, hq, abq);                                   12
}                                                                            13
```

Then, we define the `mul512` function that receives two 512-bit zmm registers (a, b) as input, multiplies them and writes the result into the two registers $zh||zl$. The function performs several permutations to reorganize the quad-words. The relevant masks are:

```
const __m512i mask0   = _mm512_set_epi64(13, 12,  5,  4,  9,  8, 1, 0);   1
const __m512i mask1   = _mm512_set_epi64(15, 14,  7,  6, 11, 10, 3, 2);   2
const __m512i mask2   = _mm512_set_epi64(3,   2,  1,  0,  7,  6, 5, 4);   3
const __m512i mask3   = _mm512_set_epi64(11, 10,  9,  8,  3,  2, 1, 0);   4
const __m512i mask4   = _mm512_set_epi64(15, 14, 13, 12,  7,  6, 5, 4);   5
const __m512i mask_s2 = _mm512_set_epi64(3,   2,  7,  6,  5,  4, 1, 0);   6
const __m512i mask_s1 = _mm512_set_epi64(7,   6,  5,  4,  1,  0, 3, 2);   7
```

The __m512i variables that are used in this function are: a) x1, xh. These hold the lower and upper parts of the 128-bit Karatsuba sub-multiplications; b) xabl, xabh, xab, xab1, xab2. These are used for the middle term of the 256-bit Karatsuba sub-multiplications; c) yl, yh, yabl, yabh, yab. These are used for middle term of the top 512-bit Karatsuba multiplication; d) t[4] that holds all the temporary products to `mul128` of the middle words.

Define

$$AX[i] = a[128(i+1) - 1 : 128i]$$
$$BX[i] = b[128(i+1) - 1 : 128i]$$
$$AY[i] = a[256(i+1) - 1 : 256i]$$
$$BY[i] = b[256(i+1) - 1 : 256i]$$

Then set

$$t[0] = AX1 \oplus AX3||AX2 \oplus AX3||AX0 \oplus AX2||AX0 \oplus AX1$$
$$t[1] = BX1 \oplus BX3||BX2 \oplus BX3||BX0 \oplus BX2||BX0 \oplus BX1$$

where

$$AX1 \oplus AX3 \| AX0 \oplus AX2 = (AX1 \| AX0) \oplus (AX3 \| AX2) = AY0 \oplus AY1$$
$$BX1 \oplus BX3 \| BX0 \oplus BX2 = (BX1 \| BX0) \oplus (BX3 \| BX2) = BY0 \oplus BY1$$

and set the lower 128 bits of t[2], t[3] to (ignoring the upper bits)

$$t[2][127:0] = AX1 \oplus AX3 \oplus AX0 \oplus AX2$$
$$t[3][127:0] = BX1 \oplus BX3 \oplus BX0 \oplus BX2$$

```
t[0] = PERM64VAR(mask_s1, a) ^ PERM64VAR(mask_s2, a);    1
t[1] = PERM64VAR(mask_s1, b) ^ PERM64VAR(mask_s2, b);    2
t[2] = t[0] ^ ALIGN(t[0], t[0], 4);                      3
t[3] = t[1] ^ ALIGN(t[1], t[1], 4);                      4
```

The implementation invokes mul128x4 three times: a) for calculating the lower and the upper 512-bit words; b) for the two middle 256-bit words; c) for the middle 512-bit word in the top-level Karatsuba. The number of invocations of VPCLMULQDQ for the entire mul512 is only 9.

```
mul128x4(&xh, &xl, a, b);              1
mul128x4(&xabh, &xabl, t[0], t[1]);    2
mul128x4(&yabh, &yabl, t[2], t[3]);    3
```

Finally, we complete the four 128-bit Karatsuba by

```
xab  = xl ^ xh ^ PERM64X2(xabl, mask0, xabh);    1
yl   = PERM64X2(xl, mask3, xh);                  2
yh   = PERM64X2(xl, mask4, xh);                  3
xab1 = ALIGN(xab, xab, 6);                       4
xab2 = ALIGN(xab, xab, 2);                       5
yl   = MXOR(yl, 0x3c, yl, xab1);                 6
yh   = MXOR(yh, 0x3c, yh, xab2);                 7
```

and the 512-bit result is

```
__m512i oxh = PERM64X2(xabl, mask1, xabh);       1
__m512i oxl = ALIGN(oxh, oxh, 4);                2
yab         = oxl ^ oxh ^ PERM64X2(yabl, mask0, yabh);  3
yab         = MXOR(oxh, 0x3c, oxl, ALIGN(yab, yab, 2)); 4
yab ^= yl ^ yh;                                  5
                                                 6
yab = PERM64VAR(mask2, yab);                     7
*zl = MXOR(yl, 0xf0, yl, yab);                   8
*zh = MXOR(yh, 0x0f, yh, yab);                   9
```

For higher efficiency, our `mul1024` Karatsuba implementation holds the data in zmm registers in order to save memory operations when invoking `mul512`.

```
void mul1024(uint64_t *cp, const uint64_t *ap, const uint64_t *bp) {    1
    const __m512i a0 = LOAD(ap);                                        2
    const __m512i a1 = LOAD(ap + 8);                                    3
    const __m512i b0 = LOAD(bp);                                        4
    const __m512i b1 = LOAD(bp + 8);                                    5
    __m512i        hi[2], lo[2], ab[2];                                 6
                                                                        7
    mul512(&lo[1], &lo[0], a0, b0);                                     8
    mul512(&hi[1], &hi[0], a1, b1);                                     9
    mul512(&ab[1], &ab[0], a0 ^ a1, b0 ^ b1);                          10
                                                                       11
    __m512i middle = lo[1] ^ hi[0];                                    12
                                                                       13
    STORE(cp, lo[0]);                                                  14
    STORE(cp + 8, ab[0] ^ lo[0] ^ middle);                            15
    STORE(cp + 16, ab[1] ^ hi[1] ^ middle);                           16
    STORE(cp + 24, hi[1]);                                            17
}                                                                      18
```

C   Fast Permutation

The inverted bit permutation $(a = map(b))$ of Sect. 4 can be implemented in a straightforward way as follows. We first convert the map to two maps bytes_map and bits_map, where bytes_map[i] is the byte index of $map(b[i])$ and bits_map[i] is the position of the relevant bit inside this byte.

```
idx = 0;                                                               1
for(int i = 0; i < r; i++)                                             2
{                                                                      3
    uint8_t t = 0;                                                     4
    for (size_t j = 0; j < 8; j++) {                                   5
        uint8_t bit = (a[pos_byte[idx]] >> pos_bit[idx]) & 1;          6
        t |= (bit << j);                                               7
        idx++;                                                         8
    }                                                                  9
    b[i] = t;                                                         10
}                                                                     11
```

A simpler way to apply the map is possible if we store every bit in a byte (that has the value `0x00` or `0x01`).

```
for(int i = 0; i < r; i++)                                             1
    b[i] = a[map[i]];                                                  2
```

This can involve a costly conversion to and from across the representations but fortunately, we can speed it up with AVX512 (when available)

```
// Converting a binary array (B) to a bytes array (A)          1
for(size_t i = 0; i < qw_len; i++)                             2
   STORE(&A[i*8], _mm512_maskz_set1_epi8(B[i], 1));            3
```

```
// Converting a bytes array (A) to a binary array (B)          1
__m512i first_bit_mask = _mm512_set1_epi8(1);                  2
for(size_t i = 0; i < qw_len; i++)                             3
   B[i] = _mm512_cmp_epi8_mask(LOAD(&A[i*8]), first_bit_mask, 0); 4
```

Note that the _mm512_bitshuffle_epi64_mask instruction can also be
used for the latter conversion (see next). This instruction requires the
AVX512_BITALG extension while the _mm512_cmp_epi8_mask instruction
requires only AVX512F which is more common.

```
// Converting a bytes array (A) to a binary array (B)          1
__m512i first_bit_mask = _mm512_set1_epi64(0x3830282018100800); 2
for(int i=0; i < qw_len; i++)                                  3
   B[i] = _mm512_bitshuffle_epi64_mask(LOAD(&A[i*8]), first_bit_mask); 4
```

References

1. Aguilar Melchor, C., et al.: Hamming Quasi-Cyclic (HQC) (2017). https://pqc-hqc.org/doc/hqc-specification_2017-11-30.pdf
2. Amazon Web Services: s2n (2020). https://github.com/awslabs/s2n. Accessed 16 Feb 2020
3. Aragon, N., et al.: BIKE: Bit Flipping Key Encapsulation (2017). https://bikesuite.org/files/round2/spec/BIKE-Spec-2019.06.30.1.pdf
4. Baldi, M., Barenghi, A., Chiaraluce, F., Pelosi, G., Santini, P.: LEDAcrypt (2019). https://www.ledacrypt.org/
5. Bernstein, D.J., Yang, B.Y.: Fast constant-time GCD computation and modular inversion. IACR Trans. Crypt. Hardw. Embed. Syst. **2019**(3), 340–398 (2019). https://doi.org/10.13154/tches.v2019.i3.340-398
6. Bos, J.W., Kleinjung, T., Niederhagen, R., Schwabe, P.: ECC2K-130 on cell CPUs. In: Bernstein, D.J., Lange, T. (eds.) AFRICACRYPT 2010. LNCS, vol. 6055, pp. 225–242. Springer, Heidelberg (2010). https://doi.org/10.1007/978-3-642-12678-9_14
7. Chien-Hsing, W., Chien-Ming, W., Shieh, M.-D., Hwang, Y.-T.: High-speed, low-complexity systolic designs of novel iterative division algorithms in $gf(2^m)$. IEEE Trans. Comput. **53**(3), 375–380 (2004). https://doi.org/10.1109/TC.2004.1261843
8. Drucker, N., Gueron, S.: A toolbox for software optimization of QC-MDPC code-based cryptosystems. J. Crypt. Eng. **9**(4), 341–357 (2019). https://doi.org/10.1007/s13389-018-00200-4
9. Drucker, N., Gueron, S., Kostic, D.: Additional implementation of BIKE. https://bikesuite.org/additional.html (2019)

10. Drucker, N., Gueron, S., Kostic, D.: QC-MDPC decoders with several shades of gray. Technical report. Report 2019/1423, December 2019. https://eprint.iacr.org/2019/1423

11. Drucker, N., Gueron, S., Krasnov, V.: Fast multiplication of binary polynomials with the forthcoming vectorized VPCLMULQDQ instruction. In: 2018 IEEE 25th Symposium on Computer Arithmetic (ARITH), pp. 115–119, June 2018. https://doi.org/10.1109/ARITH.2018.8464777

12. Gueron, S.: October 2018. https://github.com/open-quantum-safe/openssl/issues/42#issuecomment-433452096

13. Guimar, A., Borin, E., Aranha, D.F., Guimarães, A., Borin, E., Aranha,D.F.: Introducing arithmetic failures to accelerate QC-MDPC code-based cryptography. Code-Based Cryptogr. **2**, 44–68 (2019). https://doi.org/10.1007/978-3-030-25922-8

14. Guimarães, A., Aranha, D.F., Borin, E.: Optimized implementation of QC-MDPC code-based cryptography. Concurr. Comput.: Pract. Exp. **31**(18), e5089 (2019). https://doi.org/10.1002/cpe.5089

15. Hülsing, A., Rijneveld, J., Schanck, J., Schwabe, P.: High-speed key encapsulation from NTRU. In: Fischer, W., Homma, N. (eds.) CHES 2017. LNCS, vol. 10529, pp. 232–252. Springer, Cham (2017). https://doi.org/10.1007/978-3-319-66787-4_12

16. Itoh, T., Tsujii, S.: A fast algorithm for computing multiplicative inverses in $GF(2^m)$ using normal bases. Inf. Comput. **78**(3), 171–177 (1988). https://doi.org/10.1016/0890-5401(88)90024-7

17. McEliece, R.J.: A public-key cryptosystem based on algebraic coding theory. Deep Space Netw. Prog. Rep. **44**, 114–116 (1978). https://ui.adsabs.harvard.edu/abs/1978DSNPR..44..114M

18. Misoczki, R.: BIKE - bit-flipping key encapsulation (2019). https://csrc.nist.gov/CSRC/media/Presentations/bike-round-2-presentation/images-media/bike-misoczki.pdf. Accessed 18 Feb 2020

19. Niederreiter, H.: Knapsack-type cryptosystems and algebraic coding theory. Prob. Contr. Inform. Theory **15**(2), 157–166 (1986). https://ci.nii.ac.jp/naid/80003180051/en/

20. NIST: Post-Quantum Cryptography (2019). https://csrc.nist.gov/projects/post-quantum-cryptography. Accessed 20 Aug 2019

21. Open Quantum Safe Project: liboqs (2020). https://github.com/open-quantum-safe/liboqs. Accessed 16 Feb 2020

22. Pierrick G., Richard Brent, P.Z., Thome, E.: gf2x-1.2, July 2017. https://gforge.inria.fr/projects/gf2x/

23. Sendrier, N., Vasseur, V.: On the decoding failure rate of QC-MDPC bit-flipping decoders. In: Ding, J., Steinwandt, R. (eds.) PQCrypto 2019. LNCS, vol. 11505, pp. 404–416. Springer, Cham (2019). https://doi.org/10.1007/978-3-030-25510-7_22

24. Shoup, V.: Number theory C++ library (NTL) version 11.3.2, November 2018. http://www.shoup.net/ntl

25. The OpenSSL Project: OpenSSL 1.1.1: The open source toolkit for SSL/TLS. https://github.com/openssl/openssl

Efficient CORDIC-Based Sine and Cosine Implementation for a Dataflow Architecture
(Extended Abstract)

Daniel Khankin$^{(\boxtimes)}$, Elad Raz, and Ilan Tayari

NextSilicon, Tel-Aviv, Israel
{daniel.khankin,e,ilan}@nextsilicon.com

Abstract. A program in a dataflow architecture is represented as a dataflow graph. The dataflow nodes in the graph represent operations to be executed on data. The edges represent a data value being transformed by a dataflow node. Such an architecture can allow exploitation of parallelism, code sharing, and out-of-order execution. The dataflow nodes include operations from a small set of operators: logical operations, switching, addition/subtraction, and multiplication. There is no arithmetic logic unit nor a floating-point unit. As a result, elementary operations for integer, and in particular floating-point, arithmetic are emulated in software. Therefore, when a more advanced functionality such as trigonometric functions is required, we find that the commonly used implementations are inefficient. The inefficiency results in an over-increased dataflow graph that directly translates to wasted area on the *silicon*, resulting in increased power consumption and lower throughput. Volder proposed the CORDIC algorithm for trigonometric functions, expressed in terms of basic rotations. In this work, we present a correctly-rounded and efficient implementation of the CORDIC algorithm for the dataflow architecture.

Keywords: Dataflow · Floating-point · CORDIC · Trigonometric functions · Elementary functions · Efficient

1 Introduction

There is a great need for making floating-point arithmetic highly efficient for artificial intelligence (AI) in hardware. The challenge is to reduce hardware overhead and lowering power usage during the design, training and inference phases of an AI system [13]. However, this is usually achieved through lowering computation precision [4,6,9,24]. Reducing computation precision, though, limits the range of representable numbers or reduces accuracy. Additionally, for non-standard lower precision it requires a custom floating-point format, which is usually not (or only partially) compliant to the standardized specifications [3,4,6,13,15].

© Springer Nature Switzerland AG 2020
S. Dolev et al. (Eds.): CSCML 2020, LNCS 12161, pp. 128–142, 2020.
https://doi.org/10.1007/978-3-030-49785-9_9

Any compute-intensive program is composed of computation building blocks. Those building blocks are the elementary arithmetic operations: addition, subtraction, multiplication and division. Based upon those building blocks are elementary functions, such as trigonometric functions, exponential and logarithmic functions, and many more. Trigonometric functions, essentially sine and cosine, are often used in general, and in particular in AI-based computations.

In most modern architectures, the arithmetic operations are carried out by hardware elements. In particular, floating-point operations and some of the common elementary functions are carried out by an integrated floating-point unit (FPU). In this work, we consider efficient implementation of trigonometric functions, namely sine and cosine, in software for a dataflow architecture.

In the architecture that we consider, there is no FPU and only a subset of arithmetic operations are supported by hardware. The subset of arithmetic supported operations include binary and unary addition, binary and unary subtraction, multiplication, and negation. In case of logical operations, the supported bitwise operations are AND, OR, and XOR. An additional supported operation is the SELECT operation, which is used for choosing one of its inputs, based on a condition and without branching.

The above set of operators may seem restrictive. However, the main purpose of using such software-defined architecture is the decoupling of the operational and computational complexity from the underlying hardware implementation. In other words, similarly to other software-defined concepts, the goal is to use generic hardware elements and off-burden the computational complexity to software.

In a dataflow architecture, a program is represented by a directed graph, called a data-flow graph (DFG). The nodes of a DFG represent operators, or functions, that are applied on data objects. Edges of a DFG represent data object movement between the operators. An operator can have several outputs and several or no inputs. The DFG is mapped by a managing software to an array of logical elements on hardware. Initially, the logical elements on hardware are *generic* and the managing software is responsible for reprogramming the generic logical elements into target operators and activating the appropriate interconnections between the logical elements.

In contrast to the approach used in common architectures, e.g., von Neumann architecture, the dataflow approach minimizes amount of resources devoted to instruction processing, allowing more resources being devoted to arithmetic operations. In addition, when no dependency exists among data objects the operators can operate in parallel on the data.

The supported arithmetic operations operate on defined data sizes. If an operation needs to be applied on a greater data size, then the data will be split into smaller chunks whose size is supported by the operators, and their output will be *glued* in order to construct the final result.

Any logical element can be configured by the managing software to only one of the mentioned operators. Consequently, any other arithmetic or logical operation that is not directly supported must be emulated in software. In particular, any floating-point support (including elementary functions) must also be emulated in software.

The commonly used solutions for implementing elementary functions in software are table lookup methods or polynomial approximations. The latter requires several of multiplications and additions/subtractions of floating-point numbers. In 1959, Volder proposed a special purpose digital computing unit known as COordinate Rotation DIgital Computer (CORDIC) [16,25]. The proposed algorithm was initially developed for trigonometric functions that were expressed in terms of basic rotations. The CORDIC algorithm computes 2D rotations using iterative equations, employing only shift and add operations.

In this work, we propose an implementation of a CORDIC algorithm for sine and cosine that is optimized for a dataflow architecture and is fully compliant to IEEE-754 single-precision floating-point format. Although we describe an implementation for single-precision, it is easily extendable to a higher precision.

There exist varying measurements and criteria for defining efficiency and utilization of programmable hardware. For example, power consumption of a mapped program, or benchmark evaluating the mapping algorithm. Our main criteria is efficient utilization of area on the hardware unit. As a measuring benchmark, we consider the approximated area to be consumed measured in terms of program's dataflow graph, namely, the graph's height and number of computing (operator) nodes. The measured area is not the actual area that will be consumed on the hardware unit. The area actually consumed by a particular program is affected by other factors such as the particular mapping of the program, types of generic logical elements, geometrical constraints and more.

Similarly to compiler optimizations the mapping software is allowed to modify the dataflow graph in order to improve its final mapping considering various constraints such as available area and hardware resources. We can safely state that the premapping DFG is equivalent to an upper bound of optimal mapping conditions. Thus, for the purpose of this work, the premapping estimation of required area from DFG dimensions is a reliable measurement of efficiency and optimization. We use this benchmark for comparison of our results and through optimization steps.

Related Work. The CORDIC algorithm is widely used in many fields and is still actively researched for being extended to other elementary functions, adaptations and applications [16,18]. The most related work is [11], where a full-precision floating-point CORDIC implementation was proposed. However, the use of floating-point operations in each rotation would cause an enormous computational overhead in a dataflow architecture.

The work [22] proposes a low-latency adaptive CORDIC algorithm. However, it requires a larger in-memory access (for full-precision) and increased use of comparison logic. Additionally, it requires the use of multiplication operations, whereas our goal of using the CORDIC algorithm is to avoid multiplication operations.

Other CORDIC variants, reviewed in [16,18,20], will result in a similar inefficiency if implemented on a dataflow architecture.

2   Preliminaries and Notations

IEEE-754 Floating-Point Numbers. Floating-point numbers are numbers of the form

$$x = (-1)^{s_x} \cdot m_x \cdot \beta^{e_x}$$

where β is an integer that represents the radix of the floating-point system, m_x is the significand[1] that satisfies $|m| < \beta$, $e_x \in \{e_{min} \ldots e_{max}\}$ is an integer that represents the exponent, and s_x is the sign. For binary floating-point numbers $\beta = 2$.

There are certain binary formats defined by IEEE-754 specifications [1]. In this paper, we discuss only *binary32* and *binary64* formats, also called *single-precision* and *double-precision* The structure of those formats is detailed below.

The sign s_x is a 1-bit field: $s_x = 0$ for positive numbers and $s_x = 1$ for negative numbers. The exponent e_x is an 8-bit field with values $-126 \leq e_x \leq 127$ in binary32, and an 11-bit field with values $-1022 \leq e_x \leq 1023$ in binary64. The exponents are stored using a biased representation, with bias b equal to 127 in binary32 and 1023 in binary64. The case when the exponent is zero is reserved for the number 0 and *denormal* (or *subnormal*) numbers. The maximal exponent value is reserved for representing the special values *infinity* and *Not a Number* (NaN), the latter of which is used to represent values that are not real numbers (for example, $\sqrt{-1}$).

For normal numbers, $m_x \in [1, 2)$. The leading bit (also called the *implicit* or the *hidden* bit) of the significand is always 1 and is not explicitly stored. The size of the significand, including the hidden bit, is the precision p of the floating-point format. In case of binary32, the precision is $p = 24$ and in case of binary64 the precision is $p = 53$.

The denormal (subnormal) numbers have $e_x = 0$ but the fraction part is different from zero. The implicit bit in this case is 0 and the exponent is set to $e_{min} = -126$ so that we obtain

$$x = (-1)^{s_x} \cdot m_x \cdot 2^{-126}$$

Correct Rounding. Generally, the result of an arithmetic operation must be rounded. A floating-point number obtained from converting an infinitely precise result using IEEE standard's method is said to be correctly-rounded [1].

What arises from rounding is inaccuracy of the approximated result. When measuring the accuracy of computer arithmetic operations, it is desirable to express the inaccuracy in terms of ulps [19]. ulp(x) is the gap between two floating-point numbers nearest x, even if x is one of them [14]. For estimating our results, we follow the definition given by Goldberg [8]:

If $\tilde{x} = m_{\tilde{x}} \cdot 2^{e_{\tilde{x}}}$ is the floating-point number that is used to approximate x, then it is in error by

$$\left| m_{\tilde{x}} - \frac{x}{2^{e_{\tilde{x}}}} \right| \cdot 2^{p-1}$$

---

[1] The significand is sometimes called the mantissa, but the use of the term mantissa is discouraged and should be used in the context of logarithms.

units in the last place. Generalizing to a real number x, $\text{ulp}(x) = 2^{\max(e, e_{min}) - p + 1}$ for any number $x \in [2^e, 2^{e+1})$ [21].

The rounding to nearest even (RN) is the IEEE-754 default rounding mode. Rounding with this mode, results in the machine number $\tilde{x}$ that is the closest to the real number x. If x is exactly halfway between two consecutive machine numbers, return the even one.

Rounding to nearest corresponds to an error of at most $\frac{1}{2}\text{ulp}(x)$ of the real value. Thus, if $\tilde{x}$ is the machine number that approximates the real number x, then $\tilde{x} = \text{RN}(x) \implies |\tilde{x} - x| \leq \frac{1}{2}\text{ulp}(\tilde{x})$.

Research shows that achieving a correctly-rounded implementation for elementary functions is difficult [20]. In order to obtain a correct rounding, one must ensure that after rounding, the exact result is on the same side of a midpoint as the approximated result [17]. The standard approach is a two-phase algorithm for correctly rounded results [2,5,17]. The first phase is a computation that produces, for most cases, a correctly-rounded result. If it is detected that the result is not correctly-rounded, then the second phase is carried out, in which the function is recomputed with much higher precision.

We carry through a similar two-phase process for computation of trigonometric functions in single-precision. First, an approximation is computed using 64-bit precision. As we show in the Evaluation section, for the vast majority of cases this is sufficient to return a correctly rounded result. For the few cases that are incorrectly rounded, their correct result is hard-coded to return without recomputation. Since there are only a few such cases, and with single-precision we can actually enumerate those cases, it is much cheaper to hard-code the correct values instead of recomputing with higher precision.

CORDIC Algorithm. The CORDIC algorithm is based on a decomposition of an angle θ on a discrete base. The decomposition is given by

$$\theta = \sum_{k=0}^{\infty} d_k w_k, \quad d_k = \pm 1, \quad w_k = \arctan(2^{-k}) .$$

There are several *modes* of operation for the CORDIC algorithm. For trigonometric functions, the *rotation mode* is used. The idea is to perform a rotation of a vector by the angle θ as a sequence of elementary rotations of the angles $d_n w_n$. Starting from (x_0, y_0), we obtain the point (x_{i+1}, y_{i+1}) by rotating the point (x_i, y_i) by angle $d_i w_i$. We choose the rotation angles such that $\tan(\omega_i) = 2^{-i}$. For each rotation, the vector is extended by $\cos(\omega_i)$. For maximal number of iterations N, the angle is computed by

$$\begin{pmatrix} x_\theta \\ y_\theta \end{pmatrix} = \cos(w_0) \begin{pmatrix} 1 & -d_i 2^0 \\ d_i 2^0 & 1 \end{pmatrix} \cdots \cos(w_N) \begin{pmatrix} 1 & -d_i 2^{-N} \\ d_i 2^{-N} & 1 \end{pmatrix} \begin{pmatrix} x_i \\ y_i \end{pmatrix}$$

or can be rewritten as

$$\begin{pmatrix} x_\theta \\ y_\theta \end{pmatrix} = \lim_{N \to \infty} K \cdot \begin{pmatrix} 1 & -d_i 2^0 \\ d_i 2^0 & 1 \end{pmatrix} \cdots \begin{pmatrix} 1 & -d_i 2^{-N} \\ d_i 2^{-N} & 1 \end{pmatrix} \begin{pmatrix} x_i \\ y_i \end{pmatrix}$$

where $K = \Pi_{i=0}^{N-1} \cos(\omega_i)$ is a scale factor. The equations used to calculate x_{i+1}, y_{i+1} are:

$$x_{i+1} = x_i - d_i y_i 2^{-i}$$
$$y_{i+1} = y_i + d_i x_i 2^{-i}$$
$$z_{i+1} = z_i - d_i \omega_i$$

for which the initial values are $x_0 = 1/K, y_0 = 0, z_0 = \theta$.

3   Design and Implementation

The standard floating-point operations are complex and require many elementary operations. For example, in floating-point multiplication one must: a) check if the input numbers are invalid (infinity or NaN), b) normalize any subnormals, c) compute the resulting exponent, d) multiply the significands, e) check for underflow, f) test if the result is subnormal, and lastly g) round and check for overflow. Seemingly, we have roughly seven actions to perform for each multiplication, while each such action constitutes a set of elementary operations. Consequently, each CORDIC iteration using floating-point is very expensive in terms of elementary operations. Since each such elementary operation will be translated to at least one logical unit, a CORDIC iteration using floating-point that consist of hundreds of elementary operations will consume a large area on chip. Therefore, taking into account the above, our goal will be to reduce the number of operations per iteration as much as possible in order to reduce the area consumed by a CORDIC iteration.

In order to obtain at least faithfully-rounded[2] calculations for the trigonometric functions, all computations must be carried out in higher than the target precision [8,20]. The logical units in our architecture support only 32-bit arithmetic operations; any computation of a higher number of bits will be subdivided into 32-bit operations, and additional gluing operations will be required for computing the final result.

Let us concentrate on the floating-point numbers and their exponents in range $I = [0, \pi/2]$. Any other number out of range I can be range-reduced by one of the known methods (see [20] for a discussion on several methods). The minimal normal number in range I is 2^{-126} which is approximately $1.17549435 \times 10^{-38}$. The greatest normal number in range I is $\pi/2$, whose unbiased exponent is 0. The following proposition will help us limit the range of exponents of interest.

Proposition 1. *For any single-precision floating-point number x for which $e_x < -12$, $\sin(x) = x$ and $\cos(x) = 1$.*

---

[2] Faithful rounding has a maximum error of one ulp, and is not defined by IEEE-754. It is mentioned for being a less precise rounding mode to emphasize the high precision requirement.

Proof. Using Taylor's approximation for a small number, we have

$$\sin(x) = x + R_3(x)$$

For any x_0 in the interval $[0, x]$, $R_3(x) = \frac{\sin^{(3)}(x_0) \cdot x^3}{6}$, and we know that $|\sin^{(3)}(x_0)| \leq 1$. We need to show that the error bound R_3 is too small relatively to the floating-point number x.

In other words, we need to find an exponent of a floating-point number x for which R_3 will be smaller than ulp(x). Let e_x be such an exponent:

$$\frac{2^{(3 \cdot e_x - 1)}}{3} < 2^{e_x} \cdot \text{ulp(x)} = 2^{e_x - p + 1}$$

For precision $p = 24$ and targeting to an error of $\frac{1}{2}$ulp we have:

$$\frac{2^{(3 \cdot e_x - 1)}}{3} < \frac{1}{2} \cdot 2^{e_x - 23}$$

solving for e_x we obtain that $e_x < -12$. Similarly, for cosine we have $\cos(x) = 1 + R_2(x)$, where $R_2(x) = \frac{\cos^{(2)}(x_0) \cdot x^2}{2}$. However, in this case, note that we are looking for values that are relatively smaller than ulp(1). As before, for precision $p = 24$ and targeting an error of $\frac{1}{2}$ulp, we have

$$\frac{2^{2 \cdot e_x}}{2} < \frac{1}{2} \cdot 2^{-23}$$

solving for e_x similarly results in $e_x < -12$.   □

Proposition 1 tells us that the actual range of exponents that we are interested in is $[-12, 0]$. Let us now turn to estimation on the number of bits and the number of iterations that are required.

Each iteration of the algorithm computes one bit of the result. The 24 bits of the argument are scaled by an exponent of value from 0 to 12, resulting in 13 exponents with 24-bits fraction to be mapped to a total of 37 bits. We need to estimate the number $k \geq 1$ of excessive bits needed to compute the approximation of the trigonometric function so that we are able to correctly round the approximation to a precision-p correctly rounded result [20]. Namely, the *hard-to-round* cases for which the bits appearing after the p bits are either

$$\overbrace{011111 \dots 11}^{k \text{ bits}} \text{xxxx} \dots$$

or

$$\overbrace{100000 \dots 00}^{k \text{ bits}} \text{xxxx} \dots$$

Muller in [20] provides a probabilistic estimation for having at least one input number leading to a value of k excessive bits. The estimation for k is given by

$$k \geq p + log_2(n_e) + 1.529$$

where p is the target precision and n_e is the number of possible exponents. The probability for having at least one input number leading to a value of k or greater is given by

$$Pr[k] = 1 - [1 - 2^{1-k}]^N$$

where N is the number of floating-point numbers in the set of input values. Substituting the target precision $p = 24$ and $n_e = 13$, we obtain

$$k \geq= 24 + log_2(13) + 1.529 \approx 29.$$

There, we need 29 bits in addition to the 37 bits computed before - for a total of at least 66 bits. The probability of having at least one hard-to-round input number is

$$Pr[k] = 1 - [1 - 2^{1-29}]^{13 \times 2^{23}} \approx 0.334.$$

However, in order to take into account 66 bits we would need to use either 128-bits size variable or two different size variables. For example, one of 64 bits and the other of 32 bits. In the first case, we would have a very low utilization of data space; in the second case, we would have much more complex computations with still low utilization of data space. For that matter, we decided to use 64-bit variables, accepting the higher chance of having hard-to-round cases. Moreover, rotation angles smaller than $\arctan(2^{-56})$ affect only the lowest 12 bits. The value of those lowest 12 bits is slightly more than the round-off error for double-precision floating-point numbers, thus, those lowest rotation angles can be discarded. Practically, this is indeed the case. In the evaluation results shown in Sect. 4, we show that 57 iterations are enough to obtain correctly-rounded results with only a few incorrectly rounded numbers with an error at most $\frac{1}{2} \cdot \text{ulp}(x)$.

Encoding. In our architecture, we do not have floating-point hardware computation elements and, as mentioned above, utilizing emulated floating-point operations in software can result in a highly inefficient implementation. Therefore, we are interested in reducing (as much as possible) the use of floating-point arithmetic. To do this, we encode each of the input angles to a scaled fixed-point format. Additionally, we encode the rotation angles and the pre-computed scaling factor. However, those must be (pre-)computed and encoded in double-precision in order to adhere to the precision that is used during intermediate computations. Thus, the encoding procedure expects its input in double-precision format. The input angle, which is in single-precision, is converted to double-precision before being encoded. Such conversion does not result in any data loss since it only positions the significand to a new location and adjusts the exponent as required by the *binary64* format.

The encoding process converts each floating-point number to a *scaled* fixed-point format such that the real magnitude of the number is preserved. Working with floating-point numbers encoded in such way has several advantages.

Mainly, intermediate (higher than the target) precision is preserved among operations. Other advantages are: a) addition/subtraction operations are exact and there are no round-off errors, b) full type range is utilized since there is no

---

Algorithm 1: Floating-Point Encoding

---

    input   : integer representation of an angle in double-precision format.
    output : 64-bit integer encoding the input X.

1 extract the unbiased exponent e_x
2 extract the significand m_x with the implicit bit ORed back
3 reposition m_x so that the leading bit is in the leftmost position
4 $encoded_x \leftarrow m_x \times 2^{-|e_x|}$
5 **return** $encoded_x$

---

exponent or sign bits and no exception reserved values, c) no exponent arithmetic happens in between operations, d) no aligning is required when performing addition/subtraction, e) no overflow (if floating-point exponent is less than the integral part of the format), and d) no underflow (due to advantage (a)).

We encode all floating-point numbers that are of interest as follows. The input value $x = m \cdot 2^e$ is represented as $x = e_{11} \ldots e_0 m_{51} \ldots m_0$:

1. The implicit leading bit of the significand is returned and the number is shifted to the left most position of a 64-bit integer, discarding the exponent bits:

$$\overbrace{1.m_{51} \ldots \ldots m_0}^{53 \text{ bits}} \overbrace{0 \ldots \ldots \ldots 0}^{11 \text{ bits}}$$

2. The number is shifted right by $|e|$ bits:

$$\overbrace{0 \ldots \ldots 0}^{|e| \text{ bits}} \overbrace{1.m_{51} \ldots \ldots m_0}^{53 \text{ bits}} \overbrace{0 \ldots \ldots \ldots 0}^{11 - |e| \text{ bits}}$$

Algorithm 1 describes the encoding algorithm. First, the exponent and the significand of the input X are extracted, and the implicit bit is ORed back. The required scale is computed by subtracting the biased exponent from the exponent bias, obtaining the absolute value of e_x, which is the required scale. We know that for all numbers belonging to I, the unbiased exponent is not greater than 0. After, the exponent bits are eliminated and the value is scaled according to its exponent.

Decoding. The decoding process is symmetrical and is described in Algorithm 2. The decoding begins by computing the number of leading zeros. The exponent is computed by subtracting the number of leading zeros from the single-precision exponent bias. The number of leading zeros tells us how much the number is scaled by a power of two, which is exactly the exponent of the floating-point format. The significand is first positioned in its target location by shifting it left as the number of leading zeros minus the exponent size, 11-bits in case of double-precision format (as those bits were used for the encoded fraction). It may be the case that the number of leading zeros is less than 11 and thus, the significand would be shifted right. Then, the significand is shifted to its final location for single-precision format. The truncated bits are evaluated for rounding decision.

If the truncated value is closer to the next floating-point number or if it is exactly halfway and the truncated number is odd, then the number is rounded to even.

CORDIC Procedure. The core CORDIC algorithm remains while we adapt it to our encoded format and to our available logical operators. The results are returned through *output* variables (for example, a pointer in C/C++ languages). The variable x is initialized to the precomputed and encoded value of $1/K$. The variables y and z are initialized as described earlier in this paper. The variable d represents the sign of the current angle (i.e., whether we need to rotate forward or backward in the next step in order to approach zero). Initially, d is set to 0, since the angle we start with is positive and we need to rotate forward.

At each step of the main computation loop, x and y are multiplied by 2^{-k} in order to compute the rotation amount. Remember that, in binary integer arithmetic a multiplication by 2^{-i} is translated into a shift right by i. Next, we add or subtract the rotation according to the desired direction. We utilize the SELECT operator and binary arithmetic, instead of branching between addition and subtraction. Either the rotation amount is left intact or one's complement is computed. The result is selected for addition operation.

The precomputed angle ω_k is subtracted from z. If the subtracted angle was greater than z, then z is inverted representing a negative value and d is inverted to account for that.

4 Accuracy and Performance Evaluation Results

We tested our implementation for the whole range of single-precision numbers. Single-precision floating-point numbers range from 0 to $3.4028234664 \times 10^{+38}$, represented in total by $2,147,483,647$ numbers (from 0 to 0x7FFFFFFF). Such an exhaustive test is feasible to execute on any modern computer. We implemented the well known Payne & Haneck range-reduction technique for numbers out of $[0, \frac{\pi}{2}]$ range. Efficient implementation of the Payne & Haneck range-reduction method is not the scope of our work; a description of the method can be found in [23].

Algorithm 2: Decoding to a Floating-Point Number

---

    input   : Y - 64-bit integer encoding the CORDIC result.

    output : integer representation of the result in single-precision format.

1 $lz \leftarrow$ the number of leading zeros of Y

2 $m_x \leftarrow Y \times 2^{lz-11}$

3 $e_x \leftarrow \mathtt{b} - lz$

4 extract and truncate the trailing 29 bits of m_x

5 mask any bits of m_x that are higher than the 23rd bit

6 pack x into binary32 with exponent e_x and significand m_x

7 round x to nearest number, in case of ties to even

8 return x

Algorithm 3: Adapted CORDIC algorithm.

---

input   : angle encoded with Algorithm 1, out variables for sine/cosine results.

1 $x \leftarrow \frac{1}{K}$ encoded with Algorithm 1
2 $y \leftarrow 0,\ z \leftarrow angle,\ d \leftarrow 0,\ N \leftarrow 57$

3 **for** $k \leftarrow 1$ **to** N **do**
4 | $x' \leftarrow y \times 2^{-k}$
5 | $y' \leftarrow x \times 2^{-k}$

6 | $x' \leftarrow$ **SELECT** x' **if** $d > 0$ **else** $\sim x'$
7 | $y' \leftarrow$ **SELECT** $\sim y'$ **if** $d > 0$ **else** y'

8 | $x \leftarrow x + x'$
9 | $y \leftarrow y + y'$

10 | $z' \leftarrow z - \omega_k$
11 | $z \leftarrow$ **SELECT** z' **if** $z \geq \omega_k$ **else** $\sim z'$
12 | $d \leftarrow$ **SELECT** d **if** $z \geq \omega_k$ **else** $\neg d$
13 **return** x as cosine and y as sine

The final computed results from our CORDIC procedure, after decoding, were bitwise-compared against the expected results computed with a multi-precision floating-point library (MPFR [7]). In the event of discrepancy, an error in ulp(x) was computed.

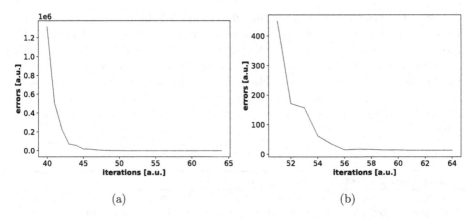

(a)   (b)

Fig. 1. (a) Total errors as a function of iterations. (b) Close-up of (a) to the last 14 iterations.

Figure 1a depicts the number of incorrect results as a function of iterations, and Fig. 1b is a close-up of the last 14 iterations. Figure 1a show that the number of errors decrease exponentially as the number of iterations grow. The rapid decrease changes to moderate around 47th iteration, when the elementary rotation angles become too small relatively to the round-off error.

The relative error curve is less smooth in general and hardly changes towards the end. This is because though the number of errors can decrease as the number of iterations increase but the maximal relative error does not necessary decrease or change. It is important to remark here, that the figures depict the combined results of sine and cosine. It may happen that the relative error was decreased in some iteration for one of the functions but not for the other. Figures 2a and 2b show the error measured in ulps.

The least number of errors occurred at iteration 57 with maximal error of $\frac{1}{2}\mathrm{ulp}(x)$, with a total of 7 errors out of $1,207,959,551$ numbers in range I. Those few hard-to-round cases can be hardcoded as literals without requiring additional memory storage (such as read-only memory or look-up table). Hardcoding the correct result for those few numbers amounts to a correctly-rounded implementation. The pattern of truncated bits for hard-to-round numbers is of the form described earlier. Thus, testing for the existence of such trailing patterns is easy to implement and can be done in parallel. Iterations greater than 57 do not improve the relative error nor the number of errors due to lower bits being truncated when such small rotation angles are encoded to scaled fixed-point format. Remember that, those rotation angles are computed in double-precision, and thus, require greater range to be properly encoded. However, in order to gain from further iterations and continue reducing the number of errors by utilizing those small rotation angles, it is necessary to use greater data types.

We have created a dataflow graph for a single-iteration of the CORDIC algorithm. The number of compute nodes that we obtained per iteration is 69, and the height of the dataflow graph is 15. This means that 15 computational instances (i.e., threads) can run through the loop in parallel. The complete algorithm can be instantiated several times, as much as (approximately) 69 compute nodes fit in the available area. Though we are interested in correctly-rounded results, in other settings it may be desirable to relax accuracy requirements. The CORDIC algorithm has a significant advantage reflected in the simplicity of adapting it to different requirements. We have calculated the number of compute nodes, and height (latency) as a function of the number of iterations. The total number of compute nodes would be approximately the number of compute nodes per iteration multiplied by the number of iterations. Practically, there would be fewer compute nodes if iterations were unrolled, since the compiler would then be able to eliminate some compute nodes during its passes. See Table 1, below, that shows the number of compute nodes and the height of the dataflow graph when iterations are unrolled.

We compared our results against a high-quality, portable, standalone mathematical library called OpenLibm [12]. The dataflow graph for the OpenLibm library has a total of $74,376$ compute nodes. Our algorithm had $8,032$ total compute nodes when all iterations were unrolled, and $1,230$ when no iterations were unrolled.

OpenLibm uses an iterative and highly inefficient range reduction process. We disabled the range reduction functionality in OpenLibm, discarding any computational errors, in order to compare the trigonometric functions themselves.

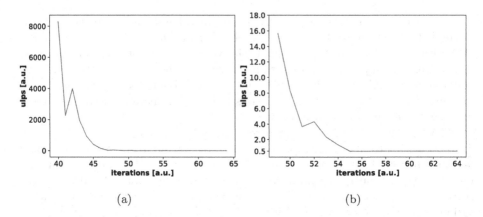

Fig. 2. (a) Error in ulps as a function of iterations. (b) Close-up of (a) for the last 14 iterations.

The main computation dataflow graph has $8,334$ compute nodes and a height of 228. This is twice as much as our algorithm fully unrolled. After, we considered only input in range $[0; \pi/4]$ so no range reduction would occur at all in Open-Libm. In that scenario, OpenLibm has a total of $25,684$ compute nodes. On the bright side, the main dataflow graph has $3,378$ compute nodes with height 217. This size of dataflow graph is comparable to our unrolled 57 iterations. However, we have much less error when 57 iterations are used. OpenLibm has a total of $24,133$ errors in the range $[0; \frac{\pi}{2}]$ and $612,217$ errors in the rest of the range, with maximal relative error slightly above $\frac{1}{2}\text{ulp}(x)$.

Table 1. Number of nodes and height as a function of unrolled iterations.

iterations	nodes	height	iterations	nodes	height	iterations	nodes	height
40	2,104	282	50	2,829	342	60	3,673	402
41	2,172	288	51	2,907	348	61	3,742	408
42	2,241	291	52	2,986	354	62	3,831	414
43	2,330	303	53	3,066	360	63	3,921	420
44	2,382	306	54	3,147	366	64	4,009	424
45	2,454	312	55	3,229	372			
46	2,527	318	56	3,312	378			
47	2,601	324	57	3,396	384			
48	2,676	330	58	3,481	390			
49	2,752	336	59	3,567	396			

5   Discussion

In this work, we described an efficient implementation of the CORDIC algorithm for a dataflow architecture. We showed that our implementation provides correctly-rounded results for sine and cosine and that the implementation is efficient compared to existing state-of-the-art software library.

The use of CORDIC is widespread over many fields. Notably, the CORDIC algorithm is used in resource-limited hardware. Furthermore, it was recently used in a large-scale neural-network system [10]. For AI-based use, a relaxing of the accuracy requirements may be necessary. The CORDIC algorithm is easily modifiable as it only requires changing the number of iterations to relax accuracy requirements. Our evaluation results provide an expectation of the number of errors and the relative errors (in terms of ulp(x)) if accuracy is to be lowered, together with the expected area utilization.

Acknowledgments. We thank Shachar Lovett for his valuable input; John Gustafson for his comments. We thank Laura Ferguson for her assistance.

References

1. IEEE Standard for Floating-Point Arithmetic. IEEE Std 754–2019 (Revision of IEEE 754–2008), pp. 1–84, July 2019. https://doi.org/10.1109/IEEESTD.2019. 8766229
2. Abraham, Z.: Fast evaluation of elementary mathematical functions with correctly rounded last bit. ACM Trans. Math. Softw. (TOMS) (1991). https://dl.acm.org/ doi/abs/10.1145/114697.116813
3. Burgess, N., Milanovic, J., Stephens, N., Monachopoulos, K., Mansell, D.: Bfloat16 processing for neural networks. In: 2019 IEEE 26th Symposium on Computer Arithmetic (ARITH), pp. 88–91, June 2019. https://doi.org/10.1109/ARITH.2019. 00022. ISSN 1063-6889
4. Courbariaux, M., Bengio, Y., David, J.P.: Low precision arithmetic for deep learning. CoRR abs/1412.7024 (2014)
5. Daramy-Loirat, C., De Dinechin, F., Defour, D., Gallet, M., Gast, N., Lauter,C.: CRLIBM. A library of correctly rounded elementary functions indouble-precision (cit. on pp. xiii, xviii, xxvi, 17, 32, 37, 64, 89) (2010). http://lipforge.ens-lyon.fr/ www/crlibm/
6. Dettmers, T.: 8-bit approximations for parallelism in deep learning. arXiv preprint arXiv:1511.04561 (2015)
7. Fousse, L., Hanrot, G., Lefèvre, V., Pélissier, P., Zimmermann, P.: MPFR: a multiple-precision binary floating-point library with correct rounding. ACM Trans. Math. Softw. (TOMS) **33**(2), 13 (2007)
8. Goldberg, D.: What every computer scientist should know about floating-point arithmetic. ACM Comput. Surv. (CSUR) **23**(1), 5–48 (1991)
9. Gupta, S., Agrawal, A., Gopalakrishnan, K., Narayanan, P.: Deep learning with limited numerical precision. In: Proceedings of the 32nd International Conference on International Conference on Machine Learning ICMLc 2015, Lille, France, vol. 37, pp. 1737–1746. JMLR.org (2015)
10. Hao, X., Yang, S., Wang, J., Deng, B., Wei, X., Yi, G.: Efficient implementation of cerebellar purkinje cell with the CORDIC algorithm on LaCSNN. Front. Neurosci. **13** (2019). https://doi.org/10.3389/fnins.2019.01078, https:// www.frontiersin.org/articles/10.3389/fnins.2019.01078/full

11. Hekstra, G., Deprettere, E.: Floating point Cordic. In: Proceedings of IEEE 11th Symposium on Computer Arithmetic, pp. 130–137, June 1993. https://doi.org/10.1109/ARITH.1993.378100

12. Jaeger, A.: OpenLibm (2016)

13. Johnson, J.: Rethinking floating point for deep learning. arXiv preprint arXiv:1811.01721 (2018)

14. Kahan, W.: A logarithm too clever by half (2004)

15. Köster, U., et al.: Flexpoint: an adaptive numerical format for efficient training of deep neural networks. In: Advances in Neural Information Processing Systems, pp. 1742–1752 (2017)

16. Lakshmi, B., Dhar, A.: CORDIC architectures: a survey. VLSI Des. **2010**, 2 (2010)

17. Maire, J.L., Brunie, N., Dinechin, F.D., Muller, J.M.: Computing floating-point logarithms with fixed-point operations. In: 2016 IEEE 23nd Symposium on Computer Arithmetic (ARITH), pp. 156–163, July 2016. https://doi.org/10.1109/ARITH.2016.24. ISSN 1063-6889

18. Meher, P.K., Valls, J., Juang, T.B., Sridharan, K., Maharatna, K.: 50 years of CORDIC: algorithms, architectures, and applications. IEEE Trans. Circuits Syst. I Regul. Pap. **56**(9), 1893–1907 (2009). https://doi.org/10.1109/TCSI.2009.2025803

19. Muller, J.M.: On the definition of ulp(x). Research Report RR-5504, LIP RR-2005-09, INRIA, LIP, February 2005. https://hal.inria.fr/inria-00070503

20. Muller, J.M.: Elementary Functions: Algorithms and Implementation, 3 edn. Birkhäuser Basel (2016). https://www.springer.com/gp/book/9781489979810

21. Muller, J.M., et al.: Handbook of Floating-Point Arithmetic, 2 edn. Birkhäuser Basel (2018). https://doi.org/10.1007/978-3-319-76526-6, https://www.springer.com/gp/book/9783319765259

22. Nguyen, H.T., Nguyen, X.T., Hoang, T.T., Le, D.H., Pham, C.K.: Low-resource low-latency hybrid adaptive CORDIC with floating-point precision. IEICE Electron. Exp. **12**(9), 20150258–20150258 (2015)

23. Payne, M.H., Hanek, R.N.: Radian reduction for trigonometric functions. ACM SIGNUM Newslett. **18**(1), 19–24 (1983)

24. Tulloch, A., Jia, Y.: High performance ultra-low-precision convolutions on mobile devices. arXiv preprint arXiv:1712.02427 (2017)

25. Volder, J.E.: The CORDIC trigonometric computing technique. IRE Trans. Electron. Comput. **3**, 330–334 (1959)

SecureMCMR: Computation Outsourcing for MapReduce Applications

Lindsey Kennard$^{(\boxtimes)}$ and Ana Milanova

Rensselaer Polytechnic Institute, Troy, NY 12180, USA
`kennal@rpi.edu, milanova@cs.rpi.edu`

Abstract. In the last decade, cloud infrastructures such as Google Cloud and Amazon AWS have grown vastly in scale and utilization. Therefore, research into the security and confidentiality of sensitive data passed through these infrastructures is of great importance. We present SecureMCMR, a system that utilizes two public clouds for privacy preserving computation outsourcing for MapReduce applications. We also present analysis of 87 MapReduce applications and the operations they use. Our results on three MapReduce applications show overhead of 160%, 254%, and 380% over plaintext execution.

1 Introduction

Encryption is a promising approach to privacy preserving computation outsourcing. First, users encrypt their sensitive data then they transform their program to work using the corresponding encryption scheme. Finally, they upload the transformed program and encrypted data to the cloud server. The final result is that they can run their program on a public cloud without leaking sensitive data. Researchers have proposed different encryption schemes to support a variety of operations, allowing for larger and larger subsets of programs to be run this way. Fully Homomorphic Encryption (FHE) [27,59] can perform arbitrary operations on encrypted data, but in its current state FHE is still prohibitively expensive [28]. An alternative to FHE is Partially Homomorphic Encryption (PHE), which scales substantially better, but cannot perform arbitrary operations. PHE is limited in the sense that a given encryption scheme supports only certain operations on ciphertexts. For example, Linearly Homomorphic Encryption (LHE) (e.g., the Paillier cryptosystem [47]) supports *addition* over ciphertexts but not multiplication or comparison. PHE has been recognized as a promising direction towards privacy preserving computation outsourcing [23,29,49,55,56,58].

The principal problem with PHE is *data incompatibility*—when a program uses one encryption scheme (e.g., Paillier) but later requires an operation that is not supported (e.g., comparison). Figure 1 illustrates.

© Springer Nature Switzerland AG 2020
S. Dolev et al. (Eds.): CSCML 2020, LNCS 12161, pp. 143–166, 2020.
https://doi.org/10.1007/978-3-030-49785-9_10

```
1   while (token.hasMoreTokens()) {
2     int value = token.nextToken(); // encrypted
3     total = total + value;
4   }
5   if (total > limit) { ... }
```

Fig. 1. Data conversion. Variables value and total are encrypted with LHE, allowing the addition in line 4. However, we cannot perform the comparison on line 6 over LHE-encrypted total.

One way to address the problem of data incompatibility is to maintain a *trusted machine* [23,58] that stores cryptographic keys and in some cases plaintext input data. The approach resolves data incompatibility by having the trusted machine perform conversion from one encryption scheme to another, or carry out the unsupported operations. For example, the trusted machine may receive data in one encryption scheme (e.g., Paillier), decrypt it, carry out the computation (e.g., multiplication, exponentiation, etc.), re-encrypt, and send the result back to the untrusted cloud server. Clearly, this approach entails communication between the server and the trusted machine. This communication restricts PHE in highly-parallel MapReduce applications, where multiple server nodes send work to the trusted machine and create a bottleneck.

In this paper, we propose SecureMCMR (Secure [M]ulti-[C]loud computation for [M]ap [R]educe). SecureMCMR falls into a line of work that makes use of PHE for computation outsourcing [23,49,55,56,58] improving the trusted-machine approach in two ways:

1. SecureMCMR replaces the trusted machine with an *untrusted cloud server*, thus eliminating the need for clients to maintain secure and computationally powerful trusted machines.
2. The untrusted cloud server is *highly parallel* thus alleviating bottlenecks that arise when multiple server nodes access a single trusted machine.

The overarching problem we address is the following. Can users take advantage of inexpensive, efficient, and convenient cloud services, while (1) preserving data privacy, and (2) retaining efficiency of computation. Our specific focus is on MapReduce applications.

SecureMCMR uses two non-colluding public clouds, cloud A (e.g., Google Cloud) and cloud B (e.g., Amazon AWS). Cloud A stores public keys and runs the MapReduce task using LHE. It runs LHE-unsupported operations (e.g., multiplication) collaboratively with cloud B, which stores private keys and can decrypt LHE-encrypted sensitive values. The key guarantee of SecureMCMR is that cloud A sees only *LHE-encrypted ciphertexts* of sensitive values, and cloud B sees only *blinded* sensitive values, which ensures that neither public cloud can retrieve sensitive input values.

We present a framework for reasoning about the security of MapReduce applications and we classify a corpus of 87 programs. We run 3 MapReduce applications under SecureMCMR in a real cloud environment, present findings and outline future directions.

This paper makes the following contributions:

- SecureMCMR, a system for privacy-preserving computation outsourcing for MapReduce applications.
- A new protocol inspired by Randomized Encoding that allows servers A and B to collaboratively compute certain LHE-unsupported operations securely.
- A study of the security of a large corpus of MapReduce applications. We study 87 MapReduce applications and the kinds of operations they use. Understanding of ways different operations are used in practice may guide development of new protocols.
- Results running MapReduce applications under SecureMCMR on Google Cloud (cloud A) and Amazon AWS (cloud B). The overhead of SecureMCMR decreases as the number of Amazon nodes increases, and it remains acceptable in our experiments at 380%.

The rest of the paper is organized as follows. Section 2 presents an overview of SecureMCMR and positions our work among related works. Section 3 presents the cryptographic primitives we make use of, including a description of our protocol for collaborative computation of unsupported operations. Section 4 presents the programming language primitives we make use of. Section 5 presents our security analysis, including our framework for reasoning about programs that use comparisons on top of LHE-encrypted execution. Section 6 details our experiments and evaluation. Section 7 concludes.

2   Overview and Related Work

2.1   MapReduce

MapReduce [19] is a highly parallel programming model created to compute "big data" problems on a large cluster of nodes. Each cluster contains one or more *master* nodes along with many *worker* nodes. A MapReduce job generally consists of 3 steps: **map**, **shuffle**, and **reduce**. The framework splits the input file into chunks where each chunk is assigned to a worker node. Each worker node calls the special map function on each line of input. The **map** phase outputs a list of key-value pairs. The **shuffle** phase sorts the values associated with each key k. Finally, the **reduce** phase runs a reduce function per each key k, collapsing the list of values associated to k into a final result. MapReduce has been implemented in different frameworks [5,6,22]; it is actively used in a wide variety of applications.

2.2   Overview of SecureMCMR

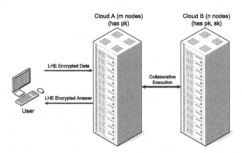

Fig. 2. Multi-cloud infrastructure: Cloud A (Google) acts as the server and computes over LHE-encrypted data. Cloud B (AWS) acts in liue of the trusted machine. It receives blinded data, decrypts it, computes over, re-encrypts and sends it back to A. A and B collaboratively compute LHE-unsupported operations.

SecureMCMR takes a MapReduce application and transforms it to work on two non-colluding, *untrusted* servers, cloud A and cloud B. Cloud A takes the input files in LHE-encrypted form, and runs LHE-supported operations locally. Whenever it encounters LHE-unsupported operations, it performs computation collaboratively with cloud B. Cloud A has access to the public key associated with the LHE scheme and cloud B has access to the public and private keys, i.e., B can decrypt the values that A sends (Fig. 2).

Clouds A and B collaboratively compute arbitrary operations that are unsupported by LHE, however, there is varying degree of security (i.e., leakage) depending on the operation. SecureMCMR computes certain operations, e.g., multiplication, *securely*. We achieve security through a protocol inspired by Randomized Encoding, which encodes multiplications in a way that server B sees only blinded sensitive values and server A sees only LHE ciphertexts. The protocol achieves statistical security as we show in Sect. 5. Other operations, particularly comparisons, inherently leak *order sequences* of sensitive values, thus creating adversarial advantage [11,12] for the servers to "guess" plaintext *values* in the sequence or *distances* between two plaintexts; a longer order sequence implies lower degree of security [11,12]. SecureMCMR computes such operations *OPE-securely*, thus realizing the guarantees of Order Preserving Encryption (OPE). Yet SecureMCMR computes other operations with leakage of aggregate values, e.g., to compute e^{-x} where x is an inner product of two input vectors, it leaks the value of x to B. Depending on the information an attacker is looking for the severity of this leak can change. For example, if the attacker is not looking for the exact value of x but only the sign of x, then leaking x reveals significant relevant information. Computing scientific operations *securely*, *precisely*, and *efficiently* is an ongoing area of research in the secure computation community. For example, [41] considers a novel approximation of the sigmoid and [3] presents implementations and benchmarking of scientific operations based on numerical approximation in the SCALE-MAMBA system [2] for secure multiparty computation.

Across 87 MapReduce programs, we find the majority can be computed securely or OPE-securely. In addition, the nature of programs is such that OPE security comes with low adversarial advantage against guessing the exact value of an OPE ciphertext or the exact distance between two OPE ciphertexts.

2.3 Related Work

The closest related work is work on computation outsourcing for MapReduce programs. MrCrypt [55] reasons about the uses of variables in the program and assigns an encryption scheme to each variable. For example, if a variable is used only in addition operations, it assigns LHE, if it is used in only a comparison, it assigns OPE, etc. MrCrypt simply gives up on programs that exhibit data incompatibility; e.g., it cannot handle the program in Fig. 1. SecureMR [23] handles certain programs that exhibit data incompatibility using a trusted machine. Our work falls in line with MrCrypt and SecureMR and their "counterparts" in the database world, CryptDB [49], which makes use of different encryption schemes for different columns, but cannot handle incompatibility and Monomi [58], which handles data incompatibility by sending unsupported operations to a trusted machine. Our work improves upon MrCrypt and SecureMR in at least two major ways: (1) it eliminates the trusted machine, and (2) it significantly expands the security analysis. Another related work is GraphSC framework [44]. It allows non-cryptography experts to write secure versions of parallel algorithms in the areas of machine learning, data mining, and graph theory. Our work differs from GraphSC in several ways. We seek to automatically transform *existing* MapReduce programs and deploy them with Hadoop, while GraphSC is a library that allows programmers to write parallel programs in a secure way. Secondly, we use LHE as the key cryptographic primitive, while GraphSC uses garbled circuits. Finally, we deploy on Google and AWS, while GraphSC deploys on AWS using two geographic regions. Additionally, the work of Dinh et. [21] is also related to secure Hadoop computation. However it focuses on hardware solutions while our work focuses on software.

Secure Multi-party Computation (MPC) is another approach to secure computation [9,15,21,30,46,60]. Our approach was inspired in part by MPC, however, we weaken the security guarantees in favor of a performance boost. In MPC two or more mistrusting parties attempt to compute a task collaboratively, without revealing their individual inputs. In our model, clouds A and B can be viewed as mistrusting parties that collaboratively compute an operation, although the premise of collaborative computation is different. There has been significant progress in MPC and adaptations of MPC that target both classical machine learning algorithms [26,29,41,45,46,52] and deep learning ones [33,38].

Building programming frameworks for MPC is an active, rapidly evolving area [31]. Early research such as Fairplay [39] (and its extension to MPC FairplayMP [8]), Sharemind [10], VIFF [17], and CBMC-GC [25] were later built upon in works like Frigate [42], and ABY [20]. VIFF [17] was specifically followed by MPyC [54], a powerful MPC framework for Python. Our frameworks differs because we target Hadoop and Java, the dominant language for MapReduce implementations. Newer compilers include HyCC [13], EzPC [14], SCALE-MAMBA (formerly SPDZ) [34], and ABY3 [40]. Unfortunately, none of these systems directly target Hadoop-like frameworks and cannot be used for the analysis, transformation and deployment of Hadoop MapReduce applications. In addition, MPC compilers (including ABY, HyCC, and EzPC) restrict loop bounds to constant values to enhance security. Thus, they cannot be applied on our benchmark programs with input dependent loop bounds.

Our system can be viewed as a variant of two-party computation (2-PC). The major difference is that SecureMCMR allows for the automatic transformation of existing MapReduce programs– we can replace LHE-supported operations with the equivalent operations over LHE-ciphertexts (e.g. plaintext $a = b + c$ becomes $LHE(a) = LHE(b) \oplus LHE(c)$), and LHE-unsupported operations with the corresponding collaborative protocol (if there is one). The program runs in Hadoop on cloud A with minimal synchronous communication with B. In contrast, existing 2-PC compilers (e.g., ABY, HyCC) do not support Hadoop. Extending such compilers to run in Hadoop is a significant research and engineering task; furthermore, automatic transformation of MapReduce to the inputs that would be accepted by those systems is unresolved as well. Despite the current state of MPC implementation, we believe that MPC is the most promising approach to secure computation, including in the parallel domain, due to its strong security guarantees. Our results stress the importance of parallelism in the two cloud systems, and study the kinds of operations used in real world MapReduce programs, which may guide development of MPC compilers and protocols for the MapReduce domain.

3   Cryptographic Primitives

This section describes the cryptographic tools we make use of, Linearly Homomorphic Encryption (Sect. 3.1), Randomized Encoding (Sect. 3.2), and Order Preserving Encryption (Sect. 3.3). Section 3.2 details our adaptation of RE for the purposes of SecureMCMR.

3.1   Linearly Homomorphic Encryption (LHE)

Given a message space M, an LHE scheme is defined, per [29], by:

1. Algorithm *Gen* generates a pair of keys, a *private key* sk and a *public key* pk given a security parameter κ: $(sk, pk) \leftarrow Gen(\kappa)$
2. Encryption algorithm *Enc* takes $m \in M$ and the public key, and generates ciphertext c: $c \leftarrow Enc(m, pk)$
3. Decryption algorithm *Dec* is a deterministic algorithm that takes c and the private key and decrypts the plaintext message corresponding to c: $m = Dec(c, sk)$

4. There is a homomorphic operation that operates on ciphertexts: $Dec(Enc$
$(m_1, pk) \oplus Enc(m_2, pk), sk) = m_1 + m_2$

As it is standard, the LHE plaintexts are in $\mathbb{Z}_N$ where N is an RSA modulus. Negative numbers are represented by the upper half of this range:

$$\left[\lceil \frac{N}{2} \rceil, N - 1\right] \equiv \left[-\lfloor \frac{N}{2} \rfloor, -1\right]$$

We assume that N is sufficiently large and computation does not overflow the modulus.

There are several known LHEs, e.g., Paillier [47], Damgård and Jurik [18], and Damgård, Geisler, and Krøigaard (DGK) [16]. Our framework uses a Java implementation of Paillier [4]. LHEs follows the standard semantic security property, which states, informally, that a computationally bounded algorithm cannot gain additional information about m given only the public key pk and the ciphertext c of m.

The key takeaway for our purposes is that LHE performs arbitrary affine transformations on ciphertexts. We can compute (the ciphertext of) $m_1 \cdot c_1 + m_2 \cdot c_2 + m_3$, where m_1, m_2 and m_3 are plaintexts and c_1 and c_2 are ciphertexts. Therefore, all affine transformations on program inputs can be computed locally on Server A. Empirically, a significant amount of computation in the MapReduce applications was affine operations.

3.2   Randomized Encoding (RE)

Standard RE. Randomized Encoding, described in [7], works as follows. Let $f(x)$ be a function. RE introduces an *encoding function* $\hat{f}(x; r)$, where r is uniformly random input, and a *decryption algorithm, Decode*. REs enforce two key properties: (1) correctness: $Decode(\hat{f}(x; r)) = f(x)$, and (2) privacy: the distribution of $\hat{f}(x; r)$ depends only on $f(x)$, i.e., it reveals only $f(x)$, and does not reveal any additional information on x. An additional property, (3) efficiency, states that computing $\hat{f}(x; r)$ is more efficient than computing $f(x)$.

An example from [7] is $f(x) = x^2 \bmod N$, where x is private input and N is a public integer. Take $\hat{f}(x; r) = x^2 + r \cdot N$, and $Decode(\hat{f}(x; r)) = \hat{f}(x; r) \bmod N$. Clearly, the randomized encoding is correct because $Decode = (x^2 + r \cdot N) \bmod N = x^2 \bmod N$. The encoding is also private, as argued by Appelbaum; this is because the distributions $\hat{f}(x; r)$ and $\hat{f}(x'; r)$ where $f(x) = f(x') = y$ (i.e., $x^2 = q \cdot N + y$, and $(x')^2 = q' \cdot N + y$), are statistically the same (intuitively, choosing r or r', s.t., $q \cdot N + y + (r-q) \cdot N = q' \cdot N + y + (r'-q') \cdot N$, is equally probable).

In traditional RE one party, say party A, may send the result of $\hat{f}(x; r)$, in our example this is the value $x^2 + r \cdot N$, to another party, say party B. Party B then retrieves the value of $f(x)$, by applying algorithm *Decode*. Party B will not learn anything additional on x (besides $x^2 \bmod N$, of course), which is guaranteed by privacy. And party A computes $\hat{f}$ more efficiently than f because modular division is expensive. Crucially, in traditional RE, both parties A and B can perform arbitrary operations and compute arbitrary functions. Therefore, neither the encryption (the encoding algorithm) nor the decryption (decoding algorithm) are constrained. In contrast, in our system *encoding of input* and *decoding of output* are constrained to only affine transformations. We build on RE, but impose different constraints.

SecureMCMR RE. Our variation of RE, which we call SecureMCMR RE, defines privacy as follows. For the rest of this paper, when we write RE, we refer to SecureMCMR RE. We require $\hat{f}(e(x;r))$, where $e(x;r)$ is an encoding of the input x such that it does not reveal anything on x. If the inputs x are of bit length l, we require that the random numbers r are drawn from the integers of bit length $\sigma + l$, where σ is a security parameter. It is an onus on the protocol designer to show that $e(x;r)$ is secure as we demonstrate for the two protocols we fit in this framework (recall that $e(x;r)$ is a ciphertext on the side of A, but a plaintext on the side of B). SecureMCMR RE defines correctness as follows: $Decode(\hat{f}(e(x;r)), x, r) = f(x)$; the decoding operation $Decode$ takes $\hat{f}(e(x;r))$, x, and r and produces the result of $f(x)$. The difference with traditional RE is that the decoder depends on x and the random inputs r used to encode x. In our setup Server A performs both the encoding and decoding, x is an LHE-encrypted ciphertext and r is a random plaintext. Server B computes $\hat{f}(e(x;r))$ over blinded inputs, thus $\hat{f}$ can perform arbitrary operations.

Encoding of Multiplication. We consider multiplication $f(x,y) = x \cdot y$. The encoding $\hat{f}(e(x;r_1), e(y;r_2)) = (x + r_1) \cdot (y + r_2) = v$. $Decode(v, x, y, r1, r2) = v - x \cdot r_2 - y \cdot r_1 - r_1 \cdot r_2$. Privacy holds, as $x + r_1$ and $y + r_2$ blind the values of x and y, and $(x + r_1) \cdot (y + r_2)$ does not reveal any additional information about x or y. Correctness holds as well, since $(x + r_1) \cdot (y + r_2) - x \cdot r_2 - y \cdot r_1 - r_1 \cdot r_2 = x \cdot y$.

To establish privacy, we show that $e(x;r)$ is at least statistically secure following the proofs of security in [20,50]. We assume that the Paillier modulus N is large enough and computations do not overflow N; this is convenient for correctness as $(x + r_1) \cdot (y + r_2)$ does not overflow the modulus and can be viewed as computation over the integers; however it limits the security of blinding, as now $x + r$ may reveal the length of x when B decrypts $x + r$. Consider the view of cloud B. The value $x + r$ may leak information about the length of x if its length is shorter than l, where l is the length of the input. The standard approach [20,50] is to use a statistical parameter σ, i.e., add σ random bits by randomly selecting padding r of bit length $\sigma + l$. We have $0 \leq r < 2^{\sigma+l}$. The only way $x + r$ reveals information about the length of x is if the σ most significant bits of r are 0, which happens with probability $2^{-\sigma}$; this is negligible in the security parameter σ. Therefore, $e(x;r)$ as applied to x and y is statistically secure. From the point of view of server A, A receives the Paillier encrypted value $(x + r_1) \cdot (y + r_2)$ which is indistinguishable from any other encrypted value by the guarantees of the Paillier cryptosystem.

We now plug in SecureMCMR RE into our system. SecureMCMR RE defines a protocol to compute LHE-unsupported function $f(x)$. It is parameterized by $\hat{f}$, $e(x, r)$, and *Decode*, meeting the above requirements.

1. Server A generates random r and computes LHE ciphertext $c = e(x; r)$. Recall that the computation uses only affine transformations on x as A holds the LHE ciphertext of x.
2. Server A sends c to B.
3. Server B decrypts c and computes $m = \hat{f}(Dec(c))$.
4. Server B encrypts $c = Enc(m)$ and sends the LHE ciphertext c to A.
5. Server A decodes $\hat{f}(c)$, computing the ciphertext of $f(x)$.

Server B receives *only* input encodings $e(x; r)$, in ciphertext. It is a requirement that $e(x; r)$ is secure, and the protocol designer must establish security of $e(x; r)$ as we did for the multiplication protocol. Server A receives $\hat{f}$ as LHE ciphertext which is secure based on the security guarantees of LHE.

As it is well known, we can approximate any function $f(x)$ by the first n terms of its Taylor series expansion. A and B can collaboratively compute each term of the expansion leaving server A to sum up the resulting ciphertexts computing $\approx f(x)$. The more terms of expansion the more accurate the Taylor series estimate. A downside of this is the inefficiency that n communication rounds entail. Therefore, we define our requirement for *efficiency* as a single round of communication, where A and B each send at most a small constant number of values. Operations are computable in our framework when we can design a protocol that fits the security and efficiency requirements; operations are *Unknown* otherwise. Section 5 has additional discussion.

One can use the framework to encode different operations. We have constructed encodings for multiplication (described above) and comparison $x \leq y$ (described below), which are necessary to run our benchmarks; we envision encoding of other operations in future work.

Encoding of Comparison. We adapt a protocol based on multiplication hiding described by Kerschbaum et al. [37]. We expand the protocol to suit our needs and argue both correctness and security (there are no proofs in ref. [37]). Recall that server A wishes to compute $x \leq y$, however, A holds both x and y as LHE-encrypted values. First, Server A computes the ciphertext $d = y - x$. (Note that computing $Enc(x)$ in either Paillier or Damgard and Jurik amounts to computing the multiplicative inverse of $Enc(x)$ in $\mathbb{Z}_{N^2}$.) Then A generates large non-negative uniformly random integers r and r' of length $\sigma + l$ such that $r' < r$ and computes $r \cdot d + r'$. As in [37], we assume the existence of such random values r and r' that the distribution of $r \cdot d + r'$ is statistically close to uniform over the set of values of d.

Server A sends the ciphertext $r \cdot d + r'$ to B.[1] B decrypts to a plaintext value v and sends True if $v > 0$ and False otherwise. In terms of SecureMCMR RE

$$\hat{f}_{x \leq y}(e(y - x; r, r')) = \begin{cases} True & \text{if plaintext } r \cdot (y - x) + r' > 0 \\ False & \text{otherwise} \end{cases}$$

$$Decode_{x \leq y}(v, x, y, r, r') = v$$

The protocol is correct: $x \leq y$ if and only if $r \cdot (y - x) + r' > 0$. Correctness follows from the assumption that the Paillier modulus N is large and computations $r \cdot d + r'$ do not overflow the modulus. Typical bit length values are $l = 32$, $\sigma = 112$, and N is 2048 bits, at least [50]. Consider the case $d < 0$ (d is negative in the integers). In Paillier, d is represented by $N - d'$ where $d' = |d|$, and $r \cdot (N - d') \bmod N = -r \cdot d'$; given the large N, $-r \cdot d'$ is in the upper half of the modulus N. Since $r' < r$ and d' is a positive integer, it follows that $-r \cdot d' + r'$ is in the upper half of the modulus, i.e., it is a negative integer. Analogously, $x > y$ implies that $r \cdot (y - x) + r' < 0$, and the equivalence follows from simple contradiction.

To prove security of $e(y - x; r, r')$ we again use the statistical parameter σ. $r \cdot d + r'$ reveals information to server B about the length of d only if the length of $r \cdot d + r'$ is less than $l + 1$. In order to have such a length, r must be 1 (and r' must be 0). The probability of selecting a random $r = 1$ is $\frac{1}{2^{\sigma+l}}$ which entails that hiding is at least statistically secure.

Encoding the rest of the comparison operations in terms of $x \leq y$ is straightforward [35].

3.3   Order Preserving Encryption (OPE)

The last cryptographic primitive that factors in our system and analysis is Order Preserving Encryption (OPE) [11,12,36]. An OPE scheme is a symmetric encryption scheme over a key space, message space M, and ciphertext space C. It is well known that OPE has weaker security than LHE, RE, and 2-PC protocols. We make use of OPE as a compromise to achieve better performance: we can encrypt values with OPE and perform comparison on server A, as opposed to sharing sensitive values between A and B and performing comparison collaboratively by A and B as is standard in MPC. OPE is defined in terms of three algorithms:

- A key generation algorithm that returns a key K
- An encryption algorithm Enc that takes a key K and a plaintext m and returns the ciphertext c
- A decrpyption algorithm Dec that takes K and a ciphertext and returns a plaintext

---

[1] The protocol assumes that x and y are integers, however, it is trivially adapted to work over fixpoint representation of real numbers as in the Java implementation of Paillier we use.

The correctness property $Dec(K, Enc(K, m)) = m$ holds for every K in the key space, and $m \in M$. The order-preserving property, if $m_1 < m_2$ then $Enc(K, m_1) < Enc(K, m_2)$, holds for every K and $m_1, m_2 \in M$.

Boldyreva et al. [11,12] study OPE and its security properties. It is well-known that since OPE schemes reveal order of plaintexts, their security is weaker than LHE or RE. Boldyreva et al. cast an OPE scheme in terms of a Random Order Preserving Function (ROPF), and describe the "ideal" behavior of an OPE scheme:

- Key generation picks a ROPF g
- *Enc* takes the key and a plaintext m and returns $g(m)$
- *Dec* takes the key and a ciphertext c and returns $g^{-1}(c)$

A secure OPE scheme, Boldyreva et al. argue, should closely "mimic" the behavior of a ROPF. In addition to the characterization of the "ideal" behavior, they propose an OPE scheme that is secure according to this definition.

Boldyreva et al. [12] give upper and lower bounds on *Window One-Wayness (WOW)*, a metric of the advantage of an adversary A trying to guess the plaintext values of OPE ciphertexts. Assuming an ideal OPE scheme, the upper bound is as follows:

$$\mathbf{Adv}^{1,z-WOW}(A) < \frac{4z}{\sqrt{M - z + 1}}$$

where M is the size of the domain of the plaintext, and z is the number of OPE challenge ciphertexts the adversary sees. $\mathbf{Adv}^{1,z-WOW}(A)$ in particular is the probability that A will find the exact value of at least one of the z challenge ciphertexts. Intuitively, the larger z is, i.e., the higher the number of *ordered* ciphertexts adversary A sees, the higher A's advantage, and hence the lower overall security. Analogous analysis applies to the adversarial advantage in guessing the distance between two OPE ciphertexts [35].

A key contribution of our work is to apply the upper bound on adversarial advantage on real-world MapReduce programs and study their OPE security, substantially expanding prior work [23,49,55,58] that has used OPE with potentially weak security guarantees.

4   Programming Primitives

We define the program execution semantics in terms of the notions of the *AST value* and *program trace*. We use these notions in Sect. 5 to reason about programs with comparisons.

AST Values. We denote values as $AST(v_1, \ldots, v_n)$, where $v_1, \ldots, v_n$ and $n \geq 1$ are *inputs*, which can be either (1) *program constants* or (2) *values read from MapReduce input files*. Inputs are plaintext or sensitive, where sensitive ones are LHE-encrypted by the client that outsources computation. For example, b0, b1, ... b5 in Fig. 3 are sensitive program constants, and rating's are sensitive

```
1   int b0, b1, b2, b3, b4, b5; // LHE—encrypted inputs (constants)
2   map(LongWritable key, Text value) {
3     int total = 0, sumRatings = 0, outValue = 0;
4     ...
5     while (token.hasMoreTokens()) {
6       int rating = token.nextToken(); // rating is LHE—encrypted input
7       sumRatings = sumRatings + rating;
8       total = total + 1;
9     }
10    if (total*b0 <= sumRatings && sumRatings <= total*b1)
11      outValue = 1;
12    else if (total*b1 <= sumRatings && sumRatings <= total*b2)
13      outValue = 2;
14    else if (total*b2 <= sumRatings && sumRatings <= total*b3)
15      outValue = 3;
16    else if (total*b3 <= sumRatings && sumRatings <= total*b4)
17      outValue = 4;
18    else if (total*b4 <= sumRatings && sumRatings <= total*b5)
19      outValue = 5;
20
21    output(outValue,1);
22  }
```

```
1   reduce(IntWritable key, Iterator<...> values) {
2     int sum = 0;
3     while (values.hasNext()) {
4       int value = values.next();
5       sum += value;
6     }
7     output.collect(key, sum);
8   }
```

Fig. 3. Histogram, adapted from PUMA, computes a histogram of ratings. The bucket interval boundaries b0, b1, ... and the rating values are LHE-encrypted inputs.

values read from the MapReduce input file. Inputs are the leaves of the Abstract Syntax Tree (AST) that computes the actual value. Our notation hints at the AST, however, we are interested in the inputs, and not the structure of the AST. For example, consider the value b0*total in line 13 in Fig. 3. Its AST notation will be $AST(b0,1,...,1)$, as it is computed from inputs b0 and the constant 1 in line 10. As a remark $v_1, \ldots, v_n$ may repeat inputs, as in the example $AST(b0,1,...,1)$.

$AST(v_1, \ldots, v_n)$ is plaintext if all inputs v_i's are plaintext; it is sensitive otherwise, i.e., there is at least one input that is sensitive. For example the AST of total, namely $AST(1,...,1)$ is plaintext, and the AST of b0*total is sensitive. A sensitive AST must be LHE-encrypted on Server A, and blinded on Server B; this is the correctness invariant enforced by our system.

Traces. An execution *trace* is the sequence of statements (e.g., x = y and x = y + z) and tests (e.g., x < y) that the program executes for a given input. For example, below is a trace for Fig. 3 that sums up the ratings in the first line of the input file and the average rating falls into the first bucket:

$$s1 = s0 + rating; total1 = total0 + 1; ...(b0 * totalN \leq sN) \wedge (sN \leq b1 * totalN); outValue = 1;$$

Here s0, s1,... stand for the partial sumRatings and r0, r1,... stand for the sequence of rating inputs, and t0, t1,... stand for the partial total.

Consider the trace view of the program: the same trace is running on A and on B. All sensitive ASTs must be "encrypted", i.e., available as LHE ciphertexts on A, and as blinded plaintexts on B. The trace view makes no distinction between arithmetic operations and comparison operations—each operation in the trace sequence is either (1) locally computable on Server A, (2) RE-enabled through communication between A and B, or (3) "unknown". We elaborate on "unknown" operations in Sect. 5.

Path Conditions. Note that a trace reveals the results of all comparisons to both servers A and B. The full sequence of comparison clauses in a trace T forms the *path condition* of T. The path condition of a trace T for our purposes is the sequence of all comparisons. For example, the path condition for the running example in Fig. 3 and the trace we showed earlier is $(b0 * total <= sumRatings), (sumRatings < b1 * total)$.

5   Security Analysis

This section presents the security analysis of SecureMCMR. We begin with stating our assumptions (Sect. 5.1). We describe the different kinds of program operations (Sect. 5.2) that give rise to the three security levels: Secure, OPE-secure, and Unknown (Sect. 5.3).

5.1   Assumptions

The goal of SecureMCMR is to distribute computation among two untrusted public clouds, cloud A (which runs the program over LHE-encrypted values) and cloud B (which helps run LHE-unsupported operations). Cloud A holds the public key pk as well as LHE-ciphertexts of sensitive ASTs. Cloud B holds the private key sk, however, it receives only statistically blinded values.

Our assumptions are:

1. Cloud A and cloud B are non-colluding, i.e., A has no access to B and vice versa.
2. We assume a passive adversary, e.g., an administrator at either cloud can monitor memory and traffic but would not attempt active attacks.
3. We assume that servers A and B consider the interval from which values are drawn to be sufficiently large, in other words, bounds on adversary advantage due to order information are driven by the size of the ordered sequence z.

We allow that the program code is known to both cloud A and cloud B. We may state an assumption that the program is *not known* to cloud B, which will strengthen our security guarantees. (In this case we will be able to send *any* value from A to B, as B does not know anything about the structure of the AST.) In practice however, cloud B may infer the program from the set of LHE-unsupported operations it is asked to perform, particularly, given that MapReduce applications typically run well-known data analytics tasks. Allowing that B knows the program code, entails that B has the exact same trace view as A. Both A and B see the AST of each value.

In addition, since both A and B observe the execution trace, they observe the number of iterations each loop takes. Thus, they observe the size of container structures. As expected, knowledge of the exact number of executions a loop takes can create side-channel leaks when the loop-bound is input dependent. We examine such leaks in our benchmarks in detail.

5.2 Kinds of Operations

We group operations on sensitive ASTs into 4 categories. Here x and y are ciphertexts and p is plaintext:

1. LHE-supported arithmetic (LHE): $x + y$ and $p \cdot x$,
2. RE-supported arithmetic (RE): $x \cdot y$ and x^p,
3. Comparison (CMP): $x \leq y$, and
4. Unsupported operations (UNK): any other operation, e.g., e^x.

LHE operations are carried out locally on Server A. RE ones are carried collaboratively by Servers A and B; as we argue in Sect. 3.2, RE operations do not leak additional information about the operands or result to either A or B. Comparisons are carried locally on A using OPE, or remotely using the encoding in Sect. 3.2. We classify a programs into one of three security levels, depending on the kinds of operations it executes. If the static analysis (a standard taint analysis described in [35]) determines that sensitive inputs reach a LHE, RE, CMP, or UNK operation, then we say that the program executes LHE, RE, CMP, or UNK operations, respectively.

5.3 Security Levels

Secure. Secure applications execute only LHE and RE operations. Server A sees only LHE-encrypted ciphertext of sensitive ASTs, and therefore SecureMCMR w.r.t. Server A is as strong as LHE encryption (i.e., we have semantic security). Server B sees statistically blinded sensitive ASTs, and thus, SecureMCMR w.r.t. Server B is at least statistically secure.

OPE-Secure. OPE-secure applications execute CMP operations (i.e., comparisons) in addition to LHE and RE ones. Comparisons present the biggest challenge to security reasoning. There are two cases, a local CMP and a remote CMP. Local CMPs have two operands that are inputs v_i (rather than ASTs of two or more leaves). Remote CMPs are ones where at least one operand is a sensitive AST. In other words, local CMPs use inputs as is, while remote CMPs perform computation/transformation on inputs. For example, the comparison in line 3 in Fig. 4 is a local CMP, as both the entryDate column value, and the constant input date are inputs; the comparisons in lines $10, 12, 14, 16$, and 18 in Fig. 3 are remote CMPs.

```
1   int date; // OPE−encrypted input (constant)
2   Integer map(Integer entryDate , Integer caloriesBurnt) {
3      if ( entryDate > date)
4         return caloriesBurnt ;
5      else
6         return 0;
7   }
8   Integer reduce ( List<Integer> caloriesBurntList ) {
9      Integer sum = 0;
10     for ( Integer caloriesBurnt : caloriesBurntList )
11        sum += caloriesBurnt ;
12     return sum ;
13  }
```

Fig. 4. A MapReduce-like program adapted from MrCrypt.

CMP-Local. We first discuss security of local CMPs, significantly expanding discussion of OPE compared to previous work [23, 49, 55, 58].

Our analysis applies Boldyreva et al's results to reason about OPE security (and order information more generally) in real programs. The actual bounds on adversary advantage depend on what order-preserving operations are executed in a program. If a program uses a large number of distinct OPE-encrypted ciphertexts, thus entailing a large z (recall Sect. 3.3), then the bound on adversary advantage is high and the program's OPE security is low. Conversely, if it uses only a few OPE-encrypted ciphertexts, then the bound on adversary advantage is low and OPE security is high.

Consider Fig. 4. Applying an OPE encryption scheme entails that all v_i's in column entryDate are encrypted using a key K. In terms of Boldyreva's analysis K is, essentially, a randomly chosen Order Preserving Function (ROPF) (recall Sect. 3.3). Thus, the bounds on the adversary advantage, depend on the size of the input file. As input files are large, that means OPE security is low—the adversary can guess the plaintext of a ciphertext with probability very close to one.

A mitigation is to encrypt each record, i.e., each entryDate with a different random key, thus associating a different random OPF with each value (i.e., rekey). This necessitates encryption of the date constant with different keys as well, and the comparison becomes

$$\text{if}(\text{entryDate}_i > \text{date}[\text{key}_i])...$$

z however is 2, since the adversary sees exactly 2 ciphertext per random function, and the bound on $\mathbf{Adv}^{1,z-WOW}(A)$ becomes $\frac{8}{\sqrt{M-1}}$. In Sect. 6 we present analysis of the adversary advantage bounds in our corpus of benchmarks.

CMP-Remote. Remote comparisons present a challenge because sequences of such comparisons combined with knowledge of the ASTs of operands may lead to side-channel leaks. Recall that remote comparisons happen when at least one of the operands of the comparison is a result of a computation. Many existing works (e.g., MrCrypt and CryptDB) do not support such programs.

To reason about CMP-remote operations we define the notion of the *interval leak*:

```
1  int start_node = Integer.parseInt(line[0]);
2  int end_node = Integer.parseInt(line[1]);
3  for(i = start_node; i <= end_node; i++) {
4    from_node_int.set( i );
5    output.collect(from_node_int, new Text("v"+initial_weight));
6  }
```

Fig. 5. Interval leak example.

Definition 1. *Consider an execution trace with corresponding path condition P. An interval leak occurs when $P \Rightarrow c_l \leq v_i$ or $P \Rightarrow v_i \leq c_u$, where c_l and c_u are plaintext constants, v_i is a sensitive input, and the implied interval is strictly included in v_i's interval.*

Figure 5 shows an example of an interval leak. The path condition implied by the execution is

$$\mathsf{start\_node} \leq \mathsf{end\_node}, ..., \mathsf{start\_node} + n \leq \mathsf{end\_node}$$

where n is the number of iterations of the loop, a value that can be observed by the servers. The above path condition implies a lower bound on $\mathsf{end\_node}$: $n \leq \mathsf{end\_node}$ and an upper bound on $\mathsf{start\_node}$: $\mathsf{start\_node} \leq M - n$, where M is the largest value that $\mathsf{start\_node}/\mathsf{end\_node}$ take. There is also an obvious leak of the difference between $\mathsf{end\_node}$ and $\mathsf{start\_node}$, however, our analysis does not take such leaks into account. We are interested in interval leaks on input values rather than interval leaks on sensitive ASTs because, by definition, every remote comparison is an interval leak on a sensitive AST. Our technical report presents additional examples of codes that exhibit interval leaks as well codes that do not have interval leaks [35].

In addition to interval leaks, we study adversarial advantage due to ordered sequences of sensitive ASTs. We call these leaks *sequence leaks*. Let path condition P imply an ordered sequence of sensitive ASTs: $a \leq b \leq ... \leq c$. $a, b, ...,$ and c can be treated as points in a Random Order Preserving Function (ROPF) $M \to N$, per Boldyreva et al. We can then make use of Boldyreva's framework to bound leakage due to such ordered sequences: each value (LHE ciphertext) in the sequence implied by the path condition is viewed as a challenge ciphertext. Thus, fixing z to be the number of ordered ciphertexts implied by the path condition, then fixing M, we can apply the bound on $\mathbf{Adv}^{1,z-WOW}(A_P)$ from Sect. 3.3.

In summary, we reason about side channels due to remote comparisons from two angles: (1) interval leaks on input values, and (2) ordered sequences of sensitive ASTs, applying Boldyreva et al.'s analysis on ordered sequences of sensitive ASTs implied by path conditions.

Unknown. Our last category includes programs with unknown security guarantees. If there is an UNK operation whose operand is a sensitive value according to our static analysis, then the program is classified as unknown. When the sensitive value is an aggregate agg (e.g., the inner product of two sensitive vectors), our framework executes the operation by having A send $Enc(agg)$ to B, where B decrypts it, runs the UNK operation over plaintext arguments, then encrypts and sends the result back to A. Our classification of Unknown means that the security guarantees of the framework are Unknown, in a sense that they depend on the kind of aggregation. B sees the aggregate sensitive value agg. In certain cases the programmer may deem safe to send the aggregate value to B; this can happen when the probability that agg leaks information about individual sensitive inputs is small (e.g., the inner product aggregate where the number of points is large). However, in other cases, the programmer may deem leaking a sensitive aggregate unsafe. The degenerate case is when agg is a sensitive input itself (e.g., the maximal element in a sequence), in which case leaking the sensitive value is clearly unsafe.

We note that any UNK function can be approximated by the first n terms of its Taylor series, as we argued earlier. Therefore, in theory the program can be run securely in terms of addition and multiplication, making use of our multiplication protocol. However, this will require multiple rounds of communication and violate the efficiency requirement. We have not considered it in our framework.

6   Experimental Results

We analyze MapReduce applications from six different benchmark suites: Pigmix2 [48], Brown, Puma [1], HiBench suite [32], TCP-H [57], and MLHadoop [43]. For details on these suites, see [35]. We chose three basic but non-trivial machine learning algorithms to run on Google Cloud and AWS: LinearRegression, LogisticRegression, and Kmeans. The results and details of our experiments are discussed in Sect. 6.3.

We address the following research questions:

RQ1. How applicable is our framework? Specifically, what percentage of applications are Secure, OPE-secure, and Unknown? Is the percentage of Unknown *low*?

RQ2. How secure are OPE-secure applications? Specifically, are bounds on lengths of ordered sequences and thus on adversary advantage *low*?

RQ3. How scalable is our framework? Is overhead of SecureMCMR over plaintext execution *low*?

Section 6.1 addresses **RQ1** and Sect. 6.2 addresses **RQ2**. Section 6.3 addresses **RQ3**; we describe experiments on Google Cloud and Amazon's AWS, and measure overhead over plaintext execution on Google Cloud.

6.1 Applicability of SecureMCMR

We apply the analysis from Sect. 5 to classify the benchmarks into security levels as described in Sect. 5.3. We present a classification of the benchmarks into one of the four categories introduced in Sect. 5.3: Secure, CMP-local, CMP-remote, and Unknown.

Based on our analysis, the majority of the analyzed benchmarks, 50.57% are Secure. 17.24% are Unkown. Table 1 summarizes the results. Results on individual benchmark suites are presented in [35]. In addition, 50.0% of all benchmarks with comparisons exhibit short ordered sequences and no interval or sequence leaks. Our Unknown category includes Grep, HadiBlock, and LogisticRegression, which depend on operations that we could not represent using RE (e.g., LogisticRegression employs the sigmoid function).

Table 1. Counts and percentages across all benchmarks for each category.

Secure	CMP-local	CMP-remote	Unknown
44	19	9	15
50.57%	21.83%	10.34%	17.24%

6.2 OPE Secure

For each benchmark in each suite we analyzed the severity of the leaks created by comparisons. We found that 63.16% of the CMP-local programs exhibit a low z value (or allow for rekeying which then entails a low z), and 22.22% of the CMP-remote programs exhibit short order sequences and no interval leaks. As mentioned earlier, this amounts to 50.0% of benchmarks with comparisons exhibiting short ordered sequences and no interval or sequence leaks. Detailed tables per benchmark suite, as well as detailed analysis and examples can be found in our technical report [35].

6.3 Scalability of SecureMCMR

To test the scalability of SecureMCMR we transformed three MapReduce programs from MLHadoop, and studied their performance. Importantly, we used two *different* cloud providers to execute the programs.

We chose Machine Learning applications, which have been an important area of research in secure computation [26,33,38,41,45,52,53]. We chose three programs from MLHadoop: LinearRegression, LogisticRegression and Kmeans. They use LHE-unsupported operations that require remote communication such as RE-supported multiplication, and they are likely to exhibit slowdown with SecureMCMR. Neither of these applications is supported by existing frameworks for MapReduce such as MrCrypt or SecureMR. We note that there is a number of applications, MLHadoop ones included that can run in SecureMCMR without any remote communication, as every operation is supported by a single encryption scheme (e.g., NaiveBaise). The benchmarks span our classification— LinearRegression is Secure, Kmeans is CMP-remote, and LogisticRegression is Unknown. LogisticRegression is classified Unknown because it computes e^{-x} as part of the sigmoid function, where x is a sensitive aggregate value. We argue that users of SecureMCMR may determine that such an aggregate leak is acceptable for their purposes.

Overhead ranges from 3.8x for Kmeans to 1.6x for LinearRegression. Importantly, as the number of cloud B nodes (Amazon) increases, running time decreases. Adding Amazon nodes improves performance if the current configuration is not able to handle the workload. Otherwise, communication dominates the cost, and adding nodes no longer improves performance. We observe taper off in Kmeans when going from 8 to 16 nodes, however, additional experiments are needed to make a robust conclusion.

For Linear regression we used the Iris Data Set [24] as a base point to generate a 240,000 data points for training. For Logistic Regression we used a real world dataset used to classify potential pulsar stars; this dataset has 179,890 points with 8 features each [51]. For Kmeans classification we created a dataset of 100,000 data points in 2D euclidean space and grouped them into 4 clusters.

We compared the running times of SecureMCMR, which uses both LHE and network communication for RE-supported operations, with the standard run on Google Cloud in plaintext. Table 2, Table 3, and Table 4 show the running times, slowdown and overhead. As expected, increasing the number of Amazon nodes decreases the overhead. We also found that fewer than 4 Amazon nodes results in 100% CPU utilization, stalls the experiment, and ultimately crashes the job. Again, we refer the reader to the technical report [35] for details on utilization and additional discussion.

Table 2. Run times: Linear Regression

	4 nodes	8 nodes	16 nodes
SecureMCMR	528 s	258 s	200 s
Slowdown	≈6.86x	≈3.35x	≈2.60x

Table 3. Run times: Logistic Regression

	4 nodes	8 nodes	16 nodes
SecureMCMR	463 s	315 s	244 s
Slowdown	≈6.71x	≈4.57x	≈3.54x

Table 4. Run times: Kmeans Classification

	4 nodes	8 nodes	16 nodes
SecureMCMR	473 s	321 s	315 s
Slowdown	≈7.2x	≈4.89x	≈4.8x

7   Conclusions

We presented SecureMCMR, a novel framework for the analysis and execution of MapReduce programs using PHE, OPE, and multiple clouds. Using multiple untrusted clouds to execute MapReduce programs removes the bottleneck created by a single trusted machine. At the time of writing of this paper our prototype is not yet publicly available, however, we plan to make SecureMCMR publicly available at https://github.com/proganalysis/type-inference alongside our previous work on SecureMR [23]. We also presented an analysis of MapReduce programs with comparisons, and the effect comparisons have on the security of the system. In the future we will continue to research MapReduce programs, parallelization, and optimization, in the context of SecureMCMR and MPC.

References

1. Ahmad, F., Lee, S., Thottethodi, M., Vijaykumar, T.N.: PUMA: Purdue MapReduce Benchmarks Suite. Technical Report. Purdue University (2012)
2. Aly, A., et al.: SCALE-MAMBA v1.6 : Documentation (2019). https://homes.esat. kuleuven.be/~nsmart/SCALE/Documentation.pdf
3. Aly, A., Smart, N.P.: Benchmarking privacy preserving scientific operations. In: Deng, R.H., Gauthier-Umaña, V., Ochoa, M., Yung, M. (eds.) ACNS 2019. LNCS, vol. 11464, pp. 509–529. Springer, Cham (2019). https://doi.org/10.1007/978-3-030-21568-2_25
4. N1 Analytics: javallier (2017). https://github.com/n1analytics/javallier
5. Apache Software Foundation: Apache CouchDB 2005–2019. https://couchdb. apache.org/
6. Apache Software Foundation: Apache Hadoop 2006–2018. https://hadoop.apache. org/
7. Applebaum, B.: Garbled circuits as randomized encodings of functions: a primer. Tutorials on the Foundations of Cryptography. ISC, pp. 1–44. Springer, Cham (2017). https://doi.org/10.1007/978-3-319-57048-8_1
8. Ben-David, A., Nisan, N., Pinkas, B.: FairplayMP: a system for secure multi-party computation. In: Proceedings of the 15th ACM Conference on Computer and Communications Security (CCS 2008), pp. 257–266. Association for Computing Machinery, New York (2008)
9. Ben-Or, M., Goldwasser, S., Wigderson, A.: Completeness theorems for noncryptographic fault-tolerant distributed computation. In: Proceedings of the Twentieth Annual ACM Symposium on Theory of Computing (STOC 1988), pp. 1–10. ACM, New York (1988)

10. Bogdanov, D., Laur, S., Willemson, J.: Sharemind: a framework for fast privacy-preserving computations. In: Jajodia, S., Lopez, J. (eds.) ESORICS 2008. LNCS, vol. 5283, pp. 192–206. Springer, Heidelberg (2008). https://doi.org/10.1007/978-3-540-88313-5_13
11. Boldyreva, A., Chenette, N., Lee, Y., O'Neill, A.: Order-preserving symmetric encryption. In: Joux, A. (ed.) EUROCRYPT 2009. LNCS, vol. 5479, pp. 224–241. Springer, Heidelberg (2009). https://doi.org/10.1007/978-3-642-01001-9_13
12. Boldyreva, A., Chenette, N., O'Neill, A.: Order-preserving encryption revisited: improved security analysis and alternative solutions. In: Rogaway, P. (ed.) CRYPTO 2011. LNCS, vol. 6841, pp. 578–595. Springer, Heidelberg (2011). https://doi.org/10.1007/978-3-642-22792-9_33
13. Büscher, N., Demmler, D., Katzenbeisser, S., Kretzmer, D., Schneider, T.: HyCC: compilation of hybrid protocols for practical secure computation. In: Proceedings of the 2018 ACM SIGSAC Conference on Computer and Communications Security (CCS 2018), pp. 847–861. ACM, New York (2018)
14. Chandran, N., Gupta, D., Rastogi, A., Sharma, R., Tripathi, S.: EzPC: programmable, efficient, and scalable secure two-party computation for machine learning. In: IEEE European Symposium on Security and Privacy (IEEE EuroS&P 2019) (2019)
15. Chaum, D., Crépeau, C., Damgard, I.: Multiparty unconditionally secure protocols. In: Proceedings of the Twentieth Annual ACM Symposium on Theory of Computing (STOC 1988), pp. 11–19. ACM, New York (1988)
16. Damgård, I., Geisler, M., Krøigaard, M.: Efficient and secure comparison for on-line auctions. In: Pieprzyk, J., Ghodosi, H., Dawson, E. (eds.) ACISP 2007. LNCS, vol. 4586, pp. 416–430. Springer, Heidelberg (2007). https://doi.org/10.1007/978-3-540-73458-1_30
17. Damgård, I., Geisler, M., Krøigaard, M., Nielsen, J.B.: Asynchronous multiparty computation: theory and implementation. In: Jarecki, S., Tsudik, G. (eds.) PKC 2009. LNCS, vol. 5443, pp. 160–179. Springer, Heidelberg (2009). https://doi.org/10.1007/978-3-642-00468-1_10
18. Damgård, I., Jurik, M.: A generalisation, a simpli.cation and some applications of Paillier's probabilistic public-key system. In: Kim, K. (ed.) PKC 2001. LNCS, vol. 1992, pp. 119–136. Springer, Heidelberg (2001). https://doi.org/10.1007/3-540-44586-2_9
19. Dean, J., Ghemawat, S.: MapReduce: simplified data processing on large clusters. In: OSDI'04: Sixth Symposium on Operating System Design and Implementation, San Francisco, CA, pp. 137–150 (2004)
20. Demmler, D., Schneider, T., Zohner, M.: ABY - a framework for efficient mixed-protocol secure two-party computation. In: NDSS (2015)
21. Dinh, T.T.A., Saxena, P., Chang, E.C., Ooi, B.C., Zhang, C.: M2R: enabling stronger privacy in MapReduce computation. In: Proceedings of the 24th USENIX Conference on Security Symposium (SEC 2015), 447–462. USENIX Association, Berkeley (2015)
22. Disco Project: disco: a Map/Reduce framework for distributed computing 2008–2019. https://github.com/discoproject/disco
23. Dong, Y., Milanova, A., Dolby, J.: SecureMR: Secure MapReduce computation using homomorphic encryption and program partitioning. In: Proceedings of the 5th Annual Symposium and Bootcamp on Hot Topics in the Science of Security, HoTSoS 2018, Raleigh, North Carolina, USA, 10–11 April 2018, pp. 4:1–4:13 (2018)
24. Fisher, R.A.: The use of multiple measurements in taxonomic problems. Ann. Eugen. **7**(1936), 179–188 (1936)

25. Franz, M., Holzer, A., Katzenbeisser, S., Schallhart, C., Veith, H.: CBMC-GC: an ANSI C compiler for secure two-party computations. In: Cohen, A. (ed.) CC 2014. LNCS, vol. 8409, pp. 244–249. Springer, Heidelberg (2014). https://doi.org/10.1007/978-3-642-54807-9_15

26. Gascón, A., Schoppmann, P., Balle, B., Raykova, M., Doerner, J., Zahur, S., Evans, D.: Privacy-preserving distributed linear regression on high-dimensional data. PoPETs **2017**(2017), 345–364 (2017)

27. Gentry, C.: Computing arbitrary functions of encrypted data. Commun. ACM **53**(3), 97–105 (2010)

28. Gentry, C., Halevi, S.: Implementing Gentry's fully-homomorphic encryption scheme. In: Paterson, K.G. (ed.) EUROCRYPT 2011. LNCS, vol. 6632, pp. 129–148. Springer, Heidelberg (2011). https://doi.org/10.1007/978-3-642-20465-4_9

29. Giacomelli, I., Jha, S., Joye, M., Page, C.D., Yoon, K.: Privacy-preserving ridge regression with only linearly-homomorphic encryption. In: Preneel, B., Vercauteren, F. (eds.) ACNS 2018. LNCS, vol. 10892, pp. 243–261. Springer, Cham (2018). https://doi.org/10.1007/978-3-319-93387-0_13

30. Goldreich, O., Micali, S., Wigderson, A.: How to play ANY mental game. In: Proceedings of the Nineteenth Annual ACM Symposium on Theory of Computing (STOC 1987), pp. 218–229. ACM, New York (1987)

31. Hastings, M., Hemenway, B., Noble, D., Zdancewic, S.: SoK: general purpose compilers for secure multi-party computation. In: 2019 IEEE Symposium on Security and Privacy (SP), pp. 479–496. IEEE Computer Society, Los Alamitos (2019)

32. Intel-bigdata: HiBench Suite 2012–2017. https://github.com/Intel-bigdata/HiBench

33. Juvekar, C., Vaikuntanathan, V., Chandrakasan, A.: GAZELLE: a low latency framework for secure neural network inference. In: Proceedings of the 27th USENIX Conference on Security Symposium (SEC 2018), pp. 1651–1668. USENIX Association, Berkeley (2018). http://dl.acm.org/citation.cfm?id=3277203.3277326

34. Keller, M., Pastro, V., Rotaru, D.: Overdrive: making SPDZ great again. In: Nielsen, J.B., Rijmen, V. (eds.) EUROCRYPT 2018. LNCS, vol. 10822, pp. 158–189. Springer, Cham (2018). https://doi.org/10.1007/978-3-319-78372-7_6

35. Kennard, L., Milanova, A.: SecureMCMR: Computation Outsourcing for MapReduce Applications. Technical report. Rensselaer Polytechnic Institute (2020). https://www.cs.rpi.edu/~milanova/docs/LindseyTR.pdf

36. Kerschbaum, F.: Frequency-hiding order-preserving encryption. In: Proceedings of the 22Nd ACM SIGSAC Conference on Computer and Communications Security (CCS 2015), pp. 656–667. ACM, New York (2015)

37. Kerschbaum, F., Biswas, D., de Hoogh, S.: Performance comparison of secure comparison protocols. In: Proceedings of the 2009 20th International Workshop on Database and Expert Systems Application (DEXA 2009), pp. 133–136. IEEE Computer Society, Washington, DC (2009)

38. Liu, J., Juuti, M., Lu, Y., Asokan, N.: Oblivious neural network predictions via MiniONN transformations. In: Proceedings of the 2017 ACM SIGSAC Conference on Computer and Communications Security (CCS 2017), pp. 619–631. ACM, New York (2017)

39. Malkhi, D., Nisan, N., Pinkas, B., Sella, Y.: Fairplay–a secure two-party computation system. In: Proceedings of the 13th Conference on USENIX Security Symposium - Volume 13 (SSYM 2004), p. 20. USENIX Association, Berkeley (2004)

40. Mohassel, P., Rindal, P.: ABY3: a mixed protocol framework for machine learning. In: Proceedings of the 2018 ACM SIGSAC Conference on Computer and Communications Security (CCS 2018), pp. 35–52. Association for Computing Machinery, New York (2018)

41. Mohassel, P., Zhang, Y.: SecureML: a system for scalable privacy-preserving machine learning. In: 2017 IEEE Symposium on Security and Privacy (SP), pp. 19–38 (2017)

42. Mood, B., Gupta, D., Carter, H., Butler, K., Traynor, P.: Frigate: a validated, extensible, and efficient compiler and interpreter for secure computation. In: 2016 IEEE European Symposium on Security and Privacy (EuroS P), pp. 112–127 (2016)

43. Punit Naik: MLHadoop 2016–2018. https://github.com/punit-naik/MLHadoop

44. Nayak, K., Wang, X.S., Ioannidis, S., Weinsberg, U., Taft, N., Shi, E.: GraphSC: parallel secure computation made easy. In: Proceedings of the 2015 IEEE Symposium on Security and Privacy (SP 2015), pp. 377–394. IEEE Computer Society, Washington, DC (2015)

45. Nikolaenko, V., Weinsberg, U., Ioannidis, S., Joye, M., Boneh, D., Taft, N.: Privacy-preserving ridge regression on hundreds of millions of records. In: 2013 IEEE Symposium on Security and Privacy, pp. 334–348 (2013)

46. Ohrimenko, O.: Oblivious multi-party machine learning on trusted processors. In: Proceedings of the 25th USENIX Conference on Security Symposium (SEC 2016), pp. 619–636. USENIX Association, Berkeley (2016)

47. Paillier, P.: Public-key cryptosystems based on composite degree residuosity classes. In: Stern, J. (ed.) EUROCRYPT 1999. LNCS, vol. 1592, pp. 223–238. Springer, Heidelberg (1999). https://doi.org/10.1007/3-540-48910-X_16

48. Pig Mix: PIGMIX2 Benchmarks (2013). https://cwiki.apache.org/confluence/display/PIG/PigMix

49. Popa, R.A., Redfield, C.M., Zeldovich, N., Balakrishnan, H.: CryptDB: protecting confidentiality with encrypted query processing. In: Proceedings of the Twenty-Third ACM Symposium on Operating Systems Principles (SOSP 2011), pp. 85–100. ACM, New York (2011)

50. Pullonen, P., Bogdanov, D., Schneider, T.: The Design and Implementation of a Two-Party Protocol Suite for SHAREMIND 3 (2012)

51. Raj, P.: Predicting a Pulsar Star (2018). https://www.kaggle.com/pavanraj159/predicting-a-pulsar-star/metadata

52. Riazi, M.S., Weinert, C., Tkachenko, O., Songhori, E.M., Schneider, T., Koushanfar, F.: Chameleon: a hybrid secure computation framework for machine learning applications. In: Proceedings of the 2018 on Asia Conference on Computer and Communications Security (ASIACCS 2018), pp. 707–721. ACM, New York (2018)

53. Rouhani, B.D., Hussain, S.U., Lauter, K., Koushanfar, F.: ReDCrypt: real-time privacy-preserving deep learning inference in clouds using FPGAs. ACM Trans. Reconfigurable Technol. Syst. **11**(3), 1–21 (2018)

54. Schoenmakers, B.: MPyC - Python Package for Secure Multiparty Computation (2018). https://www.win.tue.nl/~berry/mpyc/

55. Tetali, S.D., Lesani, M., Majumdar, R., Millstein, T.: MrCrypt: static analysis for secure cloud computations. In: Proceedings of the 2013 ACM SIGPLAN International Conference on Object Oriented Programming Systems Languages and Applications, pp. 271–286 (2013)

56. Tople, S., et al.: AUTOCRYPT: enabling homomorphic computation on servers to protect sensitive web content. In: Proceedings of the 2013 ACM SIGSAC Conference on Computer and Communications Security (CCS 2013), pp. 1297–1310 (2013)
57. TPC: TPC-H 2001–2019. http://www.tpc.org/tpch/
58. Tu, S.L., Kaashoek, M.F., Madden, S.R., Zeldovich, N.: Processing analytical queries over encrypted data. In: Proceedings of the 39th International Conference on Very Large Data Bases (VLDB 2013), pp. 289–300 (2013)
59. van Dijk, M., Gentry, C., Halevi, S., Vaikuntanathan, V.: Fully homomorphic encryption over the integers. In: Gilbert, H. (ed.) EUROCRYPT 2010. LNCS, vol. 6110, pp. 24–43. Springer, Heidelberg (2010). https://doi.org/10.1007/978-3-642-13190-5_2
60. Yao, A.C.: Protocols for secure computations. In: 23rd Annual Symposium on Foundations of Computer Science (SFCS 1982), pp. 160–164 (1982)

Evasion Is Not Enough: A Case Study of Android Malware

Harel Berger[1]([✉]) [ID], Chen Hajaj[2] [ID], and Amit Dvir[3] [ID]

[1] Ariel Cyber Innovation Center, CS Department, Ariel University,
Kiryat Hamada, 40700 Ariel, Israel
harel.berger@msmail.ariel.ac.il
[2] Ariel Cyber Innovation Center, Data Science and Artificial Intelligence
Research Center, IEM Department, Ariel University, Ariel, Israel
chenha@ariel.ac.il
https://www.ariel.ac.il/wp/chen-hajaj/
[3] Ariel Cyber Innovation Center, CS Department, Ariel University, Ariel, Israel
amitdv@ariel.ac.il
https://www.ariel.ac.il/wp/amitd/

Abstract. A growing number of Android malware detection systems are based on Machine Learning (ML) methods. However, ML methods are often vulnerable to *evasion attacks*, in which an adversary manipulates malicious instances so they are classified as benign. Here, we present a novel evaluation scheme for evasion attack generation that exploits the weak spots of known Android malware detection systems. We implement an innovative evasion attack on Drebin [3]. After our novel evasion attack, Drebin's detection rate decreased by 12%. However, when inspecting the functionality and maliciousness of the manipulated instances, the maliciousness rate increased, whereas the functionality rate decreased by 72%. We show that non-functional apps, do not constitute a threat to users and are thus useless from an attacker's point of view. Hence, future evaluations of attacks against Android malware detection systems should also address functionality and maliciousness tests.

Keywords: Cyber security · Android security · Malware detection

1 Introduction

Android malware evolves over time, such that malicious versions of popular Android application PacKages (APKs) can propagate to various Android markets. One of the most popular techniques in the malware detection domain is Machine Learning (ML) based detection of malicious entities, where some techniques' detection rates exceed 99% at times. However, Szegedy et al. [7] showed that some ML methods (including malware detection systems) are vulnerable to *adversarial examples*. A special case of adversarial examples involves using *evasion attacks*. Evasion attacks take place when an adversary modifies malware

© Springer Nature Switzerland AG 2020
S. Dolev et al. (Eds.): CSCML 2020, LNCS 12161, pp. 167–174, 2020.
https://doi.org/10.1007/978-3-030-49785-9_11

code so that the modified malware is categorized as benign by the ML, but still successfully executes the malicious payload.

The main contribution of this work is our analysis of functionality and maliciousness tests for Android evasion attacks that change existing features. To the best of our knowledge, none of the evasion attacks that changed existing features of malicious apps has been evaluated in terms of either functionality or malicious content maintenance, which raises the question of whether "efficient" attacks result in nonfunctional apps that would not be malicious as intended.

2   Related Work

In this section, we survey well known ML-based detection systems for Android malware. We also depict several popular evasion attacks targeting the detection systems. Then, we examine the functionality and maliciousness tests of Android malware. As far as we know, they have not been fully explored in previous studies in the Android malware field.

2.1   Android Malware ML-Based Detection Systems

One of the best known Android malware detection systems is Drebin [3], a lightweight Android malware detector (it can be installed on mobile phones). Drebin collects 8 types of features from the APKs. From the Manifest file, Drebin extracts permissions requests, software/hardware components and intents, and from the smali code, it extracts suspicious/restricted API calls, used permissions in the app's run and URL addresses. A different approach is found in MaMaDroid [14], which extracts features from the Control Flow Graph (CFG) of an application. MaMaDroid creates a tree of API calls based on package and family names. After abstracting the calls, the system analyzes the API call sequence performed by an app, to model its true nature. The third approach which inspects system features was introduced in Andromaly [19].

2.2   Evasion Attacks on ML-Based Detection Systems

Evasion attacks against ML-based detection systems can take multiple courses. One course of action is to camouflage specific parts of the app. One well-known example of camouflage is the use of obfuscation or encryption, which was implemented in Demontis et al. [6]. Reflection, which allows a program to change its behavior at runtime, is also a classic evasion method, which was exampled in Rastogi et al. [16]. A typical approach to evasion attacks on ML-based detection systems involves adding noise to the app, thus misleading the classifier's assignment of benign and malicious app. An example of the use of this approach can be found in Android HIV [5] where the authors implemented non-invoked dangerous functions against Drebin and a function injection against MaMaDroid. Changing the app flow is another approach, where a detection system that is based on analyzing the app flow, such as MaMaDroid, fails to detect the malicious app [5,11].

2.3 Functionality and Maliciousness Tests

An evasion attack's main goal is to evade detection by malware detection systems. However, two tests can be conducted to identify an attack. The first is functionality, and the second is maliciousness. These features were explored in Repackman [18], a tool that automates the repackaging attack with an arbitrary malicious payload. The authors performed 2 relevant tests for their repackaging attack, all using Droidutan [17]. For the functionality test (which they termed **feasibility**), they used random UI actions. For maliciousness, which they termed **reliability**, they measured the apps that successfully executed their payload via recorded screenshots. To the best of our knowledge, these functionality and malicious content tests have not been mentioned in previous evasion attack studies.

3 Evaluation Metrics

This study involves a number of metrics. These metrics are used to define our app dataset, evaluate the effectiveness of the attacks against the detection systems, and formulate insights about our findings. First, we describe the dataset we gathered and its verification tool. In addition, we discuss functionality and maliciousness tests for Android evasion attacks. The metrics are:

- **Data collection:**
    - **Benign apps:** We combine apps from the AndroZoo dataset [1], chosen from the GooglePlay [8] market, and Drebin's [3] dataset.
    - **Malicious apps:** We use the malicious apps from the Drebin dataset [3], CICAndMal2017 [12], AMD [22] and StormDroid [4] datasets.
    - **Verification:** We use VirusTotal (VT) [21] to verify that our apps are correctly labeled. We define benign apps as apps that are not marked as malicious by any scanner. Malicious apps are apps that are identified as malicious by at least 2/4 scanners [3,15]. In our study, we use malicious apps that are identified by at least two scanners.
- **Eliminating dataset biases:** Android ML-based detection systems suffer from temporal and spatial biases [15]. Spatial bias refers to unrealistic assumptions about the ratio of benign to malicious apps in the data. Temporal bias refers to temporally inconsistent evaluations that integrate future knowledge about the test data into the training data. To avoid these dataset biases, we follow the properties suggested in [15]. For example, 90% of our dataset is composed of benign APKs, and the remaining 10% is malicious, similar to the distribution of global apps [9,13], thus accounting for the spatial bias. To prevent temporal bias, we train the classifiers with apps whose timestamp is prior to the test data.
- **Robustness evaluation:** To evaluate robustness, we compute the proportion of instances for which the classifier was evaded; this is our metric of *evasion robustness*, with respect to the robustness of the detection system (similar to the analysis provided in [20]). Thus, evasion robustness of 0% means that the classifier is successfully evaded every time, whereas evasion

robustness of 100% means that the evasion fails in every instance. We compare the evasion robustness of our evasion attack compared to the original malicious APKs detection rate.

- **Functionality:** In an evasion attack, the attacker tries to conceal the malicious content from the detection system. Constructing an evasion attack with the use of existing Android malware includes manipulation of the APK, which is a sensitive task. It may result in any kind of error, thus resulting in a crash. If the crash occurs in the initial stages of the app's run, the malicious content will probably not harm the user at all. Therefore, evaluation of the apps' functionality is vital when generating an APK evasion attack. The functionality check includes a test where the app is installed and run on an Android emulator [10]. If the app crashes, this suggests it is not functional. A manipulated app that passes this test is declared a functional app.

- **Malicious Activity/Maliciousness:** While a manipulated app that passes the previous check can be considered a threat to the user, it does not guarantee that the previous malicious content will run similarly to the previous Android malware. Therefore, a test for the maliciousness of the app is needed. We evaluate malicious activity with the following test: We scan the app using VT. If the number of scanners that indicate the manipulated app to be malicious is less or equal to the number of scanners identifying the original app as malicious, this app is said to pass our simple maliciousness test.

4   Case Study

In this section, we demonstrate the use of our tests. We chose Drebin as a test case for this inquiry, which is one of the best known Android malware detection systems. For a full description of the Drebin classifier, see [3] (implementation is available at [2]). First, we depict our attack, which decreases Drebin's accuracy. Then, we run our additional tests (see Sect. 3) on the original and manipulated apps.

4.1   Attacker Model

The attacker has a black-box access to the input and output of the trained classifier. As can be seen in Fig. 1, The first input (denoted 1 in Fig. 1) for the classifier is malicious APK samples available to the attacker. Based on this input, the Drebin classifier outputs a report on these APKs (denoted 2 in Fig. 1), and an accuracy rate of the classification. The attacker receives this report (denoted 3 in Fig. 1), and manipulates the APKs that Drebin identified as malicious, and sends them as a second input to the classifier (denoted 4 in Fig. 1). Note that the attacker aims to modify the APKs such that the final report (denoted 5 in Fig. 1) will label the malicious APKs as benign and the accuracy rate will be lower than the initial accuracy rate. While doing so, it verifies the malicious behavior of the APKs.

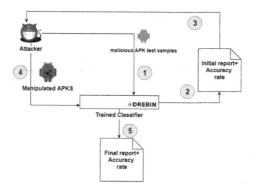

Fig. 1. Attacker model. The attacker sends malicious APKs as input to the classifier (1). The classifier produces an initial report and an accuracy rate (2). The attacker receives the output report (3), manipulates the APKs and sends them as a second input to the classifier (4). Finally, the classifier produces a final report and an accuracy rate (5).

4.2   Attack Description

Given malicious APKs to manipulate, and the observations from Drebin, the attacker attempts to conceal the appearance of the observations obtained from the classifier, while still using them to activate the malicious content. It depackages each APK into its subordinate files. We describe the attack in two stages. The input for the first stage is a string. It can resemble a URL address or an API call.

1. **First stage - Encoding:** The attacker analyzes Drebin's observations. It searches for strings in the smali code that are included in the report. The attacker replaces the string with its base64 encoding. It stores the encoded string in the variable of the previous string. Then, the attacker runs a decode function to translate the encoded string back to its previous representation. It stores the decoded string in the previous variable of the string.
2. **Second stage - Reflection:** This stage is only pertinent to encoded strings that resemble an API call, since strings that resemble a URL skip this stage. In this stage, the attacker creates a reflection call. The reflection call creates a general object with the target object from the API call. The next step is invoking the general object with the specific method name from the API call.

5   Results

We evaluated the effectiveness of our attack and the metrics from Sect. 3. We used ~75 K benign apps and ~32 K malicious apps (for more details on the source of our data, see Sect. 3). In order to account for a realizable ratio between benign and malicious files [15], we used a proportion of 90/10 between benign and malicious apps in our evaluation. Because we had more malicious apps than one-tenth of the benign apps', we randomly split the malicious data into 5 parts and use the whole benign dataset with each part separately.

In addition, we used a ratio of 80/20 between the train and test data. We did not use the benign samples of the test data while assessing the attack's evasion rate. Overall, we used ~60 k benign apps and ~25 k malicious apps as train data, and ~6 k malicious apps as test data. To account for variations in the data, we used 5-fold CV.

5.1   Evasion Robustness

To get a clearer view of the evasion robustness, we evaluated two cases: the original apps and the evasion attack apps. Any app that triggered an error in the evasion attack's construction was not included in the manipulated test data. Some of the errors we encountered were a result of corrupted APKs that we could not depackage or repackage. Other errors were a consequence of faults in the manipulation process. Overall, the error rate did not exceed 10% of the test data. The results are summarized in Table 1. This table documents the number of malicious apps in each case and the accuracy rate (including the standard deviation). Because the standard deviation was marginal (i.e., <0.02), the evasion robustness rate in each of the splits is similar.

Table 1. Evasion robustness for each case

	Number of applications	Evasion robustness (SD)
Original	6327	0.964 (0.009)
Evasion attack	5817	0.84 (0.012)

5.2   Functionality and Maliciousness Tests

As stated in Sect. 3, our goal was to test whether our evasion attack would damage the functionality and maliciousness of the previous Android malware. We implemented the functionality test on our apps in an emulator using Pixel 2 XL image with SDK 27. We implemented a functionality test on each app before the manipulation (see Sect. 4.2) and after it. For each app, our functionality test was implemented as follows: (1) Cleaning of the emulator log; (2) Installation of the app; (3) Running the app for 1 second; (4) Termination of the app; (5) Uninstallation of the app; (6) Inspection of the emulator log for crashes. We removed ~28% of the apps that were old or faulty, which led to an interesting insight. Before our evasion attack, 90% of the apps did not crash. After our attack, only 18% of the apps did not crash. Although a nonfunctional app does not attack the user who runs it, we implemented the maliciousness test (see Sect. 3) on the evasion attack apps. After the manipulation, 0.06% of the apps were identified by an equal number of scanners, and 0.1% apps were identified by more scanners than before the manipulation. 99.8% of the apps were identified by a smaller number of scanners than before the manipulation, thus resulting in an increase of ∼9.5 scanners, on average, that did not identify the manipulated apps. While the evasion attack proved to be malicious and decreased the accuracy rate of Drebin, it constitutes a minor threat to the Android user community due to the low level of functionality.

6 Discussion and Conclusion

In this study, we suggested the inclusion of functionality and maliciousness tests in the evaluation of manipulated apps. In addition, we proposed a novel evasion attack that achieved a 12% evasion rate. The maliciousness test we implemented proved that the evasion attack's apps maintained high malicious value, with an additional ∼9.5 VT scanners on average that did not recognize the apps as malicious. However, our functionality test proved that the generated apps' functionality suffered a tremendous loss, from 90% functional apps to 18% functional apps. In a classic analysis, such an attack was considered very powerful and dangerous, and may even result in a urgent update of the classifier. In contrast, the methodology we present proves that the defender has no reason to take steps in the face of such an attack, because its output is deficient in the functional side. To the best of our knowledge, this is the first study to consider these tests for the Android evasion attacks domain. We suggest future works based on our methodology to engineer sophisticated and efficient attacks against well known Android malware detection systems. While doing so, the authors should make sure to maintain high levels of both functionality and maliciousness activity.

Acknowledgement. This work was supported by the Ariel Cyber Innovation Center in conjunction with the Israel National Cyber directorate in the Prime Minister's Office.

References

1. Allix, K., Bissyandé, T.F., Klein, J., Le Traon, Y.: Androzoo: collecting millions of android apps for the research community. In: Proceedings of the 13th International Conference on Mining Software Repositories, MSR 2016, pp. 468–471 (2016)
2. Arp, D.: Drebin implementation. github (2014). https://github.com/MLDroid/drebin/
3. Arp, D., Spreitzenbarth, M., Hubner, M., Gascon, H., Rieck, K., Siemens, C.: Drebin: effective and explainable detection of android malware in your pocket. In: NDSS, vol. 14, pp. 23–26 (2014)
4. Chen, S., Xue, M., Tang, Z., Xu, L., Zhu, H.: Stormdroid: a streaminglized machine learning-based system for detecting android malware. In: Proceedings of the 11th ACM on Asia Conference on Computer and Communications Security, pp. 377–388. ACM (2016)
5. Chen, X., et al.: Android HIV: a study of repackaging malware for evading machine-learning detection. IEEE Trans. Inf. Forensics Secur. **15**, 987–1001 (2019)
6. Demontis, A., et al.: Yes, machine learning can be more secure! a case study on android malware detection. IEEE Trans. Dependable Secure Comput. **16**(4), 711–724 (2017)

7. Goodfellow, I.J., Shlens, J., Szegedy, C.: Explaining and harnessing adversarial examples. arXiv preprint arXiv:1412.6572 (2014)
8. Google: GooglePlay app market. GooglePlay website (2008). https://play.google.com/store/apps/
9. Google: Android Security 2017 Year In Review. Google website (2017). https://source.android.com/security/reports/Google_Android_Security_2017_Report_Final.pdf
10. Google: Run apps on the Android Emulator. Google developers website (2019). https://developer.android.com/studio/run/emulator
11. Ikram, M., Beaume, P., Kaafar, M.A.: Dadidroid: An obfuscation resilient tool for detecting android malware via weighted directed call graph modelling. arXiv preprint arXiv:1905.09136 (2019)
12. Lashkari, A.H., Kadir, A.F.A., Taheri, L., Ghorbani, A.A.: Toward developing a systematic approach to generate benchmark android malware datasets and classification. In: International Conference on Security Technology, pp. 1–7 (2018)
13. Lindorfer, M.: AndRadar: fast discovery of android applications in alternative markets. In: Dietrich, S. (ed.) DIMVA 2014. LNCS, vol. 8550, pp. 51–71. Springer, Cham (2014). https://doi.org/10.1007/978-3-319-08509-8_4
14. Onwuzurike, L., Mariconti, E., Andriotis, P., Cristofaro, E.D., Ross, G., Stringhini, G.: Mamadroid: detecting android malware by building markov chains of behavioral models. Trans. Privacy Secur. **22**(2), 14 (2019)
15. Pendlebury, F., Pierazzi, F., Jordaney, R., Kinder, J., Cavallaro, L.: {TESSERACT}: Eliminating experimental bias in malware classification across space and time. In: 28th Security Symposium Security, vol. 19. pp. 729–746 (2019)
16. Rastogi, V., Chen, Y., Jiang, X.: Droid chameleon: evaluating android anti-malware against transformation attacks. In: ACM Symposium on Information, Computer and Communications Security, pp. 329–334. ACM (2013)
17. Salem, A.: Droidutan the android orangutan is a smart monkey that analyzes and tests android applications. https://github.com/aleisalem/Droidutan (2018)
18. Salem, A., Paulus, F.F., Pretschner, A.: Repackman: a tool for automatic repackaging of android apps. In: Proceedings of the 1st International Workshop on Advances in Mobile App Analysis, pp. 25–28. ACM (2018)
19. Shabtai, A., Kanonov, U., Elovici, Y., Glezer, C., Weiss, Y.: "andromaly": a behavioral malware detection framework for android devices. J. Intell. Inf. Syst. **38**(1), 161–190 (2012)
20. Tong, L., Li, B., Hajaj, C., Xiao, C., Zhang, N., Vorobeychik, Y.: Improving robustness of {ML} classifiers against realizable evasion attacks using conserved features. In: 28th Security Symposium Security (19), pp. 285–302 (2019)
21. Total, V.: Virustotal-free online virus, malware and url scanner (2012). https://www.virustotal.com/en
22. Wei, F., Li, Y., Roy, S., Ou, X., Zhou, W.: Deep ground truth analysis of current android malware. In: International Conference on Detection of Intrusions and Malware, and Vulnerability Assessment, pp. 252–276 (2017)

Toward Self-stabilizing Blockchain, Reconstructing Totally Erased Blockchain (Preliminary Version)

Shlomi Dolev and Matan Liber(✉)

Department of Computer Science, Ben-Gurion University of the Negev, Beersheba, Israel
dolev@cs.bgu.ac.il, matanli@post.bgu.ac.il

Abstract. Blockchains, that are essentially distributed public ledgers, are extremely popular nowadays and are being used for many applications. One of the more common uses is for crypto-currencies, where they serve as a structure to store all the transactions publicly, securely, and hopefully irreversibly. Blockchains can be permissionless, where everyone can join and potentially contribute the blockchain, and permissioned, where only a few members (usually, much less than a permissionless blockchain) can push new transactions to the chain. While both approaches have their advantages and disadvantages, we will focus on a weakness of permissioned blockchains. The known boundary on the number of faulty participants − up to f for $3f + 1$ participants − may be surpassed, causing the BFT algorithm to fail. A situation where a malicious adversary compromises/corrupts enough nodes to harm the blockchain may lead to the complete corruption of the ledger and even to the destruction of ledger copies the nodes hold. We will suggest a solution for the reconstruction of the blockchain in the event of such an attack. Our solution will include a mandatory publication of additional information by the private users when submitting transactions and will require them to store their transaction history. We will present a technique, using verifiable secret sharing (VSS), that will make our solution trust-less, immediate and per-user independent. Our technique will prevent the private user from lying, by making such an act enable the possible exposure of the user's secret key.

Keywords: Self-stabilization · Blockchain · Public threshold commitment

1 Introduction

Since the introduction of blockchains [16] they are widely in use. As a public ledger, the blockchain can be viewed by all of the participants, and after a new

We thank the Lynne and William Frankel Center for Computer Science, the Rita Altura Trust Chair in Computer Science. This research was also supported by a grant from the Ministry of Science & Technology, Israel & the Japan Science and Technology Agency (JST), Japan, and DFG German-Israeli collaborative projects.

© Springer Nature Switzerland AG 2020
S. Dolev et al. (Eds.): CSCML 2020, LNCS 12161, pp. 175–192, 2020.
https://doi.org/10.1007/978-3-030-49785-9_12

block is added, it should be hard to revert the change. A new block is usually added after the nodes perform a BFT (Byzantine Fault Tolerance) consensus algorithm [15] and decide upon a new block to add. The BFT algorithm is used to prevent bad blocks from being added to the blockchain, as long as less than f members are malicious, where $3f + 1$ is the total number of members [17]. This keeps the blockchain trust-able when only some members are malicious at any given time (because they were bad members to begin with, or because they are good members that were taken over temporarily by an adversary). The bound f on the maximal number of Byzantine participants [17] is common knowledge and an obvious target for the adversary. Given the assumption that the adversary can compromise several participants, the adversary will surely be motivated to compromise more than the known number the system can tolerate.

Blockchain Types. In the case of permissionless blockchains, there are many members and every time a new block is to be added, only a few are selected to participate in the BFT algorithm and decide upon the new block [14]. In the permissioned case, there are fewer members and usually, they all participate in the BFT algorithm and only the leader of the BFT may change from block to block [5,19]. In those cases, it is assumed that the members are not malicious to begin with (if each member is a big company, like a bank, it is unlikely that the members will risk their reputation by deviating from the protocol on purpose), but may be overtaken by an adversary from time to time, until control over them is restored (a software/state update that fixes a security bug that exposed the nodes to attacks, see e.g., [2,4,8,9]). When the blockchain is permissioned, only the permissioned members directly contribute to the ledger. Although unpermissioned participants (private wallets) can view the state of the blockchain and ask to add transactions through queries to the members, the ledger is run by, and kept at, the members' databases.

This centralization has its advantages, such as trust efficiency in processing transactions, while still enjoying the accumulated trust in the participating companies; companies that act as the operators of the blockchain. Permissioned blockchains are also more resilient to Sybil attacks, since new private users are usually checked (bank clients, businesses in a managed supply chain, etc.), so creating many pseudonymous identities is hard. Moreover, since the private users have no voting power in the BFT algorithm, an adversary holding many private users has very limited control of the ledger. Forging identities of permissioned nodes is even more unlikely, since there is a fixed (or a mostly constant) number of nodes participating in the blockchain management, each one representing a company or a server, with a known and published corresponding public key, i.e., new permissioned parties most certainly cannot be created in large numbers.

In such scenarios, where few delegated nodes control the blockchain, and the other private participants are only clients of the blockchain, the only important copies of the ledger are those in the databases of the permissioned members since new blocks will be added to the blockchain only if they comply with those copies.

Weakness of Permissioned Blockchains. This system, of a server-client like relationship, where the center of power lies at the member nodes, is of course, vulnerable to many types of attacks. Permissioned blockchain usually consists of a small number of nodes, thus surpassing the bound f does not require an adversary to compromise many members. In those cases, the blockchain is vulnerable to undesired changes, illegal transactions and forks. If an adversary successfully overtakes the blockchain, it may prevent transaction approvals, thus stopping the regular operating of the services relying on the blockchain (bank transactions, etc.). The adversary may even eliminate records of past transactions, enabling double-spending. In an extreme (yet possible) case of an attack, all of those permissioned members can be attacked, and their databases can be destroyed or get severely damaged. The goal of the attack in this case is obvious, to destroy the blockchain, by deleting all the ledger copies. Those attacks may lead to important information held in the ledger getting lost, thus harming both the managing parties of the blockchain and the end-users.

Trustless Restoration Solution. The solution we propose, where the ledger is reconstructed from information held at the private users, may be used by the administrators of the blockchain to ensure self-stability and a promise for the clients that their balances will not be deleted, even in cases of such severe attacks. We ask to only save information of transactions where the user is the payer or the payee, i.e., the user is involved in. The restoration of the user's balance will depend only on the user presenting the relevant information to the permissioned members. At any given time, the nodes may decide to perform a BFT consensus algorithm over a *reconstructing transaction* submitted by a user to decide if reconstruction is needed and publish a call to the users. Another possibility for initiating a reconstruction is a situation where a node did retain a valid copy of the ledger after an attack, but other nodes do not hold a valid copy (or any copy). This inconsistency will surely lead to (and be detected by) problems in the performing of the BFT algorithm. I those cases a node may also suggest a reconstruction.

If the user acts honestly, the user's balance may be restored immediately after, without the need for any other users to act and share information. We enforce the users to be honest concerning the (last) sequence of their transactions, by a technique that exposes their private key if a suffix of the sequence is hidden. This will also ensure that the blockchain can be gradually reconstructed, wallet by wallet, and there will be no need for a global and finite time period for users to restore their wallet balances. As far as we know, we are the first to address this issue, and the solutions we present for the trustless restoration may be applied in other scopes as well.

The rest of the paper is structured as follows: In Sect. 2, we will describe the system that we work with, the relationship between the permissioned nodes and the private users, and some general characteristics of the BFT algorithm used. In Sect. 3, we will describe a general solution that uses this system, which requires the users to publish additional data alongside their transactions and ensures that the private users keep the necessary information during the regular flow of the blockchain for later reconstruction after a full wipeout attack. In Sect. 4, we will introduce the conditions that such data must meet, which will enable trustless proof of currentness when the permissioned members of the blockchain want to restore the balances of the wallets after the deletion of their databases. In Sect. 5, we will show how using verifiable secret sharing (VSS), one can generate such data that meets those requirements when an appropriate digital signature scheme is used in the blockchain. In Sect. 6, we will present the formal protocols for both submitting a transaction request and for restoring a user's balance in the reconstructing phase, as well as address how to continue after a restoration. Finally, in Sect. 7, we will conclude the general ideas introduced in this paper and where else they can be applied. Due to page limitations many details are excluded from this preliminary version.

2 Preliminaries

The Blockchain Settings. We will discuss blockchains run by a few permissioned members (nodes). Those nodes collect transactions submitted by users to be added to the blockchain. They run a BFT consensus algorithm that may be led by a different node every time, to decide which transaction to accept and add to the blockchain. During the execution of the algorithm, the nodes validate the transactions by checking their structure, by verifying that the wallet's current balance can support such transaction, and by validating their signature. After the nodes vote and accept a new block, the algorithm outputs a collective signature on the new ledger state, and this signature can be used by the users to trust the blockchain's state [1]. The private user accesses the blockchain through a permissioned node, for both submitting a transaction and for querying the state of the blockchain. We assume that the public ledger is stored in such a way, that all of the past transactions, their order, and the nodes signature on them, are accessible, and thus, can be queried and stored by the user.

Using Digital Signatures. A new user generates a secret/public key pair (s, y), where s is used by the user to sign transactions and y is used by the permissioned members or other users to verify those signatures [7]. The key pair is generated for a chosen signature scheme and is used to ensure that no other user can perform transactions on behalf of this wallet. By using the secret/public key digital signature scheme, we assume both users and nodes have their public keys published off-chain (not in the ledger itself), thus will not be deleted even in case of complete deletion of the ledger copies. This is important for the reconstruction phase, where the nodes will be presented with transactions approved and signed by them in the past, and with some data proving that a transaction history of a user is up-to-date. The public keys must still be accessible by the nodes to make sure all of this data was not forged, and for the nodes to be able to acknowledge their past signings.

3 Transaction Requests Submission and Balance Restoration

In case of complete deletion of the databases of the permissioned members, we would like the users to have enough information to enable the nodes to restore their wallet balance. Users will keep information on transactions they participated in, meaning transactions they created for paying other users, and transactions where they were paid, i.e., created by the paying user. All of the transactions are of course saved alongside the nodes' collective signature on them. By saving all of this information and later presenting the information to the nodes, a user will be able to prove its current balance since the entire history of payments and incomes is submitted. We must address the problem of users presenting only a partial history to the nodes, for example, hiding some big payments they made, and taking advantage of the fact that the nodes have no valid records of the blockchain history (or no records at all) after the attack.

Requirements for a Solution. To solve this problem we must ensure that (1) the user will present an ordered history of its transactions, where the transactions are of an increasing index, without a single index skipped from the first transaction to the most current one, and (2) that the last transaction in this ordered history is indeed the most up-to-date, meaning no suffix of the history is omitted by the user. Regarding requirement (2), it can be claimed that if a user chooses to hide a suffix of the transaction history, probably some lawn made by the user to other users, the other users will expose this dishonest behavior by presenting the transaction (a transaction where there transfer money) when they will come forward to restore their balance. In this case, a way to settle the arising dispute may be using digital arbitrators [12], possibly other users with high reputation, who have records of the ledger as well. We aim for trustless, per-user independent and immediate method, to restore the balances. Since both relying on other users to expose dishonest behaviors and using trust-able arbitrators to restore a user's balance violate those goals, we have to find other solutions.

To meet requirement (1), meaning a user can and must preset an ordered history of its transactions without any transaction omitted when coming to restore its balance, we will introduce a general protocol to be followed by the users and the nodes during the regular flow of the blockchain. The goal of this protocol is to ensure that the nodes indeed accept and sign every transaction kept in the user's history database. We will also force the user to publish some additional data with every submitted transaction request. This data, together with proof that the user will have to publish when the balance is to be restored, will make sure requirement (2) is met. This will enable the nodes to later accept the history presented by the user to them, as valid proof for the user's transactions, and therefore its current balance. We will use a linked-list as a database for the user to keep a payment transactions "backup" (payments linked list – PLL), and another one to keep the transactions of payments received (incomes linked list – ILL). We will assume users have no incentive to hide transactions that increases their balance, namely, transactions in which they were paid and will make sure the users do not hide any transaction in which they paid others. Every user will have a current transaction number i that will increase with every transaction request submitted, approved by the nodes and added to the blockchain. The nodes will also keep track of this index for every user, so that they can validate that when a user submits a transaction request, it is of the current index i.

Additional Submitted Data. For every transaction, T_i, the user wants to submit, additional information D_i will be added. This means that the user requests $R_i = (T_i, D_i)$ to be added to the blockchain. The nodes will check that R_i is valid, meaning T_i can be made by the user and that D_i corresponds to the latest index i of the user and is of a correct form. If all conditions are met and the nodes indeed approve, sign and add R_i to the blockchain, then they increase the index they keep for that user to $i + 1$. Then the user itself should check whether its transaction was approved and add R_i and the collective signature of the nodes on it to its PLL, as well as increase the transaction requests index. When the user wishes to do so, probably before submitting transactions, the user will query the nodes for the state of the blockchain and will check for any transactions where it was paid and add them to the ILL. Checking for such income transactions will let the user know its current balance, and adding them to the ILL will be useful when coming to restore the balance.

Restoration Process. When coming to restore the wallet's balance, the user will present its PLL and ILL to the nodes, thus enabling them to verify that the history shown to them is indeed complete, and was approved and signed by them in the past. To make sure that the history is unaltered, an additional proof will be published, so that, if a user claims that $R_m = (T_m, D_m)$ is the last request submitted and approved, the user will also have to supply a proof P_m. The data and proof are structured in such a way, that a user will have the incentive to be honest and not try to claim that $R_{m'}$ was the last request and publishing $P_{m'}$ when $m > m'$ is the actual most current transaction index.

4   Enforcing Current Balance Reveal

The Problem. We describe a scenario, where we have a player A that holds a secret key s and a public key y. The player publishes a series of data D_i to a group C of computationally limited players. At some point ($i = m$, meaning D_m was the last data published), the player needs to prove to a third party B, that may have invalid records or no records of the D_i, that m is indeed the most current index of data that was published, by publishing both the data history up to D_m and some proof P_m. A knows this point of time may come, and A may want to cheat by proving that $m' < m$ is the most current index of data that was published. A may do so by publishing the history up to $D_{m'}$ and a corresponding proof $P_{m'}$.

In our case, A is the user that wants to restore the wallet's balance. C is the group of other private users that can view and store any data A publishes. B is a node presented with A's history and needs to be able to accept what is published and restore A's crypto-currency wallet balance. B was attacked, i.e., B cannot trust the ledger, possibly due to the fact that all records of the public ledger have been destroyed, so B has invalid records or no records of the D_i. The data D_i is the additional data that A is required by the protocol to add to any of the transaction requests. Finally, P_i is a proof that A will have to publish to claim that R_i is the most current one submitted. The incentive of A to claim m' as the most current index of data published is clear, since requests $R_{m'+1}, ..., R_m$ may contain payments A made and wants to be forgotten so that A can double spend the crypto-currency (Fig. 1).

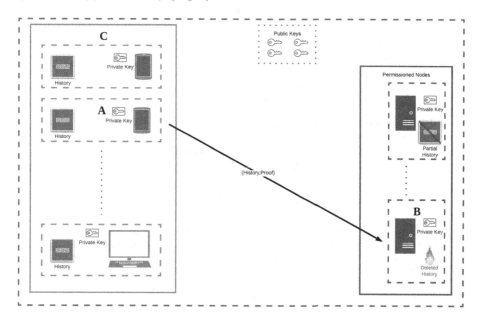

Fig. 1. C is the group of private users, that may have recorded some of the ledger's history, including A transactions. B is a permissioned node with deleted ledger copies. A sends the history and proof the history is up-to-date to B. The private key and history are directly accessible only by their holder and the public keys of all parties are accessible by everyone.

Conditions for a Solution. We will introduce some conditions on D_i and P_i:

(a) Only A, the holder of s, can generate D_i, P_i, for every $i \in \mathbb{N}$.
(b) By viewing $H(m) = \{D_i | 1 \leq i \leq m\} \cup P_m$, a player $c \in C$ learns no additional information on s.
(c) If a player c knows $H(m) \cup P_{m'}$ for some $m' < m$, then it can recover s.
(d) For every $i \in \mathbb{N}$, it can be verified that a data D_i or a proof P_i are valid.[1]

---

[1] By valid we mean they were generated by A and will indeed enable a player c to recover s if A did not act honestly.

Condition (a) is necessary to ensure that the data and proof were indeed generated by A, thus allowing the nodes to accept requests, knowing A is the real source of them. Furthermore, when the reconstructing process is taking place, the nodes can be certain that A is the one trying to restore that balance. To make the publication of the additional data D_i and the proof P_i are safe for an honest user, we must ensure no information about s is leaked if one does not try to hide parts of its history. If m is the most current index of transactions an honest user A submitted before the wipeout attack, it has published $\bar{H}(m) = \{D_i | 1 \leq i \leq m\}$ when the blockchain was alive and P_m when it tried to restore its balance. The total information it published is $H(m)$, and again, we do not want the honest user to be at risk, hence condition (b) is necessary.

The main idea behind our suggestion lies in condition (c) since we want to solve the problem of users hiding suffix of their transaction history. In our case, try to prove $R_{m'} = (T_{m'}, D_{m'})$ is their most current request submitted and approved by publishing $P_{m'}$ for some $m' < m$ where R_m is the actual most current approved request. This condition should deprive A of acting this way, by putting s at risk if it does. If all of the users know that condition (c) holds then we expect users to act honestly since they know other users, that may have stored their entire publishing history, will learn their secret key s if they decide to misbehave. Then, those users may use s as they wish (for example, transfer all of the wallet's crypto-currency to their own wallet). If the nodes know that condition (c) holds, it should help them accept the information presented by the user in the reconstruction phase as legitimate, and restore the claimed balance, since they know the user will have put the secret key to its wallet at risk otherwise. This idea, of one revealing its own secret key in case of misbehavior, is similar to [3,13].

Condition (d) is required for the nodes to be able to verify any request a user submits. If it is impossible to determine whether D_i and P_i are valid, a user may publish additional information and proof that compromises condition (c). Then the user will be able to publish a proof of any transaction index and hide the transactions history suffix, thus restoring a greater balance than deserved.

By embedding data that meets all of those conditions into the transaction requests and proofs, we will be able to achieve our desired goal, of trust-less and immediate restoration of a user's balance, in an independent way, i.e., that does not rely on other participants of the blockchain, thus proving those conditions are sufficient.

5   Verifiable Secret Public Sharing

Shamir [18] introduced Shamir's secret sharing (SSS) as a method to divide a secret into parts (shares), which are generated by the secret owner (dealer), and distributed amongst a group of participants (shareholders). In a (t, n)-threshold (t-out-of-n) secret sharing scheme, n participants, each holding a share, can reconstruct the secret only if t or more of them combine their shares. Moreover, any group of strictly less than t shareholders, learn nothing about the secret.

Verifiable secret sharing (VSS) was introduced by Chor, Goldwasser, Micali and Awerbuch [6], as a secret sharing scheme where every participant can verify that secret shares are consistent. This is important for preventing a malicious dealer from sending shares to different participants, which do not define a (single) secret.

In our use of VSS, the dealer does not deal shares to individual shareholders, but rather publishes them by including them in the D_i it appends to the transactions it wishes to submit. This means, that after a user A submits a request $R_i = (T_i, D_i)$ for a transaction, and the nodes approve it, some shares of the wallet's secret key s are published on the blockchain. The main idea is, that for every transaction, the user A generates three shares of the secret for a 3-out-of-3 verifiable secret sharing scheme, and publishes one to the blockchain. If A is honest, at no given point in time, all three of those shares will be published, so if the scheme is secure, no additional information about s is leaked. However, for a A to try and hide a suffix of its transaction history, it will imply revealing all three shares of a single 3-out-of-3 verifiable secret sharing scheme shares generation. By displaying some $R_{m'} = (T_{m'}, D_{m'})$ as its most current request, combined with the publishing of $P_{m'}$, its secret key s will be reconstructable. If a different user $c \in C$ was to save both $D_{m'}$ and $D_{m'+1}$ (that exists since m' is not the most up-to-date index of transactions that A submitted) from the blockchain, then by seeing $P_{m'}$ as well, c will have three shares of s, one share from each data piece.

It is important to note that it is indeed required to be able to verify that the shares correspond to s, since otherwise, A may use this weakness, publish some random shares, and will have nothing to hold it back from presenting any prefix of the transaction history to the nodes after they lost their ledger records.

5.1 Digital Signature

Digital signatures [7] are used to verify the authenticity of digital messages, that is, to know with a high level of certainty, that a digital message was created by a known sender and was not altered in any way. In our scenario, they are used by the nodes, to sign transactions as approved to be published on the blockchain. This makes it possible for private users to verify their transaction was accepted and makes it impossible for the nodes to claim they did not approve a specific transaction. The users use digital signatures when signing the transactions submitted. This allows both other users and the nodes to be certain that a transaction request was submitted by the real owner of the wallet, i.e., the real owner of the secret key.

Digital signatures use asymmetric cryptography, where the signer has a secret signing key for signing messages, and a respective published public key, to be used by the recipient of the signed message, to verify the message origin and integrity. This also applies to our scenario, where we assume the public keys of every user and all the permissioned members are published and are not compromised, even if the databases that hold the public ledger are attacked. Those schemes usually consist of a *key generation* algorithm, that outputs a random secret key s and a corresponding public key y, a *signing* algorithm, that given a message to sign and a secret key outputs a signature on the message, and a *signature verification* algorithm, that given a message, a signature, and a public key accepts only if the signature is indeed the output of *signing* on the supplied message with the corresponding secret key as an input, with high probability.

We will use the Digital Signature Algorithm (DSA) [11] as a digital signature scheme, which is based on the mathematical concepts of modular exponentiation and the discrete logarithm problem. DSA uses several global parameters for digital signing:

1. A prime modulus p.
2. A prime divisor of $(p-1)$, q, of bit length N.
3. A generator g of a subgroup of order q in the multiplicative group of $GF(p)$, such that $1 < g < p$.
4. A hash function h with an output block bit length of *outlen*.

Nodes (when the blockchain is created) and new users (when joining the blockchain) will invoke DSA_Key_Gen, i.e., will randomly or pseudorandomly generate a secret key s, such that $0 < s < q$, i.e, s is in the range $[1, q-1]$. The corresponding public key published is $y = g^s \bmod p$ for a total DSA key pair of (s, y). One can sign a given message m using DSA_s. Verification of signatures, that require the message, the signature and the public key of the signer, can be achieved using DSA_Verify^2.

5.2   Verifiable Secret Sharing Scheme

We will introduce a suggestion based on the ideas of [6, 10, 18], for the structure of D_i and P_i, that combined with DSA as a digital signature scheme, will meet all of the four conditions described in Sect. 4, and enable us to force the reveal of the current balance by the user.

An (t, n)-threshold secret sharing scheme, consists of a probabilistic polynomial-time algorithm (PPTA) $Share_G$ and a polynomial-time algorithm (PTA) $Recover_G$, for some global parameters G. The global parameters G will be clear from the context so we will drop G from the notation. The algorithm $Share(s) \rightarrow \{(1, s_1), (2, s_2), \ldots, (n, s_n)\} = S(s)$ takes a secret key s as an input and outputs n shares $(1, s_1), (2, s_2), \ldots, (j, s_j), \ldots, (n, s_n)$ where j is the share's index and s_j is the share's value. The algorithms $Recover((a_1, s_{a_1}), (a_2, s_{a_2}), \ldots, (a_t, s_{a_t})) \rightarrow s$ takes as an input any t valid distinct shares with share indices $\{a_1, \ldots, a_t\} \subseteq [1, n]$ and outputs the original secret s. Formally,

$$\forall s.Share(s) \rightarrow S(s) \implies \forall T' \in \{T \subseteq S(s) |\ |T| = t\}, Recover(T') = s$$

We will use a $(3, 3)$-threshold secret sharing scheme, or a 3-out-of-3 scheme, in our construction of D_i and P_i, i.e., $Share(s)$ generated three shares of s, and all three

---

[2] See [11] for full details about random or pseudorandom integer generation and for formal definitions of DSA_s and DSA_Verify.

are required to reconstruct s. We will use p, q, g and h as defined by DSA as the global parameters G. To create the shares of a given s, the user will randomly or pseudorandomly generate two integers c_1 and c_2 such that $0 < c_1, c_2 < q$. Those integers, that should be kept as a secret by the user, together with s itself, will define a polynomial $Pol(x) = s + c_1 x + c_2 x^2$. In respect to $Pol(x)$, the ith share of s is $s(i) = (i, Pol(i) \bmod q) = (i, s + c_1 i + c_2 i^2 \bmod q)$. The $Recovery$ algorithm takes t shares, and performs polynomial interpolation [18], to eventually find $Pol(0) = s$.

This scheme is secure[3] since every two or less distinct shares look just like random points, yet three shares uniquely define the polynomial $Pol(x)$. To make this scheme verifiable, we will introduce two additional PTAs. $Commit(c) \to C$ that takes a coefficient generated by the user and outputs a commit C for it, and $Verify(s(i), C_1, C_2, y) \to res \in \{ACCEPT, REJECT\}$ that takes a share, commits for both of the polynomial's coefficients, and the public key of the user, and ACCEPTs if the share is valid or REJECTs otherwise. We will define:

- $Commit(c) = g^c \bmod p$
- $Verify((i, s_i), C_1, C_2, y) = \text{ACCEPT} \iff g^{s_i} \bmod p = g^{s + c_1 i + c_2 i^2 \bmod q} = g^s \cdot (g^{c_1})^i \cdot (g^{c_2})^{i^2} = y \cdot C_1^i \cdot C_2^{i^2} \bmod p$

Corollary 1. *If $Verify((i, s_i), C_1, C_2, y)$ returns $ACCEPT$, the verifier knows that with high probability $s_i = Pol(i) \bmod q$ and that s is the free coefficient of Pol.*

5.3 Data and Proof Structure

Now, after defining the digital signature scheme and the verifiable secret sharing scheme, we may suggest a structure for D_i and P_i. For each user, the public parameters of p, q, g and h, as well as the public key y, will be published and known by both the nodes and the other private users. For the ith transaction, the user will randomly or pseudorandomly generate c_{i1} and c_{i2} as described in our proposed VSS scheme. Those will define the polynomial $Pol_i(x) = s + c_{i1} x + c_{i2} x^2$. We will define $C_{ij} = g^{c_{ij}} \bmod p$ as the commit for the jth coefficient of $Pol_i(x)$, and $s_i(j) = (j, Pol_i(j) \bmod q)$ as the jth share of s regarding the polynomial $Pol_i(x)$. The additional data that will be added to the transaction T_i to create the request $R_i = (T_i, D_i)$, and the proof to be published to claim R_i is the most current request will be:

- $D_i = (s_i(1), s_{i-1}(2), C_{i1}, C_{i2}, C_{(i-1)1}, C_{(i-1)2})$ [4]
- $P_i = (s_i(v), C_{i1}, C_{i2})$, where $2 \leq v \leq q - 1$ is a random value

So D_i will contain the first share and commitments regarding the current polynomial and the second share and commitments regarding the previous polynomial (the same commitments published in D_{i-1}). P_i will contain a share with an random index $2 \leq v \leq q - 1$ and the commitments regarding the current polynomial

---

[3] For a full proof of the scheme security see [18].
[4] $D_1 = (s_1(1), C_{11}, C_{12})$.

(the same commitments published in D_i). We will discuss the importance of v in Sect. 6.2.

Theorem 1. *The suggested structure for D_i and P_i meets all four conditions defined in Sect. 4.*

Proof Sketch. Since both D_i and P_i contain shares of a user's secret key s, only the user can generate them, so condition (a) is met. If a user is honest, it will only publish $H(m) = \{D_i | 1 \leq i \leq m\} \cup P_m$ where m is the index of the latest request it submitted, before the nodes were attacked. This means, that even if a different user c kept all of $H(m)$, c knows only $s_i(1)$ from D_i and $s_i(2)$ from D_{i+1} for $1 \leq i \leq m - 1$. Regarding the last index m, c knows only $s_m(1)$ from D_m and $s_m(v)$ from P_m. In total, c does not hold more than two shares for any given index $1 \leq i \leq m$. The commitments $C_{ij} = g^{c_{ij}}$ also does not add any additional information about s, so no information about s is leaked beyond what is implied from $y = g^s$, hence condition (b) is met (due to page limitation, the full security details are omitted from this preliminary version).

If a user is not honest, i.e., although the published history is $\bar{H}(m) = \{D_i | 1 \leq i \leq m\}$, the user decides to publish a proof $P_{m'}$ for some $m' < m$, then a different user c that kept $\bar{H}(m)$ and sees the published $P_{m'}$ knows $s_{m'}(1)$ from $D_{m'} \in \bar{H}(m)$, $s_{m'}(2)$ from $D_{m'+1} \in \bar{H}(m)$ (again, since $m' < m$, $D_{m'+1}$ was published), and $s_{m'}(v)$ from $P_{m'}$. Condition (c) is met since those three shares put together, can be used as an inputs for *Recovery* to reconstruct s. The final condition (d) is met since D_i contains enough information to validate it was generated by the holder of s and that the shares indeed correspond to s by running $Verify(s_i(1), C_{i1}, C_{i2}, y)$ and $Verify(s_{i-1}(2), C_{(i-1)1}, C_{(i-1)2}, y)$ and check that both return ACCEPT. The same can be done regarding P_i by running $Verify(s_i(v), C_{i1}, C_{i2}, y)$. □

6 Transaction Requests Submission and Balance Restoration Protocols

Now, that we have structured D_i and P_i in a way that meets all of the conditions to enforce a user to reveal the real transactions history, i.e., ask to restore its real balance before the permissioned participants were attacked, we may present the full protocols to be followed by both the users and the nodes.

6.1 Request Submission

First, we introduce the protocol for the submission process of a request by a user, and its validation by the nodes, before adding it to the blockchain. We assume accessibility to the public keys and the corresponding DSA domain parameters p, q, g and h of the participants.

The Protocol. The user constructs a request and submits it to a node using Submit_To_Node() (lines 1.a–1.j). The node verifies the DSA signature on the transaction using DSA_Verify(), the validity of the transaction itself (that the transaction is between existing wallets, that the payer has sufficient balance, or any other requirements of the specific blockchain) using Transaction_Verify() and then verifies the shares using Verify() (lines 2.a–2.d.iii). If the transaction verification passes, the node will add it to the pool of pending requests by using Add_To_Requests_Pool() (line 2.e.i). Then, the nodes perform the BFT algorithm and the request may be accepted and published on the ledger.

The user will be able to query the state of the blockchain and see if the request was indeed published using Check_Request_Accepted() (line 4.a). The user will get the nodes' collective signature on the transaction from the blockchain using Get_Nodes_Signature() and will add both the request and the signature to the PLL using Add_To_PLL() (lines 4.a.i–4.a.iii). This will enable the user to later prove to the nodes that the request accepted into the blockchain and signed by them. If all of the steps above pass, both the user and the nodes increase the user's current transaction number by one.

Protocol 1. Transaction Request Submission

Input: Both the user and the nodes hold the current transaction index of the user i and the user's public key y, as well as the user's DSA domain parameters p,g,g,h. Only the user holds its secret key s and $c_{(i-1)1}$, $c_{(i-1)2}$.

The protocol:

1. **Submitting a Request (User).**
    (a) Randomly or pseudorandomly generate two integers c_{i1},c_{i2} s.t. $0 < c_{i1}, c_{i2} < q$
    (b) $C_{i1} \leftarrow g^{c_{i1}} \bmod p$, $C_{i2} \leftarrow g^{c_{i2}} \bmod p$.
    (c) $Pol_i(x) \leftarrow s + c_{i1}x + c_{i2}x^2$.
    (d) $s_i(1) \leftarrow (1, Pol_i(1) \bmod q)$
    (e) if $i = 1$:
        (i) $D_i \leftarrow (s_i(1), C_{i1}, C_{i2})$
    (f) else :
        (i) $s_{i-1}(2) \leftarrow (2, Pol_{i-1}(2) \bmod q)$
        (ii) $D_i \leftarrow (s_i(1), s_{i-1}(2), C_{i1}, C_{i2}, C_{(i-1)1}, C_{(i-1)2})$
    (g) $t_i \leftarrow transaction\_to\_submit$
    (h) $T_i \leftarrow (t_i, DSA_s(t_i))$
    (i) $R_i \leftarrow (T_i, D_i)$
    (j) Submit_To_Node(R_i)
2. **Verifying a Request (Node).**
    (a) $dsa\_v \leftarrow$ DSA_Verify(T_i, y)
    (b) $trans\_v \leftarrow$ Transaction_Verify(T_i)
    (c) if $i = 1$:
        (i) $ss\_v \leftarrow$ Verify($s_i(1), C_{i1}, C_{i2}, y$)
    (d) else :
        (i) $ss_i\_v \leftarrow$ Verify($s_i(1), C_{i1}, C_{i2}, y$)

(ii) $ss_{i-1}\_v \leftarrow \texttt{Verify}(s_{i-1}(2), C_{(i-1)1}, C_{(i-1)2}, y)$

(iii) $ss\_v \leftarrow ss_i\_v \land ss_{i-1}\_v$:

(e) if $dsa\_v \land ss\_v \land trans\_v$:

    (i) $\texttt{Add\_To\_Requests\_Pool}(R_i)$

(f) else :

    (i) REJECT

3. **Perform BFT (Nodes).**

The nodes perform the BFT algorithm and the request R_i may get published on the blockchain. If it does, both the request and the nodes signatures on it - $Sign(R_i)$ - are published on the public ledger and the nodes should increase the transactions counter of the user by one.

4. **Record Accepted Request (User).**

(a) if $\texttt{Check\_Request\_Accepted}(R_i)$:

    (i) $Sign_i \leftarrow \texttt{Get\_Nodes\_Signature}(R_i)$

    (ii) $\texttt{Add\_To\_PLL}(R_i, Sign_i)$

    (iii) $user\_current\_transaction\_number \leftarrow i+1$

6.2   Balance Restoration

We assume the permissioned members have been attacked and may hold no records of the public ledger. We do require that they still hold their secret and public keys, as well as having access to the public keys of the users and their respective DSA domain parameters.

Conditions for Continuing After Restoration. We must remember that users will want to continue and submit transaction requests using their secret key after the restoration of the balance. Since the users published $s_m(1)$ in D_m and we require that they publish P_m in the restoration process, $s_m(v)$ will be published as well. This means that $s_m(2)$ shall not be published at all, otherwise, even an honest user will expose the secret key. If the blockchain is attacked again, and another reconstruction will be necessary, the user may try to claim m is still the most current index of a submitted request, even though other transactions have been submitted since. If the share index of the proof was a constant, e.g., 3, then publishing P_m again (that contains $s_m(3)$), would have kept $s_m(1)$ and $s_m(3)$ as the only shares regarding Pol_m that have been exposed. We will require that a new reconstruction will mean a new random $2 \leq v' \leq q-1$ share index, that will be different from v with high probability, so 3 different shares - $s_m(1)$, $s_m(v)$, $s_m(v')$, will have to be published by a dishonest user.

When we reconstruct the ledger, we assume that an honest majority will have been restored, i.e., no more than f out of the $3f+1$ nodes are byzantine. If a reconstruction of the ledger is required once again, a malicious user may know which node is byzantine, and submit the restoration request to this node. The byzantine node can purposely ask the user to present a proof with $v' = v$, and the user will be able to claim m as the most current transaction index. To solve this, each node will publish a random value $2 \leq \hat{v}_{node} \leq q-1$ and its DSA signature $sign(\hat{v}_{node})$ off-chain. The user will have to choose $f + 1$ nodes, ask them to generate another pair $(v_{node}, sign(v_{node}))$ and use all of those values bit-wise XOR as the published share's index.

Lemma 1. *By requiring the user to collect $f + 1$ different values from $f + 1$ different nodes, and publishing a share with the values bit-wise XOR as an index, we prevent, with high probability[5], the user from claiming m as the most current transaction index.*

Proof Sketch. Even if there are f byzantine nodes, and the user knows who all of them are, at least one value will be a random value generated by an honest node. Let us assume a user receives $\{(v'_1, sign(v'_i)), \ldots, (v'_{f+1}, sign(v'_{f+1}))\}$ and w.l.o.g only $(v'_{f+1}, sign(v'_{f+1})$ was generated by an honest node. In the worst case, the user can control the other f nodes so the user can choose $\bigoplus_{i=1}^{f}(v'_i \oplus \hat{v}'_i) = v''$. Since we assume $v'_{f+1} \oplus \hat{v}'_{f+1} = v''_{f+1}$ is a random value the user cannot control, we will get that $(v'' \oplus v''_{f+1})\ mod\ q = v'$ is again a random value that the user cannot control and that does not equal the previous value v. Since the user already holds $f + 1$ signed pairs $(v_{node}, sign(v_{node}))$ from the previous restoration, the user may try to cheat and use the same v, so we use the newly published values $\hat{v}_{node}$ in the XOR to ensure a true new random value is enforced.

Finally, we will discuss a case where a user did not submit any request between two reconstructions. Again, we want an honest user to be able to restore the wallet's balance once more, without exposing the secret key s. Since publishing P_m again, that contains $s_m(v')$, will probably expose s, we will generate Pol_{m+1} and publish corresponding shares together with the proof and will also increase the transactions index to $m + 2$ after restoration (submit an additional data for a "shadow" transaction). Now, an honest user that has submitted no real transactions between two attacks will no longer face this issue.

The Protocol. When the user wants to restore the balance, the user will first collect $f + 1$ pairs $(v_{node}, sign(v_{node}))$ of random values and their signatures (signed by the public key y_{node}) generated by $f + 1$ different nodes, by using Collect_Values(). The user will collect the corresponding $f + 1$ nodes' public values using Collect_Public_Values(). Then the user will calculate the bit-wise XOR of the values (lines 1.a–1.c). A special transaction request will be submitted by the user using Submit_To_Node() (lines 1.d–1.l). This transaction will include the PLL, ILL, the corresponding proof for the claimed most current index (that contains a share with the XOR value as the index), the first share regarding a new polynomial and the commitments for the new polynomial's coefficients, as well as the collected values and public values.

The node will verify that the PLL is complete, i.e., contains a continuous history of transaction requests of increasing index up to some index m and that

---

[5] DSA defines $2^{N-1} \le q \le 2^N$ where $N \in \{160, 224, 256\}$ is the bit length of q.

the appended signatures and additional data are valid, using `Verify_PLL()`. The node will also verify that the ILL contains signed transactions and that the user is the payee in all of the transactions using `Verify_ILL()` (lines 2.a–2.b). The proof supplied by the user will be verified as well, i.e., matches m, the values' signatures will be verified using `DSA_Verify()`, and the XOR will be verified using `Verify_XOR()`. The proof share and the first share of the next polynomial will be verified using `Verify()` (lines 2.c–2.f). The node can be sure that if the user decided to include P_m in the request, there is no missing suffix in the presented PLL. If all verifications pass, the node adds the request to the pool of pending requests by using `Add_To_Requests_Pool()` (line 2.g.i).

Then, the nodes perform the BFT algorithm, where those conditions are checked by the other nodes as well and the request may be accepted and published on the ledger. This means that the nodes accept the requested balance (the outcomes from the PLL subtracted from the incomes from the ILL) as the user's balance, the presented index as the user's transaction index and the user may continue to participate in the blockchain without losing any crypto-currency.

The user will check whether the restoration request was accepted into the blockchain and act similarly to **Protocol 1**.

Protocol 2. Balance Restoration

Input: Both the user and the nodes hold the user's public key y, as well as the user's DSA domain parameters p,g,g,h. Only the user holds its secret key s, the polynomial $P_m(x)$ and the corresponding coefficients commits C_{m1}, C_{m2} as well as its PLL (with transactions up to index m) and its ILL.

The protocol:

1. **Submitting a Restoration Request (User).**
   (a) $V = \{(v_1, sign(v_i)), \ldots, (v_{f+1}, sign(v_{f+1}))\} \leftarrow$ `Collect_Values()`
   (b) $PV = \{(\hat{v}_1, sign(\hat{v}_i)), \ldots, (\hat{v}_{f+1}, sign(\hat{v}_{f+1}))\} \leftarrow$ `Collect_Public_Values()`
   (c) $v \leftarrow (\bigoplus_{i=1}^{f+1} (v_i \oplus \hat{v}_i)) \bmod q$
   (d) $s_m(v) \leftarrow (v, Pol_m(v) \bmod q)$
   (e) $P_m \leftarrow (s_m(v), C_{m1}, C_{m2})$
   (f) Randomly or pseudorandomly generate two integers $c_{(m+1)1}, c_{(m+1)2}$ s.t. $0 < c_{(m+1)1}, c_{(m+1)2} < q$
   (g) $C_{(m+1)1} \leftarrow g^{c_{(m+1)1}} \bmod p$, $C_{(m+1)2} \leftarrow g^{c_{(m+1)2}} \bmod p$
   (h) $Pol_{m+1}(x) \leftarrow s + c_{(m+1)1}x + c_{(m+1)2}x^2$
   (i) $s_{m+1}(1) \leftarrow (1, Pol_{m+1}(1) \bmod q)$
   (j) $D_{m+1} \leftarrow (s_{m+1}(1), C_{(m+1)1}, C_{(m+1)2})$
   (k) $R_{m+1} \leftarrow (PLL, ILL, P_m, V, PV, D_{m+1})$
   (l) `Submit_To_Node`(R_{m+1})
2. **Verifying a Restoration Request (Node).**
   (a) $PLL\_v \leftarrow$ `Verify_PLL`(PLL)
   (b) $ILL\_v \leftarrow$ `Verify_ILL`(ILL)
   (c) $sign\_v \leftarrow \bigwedge_{i=1}^{f+1}$ `DSA_Verify`$(V_i = (v_i, sign(v_i)), y_i)$
   (d) $p\_sign\_v \leftarrow \bigwedge_{i=1}^{f+1}$ `DSA_Verify`$(PV_i = (\hat{v}_i, sign(\hat{v}_i)), y_i)$

(e) $xor\_v \leftarrow \texttt{Verify\_XOR}(v_1, \hat{v}_1, \ldots, v_{f+1}, \hat{v}_{f+1}, v)$

(f) $ss\_v \leftarrow \texttt{Verify}(P_m, y) \wedge \texttt{Verify}(D_{m+1}, y)$

(g) if $PLL\_v \wedge ILL\_v \wedge ss\_v \wedge sign\_v \wedge p\_sign\_v \wedge xor\_v$:

   (i) $\texttt{Add\_To\_Requests\_Pool}(R_{m+1})$

(h) else :

   (i) REJECT

3. **Perform BFT (Nodes).**

The nodes perform the BFT algorithm and the request R_{m+1} may be published on the blockchain if it passes the other nodes validations as well. If it does, both the request and the nodes signatures on it - $Sign(R_{m+1})$ - are published on the public ledger and the nodes should set the transactions counter of the user to $m+2$ and then the user balance is restored.

4. **Record Accepted Request (User).**

(a) if $\texttt{Check\_Request\_Accepted}(R_{m+1})$:

   (i) $Sign_{m+1} \leftarrow \texttt{Get\_Nodes\_Signature}(R_{m+1})$

   (ii) $\texttt{Add\_To\_PLL}(R_{m+1}, Sign_{m+1})$

   (iii) $user\_current\_transaction\_number \leftarrow m+2$

7 Conclusion

We have addressed one of the problems of permissioned blockchains, the fact that the ledger is held only in the databases of the permissioned members. Being so, this weakness becomes a point of failure, when those databases are attacked or destroyed. We have introduced a way to reconstruct each user's balance, without the need for other users to contribute information and without requesting the nodes to trust the private users. We have done so by neutralizing the incentive for users to hide payments they made, with the risk of exposing their secret key, using the digital signature used in the blockchain and VSS. Our technique, is publishing additional data with every publication, and then supplying proof of currentness to a third party, that knows that the secret key of the publisher may be exposed in case of dishonesty. This technique may be applied in other scopes as well, such as general proof of currentness.

References

1. Amsden, Z., et al.: The libra blockchain (2019). https://developers.libra.org/docs/assets/papers/the-libra-blockchain.pdf

2. Binun, A., et al.: Self-stabilizing Byzantine-tolerant distributed replicated state machine. In: Bonakdarpour, B., Petit, F. (eds.) SSS 2016. LNCS, vol. 10083, pp. 36–53. Springer, Cham (2016). https://doi.org/10.1007/978-3-319-49259-9_4

3. Błaśkiewicz, P., Kubiak, P., Kutyłowski, M.: Two-head dragon protocol: preventing cloning of signature keys. In: Chen, L., Yung, M. (eds.) INTRUST 2010. LNCS, vol. 6802, pp. 173–188. Springer, Heidelberg (2011). https://doi.org/10.1007/978-3-642-25283-9_12

4. Castro, M., Liskov, B.: Practical byzantine fault tolerance and proactive recovery. ACM Trans. Comput. Syst. (TOCS) **20**(4), 398–461 (2002)

5. Castro, M., Liskov, B., et al.: Practical byzantine fault tolerance. In: OSDI 1999, pp. 173–186 (1999)
6. Chor, B., Goldwasser, S., Micali, S., Awerbuch, B.: Verifiable secret sharing and achieving simultaneity in the presence of faults. In: 26th Annual Symposium on Foundations of Computer Science (sfcs 1985), pp. 383–395. IEEE (1985)
7. Diffie, W., Hellman, M.: New directions in cryptography. IEEE Trans. Inf. Theory **22**(6), 644–654 (1976)
8. Dolev, S., Eldefrawy, K., Garay, J.A., Kumaramangalam, M.V., Ostrovsky, R., Yung, M.: Brief announcement: secure self-stabilizing computation. In: Proceedings of the ACM Symposium on Principles of Distributed Computing. PODC 2017, Washington, DC, USA, 25–27 July 2017, pp. 415–417. ACM (2017)
9. Dolev, S., Georgiou, C., Marcoullis, I., Schiller, E.M.: Self-stabilizing Byzantine tolerant replicated state machine based on failure detectors. In: Dinur, I., Dolev, S., Lodha, S. (eds.) CSCML 2018. LNCS, vol. 10879, pp. 84–100. Springer, Cham (2018). https://doi.org/10.1007/978-3-319-94147-9_7
10. Feldman, P.: A practical scheme for non-interactive verifiable secret sharing. In: 28th Annual Symposium on Foundations of Computer Science (sfcs 1987), pp. 427–438. IEEE (1987)
11. Gallagher, P.: Digital signature standard (DSS). Federal Information Processing Standards Publications, volume FIPS 186–3 (2013)
12. Hermoni, O., Gilboa, N., Dolev, S.: Digital arbitration, 21 October 2014, US Patent 8,868,903
13. Krzywiecki, Ł., Kubiak, P., Kutyłowski, M.: Stamp and extend – instant but undeniable timestamping based on lazy trees. In: Mitchell, C.J., Tomlinson, A. (eds.) INTRUST 2012. LNCS, vol. 7711, pp. 5–24. Springer, Heidelberg (2012). https://doi.org/10.1007/978-3-642-35371-0_2
14. Lamport, L.: Using time instead of timeout for fault-tolerant distributed systems. ACM Trans. Program. Lang. Syst. (TOPLAS) **6**(2), 254–280 (1984)
15. Lamport, L., Shostak, R., Pease, M.: The Byzantine generals problem. ACM Trans. Program. Lang. Syst. **4**, 382–401 (1982)
16. Nakamoto, S., et al.: Bitcoin: A peer-to-peer electronic cash system (2008)
17. Pease, M., Shostak, R., Lamport, L.: Reaching agreement in the presence of faults. J. ACM (JACM) **27**(2), 228–234 (1980)
18. Shamir, A.: How to share a secret. Commun. ACM **22**(11), 612–613 (1979)
19. Yin, M., Malkhi, D., Reiter, M.K., Gueta, G.G., Abraham, I.: HotStuff: BFT consensus with linearity and responsiveness. In: Proceedings of the 2019 ACM Symposium on Principles of Distributed Computing, pp. 347–356 (2019)

A Recommender System for Efficient Implementation of Privacy Preserving Machine Learning Primitives Based on FHE

Imtiyazuddin Shaik$^{(\boxtimes)}$, Ajeet Kumar Singh, Harika Narumanchi, Nitesh Emmadi, and Rajan Mindigal Alasingara Bhattachar

Cyber Security and Privacy Research Group, TCS Research and Innovation, Tata Consultancy Services, Hyderabad, India
{imtiyazuddin.shaik,ajeetk.singh1,h.narumanchi, nitesh.emmadi1,rajan.ma}@tcs.com

Abstract. With the increased dependence on cloud computing, there is growing concern for privacy of data that is stored and processed on third party cloud service providers. Of many solutions that achieve privacy preserving computations, fully homomorphic encryption (FHE) is a promising direction. FHE has several applications that can be used to perform computations on encrypted data without decrypting them. In this paper, we focus on realizing privacy preserving machine learning (PPML) using FHE. Our prime motivation behind choosing PPML is the increased use of machine learning algorithms on end-user's data for predictions or classification, where privacy of end-user's data is at stake. Given the importance of PPML and FHE, we formulate a recommender system that enables machine learning experts who are new to cryptography to efficiently realize a machine learning application in privacy preserving manner. We formulate the recommender system as a multi objective multi constraints optimization problem along with a simpler single objective multi constraint optimization problem. We solve this optimization using TOPSIS based on experimental analysis performed on three prominent FHE libraries HElib, SEAL and HEAAN from the PPML perspective. We present the observations on the performance parameters such as elapsed time and memory usage for the primitive machine learning algorithms such as linear regression and logistic regression. We also discuss the technical issues in making the FHE schemes practically deployable and give insights into selection of parameters to efficiently implement PPML algorithms. We observe that our estimates for matrix multiplication and linear regression correlate with the experimental analysis when assessed using an optimizer. The proposed recommendation system can be used in FHE compilers to facilitate optimal implementation of PPML applications.

Keywords: Homomorphic encryption · Privacy preserving machine learning · Linear regression · Logistic regression · Secure outsourcing

Regular Submission, CSCML 2020.

© Springer Nature Switzerland AG 2020
S. Dolev et al. (Eds.): CSCML 2020, LNCS 12161, pp. 193–218, 2020.
https://doi.org/10.1007/978-3-030-49785-9_13

1   Introduction

The evolution of data driven digital transformation has led the way to increased dependence on cloud service providers (CSPs). Organizations are embracing third-party cloud computing services to outsource storage and computations which can be easily managed with low cost overhead. In the recent years, there has been exponential increase of data in existence as well as the corresponding cloud services usage. This has lead to growing concern for data privacy. For privacy and confidentiality, data can be encrypted and stored on the CSP. However, the existing non-FHE encryption schemes restrict computations on the encrypted data. To enable computations while still preserving confidentiality and privacy of data, several privacy preserving computation methodologies have evolved, of which prominent ones are trusted execution environments (TEE) [1], multi-party computations (MPC) [2], Garbled circuits [3] and fully homomorphic encryption (FHE) [4]. Of these, homomorphic encryption has been the most promising option. Though fully homomorphic encryption has been an open problem since long [5], it is only with Gentry's scheme (2009) [4] that the pace of development has increased. Since then, consequent advances in homomorphic encryption schemes has garnered lot of interest to practically develop privacy preserving applications with use of homomorphic encryption schemes. Hence the scope of our study is limited to FHE based implementations.

FHE enables clients to securely outsource data storage to CSPs while still allowing computations on the encrypted data without the need for decryption. FHE comes with a wide range of applications to perform computations without revealing underlying data to the third party. In this direction, we focus on one such application, privacy preserving machine learning (PPML), that has great impact in current information age. At present, machine learning (ML) is of great interest to the organizations to improve their services by making their systems to automatically learn through the ML algorithms without the need for explicit programming. However, existing ML models operate at the cost of user's privacy as their sensitive data is stored at third party organizations without any safeguards from the service provider. To enable privacy of client's data, there is a need to perform privacy enabled ML, where FHE can be leveraged to develop private machine learning paradigms that preserve privacy and confidentiality of users' data.

The existing literature focuses on implementing PPML algorithms to solve specific problems such as private genomic sequencing or encrypted computation on genomic data and so on in privacy preserving manner. However these algorithms are optimized for a given usecase. Therefore, there is a need for generic framework that enables end-users to select an appropriate FHE scheme and it's parameter set based on PPML application needs. Thereby PPML applications can be implemented in an efficient manner.

There are several FHE libraries which implement various FHE schemes and optimizations. But for a machine learning expert, working with FHE libraries can be challenging. Using FHE libraries for PPML requires understanding of how the computations happen to make the implementations more efficient and get optimal performance. Hence, there is need for Recommendation system for machine learning experts on FHE libraries. In order to do this, one has to study various implementations of FHE libraries to see which one suits better based on the application.

Hence to address this, there are compilers such as CHET, which facilitates to build applications which requires Privacy preserving computation based on specific homomorphic encryption scheme/library. However, PPML applications might need to depend on different libraries and schemes for optimal performance. To facilitate this, we propose a generic framework that recommends users to select best the FHE library and FHE scheme (along with parameter configurations) supported by it among several FHE libraries to build PPML application efficiently.

1.1 Our Contribution

Our contribution in this paper can be categorized as follows:

– **Recommender system for FHE:** We present a novel framework for a recommender system for FHE libraries which suggests the optimal parameter set for a given application. We theoretically analyze the proposed recommendation system and investigate FHE schemes from PPML perspective. For a thorough investigation, we follow a two step approach wherein:
  • We come up with an optimal recommendations on library and scheme to use along with settings like packing, bootstrapping and parameter selection for primitive ML computations.
  • We provide estimates for computations such as matrix multiplication, linear regression based on primitive operations. Our estimates and actual computation times for matrix multiplication and linear regression are given as input to the optimizer (TOPSIS [6]). We note that optimizer is recommending the same in both these cases.

This study is intended for programmers and machine learning experts who are new to cryptography and plan to implement machine learning applications in a privacy preserving manner based on FHE. From PPML perspective, we need to configure the parameters by taking into account aspects such as accuracy required, whether the application needs to be interactive or non-interactive, packing is required or not, security levels and noise threshold. We recommended parameter choices for existing FHE libraries to achieve optimal performance.

1.2 Related Work

Ever since the first fully homomorphic encryption scheme was proposed in 2009, there had been significant advances in devising more efficient schemes as well as improving efficiency of applications built on FHE encrypted data. One of the most important benchmarking platform was provided by iDash - a Genome sequence competition [7], which emphasized on efficient application of machine learning algorithms on private genome datasets for prediction or classification in a privacy preserving manner. The entries into this competition have seen many HE implementations with optimizations making them ready for practical use. In the context of secure computation on genomic data, most notable work in iDash 2015 [8] investigated private genome analysis over encrypted data based on the BGV [9] and YASHE schemes [10]. While the BGV implementation efficiently evaluated circuits of larger depths (like the Hamming distance algorithm or approximate Edit distance algorithm), low depth circuits (such as minor allele frequencies or c2 test statistic in a case-control study) evaluation was more efficient in YASHE instantiation. [11] studies Privacy-preserving genome-wide association on cloud environment using fully homomorphic encryption. They demonstrate with experimentation that secure outsourcing computation of one c2 test and evaluation of one linkage disequilibrium with 10,000 subjects takes 35 ms and 80 ms respectively. Zhang *et al.* [12] proposed a framework to enable secure division over encrypted data by introducing two division protocols with a trade-off between complexity and accuracy in computing chi-square statistics. In 2016, Çetin *et al.* [13] demonstrated the feasibility of privacy preserving queries (single/multi query) on homomorphically encrypted genomic data using SEAL based implementation for queries over large datasets of sizes ranging from 10,000 to 100,000 rows [13].

Machine learning techniques like logistic regression over encrypted data was investigated in 2017 [14,15]. The implementation of [14] encodes the whole dataset into a single ciphertext using the packing technique and uses approximate arithmetic over encrypted data which allows computation for the required accuracy. Here nestrov gradient descent method is used for faster convergence for logistic regression in non interactive way. They also proposed an iterative method for performing logistic regression for larger datasets. [15] implementation uses scale factors and "combining bootstrapping with scaling" approach to achieve fixed point arithmetic on encrypted data. They used gradient descent using sigmoid function (approximated using Taylor series). However their solution took much longer time compared to [14]. iDash-2018 competition explored Genome Wide Association Studies (GWAS) based on homomorphically encrypted data for large datasets which was efficiently computed in 0.09 min by [16]. They computed Fisher scoring and semi-parallel GWAS algorithms over homomorphically encrypted data with several optimization methodologies. They implemented using HEAAN. It requires 30 to 40 min for 245 samples containing 10,000 to 15,000 SNPs (Single Nucleotide Polymorphism) and gives high accuracy.

Other most prominent works in literature that focus on logistic regression on encrypted data include [17–23] and PPML on cloud [24]. For more general information on HE and machine learning over encrypted data refer [25–29].

Prominent open source implementations of FHE include HElib, SEAL, HEAAN, PALISADE [30], TFHE [31] and nGraph-HE [32]. HElib is one of the first libraries for FHE by IBM. It's main advantage is working with binary (bitwise) data as it supports bootstrapping for binary inputs. SEAL was developed by Microsoft to provide support for integer and floating point arithmetic on encrypted data. However, SEAL doesn't support packing for floating point and negative numbers which is required for PPML. HEAAN has support for this and also provides support for bootstrapping. PALISADE library supports wide variety of cryptographic primitives, however does not support bootstrapping. TFHE library works primarily for binary inputs with support for bootstrapping. The existing state-of-art has research on homomorphic compilers that deal with a specific FHE library or a scheme. CHET [33] takes computation as input from the user, calculates the optimal parameters required for the computation and gives a code snippet which implements the computation. The code snippet is generated using CKKS scheme implemented in (i) HEAAN (ii) SEAL. Alchemy [34] is a compiler that converts code in domain specific language to its corresponding optimized homomoprhic encryption code which doesn't require knowledge on FHE. It supports BGV-style [9] cryptosystem as defined and implemented in [35], a recent Haskell framework for FHE and lattice-based cryptography more generally. Out of these, HElib, SEAL and HEAAN have been widely used in the recent times for PPML. Hence, we consider these three libraries for our experiments.

In Sect. 2, we briefly describe the basics of FHE and models of PPML based on FHE. Section 3 describes the state of the art opensource implementations of FHE and summarizes the implementation aspects in making the current FHE schemes practical. In Sect. 4 we illustrate the machine learning case studies such as matrix multiplication, linear regression and logistic regression and present the experimental results in terms of elapsed time (ET) and memory usage. We also suggest from PPML perspective what support is needed for PPML algorithms to be implemented. In Sect. 5 we propose a novel framework for a recommendation system for PPML applications based on FHE. We provide our analysis on computations like matrix multiplication and linear regression and solve them using TOPSIS optimizer.

2   Brief Overview of FHE and PPML

FHE allows arbitrary computations on encrypted data without decrypting them. Given a set of ciphertexts $\{c_1 \ldots c_n\}$ corresponding to messages $\{m_1 \ldots m_n\}$, one can compute a function $\mathcal{F}\{c_1 \ldots c_n\}$ resulting in an encrypted output, which when decrypted is equal to the result of computation $\mathcal{F}(m_1 \ldots m_n)$. A typical public key encryption algorithm ξ has KeyGen_ξ, Encrypt_ξ, Decrypt_ξ functions that perform generation of public and private key pairs, encrypting a message with public key and decrypt a message with private key respectively. In addition to these functions, FHE encryption algorithms have an Eval_ξ function that evaluates a given function $\mathcal{F}$ over a set of input ciphertexts $c = \{c_1 \ldots c_n\}$. Operations supported by FHE encryption schemes depend on the underlying mathematical structure of the ciphertexts.

Applications based on homomorphic encryption can use either bit-wise encryption instantiation or integer-wise encryption instantiation to encrypt data, however bit-wise encryption increases the size of data sets. The space required to store the ciphertext of an l-bit integer in bit-wise encryption instantiation is l-ciphertext units where as integer-wise encryption requires only one ciphertext unit. Studies like [36] suggest that through optimizations integer wise encryption is more efficient than bit-wise encryption. The challenge is to bring a balance between space and performance.

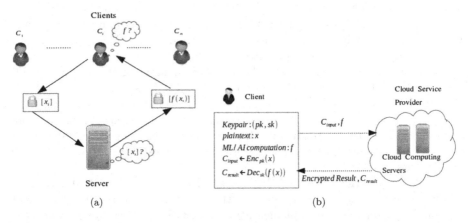

Fig. 1. (a) Computation as a Service (b) Prediction as a Service. Diagram inspired from [37]

2.1   Computational Models for PPML Based on FHE

FHE can be applied to ML in two scenarios: computation as a service and prediction as a service. In computation as a service model (See Fig. 1a), client wants to outsource ML computations to the CSP but does not want to reveal data to it. Here, client knows what ML algorithm it is outsourcing and sends the algorithm and encrypted data to the CSP. The CSP performs the computations on the ciphertexts and sends the encrypted result back to the client. In prediction as a service scenario (See Fig. 1b), the service provider has proprietary machine learning algorithms which he does not wish to share with the client. In the same way, the client does not wish to share confidential data to the service provider. Hence, using FHE, the client can provide encrypted inputs to the cloud service provider, who then feeds these encrypted inputs to the proprietary ML algorithm and develop model parameters. The CSP can then use this encrypted model to provide prediction as a service to the client. This way objectives of both client and server are realized.

Though there is subtle difference in the two scenarios, the common part of the two is the computation hosted on the server side. For efficiency of the services, these computations has to be efficient, which is focus of our study. In this paper, we analyze algorithms from both computation as a service as well as prediction as a service perspective.

2.2   Limitations of FHE

Noise management is a major limitation of FHE. Every ciphertext has inherent noise associated which increases with number of computations. There are two ways for noise management, (*i*) Bootstrapping and (*ii*) Modulus Switching. Bootstrapping is used to reduce the noise and get fresh ciphertext homomorphically at the expense of computation time. Modulus Switching helps in reducing noise but to certain extent only. This limits the use of FHE to applications which require only operations which are linear in nature. *Hence, we require linear approximation of non-linear functions.* Recent advances have seen use of approximation of non linear functions, like calculating the exponent, with reduced computational complexity. For instance [15] uses approximation of Sigmoid function to polynomial evaluation upto degrees 3, 5 and 7 depending on the accuracy needed.

Another important consideration is Parameter optimization. It is essential to find the optimal set of values for the parameters mentioned in Sect. 3. These parameters, in particular the Polynomial modulus (N) and the Coefficient modulus (q) have significant impact on performance. For instance, higher N value is better for Bootstrapping, however doubling N value will also double the size of the ciphertext and the time taken for computations. *Current fully homomorphic encryption schemes are computationally expensive and memory intensive.* Encrypted computations using first homomorphic encryption scheme by Craig Gentry from 2009 [4], was **100 trillion times slower** than plaintext operations. Over the last decade, the performance has seen significant process now reaching **million times** level [38,39]. The progress is optimistic and we can expect more efficient schemes in the future.

In the next section we present some insights into technical aspects of FHE implementations and discuss issues which are important in making FHE based PPML applications efficient.

3   FHE Libraries and Implementation Aspects

In this section we mainly focus on three FHE libraries namely HElib, SEAL and HEAAN. We talk about the pros and cons of these libraries, parameter settings and features like packing and bootstrapping.

3.1   The Trio

HElib, SEAL and HEAAN are among the most widely used open source libraries for FHE. While all three libraries support CKKS scheme, HElib additionally supports BGV and SEAL supports BFV. Summary of operations supported by each of these libraries are given in Table 1. HElib supports bootstrapping for Bit-wise encryption and HEAAN for both Bit-wise and Integer-wise (floating point) encryption respectively. SEAL has automatic parameter selection, while HEAAN allows fine grained control over parameter selection for any PPML application.

3.2   Other Libraries

Other prominent publicly available FHE libraries include PALISADE, TFHE
and nGraph-HE. PALISADE library supports a wide range of cryptographic
primitives including public-key encryption, homomorphic encryption, digital
signatures, proxy re-encryption, identity-based encryption, and attribute-based
encryption. iDash 2018 winning entry uses PALISADE for its implementation.
TFHE implements a ring variant of the GSW cryptosystem. It implements a very
fast gate-by-gate bootstrapping. It allows users to give a circuit for computation.
nGraph is Intel's graph compiler for Artificial Neural Networks. nGrpah-HE is
a backend for nGraph to support computations on encrypted data.

Table 1. Comparing libraries

Scheme	Integer-wise	Bit-wise	Negative numbers	Fractional numbers	Bootstrapping	Packing
HElib	✓	✓	✗	✗	✓	✓
SEAL	✓	✓	✓	✓	✗	✓
HEAAN	✓	✓	✓	✓	✓	✓

3.3   Parameters and Considerations

FHE schemes primarily rely on hardness of three types of hardness assumptions:

1. **Lattice:** These type of schemes rely on hardness of lattice problems like
   Shortest Vector Problem (SVP) and Closest Vector Problem (CVP).
2. **LWE:** These type of schemes rely on hardness of Learning With Errors problem. The problem with these schemes is that the key sizes are much larger.
3. **RLWE:** These type of schemes rely on hardness of Ring LWE problem which
   is efficient due to the underlying ring structure.

Ring based Learning with Errors (RLWE) is the basis for most of the efficient
FHE schemes. Typical parameters in RLWE based FHE schemes are:

- M - the cyclotomic polynomial
- N - degree of cyclotomic polynomial $N = \phi(M)$
- p - modulus for coefficients in the plaintext
- $t = p^r$ - plaintext modulus, for an exponent r
- h - 1-norm of the secret key (For example, 1-norm of vector x is $\sum_{i=1}^{n} |x_i|$)
- $q = q_1 * q_2 \ldots q_l$ where $l = 1 \ldots L$ and L is the number of primes and q is the
  coefficient modulus for ciphertext and $q_1 \ldots q_l$ are small primes
- α - the width of Gaussian distribution for sampling error
- χ - the error distribution.

As part of the HE standardization, the suggested parameters sets are available at [40]. We have performed the experimentation using these parameter sets. Parameter selection plays a crucial part in performance of any FHE application. There can be different parameter sets subjecting to same level of security. However, the challenge is to choose a set that is suitable for a particular application (or depth). The analysis on optimal choice of parameters is an active research area and there are some results available in the literature [41].

The parameters that have significant effect on the performance of FHE applications are lattice dimension N, q. The parameter q should be large which sets the noise limit to a higher level and enables us to do more computations. It can also be computed as product of a set of small primes. The small primes $q_1 \ldots q_l$ are a chain of moduli of decreasing sizes $q_1 > q_2 > \ldots q_l$ which can be used for modulus switching. During homomorphic evaluation, the modulus can be switched to lower level which helps in reducing noise as well to certain extent. For example, in FV scheme (implemented in SEAL library [42]), to perform 10 multiplications, requires a polynomial modulus degree of 8124 and plaintext modulus of at least 2^{243} for a fractional encoding in base 3 [41]. The parameters N and p determine the number of plaintext slots, which specifies how many elements can be packed in a single ciphertext. The number of plaintext slots depends on the cyclotomic polynomial which is a product of d-irreducible factors. Each factor corresponds to a plaintext slot in plaintext modulus and is of degree $\phi(M)/d$.

Some libraries such as HEAAN (implementation of CKKS scheme) has a provision to specify accuracy of the approximate arithmetic on ciphertexts. This accuracy depends on plaintext modulus. Higher plaintext modulus gives more accuracy. The error distribution and sparse secret should be small which in-turn reduces the noise. The parameter selection criteria depends on the type of application and its circuit depth, multiplicative depth and the level of accuracy required. Depending on the type of application such as private computation on encrypted genomic data or private search, challenge is to choose an optimal parameter set that achieves better performance.

3.4 Ciphertext Packing

It is a technique where a vector of plaintexts are packed into a single ciphertext to get the advantage of space or computational efficiency. This enables computations to be performed parallelly in a Single Instruction Multiple Data (SIMD) manner. There are several ciphertext packing techniques available in literature [43–46]. All these techniques are based on polynomial Chinese Reminder Theorem (CRT) plaintext packing that has plaintext space $\mathcal{M}$ which is represented as a n-dimensional vectors in R^n over ring R using encoding or decoding methods [47]. One can encode an element of R^n into a ciphertext and perform component wise multiplication over the plaintext slot where each plaintext slot corresponds to each of the l irreducible factors with degree $\phi(M)/l$ and in plaintext modulus of the cyclotomic polynomial [47]. This enables us to parallelize the computations. However, the main drawback of packing is it not possible to access inputs in individual slots. To overcome this problem, we need to perform the rotation operation on plaintext slots where we can define the rotation operation on a encryption ct of $m = \{m_0 \ldots m_{n-1}\}$ as $\{m_l \ldots m_{n-1}, m_0, \ldots m_{l-1}\}$ for l-rotations. The rotation operation is usually required while performing matrix operations on packed ciphertexts. Performing computations on specific slots is expensive as it requires large number of rotations and constant multiplications. Therefore, there is a need to homomorphically unpack the ciphertext on the fly, perform operations on the individual elements and homomorphically pack the elements back into the ciphertext [45]. Table 2 summarizes the complexities of the packing techniques.

Table 2. Comparison of matrix multiplications for a d-dimension matrix with and without packing, This table is taken from [47]

Scheme	No of ciphertexts	Complexity	Circuit depth	Rotation required?
Without packing	d^2	$O(d^3)$	1 $mult$	✗
Halevi-Shoup [39]	d	$O(d^2)$	1 $mult$	✓
JKLS [47]	1	$O(d)$	1 $mult + 2$ $Cmult$	✓

For matrix multiplication algorithm $(d \times d)$ without using packing technique, we encrypt each element of a matrix to get d^2 ciphertexts (complexity of the algorithm is $O(d^3)$). Halevi-Shoup used packing technique (for matrix vector multiplication) to pack matrix diagonally, which requires only d ciphertexts and complexity reduces to $O(d^2)$. However, recent packing techniques like JKLS encrypts the whole matrix into a single ciphertext hence reducing the complexity to $O(d)$ (requires rotations to add results). All these packing methodologies are agnostic to any FHE scheme.

From PPML perspective, packing is required inorder to improve the space efficiency and speed up the computation process of ML algorithms. To make these algorithms non-interactive, bootstrapping is required, which is expensive. However, to make ML algorithms more efficient and non-interactive, methodologies have to be designed to perform light weight bootstrapping on the packed ciphertexts. Furthermore, server can save computation time by packing different user's encrypted data into single ciphertext (i.e. Ciphertext packing) and do the common operation that needs to be performed and then unpack to individual user's ciphertexts and carry out the remaining operations (referred to as on-the-fly packing). Efficient on-the-fly packing is necessary in ML applications.

3.5   Bootstrapping

Noise management is one of the crucial parts in making any HE scheme practical. In homomorphic encryption, every ciphertext has some noise associated with it. This noise increases with every computation and the decryption fails if the noise crosses certain threshold value. The threshold value usually depends on the type of homomorphic encryption scheme and its parameter values. The number of homomorphic operations that can be performed depends on the threshold value.

Therefore, to be able to use homomorphic encryption in practical applications, there has to be new techniques in order to improve the number of operations that can be performed on ciphertexts, such as modulus switching. However the noise grows with every operation. To address the problem of growing noise in ciphertexts, bootstrapping has been introduced which can homomorphically decrypt the ciphertext and produce a ciphertext with lesser noise. However, bootstrapping is an expensive operation.

Currently, the most promising bootstrapping schemes for integer-wise encryption are the BGV, FV and CKKS. Out of these CKKS seems to be the most practical scheme. CKKS involves re-scaling the obtained message after computation using modulus switching to get a message with reduced error value (Table 3).

Table 3. Summary of Bootstrapping Schemes, h is 1-norm of the secret key and $t = p^r$ is the plaintext modulus, K is a small constant related to security parameter

Scheme	Parameters	Security level (in bits)	Circuit depth	Time (in secs)
BGV [48]	$n =$ 16384, $slots =$ 1024, $\log\ p =$ 16	76	$O(2\ \log(t) + \log(h))$	320
Improved BGV [49]	–	80	$O(\log(t) + \log(h))$	–
FV [49]	$n =$ 16384, $slots =$ 64, $\log\ q =$ 558	92.9	$O(\log(\log(t)) + \log(h))$	193
Slim method for FV [49]			–	6.75
CKKS [50]	$\log N =$ 15, $slots =$ 64, $\log\ p =$ 23, $\log\ q = 29$	80	$O(\log\ K_q)$	24.6
Improved CKKS [51]	$\log N =$ 15, $slots =$ 10, $\log\ p =$ 25, $\log\ q = 29$		$max(\log\ K + 2, \log(\log\ q))$	0.04

From PPML perspective, homomorphically estimating the model parameters is computationally expensive as it requires many iterations to get the desired accuracy. For example, linear regression requires two multiplications for each iteration and suppose that the Recrypt (getting a fresh ciphertext by bootstrapping (non-interactive mode) or decrypt/encrypt (interactive mode)) operation takes x seconds. Recrypt has to be performed after every iteration or some y iterations to get a fresh ciphertext depending on the multiplicative depth of each iteration. Therefore, the execution time for 100 iterations will be $a + 100x/y$ where a is the time taken for each iteration. Therefore, even a small execution time of Recrypt will be a multiple of the number of iterations which hinders the performance of AI applications.

4 Case Studies

In this section we experimentally evaluate machine learning primitives for PPML and also give recommendations for each computation. All experiments are done on Intel Xeon Gold CPU clocked at 2.4 Ghz with 64 GB RAM and 32 cores. Input sizes for all our experimental analysis is 64 bits. All parameters are configured to enable 80-bit security.

4.1 FHE Primitive Operations

Table 4 shows the timings of primitive operations implemented using HElib, SEAL and HEAAN libraries.

Table 4. Performance of Primitive operations

Operation	HElib (ms)	SEAL (ms)	HEAAN (ms)	Plain(Unencrypted) (ns)
Add	0.96	0.28	0.98	99
Sub	1	0.22	3.4	107
Mul	16.66	14.5	31.3	121

This clearly shows that SEAL is the fastest among the three libraries for primitive operations. It is important to point out that result of any computation in HElib is in the range $[0, p-1]$, whereas for SEAL and HEAAN it is in the range $[-(p-1)/2, (p-1)/2]$. So negative integer results from HElib lie in the second half of the range and has to be re-interpreted after the computation. We infer from Table 4 that primitive operations on encrypted data are 10^6 times slower than the operations on plaintext.

From PPML perspective, it is important to have support for floating point arithmetic and negative numbers as most computations require support for them. HElib natively doesn't support neither of them. We will need an additional NTL wrapper on top of HElib library to support this. Hence, for further comparisons we only go with SEAL and HEAAN.

Division: All the three libraries support division of ciphertext by a power of 2. However, HElib does not have support for division by a non power of 2 number. In SEAL and HEAAN, if we want to perform division by a number 'x', then we can encode and encrypt it as a fractional number '1/x' and then do the multiplication. However efficient division of ciphertexts is still an open problem.

Recommendation: From PPML perspective, SEAL and HEAAN libraries are more suitable as they provide support for floating point arithmetic and negative numbers. For primitive operations, SEAL is faster. However for packing support to floating point and negative numbers, HEAAN is preferred.

We now present recommendation of library and FHE scheme for PPML through experimental analysis for PPML primitives such as Matrix multiplication and Linear regression operations. We validate this recommendation by solving our proposed optimization problem through TOPSIS.

4.2   Matrix Multiplication

Matrix multiplication is perhaps the most basic operation for any machine learning algorithm. We demonstrate how timings for matrix multiplication vary based on the underlying hardware support, primarily the number of cores available for processing, so that it helps in deciding the appropriate level of hardware for a particular PPML algorithm based on the scale of inputs.

Table 5. Matrix multiplication - memory usage (in GB)

Dim	HElib	SEAL	HEAAN
10×10	0.19	0.12	0.22
20×20	0.75	0.175	0.777
25×25	1.2	0.291	1.2
30×30	1.7	0.524	1.6
50×50	2.68	1.18	4.2
100×100	11.4	3.78	17.78

Figure 2 and 3 shows matrix multiplication performance on a 8, 16 and 32 core CPUs. For all these configurations, SEAL performs better than HElib and HEAAN. Our intuition is that HEAAN is taking more time as it has support for negative numbers as well as floating point numbers.

Table 5 shows statistics on memory consumption of each of these libraries for matrix multiplication operation. It is important to point out that ciphertext memory consumption is less in SEAL when compared to HElib and HEAAN. We implemented matrix multiplication using Intel's TBB for parallelization. SEAL fares better in terms of memory consumed for matrix multiplication.

Table 5 shows the high computational requirements for FHE even for primitive operations like matrix multiplication. However, from PPML perspective, typical datasets have columns in the range 100 to 200 while the number of rows go beyond 100,000. Packing based solutions for FHE are recommended for working with such datasets.

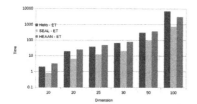 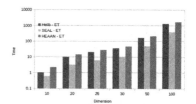

Fig. 2. Matrix multiplication performance - 8 and 16 core CPU - time (secs)

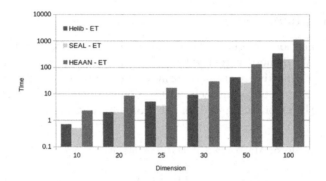

Fig. 3. Matrix multiplication performance - 32 core CPU - time (secs)

Recommendation: SEAL performs better in terms of memory and time. However for working with larger datasets in the case of PPML, packing based implementations are needed where HEAAN fares better and easier to use.

Packed Matrix Multiplication: Machine learning algorithms typically require to work on large datasets. This will be difficult to support for FHE libraries as the memory requirements are too huge to encrypt and work with such large datasets. To overcome this, FHE libraries provide support for packing. Packing technique packs multiple plaintext elements into a single ciphertext to allow SIMD operation. We demonstrate the use of packing for Matrix multiplication.

For packed matrix mult, we compare SEAL and HEAAN CKKS scheme implementations. To encode 100×100 matrix, we need 10000 slots. To get this we need to set $N = 32768$. We observed that while HEAAN takes less memory per ciphertext to represent this, while SEAL is faster in computation. Hence, for PPML applications with larger datasets it is recommended to choose HEAAN.

From memory perspective the packing based solution looks promising, however the operations on packed ciphertext are very restrictive. For example, to complete the matrix multiplication we have to perform rotations and additions. However, the operations have to be carefully mapped to individual slots for packing to be effective which might not be the case for a generic computation.

4.3   Linear Regression

Linear Regression is one of the most basic machine learning algorithms used for modeling the relationship between a scalar response (or dependent variable) and one or more explanatory variables. We implemented the basic version of linear regression with gradient descent using SEAL and HEAAN libraries.

We observed that, configuring noise budget (which determines number of multiplications that can be done before bootstrapping or interaction is needed) is much easier in HEAAN library. The default parameters in SEAL for $N = 8192$

Table 6. Linear Regression per iteration performance for SEAL (on 32-core CPU), E.T - Elapsed Time, Communication Cost is the one way cost of sending θ values per interaction, Memory consumption for N = 8192 parameter level for 150×4 dataset is 1.1 GB and for 265×10 dataset is 2.5 GB, Higher parameters give more multiplicative depth hence allowing us to use interaction in step-wise manner.

N(Poly mod)	x:Input	θ:Params	y:Target	SEAL E.T	Comm. Cost
8192	150×4	4×1	150×1	10 s	484 KB
16384	150×4	4×1	150×1	48.9 s	968 KB
8192	265×10	10×1	265×1	29.4 s	484 KB
16384	265×10	10×1	265×1	146.2 s	968 KB

Table 7. Linear Regression per iteration Timings using packing for HEAAN (on 32-core CPU) BS represents bootstrapping operation; Communication Cost is the one way cost of sending θ value per interaction
Memory consumption for 150×4 dataset reduced to 120 MB and for 265×10 reduced to 450 MB. In HEAAN, we achieve non-interactive model using bootstrapping.

N(Poly mod)	x:Input	θ:Params	y:Target	E.T w/o BS	Comm. Cost
2048	150×4	4×1	150×1	7.4–2.3 s	273 KB
8192	265×10	10×1	265×1	92.8–34.5 s	1.1 MB

allowed us to do only 3–4 multiplications before noise budget was exhausted. Hence interaction was needed in almost every iteration. HEAAN facilitates easier configuration of parameters for higher noise budget, hence allowing us to go for interaction once in every five iterations. This is done by setting log q parameter in HEAAN to a higher value. From a cloud service perspective, having lesser interaction is very important.

Linear regression algorithm typically runs for multiple iterations and then terminates based on the stopping criteria. The number of iterations also depends on the initial values for the model. With a good understanding of the dataset, these values can be optimally set to minimize the number of iterations.

Packed Linear Regression Without Bootstrapping: The important thing to remember in packed implementation of any algorithm is the data movement between the slots, as the entire matrices are represented as just a single vector of values in each slot. This is explained in the Appendix 6. Table 6 and 7 presents the experimental results for linear regression per iteration using SEAL and HEAAN respectively on a 32-core CPU. Without bootstrapping, we need smaller parameter settings. In HEAAN, after every multiplication, we do a modular switching operation to reduce parameter to a lower ciphertext modulus. Therefore, the computation time also decreases.

Packed Linear Regression with Bootstrapping: With bootstrapping, it is possible to achieve non-interactive model. We experimented this with HEAAN library. For bootstrapping we need to set parameters very high, like $\log N$ should be set to atleast 15 and we need more noise budget. Under this setting, 150×4 data set takes 320–240 s per iteration and 265×10 dataset takes 950–500 s. The performance increases as we switch to a lower modulus.

Recommendation: PPML algorithms like Linear regression require lots of iterations to converge. However FHE requires recrypt procedure to handle noise. SEAL runs faster but needs interaction with client for recrypt (decrypt then encrypt). For enabling bootstrapping, we need $\log N$ to be 15. HEAAN is slower but has support for bootstrapping which makes it non interactive.

4.4   Logistic Regression

Logistic Regression is simple machine learning algorithm widely used for classification of data. It uses a sigmoid function which evaluates exponents. However, calculating exponents in FHE domain can be very expensive. Several studies have proposed using approximations of sigmoid function using Taylor series upto a certain degree of polynomial [14, 15]. This helps in achieving the accuracy as well as reducing the computational complexity.

We trained and tested logistic regression implementation for low birth weight dataset [52] which had 189 rows and 8 features and a binary output for classification. The dataset is used to identify the risk factors associated with giving birth to low birth weight baby (weighing less than 2.5 Kgms). The dataset is used to predict the birth weight of babies based on some behavioral variables. Our implementation follows closely the implementation of [14]. The total running time for getting model parameters was 14.5 s for 7 iterations and we got AUC of 0.785.

For this, we set the N value to 8192 which gives us 4096 slots for packing. We packed the dataset into a single ciphertext by padding extra zeroes to make dimensions as 256×16. This is done to ensure correct data movement in slots as explained in [14]. The $\log q$ was set to sufficiently high value such that no interaction was needed. This can be calculated as per guidelines in [14].

Recommendation: Noise budget can be set appropriately in HEAAN to ensure no interaction is needed for certain number of iterations. For larger datasets, we can divide the dataset column wise and then do PPML algorithm iteratively.

4.5   Bootstrapping

In this section, we describe the experimental results of bootstrapping technique in HEAAN library. Figure 4b illustrates the error deviation ($\pm$ actual value) after bootstrapping operation for different input values and parameter values such as $\log p$ and slots. Here $\log p$ denotes the accuracy of the computation and slots represent the number of values that can be packed. For bootstrapping to work, we require $(\log p + \log (input)) < (\log q)$, this is because of the depth of the bootstrapping circuit. We note that the time taken for bootstrapping operation remains constant with varying log p value. It takes 5.2 s and 5.7 s for 8 and 16 slots respectively. Figure 4a shows the time taken for bootstrapping operation with increasing number of slots value. We observe that bootstrapping time grows exponentially with respect to the number of slots.

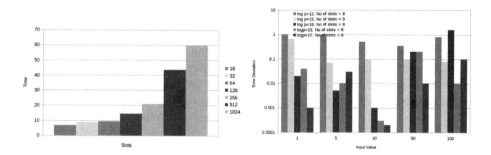

Fig. 4. (a) Slots vs Time (b) Input values vs Error Deviation; For 8 slots

Recommendation: HEAAN library has support for Bootstrapping. log p determines precision of arithmetic computations. Lesser log p gives less precision, however larger log p is not suitable to bootstrapping as it has to follow log $p + $ log $(value) < (\log q)$, i.e. log $p < \log (q/value)$ Therefore, log p around 23–30 is suitable for most PPML applications if the range of input values is fixed. However, for unknown input values lower log p can be used.

Summary: For primitive operations on FHE data such as addition, subtraction, multiplication and matrix multiplication, SEAL outperforms HElib and HEAAN. Hence, SEAL is recommended for non-packing based implementations. We recommended HEAAN for packing based implementations as it supports packing floating point numbers as well as negative numbers. We also recommended HEAAN for the linear/logistic regression algorithms as it allows us to make the interaction with the client once in every five iterations which makes it semi-interactive model. For bootstrapping operation, HEAAN is recommended. To set parameter n we need $n = 2^k$, $S.T$ $n \geq ab$, where ab is dimension of matrix to be encrypted, parameter N has to be (atleast) $2n$. log p is for precision which we recommend for PPML applications to be between 23–30. log Q can be set as log $p + log(value) < log$ q.

Compilers like CHET and Alchemy estimate parameters for a specific computation and using a specific FHE scheme. Hence there is need for a generic framework to estimate the best scheme and parameter combinations for any PPML computation. In the next section, we propose a novel framework for a recommender system for PPML applications based on FHE. We provide experimental analysis with our recommendation system for matrix multiplication and linear regression to validate our observations in Sects. 3 and 4.

5 Recommendation System for FHE

In this section, we formally define our recommender system and provide the description on how we evaluate the inputs provided by the users.

5.1 Formulation

Given an input application which is represented as a computing function $\mathbf{F}$ with input data set and its associated constraints such as computation time τ_f, memory $\mathbf{m_f}$, communication cost $comm_f$, computation cost ξ_f and security level λ, objective of the proposed recommendation system is to find an optimal recommendation (w.r.t. τ_f, $\mathbf{m_f}$, $comm_f$, ξ_f and λ) to efficiently implement an application in a privacy preserving manner using any of the available FHE libraries. Let $\mathcal{L} = \{l_1 \ldots l_\alpha\}$ be the set of FHE libraries available and each library l_q with security level λ_j supports set of $S_{l_q} = \{s_{q_1}, s_{q_2}, \ldots, s_{q_{\rho_q}}\}$ FHE schemes. We assume that an application is represented as $\mathbf{F}$, wherein $\mathbf{F} = \{f_1, f_2, f_3, \ldots f_n\}$ is represented as an arithmetic expression tree and each $f_i \in \mathbf{F}$ are the nodes (sub computations of $\mathbf{F}$) of the tree. Note that $f_{ijk}^\tau, f_{ijk}^m, f_{ijk}^{comm}$ and f_{ijk}^ξ are the computation time, memory, communication cost and computation cost requirement to compute f_i using library l_j and FHE scheme $S_{l_{j_k}}$ respectively. Now the proposed recommendation system is modeled as a multi objective and multi criterion optimization problem with a goal to minimize computation time τ, memory consumption m, communication cost $comm$ and computation cost of a function F in a privacy preserving manner.

$$\mathcal{F}_\tau{}^* = \operatorname{argmin}\{F_j^\tau | F_j^\tau = \operatorname{argmin}\{F_{jk}^\tau | \lambda_j > \lambda\}_{k \in S_{l_j}}, l_j \in \mathcal{L}\} \tag{1}$$

$$\mathcal{F}_m^* = \operatorname{argmin}\{F_j^m | F_j^m = \operatorname{argmin}\{F_{jk}^m | \lambda_j > \lambda\}_{k \in S_{l_j}}, l_j \in \mathcal{L}\} \tag{2}$$

$$\mathcal{F}_\xi{}^* = \operatorname{argmin}\{F_j^\xi | F_j^\xi = \operatorname{argmin}\{F_{jk}^\xi | \lambda_j > \lambda\}_{k \in S_{l_j}}, l_j \in \mathcal{L}\} \tag{3}$$

$$\mathcal{F}_{comm}^* = \operatorname{argmin}\{F_j^{comm} | F_j^m = \operatorname{argmin}\{F_{jk}^{comm} | \lambda_j > \lambda\}_{k \in S_{l_j}}, l_j \in \mathcal{L}\} \tag{4}$$

$$F_{jk}^\tau = \sum_{i=1}^{|\mathcal{F}|} f_{ijk}^\tau x_{ijk} \leq \tau_f, F_{jk}^m = \sum_{i=1}^{|\mathcal{F}|} f_{ijk}^m x_{ijk} \leq m_f \tag{5}$$

$$F_{jk}^{comm} = \sum_{i=1}^{|\mathcal{F}|} f_{ijk}^{comm} x_{ijk} \leq comm_f, F_{jk}^\xi = \sum_{i=1}^{|\mathcal{F}|} f_{ijk}^\xi x_{ijk} \leq \xi_f \tag{6}$$

$$x_{ijk} = \begin{cases} 1 & \text{If } f_i \text{ can be computed using library } l_j \text{ and FHE scheme } S_{l_{j_k}} \\ 0 & \text{otherwise} \end{cases}$$

$$\sum_{k=1}^{|\mathcal{F}|} x_{ijk} = |\mathcal{F}| \tag{7}$$

The above described multi objective optimization can be converted into single objective function, which is described as follows

$$\mathcal{F}^* = \mathtt{argmin}\{F_j|F_j = \mathtt{argmin}\{F_{jk}|\lambda_j > \lambda\}_{k \in S_{l_j}}, l_j \in \mathcal{L}\} \tag{8}$$

$$F_{jk} = \sum_{i=1}^{|\mathcal{F}|} f_{ijk} x_{ijk} \tag{9}$$

$$f_{ijk} = \mathcal{W}_\tau * f_{ijk}^\tau + \mathcal{W}_m * f_{ijk}^m + \mathcal{W}_{comm} * f_{ijk}^{comm} + \mathcal{W}_\xi * f_{ijk}^\xi \tag{10}$$

$$\mathcal{W}_\tau + \mathcal{W}_m + \mathcal{W}_{comm} + \mathcal{W}_\xi = 1 \tag{11}$$

$$\sum_{i=1}^{|\mathcal{F}|} f_{ijk}^\tau x_{ijk} \le \tau_f, \sum_{i=1}^{|\mathcal{F}|} f_{ijk}^m x_{ijk} \le m_f \tag{12}$$

$$\sum_{i=1}^{|\mathcal{F}|} f_{ijk}^{comm} x_{ijk} \le comm_f, \sum_{i=1}^{|\mathcal{F}|} f_{ijk}^\xi x_{ijk} \le \xi_f \tag{13}$$

$$x_{ijk} = \begin{cases} 1 & \text{If } f_i \text{ can be computed using library } l_j \text{ and FHE scheme } S_{l_{jk}} \\ 0 & \text{otherwise} \end{cases}$$

$$\sum_{k=1}^{|\mathcal{F}|} x_{ijk} = |\mathcal{F}| \tag{14}$$

These inputs can be fed into the system through various methods. For example, a configuration file or a mathematical formula. Based on the given inputs, the optimization problem can be modelled in two ways:

- Model A: User provides all the constraints based on which recommendation is provided.
- Model B: User provides only the computation to be performed where our system comes up with different set choices for the user to choose based on the requirement.

5.2 Analysis

We now present our analysis for a recommendation system using formulation mentioned earlier. The optimization is multi-objective since we want to reduce computation time, memory requirement at the same time keeping parameters as low as possible which depends on packing required or not, bootstrapping for interactive or non interactive etc. However solving multi objective optimization is believed to be hard problem [53–55]. Hence we present our analysis for a single objective optimization problem using TOPSIS optimizer (Tables 8 and 9).

Table 8. Analysis for 100×100 Matrix Mult, * includes memory for keys, temporary storage etc. for $logN = 12$

Operation	Calculated estimates			Practical w/o packing			Practical with packing	
	HElib	SEAL	HEAAN	HElib	SEAL	HEAAN	SEAL2	HEAAN2
Add + Mul (millisecs)	16	13.5	28.9	16	13.5	28.9	30	283
100×100 Matrix mult on 32 cores (secs)	330	200	1100	680	278	745	11.7	22.5
Memory per ciphertext (KB)	443	16	106	443	16	106	262144	1048
Memory for 100×100 matrix mult (GB)	4.4	0.16	1.06	11.4*	3.78*	17.78*	0.8*	0.14*
Rank - Time and Mem equal weight	2	1	3	4	3	5	1	2
Rank - Mem more weight than Time	3	1	2	4	3	5	2	1

We gave two sets of inputs to the recommendation system optimization solver (TOPSIS), set-I is Columns $\{2, 3 \ and \ 4\}$ and set-II is Columns $\{5 - 10\}$. Set-I give estimates of each of the operations based on the computation of basic primitive operations. Using this the optimizer gave SEAL library as the optimal solution for matrix multiplication. For set-II, if time and memory consumption are given same weightage by the user, the optimizer gives SEAL-2 as the optimal solution, with HEAAN 2 as the second preference and SEAL as third. However, if memory is given higher weightage, then optimizer returns HEAAN-2 as the optimal solution, SEAL-2 and SEAL as second and third preference respectively.

Table 9. Analysis for Linear Regression for 150×4, *includes memory for keys, temporary storage etc. $logN$ for SEAL is 8192 and HEAAN is 2048 as explained in Sect. 4.4

Operation	Calculated estimates		Practical	
	SEAL	HEAAN	SEAL	HEAAN
Add (millisecs)	2	0.88	2	0.88
Mul (millisecs)	62.8	470	62.8	470
Time - Linear Regression - 150×4 dataset (secs)	2	1.8	10	7.7
Memory per ciphertext (KB)	64	524	64	524
Memory for LR (MB)	151	0.01	921*	0.469*
Rank	2	1	2	1

We gave two sets of inputs to the recommendation system optimization solver (TOPSIS), set-I Columns $\{2 \ and \ 3\}$ and set-II Columns $\{4 \ and \ 5\}$. The optimizer gives HEAAN as the best solution for both the sets.

6 Conclusion

Privacy is a growing concern, especially when it comes to who is processing our data. FHE seems to be the most promising solution to this problem. In this regard, we have considered three prominent libraries for machine learning over encrypted data namely HElib SEAL and HEAAN and compared them for various usecases to demonstrate the usability of each of these libraries for specific scenarios. We proposed a novel framework for a recommendation system as a multi objective multi constraint optimization problem, along with a simpler version of it as a single objective multi constraint optimization problem. We supported our formulation with calculated estimates and actual computation times for matrix multiplication and linear regression and solving single objective multi constraint optimization using TOPSIS optimizer. The proposed recommendation system can be used in FHE compilers to facilitate optimal implementation of PPML applications. As part of our future work, we will be continuously evaluating more computations using our framework.

Acknowledgement. We would like to thank the anonymous reviewers for their valuable feedback and comments on improving this paper.

Appendix

In this section, we describe the data movement in slots in packed linear regression algorithm.

Packed Linear Regression

Input matrix X is encrypted in a single ciphertext where $m \times n < N/2$. The model values w are encoded and encrypted in a single ciphertext by duplicating the values m times.

$$X_{m\times n} = \begin{bmatrix} x_{11} & \cdots & x_{1n} \\ x_{21} & \cdots & x_{2n} \\ \cdot & \cdots & \cdot \\ \cdot & \cdots & \cdot \\ x_{m1} & \cdots & x_{mn} \end{bmatrix}_{m\times n} \qquad w_{n\times 1} = \begin{bmatrix} w_1 \\ w_2 \\ \cdot \\ \cdot \\ w_n \end{bmatrix}_{n\times 1}$$

$$\mathrm{Enc}[X_{m\times n}] = \mathrm{Enc}\begin{bmatrix} x_{11} & \cdots & x_{1n} \\ x_{21} & \cdots & x_{2n} \\ \cdot & \cdots & \cdot \\ \cdot & \cdots & \cdot \\ x_{m1} & \cdots & x_{mn} \end{bmatrix}_{m\times n} \qquad \mathrm{Enc}[w_{n\times 1}] = \mathrm{Enc}\begin{bmatrix} w_1 & w_2 & \cdots & w_n \\ w_1 & w_2 & \cdots & w_n \\ \cdot & & & \\ \cdot & & & \\ w_1 & w_2 & \cdots & w_n \end{bmatrix}_{m\times n}$$

The subscripts are written only to provide clarity of how values in slots need to be mapped for operations to be done correctly.

The output matrix is encoded by placing each y_i value at index multiples of n.

$$Y_{m \times 1} = \begin{bmatrix} y_1 \\ y_2 \\ . \\ . \\ y_m \end{bmatrix}_{m \times 1} \implies \text{Enc}[Y_{m \times 1}] = \text{Enc} \begin{bmatrix} y_1 & 0 \dots 0 \\ y_2 & 0 \dots 0 \\ . \\ . \\ y_m & 0 \dots 0 \end{bmatrix}_{m \times n}$$

Now we begin the computation of following LR algorithm:

$$\theta_{update} = \theta - \alpha[Y - wX]X^T$$

– Computing wX. Multiplying two ciphertexts X and w multiplies values in each slots respectively. To complete the multiplication, rotate the slots $n - 1$ times and add to the original result.

To remove the garbage values in other slots, multiply by 1 matrix defined as follows:

$$\text{Enc}[wX] = \text{Enc} \begin{bmatrix} x_1 \times W & * \dots * \\ x_2 \times W & * \dots * \\ . \\ . \\ x_m \times W & * \dots * \end{bmatrix}_{m \times n} \times \text{Enc} \begin{bmatrix} 1 & 0 \dots 0 \\ 1 & 0 \dots 0 \\ . \\ . \\ 1 & 0 \dots 0 \end{bmatrix}_{m \times n} = \text{Enc} \begin{bmatrix} x_1 \times W & 0 \dots 0 \\ x_2 \times W & 0 \dots 0 \\ . \\ . \\ x_m \times W & 0 \dots 0 \end{bmatrix}_{m \times n}$$

– Compute $Y - wX$. Since the y_i values are in their respective slots, we can proceed with subtraction operation.

The result of the subtraction is as follows:

$$\text{Enc} \begin{bmatrix} A_1 & 0 \dots 0 \\ A_2 & 0 \dots 0 \\ . \\ . \\ A_m & 0 \dots 0 \end{bmatrix}_{m \times n} \qquad where \ A_i = y_i - (x_i \times W)$$

– Compute $[Y - wX] \times X^T$. As we can see, there is a mismatch in the values in each slots of $Y - wX$ and X^T and we cannot simply proceed with the multiplication. Now we have to move the data between the slots to get the following transformation:

$$\text{Enc} \begin{bmatrix} A_1 & A_2 \dots A_m \\ A_1 & A_2 \dots A_m \\ . \\ . \\ A_1 & A_2 \dots A_m \end{bmatrix}_{n \times m}$$

This is done using the following steps which takes much computation time. Let B=(Y-wX), sum ← Enc(0), A ← Enc(0). Let set(i) denote function which sets i^{th} slot of vector as 1 and remaining as 0 and gets an encryption of this vector

```
for i ← 0 to m-1
    Add(sum, mul(rotate − left(B, i*n-i),set(i)))
for i ← 1 to n-1
    Add(A, rotate-right(sum, i*m))
```

`set(i)` is used to get the A_i value and then it is rotated to the appropriate location and added to sum. This completes getting all m values together. The we again rotate these values and add $n-1$ times to complete the transformation. Efficient on-the fly packing will be useful to solve this issue of data movement in between operations.

$$\text{Enc} \begin{bmatrix} A_1 \times x_{11} & A_2 \times x_{21} & \ldots & A_m \times x_{m1} \\ A_1 \times x_{12} & A_2 \times x_{22} & \ldots & A_m \times x_{m2} \\ . & & & \\ . & & & \\ A_1 \times x_{1n} & A_2 \times x_{2n} & \ldots & A_m \times x_{mn} \end{bmatrix}_{n \times m}$$

Now we perform rotation of matrix to complete multiplication and multiply with 1 matrix to get:

$$\text{Enc} \begin{bmatrix} A_1 \times X_1 & 0 \ldots 0 \\ A_2 \times X_2 & 0 \ldots 0 \\ . & 0 \ldots 0 \\ . & 0 \ldots 0 \\ A_n \times X_n & 0 \ldots 0 \end{bmatrix}_{n \times m} \qquad where \; A_i X_i = \sum_{j=1}^{m} A_j x_{jk} \; for \; k \in [1, n]$$

– Multiply $[Y - wX]X^T$ with α, the learning rate Now the values of gradient have to be mapped to respective slots for theta updation as follows:

$$\theta_{update} = \text{Enc} \begin{bmatrix} w_1 - A_1X_1\alpha & w_2 - A_2X_2\alpha & \ldots & w_n - A_nX_n\alpha \\ w_1 - A_1X_1\alpha & w_2 - A_2X_2\alpha & \ldots & w_n - A_nX_n\alpha \\ . & . & \ldots & . \\ . & . & \ldots & . \\ w_1 - A_1X_1\alpha & w_2 - A_2X_2\alpha & \ldots & w_n - A_nX_n\alpha \end{bmatrix}_{m \times n}$$

The algorithm is repeated until θ converges.

References

1. Trusted execution environment specification (2015). https://globalplatform.org/specs-library/tee-initial-configuration-v1-1/
2. Goldreich, O.: Secure multi-party computation. Manuscript. Preliminary version, 78 (1998)
3. Huang, Y., Evans, D., Katz, J., Malka, L.: Faster secure two-party computation using garbled circuits. In: USENIX Security Symposium, vol. 201, pp. 331–335 (2011)
4. Gentry, C., Boneh, D.: A fully homomorphic encryption scheme. Stanford University (2009)

5. Rivest, R.L., Adleman, L., Dertouzos, M.L.: On data banks and privacy homomorphisms. Found. Secure Comput. **4**, 169–180 (1978)
6. Technique for order of preference by similarity to ideal solution. https://decision-radar.com/Topsis.html
7. iDash competition (2019). http://www.humangenomeprivacy.org/2019/
8. Kim, M., Lauter, K.: Private genome analysis through homomorphic encryption. BMC Med. Inform. Decis. Mak. **15**, S3 (2015)
9. Brakerski, Z., Gentry, C., Vaikuntanathan, V.: (leveled) fully homomorphic encryption without bootstrapping. ACM Trans. Comput. Theory (TOCT) **6**(3), 13 (2014)
10. Bos, J.W., Lauter, K., Loftus, J., Naehrig, M.: Improved security for a ring-based fully homomorphic encryption scheme. In: Stam, M. (ed.) IMACC 2013. LNCS, vol. 8308, pp. 45–64. Springer, Heidelberg (2013). https://doi.org/10.1007/978-3-642-45239-0_4
11. Lu, W.-J., Yamada, Y., Sakuma, J.: Privacy-preserving genome-wide association studies on cloud environment using fully homomorphic encryption. BMC Med. Inform. Decis. Mak. **15**, S1 (2015)
12. Zhang, Y., Dai, W., Jiang, X., Xiong, H., Wang, S.: FORESEE: fully outsourced secure genome study based on homomorphic encryption. BMC Med. Inform. Decis. Mak. **15**, S5 (2015)
13. Çetin, G.S., Chen, H., Laine, K., Lauter, K., Rindal, P., Xia, Y.: Private queries on encrypted genomic data. BMC Med. Genom. **10**(2), 45 (2017)
14. Kim, A., Song, Y., Kim, M., Lee, K., Cheon, J.H.: Logistic regression model training based on the approximate homomorphic encryption. BMC Med. Genom. **11**(4), 83 (2018)
15. Chen, H., et al.: Logistic regression over encrypted data from fully homomorphic encryption. BMC Med. Genom. **11**(4), 81 (2018)
16. Duality tech. https://duality.cloud/duality-wins-idash-competition-fastest-computations-genomic-data/
17. Han, K., Hong, S., Cheon, J.H., Park, D.: Efficient logistic regression on large encrypted data. Technical report, Cryptology ePrint Archive, Report 2018/662. https://eprint.iacr.org/2018/662 (2018)
18. Bergamaschi, F., Halevi, S., Halevi, T.T., Hunt, H.: Homomorphic training of 30,000 logistic regression models. In: Deng, R.H., Gauthier-Umaña, V., Ochoa, M., Yung, M. (eds.) ACNS 2019. LNCS, vol. 11464, pp. 592–611. Springer, Cham (2019). https://doi.org/10.1007/978-3-030-21568-2_29
19. Kim, M., Song, Y., Li, B., Micciancio, D.: Semi-parallel logistic regression for GWAS on encrypted data (2019)
20. Crawford, J.L.H., Gentry, C., Halevi, S., Platt, D., Shoup, V.: Doing real work with FHE: the case of logistic regression. In: Proceedings of the 6th Workshop on Encrypted Computing & Applied Homomorphic Cryptography, pp. 1–12. ACM (2018)
21. Kim, M., Song, Y., Wang, S., Xia, Y., Jiang, X.: Secure logistic regression based on homomorphic encryption: design and evaluation. JMIR Med. Inform. **6**(2), e19 (2018)
22. Wang, S., et al.: HEALER: homomorphic computation of exact logistic regression for secure rare disease variants analysis in GWAS. Bioinformatics **32**(2), 211–218 (2015)
23. Private AI resources. https://github.com/OpenMined/private-ai-resources
24. Hesamifard, E., Takabi, H., Ghasemi, M., Jones, C.: Privacy-preserving machine learning in cloud. In: Proceedings of the 2017 on Cloud Computing Security Workshop, pp. 39–43. ACM (2017)

25. Martins, P., Sousa, L., Mariano, A.: A survey on fully homomorphic encryption: an engineering perspective. ACM Comput. Surv. (CSUR) **50**(6), 83 (2018)
26. Hallman, R.A., Diallo, M.H., August, M.A., Graves, C.T.: Homomorphic encryption for secure computation on big data. In: IoTBDS, pp. 340–347 (2018)
27. Bost, R., Popa, R.A., Tu, S., Goldwasser, S.: Machine learning classification over encrypted data. In: NDSS, vol. 4324, p. 4325 (2015)
28. Du, Y., Gustafson, L., Huang, D., Peterson, K.: Implementing ML algorithms with HE. In: MIT Course 6. 857: Computer and Network Security (2017)
29. Barthelemy, L.: Blog post on FHE (2016). https://blog.quarkslab.com/a-brief-survey-of-fully-homomorphic-encryption-computing-on-encrypted-data.html
30. PALISADE library (2018). https://git.njit.edu/palisade/PALISADE
31. TFHE: fast fully homomorphic encryption over the torus. https://tfhe.github.io/tfhe/
32. nGraph-HE: HE transformer for nGraph. https://github.com/NervanaSystems/he-transformer
33. Dathathri, R., et al.: CHET: compiler and runtime for homomorphic evaluation of tensor programs. arXiv preprint arXiv:1810.00845 (2018)
34. Crockett, E., Peikert, C., Sharp, C.: ALCHEMY: a language and compiler for homomorphic encryption made easy. In: Proceedings of the 2018 ACM SIGSAC Conference on Computer and Communications Security, pp. 1020–1037 (2018)
35. Crockett, E., Peikert, C.: Functional lattice cryptography. In: Proceedings of the 2016 ACM SIGSAC Conference on Computer and Communications Security, CCS 2016, pp. 993–1005. Association for Computing Machinery, New York (2016)
36. Çetin, G.S., Doröz, Y., Sunar, B., Martin, W.J.: Arithmetic using word-wise homomorphic encryption (2016)
37. Sanyal, A., Kusner, M.J., Gascon, A., Kanade, V.: TAPAS: tricks to accelerate (encrypted) prediction as a service. arXiv preprint arXiv:1806.03461 (2018)
38. Chirgwin, R.: IBM's homomorphic encryption accelerated to run 75 times faster (2018). Retrieved from The Register: https://www.theregister.co.uk/2018/03/08/ibm_faster_homomorphic_encryption
39. Halevi, S., Shoup, V.: Faster homomorphic linear transformations in HElib. In: Shacham, H., Boldyreva, A. (eds.) CRYPTO 2018. LNCS, vol. 10991, pp. 93–120. Springer, Cham (2018). https://doi.org/10.1007/978-3-319-96884-1_4
40. Homomorphic encryption standard (2019). https://eprint.iacr.org/2019/939.pdf
41. Chialva, D., Dooms, A.: Conditionals in homomorphic encryption and machine learning applications. arXiv preprint arXiv:1810.12380 (2018)
42. Chen, H., Laine, K., Player, R.: Simple encrypted arithmetic library - SEAL v2.1. In: Brenner, M., et al. (eds.) FC 2017. LNCS, vol. 10323, pp. 3–18. Springer, Cham (2017). https://doi.org/10.1007/978-3-319-70278-0_1
43. Brakerski, Z., Gentry, C., Halevi, S.: Packed ciphertexts in LWE-based homomorphic encryption. In: Kurosawa, K., Hanaoka, G. (eds.) PKC 2013. LNCS,-vol. 7778, pp. 1–13. Springer, Heidelberg (2013). https://doi.org/10.1007/978-3-642-36362-7_1
44. Carpov, S., Sirdey, R.: A compression method for homomorphic ciphertexts. IACR Cryptology ePrint Archive, 2015:1199 (2015)
45. Doröz, Y., Sunar, B., Çetin, G.S.: On-the-fly homomorphic batching/unbatching (2015)
46. Smart, N.P., Vercauteren, F.: Fully homomorphic SIMD operations. Designs Codes Cryptography **71**(1), 57–81 (2012). https://doi.org/10.1007/s10623-012-9720-4
47. Jiang, X., Kim, M., Lauter, K., Song, Y.: Secure outsourced matrix computation and application to neural networks (2018)

48. Halevi, S., Shoup, V.: Bootstrapping for HElib. In: Oswald, E., Fischlin, M. (eds.) EUROCRYPT 2015. LNCS, vol. 9056, pp. 641–670. Springer, Heidelberg (2015). https://doi.org/10.1007/978-3-662-46800-5_25

49. Chen, H., Han, K.: Homomorphic lower digits removal and improved FHE bootstrapping. In: Nielsen, J.B., Rijmen, V. (eds.) EUROCRYPT 2018. LNCS, vol. 10820, pp. 315–337. Springer, Cham (2018). https://doi.org/10.1007/978-3-319-78381-9_12

50. Cheon, J.H., Han, K., Kim, A., Kim, M., Song, Y.: Bootstrapping for approximate homomorphic encryption. In: Nielsen, J.B., Rijmen, V. (eds.) EUROCRYPT 2018. LNCS, vol. 10820, pp. 360–384. Springer, Cham (2018). https://doi.org/10.1007/978-3-319-78381-9_14

51. Chen, H., Chillotti, I., Song, Y.: Improved bootstrapping for approximate homomorphic encryption. In: Ishai, Y., Rijmen, V. (eds.) EUROCRYPT 2019. LNCS, vol. 11477, pp. 34–54. Springer, Cham (2019). https://doi.org/10.1007/978-3-030-17656-3_2

52. Low birth weight (2018). https://data.unicef.org/topic/nutrition/low-birthweight/

53. Deb, K.: Multi-objective optimisation using evolutionary algorithms: an introduction. In: Wang, L., Ng, A., Deb, K. (eds.) Multi-objective Evolutionary Optimisation for Product Design and Manufacturing, pp. 3–34. Springer, London (2011). https://doi.org/10.1007/978-0-85729-652-8_1

54. Monsef, H., Naghashzadegan, M., Jamali, A., Farmani, R.: Comparison of evolutionary multi objective optimization algorithms in optimum design of water distribution network. Ain Shams Eng. J. 10(1), 103–111 (2019)

55. Greco, S., Klamroth, K., Knowles, J.D., Rudolph, G.: Understanding complexity in multiobjective optimization (dagstuhl seminar 15031). In: Dagstuhl Reports, vol. 5. Schloss Dagstuhl-Leibniz-Zentrum fuer Informatik (2015)

Comparison of DNS Based Methods
for Detecting Malicious Domains

Eyal Paz[1] and Ehud Gudes[1,2(✉)]

[1] The Open University of Israel, Raanana 43107, Israel
`eyalsus@gmail.com`, `ehudgu@openu.ac.il`
[2] Department of Computer Science, Ben-Gurion University, Beer-Sheva, Israel
`ehud@cs.bgu.ac.il`

Abstract. The Domain Name System (DNS) is an essential component of the internet infrastructure, used to translates domain names into IP addresses. Threat actors often abuse this system by registering and taking over thousands of Internet domains every day. These serve to launch various types of cyber-attacks, such as spam, phishing, botnets, and drive-by downloads. Currently, the main countermeasure addressing such threat is reactive blacklisting. Since cyber-attacks are mainly performed for short periods, reactive methods are usually too late and hence ineffective. As a result, new approaches to early identification of malicious websites are needed. In the recent decade, many novel papers were published offering systems to calculate domain reputation for domains that are not listed in common black-lists. This research implements three such approaches and evaluates their effectiveness in detecting malicious phishing domains. The social network analysis technique performed best, as it achieved a 60.71% detection rate with a false positive rate of only 0.35%.

Keywords: Cyber security · DNS · Reputation system · Attack · Phishing · Social network analysis · Privacy-preserving security

1 Introduction

In current days, information security is an important aspect of any organization's business. Finding a cyber-attack in an enterprise network is often analogous to finding the needle in the haystack. Analysis of DNS traffic can be helpful for such quests, as it can provide high quality, cheap and fast attack detection.

Information security usually comes with three price tags: network performance, privacy violation, and false-positive alerts. Network performance impact is caused by deep traffic inspection. Privacy violation is caused by the need to decrypt private encrypted traffic for inspection. False-positive alerts are due to the variance of each network, that challenges any system's ability to generalize. Attack discovery by analysis of DNS traffic can reduce the price tag of all three aspects. DNS is a very simple plaintext protocol containing short messages, usually over UDP protocol. Hence its analysis is simple and fast. On the other hand, its true positive detection would always be inferior to the detection that can be achieved by full packet inspection.

© Springer Nature Switzerland AG 2020
S. Dolev et al. (Eds.): CSCML 2020, LNCS 12161, pp. 219–236, 2020.
https://doi.org/10.1007/978-3-030-49785-9_14

The research presented here covers three major techniques of discovering cyber-attacks via analysis of DNS: passive DNS analysis, domain registration WHOIS record analysis, and predictive domain names blacklisting. To cover as much ground as possible, we employed three approaches that have already appeared in the literature: social network analysis, machine learning, and Markov chain model. These three approaches were implemented in a single system and were compared in an extensive experimental evaluation.

The rest of this paper is structured as follows. Section 2 presents the background and discusses the related work. Sections 3, 4, and 5 describe the experimental evaluation, where Sect. 3 describes the datasets used, Sect. 4 discusses in detail the implemented algorithms, and Sect. 5 presents the results of the experiments. Section 6 concludes the paper and outlines future work.

2 Background and Related Work

This section is divided into three subsections, each surveys a different approach for detecting malicious internet domains.

2.1 Machine Learning

Machine Learning is the science of getting a computer to learn and act like humans do and improve their learning over time in an autonomous fashion, by feeding it data and information in the form of observations and real-world interactions. Machine learning algorithms are commonly divided into supervised learning and unsupervised learning. Supervised learning is algorithms that are useful when there is a large dataset with target labels. While unsupervised learning is useful when there are no labels of a given dataset.

Passive DNS (pDNS) [1] is a collection system that harvests DNS responses. The harvesting is deployed between a DNS server and a higher hierarchy DNS server. pDNS approach advantage is that it keeps the user data private, since there is no visibility to which host had issued each query. The drawback is a lack of ability to correlate different suspicious activity to a specific host. [2, 3] describe systems, which are respectively named EXPOSURE and Notos. Both systems train a supervised machine learning algorithm over a dataset of known benign and malicious domains extracted from a pDNS feed. The trained models are used to compute a reputation score for newly observed domains to indicate whether the newly observed domains are benign or malicious. EXPOSURE features are mostly based on the anomalous DNS behavior of cyber-attacks. An empirical reexamination of global DNS behavior [4] published two years after EXPOSURE paper was published, shows that most of the EXPOSURE major features have become obsolete. Notos uses features mostly based on reuse of the threat actor infrastructures i.e. network subnets. Unlike EXPOSURE, Notos concept leverage threat actor infrastructure reuse is still valid. A major drawback of the Notos system is the need for a vast pDNS repository available with constant classifier retraining.

WHOIS data describes the registration of the domain such as registration date, last modified date, expiration date, registrant contact information, registrar contact information and name server domain. Once the domain has been registered, the relevant registry is the owner of the WHOIS record. The advantage of the WHOIS-based reputation approach is that it could be the first line of defense in detecting new malicious domains. It also enables following threat actors that are reusing registrant strings. Its drawback is that WHOIS information is often anonymized or only partly available, as each registry information is not standard for WHOIS record completeness. PREDATOR [5] is a system aimed to achieve early detection of malicious domains by using only WHOIS records as input. The paper referenced below describes the process for feature engineering. It results in 22 features that help distinguish abusive domain registration behavior characteristics from legitimate registration behavior, 16 of which have not been identified or analyzed in previous work. These features are fed into a state-of-the-art supervised learning algorithm.

2.2 Social Network Analysis

Social network analysis (SNA) is the process of investigating social structures using networks and graph theory. It characterizes networked structures in terms of nodes and edges of a graph. Social network analysis has also been applied to understanding behavior by individuals, organizations, and relationships between websites. Hyperlink analysis can be used to analyze the connections between websites or web pages to examine how information flows as individuals navigate the web. PageRank algorithm [6] which performs social network analysis is used by Google to decide which search results return for their users' search query. In the PageRank algorithm any reference, e.g. hyperlink to web pages, are edges. Node importance is increased by two factors: the in-degree and the importance of the referred nodes. [7] suggested a PageRank approach to detect Phishing websites. A topology-based flow model for computing domain reputation [8] is a reputation system based on the pDNS dataset. It relies on the Domain-IP relationships which were proven to be useful for calculating a domain reputation score by the Notos system [3]. However, instead of using a machine learning classifier, it uses an interesting approach based on a flow algorithm, commonly used for computing trust in social networks and virtual communities. The goal of the flow algorithm is to assign domains with reputation scores given an initial list of domains with a known reputation, benign or malicious. Our social analysis implementation is based on this approach.

2.3 Markov Chain

A Markov chain is a stochastic model describing a sequence of possible events in which the probability of each event depends only on the state attained in the previous event. Each possible transition between two states can be taken with a transition probability. Proactive Discovery of Phishing Related Domain Names [9] describes a system that generates a blacklist of domains by using a Markov chain model and relevant lexical features extracted from a semantic splitter. Domain-specific knowledge is added from semantic tools. The model leverages the fact that threat actor commonly reuses the string pattern used when registering domains for the purpose of a Phishing campaign.

In the experimental evaluation presented below, we compare and evaluate the above three approaches.

3 Experimental Evaluation – The Dataset

This section describes the dataset collection and enrichment made for the domain classifiers' training and testing.

3.1 Data Collection

Data for this project was gathered from 4 free origins: Cisco Umbrella 1 Million popular DNS records and Alexa top 1 Million popular sites were used for benign domain collection, OpenPhish and PhishTank were used for malicious domains collection. All the mentioned origins publish a CSV file which is updated at least daily. Alexa dataset is designed to be an estimate of a website's popularity. As of May 2018, Alexa claims the ranking is calculated from a combination of daily visitors and pageviews on a website over a 3-month period. Cisco Umbrella, formally known as OpenDNS, the dataset is based on the Umbrella global network of more than 100 Billion DNS queries per day, across 65 million unique active users, in more than 165 countries. Although the data source is quite different from Alexa's, it's arguably considered to be more accurate as it's not based on only HTTP requests from users with browser additions.

Figure 1 shows the clear difference between the feeds. For example, while Netflix owns 10 out of the top 15 domains in the Cisco Umbrella ranking, the first entry of a Netflix domain in Alexa ranking on the same day is at the rank of 22. Another example is Microsoft's Windows updates domains that have 3 out of the top 15 domains in the Cisco Umbrella ranking but get much lower ranks on the Alexa ranking.

```
1,google.com                1,netflix.com
2,youtube.com               2,api-global.netflix.com
3,tmall.com                 3,prod.netflix.com
4,baidu.com                 4,push.prod.netflix.com
5,qq.com                    5,ftl.netflix.com
6,sohu.com                  6,prod.ftl.netflix.com
7,facebook.com              7,ichnaea.netflix.com
8,taobao.com                8,nrdp.prod.ftl.netflix.com
9,login.tmall.com           9,google.com
10,yahoo.com                10,secure.netflix.com
11,jd.com                   11,microsoft.com
12,amazon.com               12,nrdp51-appboot.netflix.com
13,wikipedia.org            13,windowsupdate.com
14,360.cn                   14,ctldl.windowsupdate.com
15,sina.com.cn              15,data.microsoft.com
```

Fig. 1. Top 15 rows of Alexa ranking and Cisco Umbrella ranking feeds respectively on both snapshots were taken on 17-Dec-2019.

OpenPhish and PhiskTank dataset are based on community trusted members who share their threat intelligence of phishing websites. It's interesting to know that PhishTank was founded by OpenDNS as the community which several years later released the Cisco Umbrella feed as well. Unlike benign domain sources, the malicious domain sources contain URLs and not domains. Therefore, before adding them to the dataset, some parsing should be made to extract the domains. Table 1 summarizes the data sources' characteristics.

Table 1. Summary of the data sources used on this project.

Attribute	Cisco Umbrella (OpenDNS)	Alexa	OpenPhish	Phish Tank
Classification	Benign	Benign	Malicious	Malicious
Update	Daily	Daily	Hourly	Hourly
Records Type	Domain	Domain	URL	URL
License	Free	Free	Free for partial content	Free
Source	DNS queries	Web page views	Community	Community
Further Context	Popularity rank	Popularity rank	Phishing objective	Phishing objective
Established	2016	1996	2014	2006

3.2 Data Enrichment

The data collected from the sources described in the previous section is enriched with DNS "A" record, DNS "NS" record, Autonomous System (AS) data, and parsed for processing convenience. DNS "A" record is the IPv4 address of the queried domain, DNS "NS" record is the nameserver of the queried domain. AS is the upper hierarchy of the IP address. an example of an enriched record is shown in Table 2. The record after enrichment contains the following fields:

- domain – the input domain.
- timestamp – the timestamp if the first time the data collection encountered the domain.
- label – '0' if the domain is benign, '1' if the domain is malicious.
- base domain – the domain as it appears on the whois registration, for example, edition.cnn.com base domain is cnn.com.
- domain name – the base domain name without the public suffix, for example, edition.cnn.com domain name is cnn.
- Domain IP – the current domain's DNS "A" record, IP address of the input domain.
- AS number – Autonomous System (AS) number of the domain's IP address.
- AS subnet – the matching subnet of the IP address's Autonomous System Number (ASN).
- AS name – the official name of the ASN owner of the domain IP address.
- Nameserver – the current base domain DNS "NS" record, nameserver of the base domain.
- NS base domain – the base domain of the nameserver.
- NS domain IP – the current domain's DNS "A" record, IP address of the nameserver.
- NS AS number – ASN of the nameserver's IP address.
- NS AS subnet – the matching subnet of the nameserver's IP address ASN.
- NS AS name – the official name of the nameserver's IP address ASN owner.

The use of the above datasets by the three algorithms will be explained next.

Table 2. The enriched record of edition.cnn.com

Attribute	Value
domain	edition.cnn.com
timestamp	2020-01-13T19:36:02.817160
label	0
base domain	cnn.com
domain name	cnn
domain IP	151.101.65.67
AS number	54113
AS subnet	151.101.64.0/22
AS name	FASTLY - Fastly US
nameserver	ns-1630.awsdns-ll.co.uk
NS base domain	awsdns-ll.co.uk
NS domain IP	205.251.198.94
NS AS number	16509
NS AS subnet	205.251.198.0/24

4 Experimental Evaluation – The Implemented Classifiers

This section describes the three algorithms used in the domain classifier models implementation.

4.1 Machine Learning

The machine learning classifier implemented for the experiment is based on the PREDA-TOR system [5]. That paper describes 22 types of features used by. These features are divided into three groups: domain profile features, registration history features, and batch correlation features. Unfortunately, the data on registration history features and batch correlation features is not publicly available. Therefore, we focus on domain profile features only. Table 3 shows the PREDATOR feature importance. From the table, we can see that the focus on domain profile features is reasonable since the top 6 features out of the 22 and the top 7 out of the top 8 are domain profile features.

The features we selected to implement in our research are:

– Authoritative nameservers (ranked #1), to increase the detection rate the base domain of the nameserver was used the feature.
– IP addresses of nameservers (ranked #3)
– ASN of nameserver IP addresses (ranked #5)

The project doesn't contain the following features that were presented in PREDA-TOR:

- Trigrams in the domain name (ranked #2) since it causes a massive increase in the number of features and led the classifier to be slow, heavy and tend for overfitting.
- Registrar (ranked #4), this feature can be extracted only from a premium paid feed. Which conflicts with one of the research's secondary goals to the classifiers to be based on free and open repositories only.
- Daily hour of registration & weekday of registration (ranked #6 and #8) since this data is simply not publicly available in any form.

The selected features are categorial, therefore they are translated into binary features since binary features are more common for training Machine Learning models. Table 4 shows an example of categorical features the model decodes into binary features. (Since

Table 3. Ranking of feature importance in PREDATOR [3] (D for domain profile category, R for registration history category, and B for batch correlation category).

Rank	Category	Feature	Score ratio
1	**D**	Authoritative nameservers	100.00%
2	**D**	Trigrams in domain name	64.88%
3	**D**	IP addresses of nameservers	62.98%
4	**D**	Registrar	61.28%
5	**D**	ASes of nameserver IP addresses	30.80%
6	**D**	Daily hour of registration	30.30%
7	**B**	Name cohesiveness	28.98%
8	**D**	Weekday of registration	22.58%
9	**R**	Dormancy period for re-registration	20.58%
10	**R**	Re-registration from same registrar	19.5.%
11	**R**	Life cycle	18.55%
12	**D**	Edit distances to known-bad domains	17.72%
13	**R**	Previous registrar	16.50%
14	**B**	Brand-new proportion	14.60%
15	**B**	Retread proportion	13.71%
16	**B**	Drop-catch proportion	12.90%
17	**D**	Containing digits	11.25%
18	**D**	Name length	10.71%
19	**D**	Ratio of the longest English word	9.60%
20	**B**	Probability of batch size	8.66%
21	**D**	Containing "-"	80.2%
22	**D**	Length of registration period	3.34%

many of the values of the features are repeating many times, the binary representation is not so sparse and not very space consuming.)

For the 18 records shown in Table 4, there is a limit of 18 * 3 = 54 decode features. Table 5 continues the example in Table 4. It shows the decoding result which ended with 11 "NS Base Domain" features, 14 "NS AS Subnet" features, and 13 "NS AS Name" features. Total of 38 features. The greater the dataset, the lower is the ratio between the maximal number of decoded features and the resulted amount. That is due to the repeatedness of the features.

For the phishing domain *paypalaccounttologinaccountsummarmay.com* the feature vector would be "ispvds.com", "94.250.248.0/23", and "THEFIRST-AS RU" set to 1. The other features would be set to 0.

Since this research didn't focus on machine learning classifiers optimization, we have tested two well-known classifiers with their out-of-the-box settings. The classifiers are Logistic Regression and XGBoost. when the latter was state-of-the-art when we started the experiments.

4.2 Social Network Analysis

This classifier was inspired by the Flow Model of [8]. The Flow Model relies on the Domain-IP relationships which were proven to be useful for calculating domain reputation scores by the Notos system [2]. However, instead of using a machine learning classifier, it uses an interesting approach based on social network analysis (SNA) algorithm, commonly used for computing trust in social networks and virtual communities. The main idea of [8] is to use Reputation as an asset which flows via the edges of the graph, wherein each iteration, for each node, the reputation from its neighboring nodes is aggregated into the current node and is normalized into a value between 0 and 1. Unlike the original paper, we found it to be more useful to work on a graph data structure than on an adjacency matrix. That is because an adjacency matrix is less intuitive and less efficient from a performance point-of-view. Another difference from the original paper is the entities we used on the graph. We leverage all the enriched data described in the "Data Enrichment" section. Adding the "NS" DNS records and ASN data, while the original paper used only "A" records. This results with differences in the meaning of edges as is explained next.

Figure 2 shows the Python function implementation involved in the training phase which constructs the graph. "train" is the model interface function. For every record in the given input dataset, it calls "_append_row_to_graph" which append a single enriched domain record to the graph. Notice that the record contains the ground truth label as well. Other than the label domain, 0 for benign and 1 for malicious, all the of the other nodes get the initial value of 0.5. Lines 7–15 are adding the nodes to the graph, lines 17–25 are adding the edges between the nodes that were previously added. This means that edges represent different types of connections, not only domain-IP connections such as IP-AS domain-Subnet, AS name-AS number and more as listed in Fig. 2. INITIAIL_VALUE is the default value for the non-labeled nodes. In the experiments described in Sect. 4, the INITIAIL_VALUE was set to 0.5.

Figure 3 shows the visualization of a populated graph. When we add the unlabeled enriched node "edition.cnn.com", additional nodes and edges are created: green nodes

Table 4. Records from the dataset for building an example model for PayPal phishing detection

Domain	NS base domain	NS AS subnet	NS AS name	Label
paypal.com.user-login.secure-id.ref939a.com	dendrite.network	45.9.148.0/24	NICEIT NL	1
paypalaccounttologinaccountsummarmay.com	ispvds.com	94.250.248.0/23	THEFIRST-AS RU	1
paypal-id-signin-customer-center-customer-locale-g-en.cf	freenom.com	104.155.00/19	GOOGLE- Google LLC US	1
paypal.com.au-dispute50043.gajsiddhiglobal.com	speedhost.in	208.91.198.0/23	PUBLIC-DOMAIN-REGISTRY-PDR US	1
paypal-limitato-conferma.kozow.com	dynu.com	45.79.208.0/20	LINODE-AP Linode LLC US	1
paypal.co.uk.3uea.icu	dnspod.com	119.28.48.0/23	TENCENT-NET-AP-CN Tencent Building Kejizhongyi Avenue CN	1
paypal.co.uk.v15m.icu	dnspod.com	180.160.0.0/13	CHINANET-SH-AP China Telecom(Group)CN	1
paypal.de-center.buzz	cloudflare.com	173.245.59.0/24	CLOUDFLARENET-Cloudflare Inc. US	1
paypal.co.uk.dii7.icu	dnspod.com	59.36.112.0/20	CHINANET-IDC-GD China Telecom(Group)CN	1
paypal-webnative.surge.sh	iwantmyname.net	83.169.54.0/23	GODADDY DE	1
checkout.paypal.com	ultradns.net	156.154.65.0/24	ULTRADNS-NeuStar Inc. US	0
c6.paypal.com.edgekey.net	akam.net	95.100.173.0/24	AKAMAI-ASN2 US	0
api-m-edge.glb.paypal.com	dynect.net	204.13.250.0/24	DYNDNS- Oracle Corporation US	0
svcs.paypal.com	ultradns.net	156.154.65.0/24	ULTRADNS-NeuStar Inc. US	0
paypal.me	dynect.net	204.13.250.0/24	DYNDNS-Oracle Corporation US	0
paypal-deutschland.de	dynect.net	208.78.70.0/24	DYNDNS-Oracle Corporation US	0
paypal.com.au	ultradns.net	156.154.65.0/24	ULTRADNS-NeuStar Inc. US	0
paypal-business.co.uk	dynect.net	208.78.70.0/24	DYNDNS-Oracle Corporation US	0

Table 5. Decoded features for the records of Table 4.

NS base domain	NS AS subnet	NS AS name
akam.net	104.155.0.0/19	AKAMAI-ASN2 US
cloudflare.com	119.28.48.0/23	CHINANET-IDC-GD China Telecom (Group) CN
dendrite.network	156.154.65.0/24	CHINANET-SH-AP China Telecom (Group) CN
dnspod.com	173.245.59.0/24	CLOUDFLARENET-Cloudflare Inc. US
dynect.net	180.160.0.0/13	DYNDNS-Oracle Corporation US
dynu.com	204.13.250.0/24	GODADDY DE
freenom.com	208.78.70.0/24	GOOGLE-Google LLC US
ispvds.com	208.91.198.0/23	LINODE-AP Linode LLC US
iwantmyname.net	45.79.208.0/20	NICEIT NL
speedhost.in	45.9.148.0/24	PUBLIC-DMAIN-REGISTRY-PDR US
ultradns.net	59.36.112.0/20	TENCENT-NET-AP-CN Tencent Building Kejizhongyi Avenue CN
	83.169.54.0/23	THEFIRST-AS RU
	94.250.248.0/23	ULTRADNS-NeuStar Inc. US

are labeled as benign, red are labeled as malicious and brown nodes are unlabeled. As expected, most of the neighbors of "edition.cnn.com" are benign or unlabeled. The only red node in the graph is a subdomain of a freemium hosting service. Freemium hosting is a service that offers free basic web services deployment and a paid fully-suite package. In this case, codeanywhere.com is a freemium service that was abused for malicious purposes.

After all enriched labeled domain records were appended to the graph, we can start the training phase. To train the graph all we need is to run several iterations of updating every node in the graph using the function described in Algorithm 1. This process propagates the reputation score of every node to its neighbors. Notice that even nodes that are initially labeled as benign could get a malicious score and vice versa. This is by design since it's known that ground truth in cyber-security is a real tough problem and often domains are falsely labeled as benign or malicious. Our analysis shows that 5 iterations are enough, [8] reached a similar conclusion on their implementation. In each iteration, every node score is set to be the average between its current score and the average score of its neighbors as described on Algorithm 1.

After building the network graph it can be used for calculating unlabeled domain reputation by following the below steps:

1. Enriched the domain as described in Sect. 3.2.
2. Append the enriched domain record to the graph as described in Fig. 2.
3. Propagate the reputation score of every node to its neighbors as described above.
4. Return the analyzed domain's current reputation score.

```
1    def _append_row_to_graph(self, row, G):
2        if 'label' in row:
3            G.add_node(row['domain'], start=row['label'], current=row['label'])
4            G.add_node(row['domain_ip'], start=row['label'], current=row['label'])
5        else:
6            G.add_node(row['domain'], start=INITIAL_VALUE, current=INITIAL_VALUE)
7            G.add_node(row['domain_ip'], start=INITIAL_VALUE, current=INITIAL_VALUE)
8
9        G.add_node(row['as_subnet'], start=INITIAL_VALUE, current=INITIAL_VALUE)
10       G.add_node(row['as_number'], start=INITIAL_VALUE, current=INITIAL_VALUE)
11       G.add_node(row['as_name'], start=INITIAL_VALUE, current=INITIAL_VALUE)
12       G.add_node(row['ns_base_domain'], start=INITIAL_VALUE, current=INITIAL_VALUE)
13       G.add_node(row['ns_as_subnet'], start=INITIAL_VALUE, current=INITIAL_VALUE)
14       G.add_node(row['ns_as_number'], start=INITIAL_VALUE, current=INITIAL_VALUE)
15       G.add_node(row['ns_as_name'], start=INITIAL_VALUE, current=INITIAL_VALUE)
16
17       if row['base_domain'] != row['domain']:
18           G.add_node(row['base_domain'], start=INITIAL_VALUE, current=INITIAL_VALUE)
19           G.add_edge(row['base_domain'], row['domain'])
20
21       G.add_edge(row['domain'], row['domain_ip'])
22       G.add_edge(row['domain_ip'], row['as_subnet'])
23       G.add_edge(row['as_subnet'], row['as_number'])
24       G.add_edge(row['as_number'], row['as_name'])
25
26       G.add_edge(row['base_domain'], row['ns_base_domain'])
27       G.add_edge(row['ns_base_domain'], row['ns_as_subnet'])
28       G.add_edge(row['ns_as_subnet'], row['ns_as_number'])
29       G.add_edge(row['ns_as_number'], row['ns_as_name'])
```

Fig. 2. Append enriched domain record to the graph function

Algorithm 1: Node v reputation score update by propagation of its neighbors' reputation

---

UpdateNode $(v, atten)$
    inputs : Node v
    output: An updated node v
    if $Degree(v) > 0$ **then**
        $NeighborsScoreSum \leftarrow 0$;
        foreach $Node\ u \in Neighbors(v)$ **do**
            $NeighborsScoreSum \leftarrow$
            $NeighborsScoreSum + u.CurrentScore$;
        $NeighborsCurrentAvg = NeighborsScoreSum/Degree(v)$;
        $v.CurrentScore \leftarrow$
        $v.CurrentScore * (1 - atten) + NeighborsCurrentAvg * atten$;
    return v;

4.3 Markov Chain

The Markov chain classifier implemented for the experiment used the name decomposition using the Compound-Word-Splitter python package. After the domain name

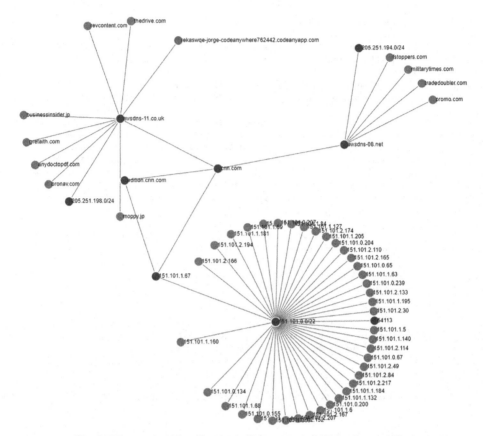

Fig. 3. Ego graph with radius 3 of edition.cnn.com (Color figure online)

decomposition phase words statistics are gathered. Figure 4 shows an example of words statistics gathering for the word "free" and the word "pay".

In the case of the word "free", the next transition in the Markov chain would be any one of the words in the "transitions" counter. Since all the following words have the same amount of appearances following the word "free", they would get the same probability for the next phase: $1/11 = 0.090909$. In the case of the word "pay," the next transition in the Markov chain would be any one of the words in the "transitions" counter. Since all the following words but the word "problems" have the same amount of appearances following the word "free", they would get the same probability for the next phase: $1/13 = 0.076923$ and the word "problems" which appeared twice, it's probability would be $2/13 = 0.153846$.

The decision to end the domain name, i.e. not to continue with another transition, is made using the "sentence_length" field in the "word statistics" data structure as shown in Fig. 4, lines 9–14 left and lines 8–13 right. The stop criterion is based on the sentence words length statistics of the last word in the generated domain name using the Markov chain, we have created a predictive blacklist of domain names similarly as described on [8]. For increased coverage the public suffix is not apart of our model, e.g. we assume

```
1   {                                          1   {
2       'appeareance': 15,                     2       'appeareance': 17,
3       'index': Counter({                     3       'index': Counter({
4           0: 8,                              4           0: 9,
5           1: 3,                              5           1: 5,
6           2: 3,                              6           3: 3
7           3: 1                               7       }),
8       }),                                    8       'sentence_length': Counter({
9       'sentence_length': Counter({           9           3: 6,
10          2: 4,                             10           4: 5,
11          3: 7,                             11           2: 5,
12          5: 1,                             12           5: 1
13          4: 3                              13       }),
14      }),                                   14       'transitions': Counter({
15      'transitions': Counter({              15           'pay': 0,
16          'free': 0,                        16           'problems': 2,
17          'liker': 1,                       17           'la': 1,
18          'o': 1,                           18           'x': 1,
19          'you': 1,                         19           'certain': 1,
20          'get': 1,                         20           'v': 1,
21          'click': 1,                       21           'pack': 1,
22          'gift': 1,                        22           'io': 1,
23          '1': 1,                           23           'you': 1,
24          'game': 1,                        24           'm': 1,
25          'ia': 1,                          25           'only': 1,
26          'host': 1,                        26           'bank': 1,
27          'movies': 1                       27           '7158': 1
28      })                                    28       })
29  }                                         29   }
```

Fig. 4. Word statistics for the words "free" and "pay" respectively

the model predicts the domain name is malicious for all public suffixes. Table 6 shows an example of domains generated by the Markov model.

5 Experimental Evaluation – The Results

This section covers the process of the experiments: data cleaning, threshold selection, and classifier result evaluation.

5.1 Data Cleaning

In the early stages of the experiment, an anomaly popped up. Many malicious domains were hosted as a subdomain of popular hosting websites such as 000webhostapp.com, azurewebsites.net, duckdns.org, no-ip.com, no-ip.org, wixsite.com. The all the mentioned domain serves a website that offers a freemium hosting platform. Threat actor takes advantage of these freemium services for their malicious purpose. Consider the enriched domain record in Table 7. The malicious domain is hosted on a legit domain infrastructure, the malicious domain is hosted on a legit domain infrastructure, i.e. the webserver IP address, and the domain nameserver are not strongly tied to the attacker. In order to avoid causing confusion to the classifiers, malicious domains hosted on the mentioned hosting providers were removed from the train and test set. It resulted in a 32% reduction in the dataset. That is not a great loss since these domains could not be analyzed by the classifier developed in this project anyway since the top domain is always benign. Therefore, we have decided the classifier should not train and test on

Table 6. Domains predicted to be malicious by the Markov model

Domain name	Words
freedompowerglobalkarma	freedom;power;global;karma
attorneyusahastudiolife	attorney;us;aha;studio;life
pastoronlinebanking	pastor;online;banking
aidecipakistantrips	aide;ci;pakistan;trips
frostemcampaigns	frost;em;campaigns
carpetsbemobilevices	carpets;be;mobile;vices
bankonlinevideos	bank;online;videos
bankonlinecentertaipei	bank;online;center;taipei
freeksbargranola	free;ks.bar;granola
freesignals	free;signals
finddeviceintpay	find;device;int;pay
paypaylogin	pay;pay;login
paymentpartner	payment;partner
applespayinfo	apples;pay;info;
paceappdomain	pace;app;domain

these hosting domain records. These kinds of malicious websites can be detected by other approaches that are not discussed in this paper such as webpage visual analysis and webpage source code analysis.

Table 7. Malicious website hosted on legit domain infrastructure

Domain	AS Subnet	AS Name	NS Base Domain
peringatanfacebook5.wixsite.com	185.230.62.0/24	WIS-COM IL	dynect.net
france-apple-store.azurewebsites.net	168.61.0.0/16	MICROSOFT-COPR-MSN-AS-BLOCK US	azuredns-prd.info
microsoft-web-gh.000webhostapp.com	145.14.144.0/23	AWEX US	000webhost.com
chasecure.duckdns.org	192.169.69.0/24	WOW-Wowrack.com US	duckdns.org

5.2 Data Separation

To decide which threshold every classifier should have We have visualized all the classifiers' verdicts into the charts seen in Fig. 5.

The classifiers' threshold selection is an important part of the experiment. The optimal threshold is the one that conducts a perfect separation between the classes. In our case the separation between benign and malicious domains. Since in real life the optimal threshold is not perfect, we'll select a threshold that maximizes true positives and at cost

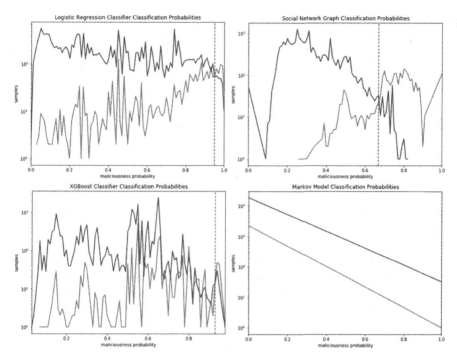

Fig. 5. Classification data separation charts. Blue represents benign sample probabilities, red are malicious sample probabilities, dashed green line is the selected threshold. (Color figure online)

of minimal false positives. In Fig. 5 we can see the places the red line is high then the blue line. For the Markov model, the threshold is a Boolean threshold, but unfortunately in the experiment, it had more false positives in any threshold. The selected thresholds are listed in Table 8.

Table 8. The selected threshold for the classifiers

Model	Threshold
SNA	0.67
XGBoost	0.93
Logistic Regression	0.95
Markov	1

5.3 Evaluation

After the classifiers' decision threshold was set its possible to translate the classifiers' probabilities results into verdicts. The evaluation was made on data collected between

17-Dec-2019 and 23-Dec-2019. In that time period, 20,640 labeled domain samples were collected. 18,148 were labeled as benign and 2,222 were labeled as malicious. The test set was collected from the origins described in Sect. 3.1. Tables 9 show the clear advantage of the SNA classifier which produced a detection rate of 83.89% at the price of 1.09% false-positive rate.

Table 9. Confusion matrixes of the Logistic Regression, XGBoost, and SNA classifiers respectively

Class	Benign	Malicious	Benign	Malicious	Benign	Malicious
Benign	98.74%	12.60%	99.74%	0.26%	98.91%	1.09%
Malicious	82.49%	17.51%	65.00%	5.00%	16.11%	83.89%

The ROC curve shown in Fig. 6, confirms the SNA model out-performed the other classifiers on any given threshold. You can see its line always above the Logistic Regression and XGBoost classifier. It's also interesting to see that the simplistic Logistic Regression algorithm outperformed the state-of-the-art machine learning algorithm XGBoost.

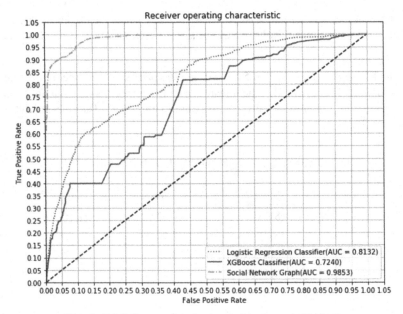

Fig. 6. ROC Curve using the thresholds shown in Table 6.

The PREDATOR [5] system baseline its evaluation of on a given FPR of 0.35%. For the results to be comparable with each other, we did the same. The experiment results are shown in Table 10. The results show that the SNA model reaches a similar detection rate to PREDATOR, while the other classifiers performed quite poorly. That is without optimization tuning of the training and testing window size as is done in the PREDATOR paper. In the experiment the SNA model was rebuilt every 2 h, that is possible since the graph construction takes less than a minute. PREDATOR paper doesn't specify how much time it takes to train the model, but I guess it's much more than a minute.

Table 10. Classifier detection rate under a 0.35% false-positive rate

Model	TPR
PREDATOR	70.00%
SNA	60.71%
XGBoost	5.40%
Logistic Regression	7.56%
Markov	0.00%

6 Conclusion

"Average uptime of phishing attacks is around 2 days and the median uptime is only 12 h. Due to this very short lifetime, reactive blacklisting is too slow to effectively protect users from phishing" [9]. This quote conveys the importance of this work. The phishing use-case is extraordinary from that perspective that it lives for a very short time. Therefore, a proactive approach is a clear requirement for detected threats.

The described experiments demonstrate it's not practical to guess the domain names to be registered. A more realistic approach would be to consistently learn the internet domains' neighborhood e.g. IP, network, ASN, nameservers, etc. while doing so, constantly calculating each node's reputation. The SNA approach was proven to be very successful reaching a detection rate of 83.89% under a 1.09% false-positive rate and 60.71% under a 0.35% false-positive rate.

Despite the fact, it reached a lower detection rate then PREDATOR [5] 70% detection rate given the same FPR it's a big achievement. That is because of the PREDATOR leverage propriety dataset which is very expensive and takes plenty of resources the manage. When all the classifiers developed in this project all rely only on open source data sources, and all the setup and software components described in Sect. 5 ran on a standard laptop. Unlike the SNA model, PREDATOR had many optimizations on the training window as shown in Table 8, where the true positive vary in the range of 58%–70%. Moreover, the SNA model obtains even better results than PREDATOR when considering high acceptable FPR.

A ground for future work can be to optimize the project models or create a meta-classifier that would combine the machine learning classifiers with the SNA classifier. We assume that any of the two would push the results higher than 70%.

References

1. Weimer, F.: Passive DNS replication. In: Proceedings of FIRST Conference on Computer Security Incident, p. 98 (2005)
2. Bilge, L., Kirda, E., Kruegel, C., Balduzzi, M.: EXPOSURE: finding malicious domains using passive DNS analysis. In: Proceedings of NDSS, pp. 1–17 (2011)
3. Antonakakis, M., Perdisci, R., Dagon, D., Lee, W., Feamster, N.: Building a dynamic reputation system for DNS. In: Proceedings of USENIX Security Symposium, pp. 273–290 (2010)
4. Gao, H., et al.: An empirical reexamination of global DNS behavior. In: Proceedings of the ACM SIGCOMM 2013 Conference, pp. 267–278 (2013)
5. Hao, S., Kantchelian, A., Miller, B., Paxson, V., Feamster, N.: PREDATOR: proactive recognition and elimination of domain abuse at time-of-registration. In: Proceedings of the 2016 ACM SIGSAC Conference on Computer and Communications Security, pp. 1568–1579 (2016)
6. Page, L., Brin, S., Motwani, R., Winograd, T.: The PageRank citation ranking: bringing order to the web. Stanford InfoLab (1999)
7. Sunil, A.N.V., Sardana, A.: A pagerank based detection technique for phishing web sites. In: Proceedings of 2012 IEEE Symposium on Computers & Informatics (ISCI), pp. 58–63. IEEE (2012)
8. Mishsky, I., Gal-Oz, N., Gudes, E.: A topology based flow model for computing domain reputation. In: Samarati, P. (ed.) DBSec 2015. LNCS, vol. 9149, pp. 277–292. Springer, Cham (2015). https://doi.org/10.1007/978-3-319-20810-7_20
9. Marchal, S., François, J., State, R., Engel, T.: Proactive discovery of phishing related domain names. In: Balzarotti, D., Stolfo, S.J., Cova, M. (eds.) RAID 2012. LNCS, vol. 7462, pp. 190–209. Springer, Heidelberg (2012). https://doi.org/10.1007/978-3-642-33338-5_10

Average-Case Competitive Ratio
of Scheduling Algorithms
of Multi-user Cache

Daniel Berend[1,2], Shlomi Dolev[2], Avinatan Hassidim[3],
and Marina Kogan-Sadetsky[2(✉)]

[1] Department of Math, Ben-Gurion University of the Negev, 84105 Beer-Sheva, Israel
[2] Department of Computer Science, Ben-Gurion University of the Negev,
84105 Beer-Sheva, Israel
{berend,dolev,sadetsky}@cs.bgu.ac.il
[3] Department of Computer Science, Bar-Ilan University, 52900 Ramat Gan, Israel
avinatan@macs.biu.ac.il

Abstract. The goal of this paper is to present an efficient realistic metric for evaluating cache scheduling algorithms in multi-user multi-cache environments. In a previous work, the requests sequence was set deliberately by an opponent (offline optimal) algorithm in an extremely unrealistic way, leading to an unlimited competitive ratio and to extremely unreasonable and unrealistic cache management strategies. In this paper, we propose to analyze the performance of cache management in a typical scenario, i.e., we consider all possibilities with their (realistic) distribution. In other words, we analyze the average case and not the worst case of scheduling scenarios. In addition, we present an efficient, according to our novel average case analysis, online heuristic algorithm for cache scheduling. The algorithm is based on machine-learning concepts, it is flexible and easy to implement.

Keywords: Concurrent cache · Competitive ratio · Scheduling algorithm

1 Introduction

A multi-user concurrent cache system should satisfy users' memory page requests. Finding an efficient cache management for these systems is of high interest and importance. A cache scheduling algorithm decides, upon each request that results in a page fault (when the cache is full), which page to evict from

We thank the Lynne and William Frankel Center for Computer Science, the Rita Altura Trust Chair in Computer Science. This research was also supported by a grant from the Ministry of Science & Technology, Israel & the Japan Science and Technology Agency (JST), Japan, DFG German-Israeli collaborative projects, and the Milken Families Foundation Chair in Mathematics.

S. Dolev et al. (Eds.): CSCML 2020, LNCS 12161, pp. 237–244, 2020.
https://doi.org/10.1007/978-3-030-49785-9_15

the cache in order to insert the newly requested page. The algorithm should minimize the number of page faults.

Offline paging strategies may align the demand periods of (known to the offline) future requests. An online strategy does not know the exact sequence of future requests. Thus, an optimal offline strategy has a significant advantage over an online strategy. The sole purpose of considering the offline case is to form a basis for comparison with the online scheduling. For example, if the competitive ratio is 1, then the online algorithm is obviously optimal, as it is not affected adversely by the uncertainty of future requests. Of course, one cannot hope for such a ratio for an online algorithm. Previous works show that, in multi-core paging, the competitive ratio of traditional algorithms in the scope of multi-cache systems, such as LRU, FIFO, CLOCK, and FWF, may be arbitrarily large.

Both [1] and [2] show that traditional online paging algorithms are non-competitive in a multi-core model. They do this by defining an extremely unrealistic request sequence chosen by an adversary, which leads to unreasonable offline cache management strategies and an unbounded competitive ratio. Thus, apparently, one cannot compare the real efficiency of (the offline and) the online algorithm. In this paper we propose an alternative version of near-optimal offline algorithm.

2   Related Work

Cache performance has been extensively studied in multi-core architectures but less so in multi-server architectures. Some proposed techniques are able to schedule requests [1] so that the paging strategy can choose to serve requests of some sequences and delay others. Thus, the order in which requests are served is algorithm dependent. Lopez-Ortiz and Salinger [2] present another technique that discards this possibility. Given a request, the algorithm must serve the request without delay. The algorithm presented in [2] is limited by a two-level non-distributed memory system. Awerbuch et al. [3] present a distributed paging algorithm for more general networks. Although the algorithm in [3] is applicable to distributed systems, it serves requests in a sequential manner: at any time a processor p may invoke a single request. In our model, requests from all the servers in the system are served simultaneously.

Competitive analysis is a method invented for analyzing online algorithms, in which the performance of an online algorithm is compared to the performance of an optimal offline algorithm that can view the sequence of requests in advance. An algorithm is competitive if its competitive ratio – the ratio between its performance and the offline algorithm's performance is bounded. The quality of an online algorithm on each input sequence is measured by comparing its performance to that of an optimal offline algorithm, which is, for an online problem, an unrealizable algorithm that has full knowledge of the future. Competitive analysis thus falls within the framework of worst-case complexity [4].

3 System Model Settings

Suppose, in general, that we have servers $S_1, S_2, ..., S_n$, and corresponding lists of possible requests $R_1, R_2, ..., R_n$, where $R_i = \{r_1^i, ..., r_{l_i}^i\}$ is of length l_i. The system contains a cache of size K, and a slow memory with access latency time of t. Denote by $R = \cup_{i=1}^n R_i$ the set of all possible requests. We implicitly assume that $K < |R|$, but in practice K is usually much smaller even than each of the $|R_i|$'s separately.

A *singleton* is a subset of size K of R, namely, any of the possible cache configurations. (The term derives from the fact that, in the process of constructing the full execution tree, we often place several possible cache configurations at a node, with the intention of resolving only later the identity of the actual configuration residing there.) Each of the singleton configurations starts an execution tree.

When expanding a node consisting of several singletons, we have branches corresponding to each of these singletons with possible request configurations. In fact, we cross out some of these branches. Namely, each of the request sequences yields some number, between 0 and n, of page faults for each of the singletons. For each request sequence, we leave only those branches yielding a minimal number of page faults and discard all others.

For each request sequence, and each singleton with a minimal number f_{min} of page faults in the current node, we need to consider those singletons we may move to. For each singleton, these are the singletons obtained from it by:

i Leaving intact all the requests that are currently in the cache and have been queried now.
ii Replacing any f_{min} requests currently in the cache, that have not been queried now, by the f_{min} missing requests.
iii Leaving the rest of the requests untouched.

Now we explain how, given a node and a request configuration, we construct the corresponding child of the node. We go over all singletons in the node. For each singleton, we find as above the set of singletons we may move to. The child consists of the union of all these sets of configurations. A node containing one singleton A is labeled by A, a node containing A and B - by AB, and so forth.

In principle, we need to expand the execution tree so as to deal with all possible sequences of request configurations. However, there is no point in expanding a node that has been encountered already. Hence, we expand the tree only until no more nodes with new content can be generated. We mention in passing that, even if the request sequence is infinite, this allows us to deal with a finite expansion of the full execution tree. In fact, the number of singletons is $\binom{|R|}{K}$. Hence the number of distinct node labels we may encounter is at most $2^{\binom{|R|}{K}}$. Hence, we will never have to expand the execution tree beyond depth $2^{\binom{|R|}{K}}$. This bound is probably way above the actual depth we will get, but serves to demonstrate that the process terminates. When we expand all the nodes, usually some potential node labels will not appear. Moreover, there may well be pairs of equivalent labels, namely, nodes having the same behavior when expanded. When several labels are found to be equivalent, we may replace any occurrence of one of them by that of a representative of the group. This tends to shorten the algorithm a great deal. Our goal is to calculate the expected number of page faults per group of simultaneously arriving requests. As we consider all possible request sequences, so that the full execution tree is infinite, we need to define what this expected number means. Suppose we expand the tree from a singleton A. Denote by $A_i, 0 \leq i < \infty$, the subtree of the full execution tree consisting of all nodes up to level i. (Thus, for example, $A_0 = A$.) We introduce the following notations:

$E_A(i)$ – number of execution paths in A_i.

$F_A(i)$ – number of page faults in A_i, i.e., the sum of the numbers of page faults over all execution paths in the tree.

$P_A(i)$ – average number of page faults per execution path in A_i.

$R_A(i)$ – average number of page faults per request in A_i.

It will be convenient in our calculations to consider also execution trees starting with nodes containing several singletons. We will use similar notations. For example, $(BC)_i$ will denote the subtree of the full execution tree consisting of all nodes up to level i, starting with BC, and $E_{(BC)}(i)$ will denote the number of execution paths in $(BC)_i$.

Out of the four quantities above – $E_A(i), F_A(i), P_A(i), R_A(i)$ – only the last is really interesting for us. In fact, we are interested mostly in the asymptotics of $R_A(i)$ as $i \to \infty$. The average of these asymptotic values over all singletons A is the baseline (offline bound) we use to calculate the competitive ratio of online algorithms. To calculate $R_A(i)$, it will be convenient to start with the other three quantities. Moreover, as hinted above, it will be convenient to calculate these quantities not only for singletons, but for sets of singletons as well.

We start with the number of execution paths $E_{A_1 A_2 \ldots A_k}(i)$, where $A_1 A_2 \ldots A_k$ is any possible cache configuration and $i \geq 0$. We construct a system of recurrence equations for these quantities as follows. Suppose we want to express $E_{A_1 A_2 \ldots A_k}(i+1)$ in terms of similar quantities, related to depth i. To this end, we need to open the node $A_1 A_2 \ldots A_k$ just once for each of the possible combinations of requests. Thus, the node has $\prod_{j=1}^{n} |R_j|$ children. Each child $B_1 B_2 \ldots B_h$ of $A_1 A_2 \ldots A_k$ contributes $E_{B_1 B_2 \ldots B_h}(i)$ to $E_{A_1 A_2 \ldots A_k}(i+1)$. We obtain a system of homogeneous linear recurrence equations with constant coefficients for the sequences $E_{A_1 A_2 \ldots A_k}(i)_{i=0}^{\infty}$, over all possible cache configurations $A_1 A_2 \ldots A_k$. The initial values $E_{A_1 A_2 \ldots A_k}(0)$ are all 1. Note that all coefficients in the resulting equations are non-negative, and their sum in each equation is the same, namely $\prod_{j=1}^{n} |R_j|$. Thus, the matrix of coefficients is a scalar multiple of a stochastic matrix, which may facilitate the calculation.

The calculation of the $F_{A_1 A_2 \ldots A_k}(i)$'s is similar, but the equations are this time non-homogeneous. That is, $F_{A_1 A_2 \ldots A_k}(i+1)$ may be expressed as a sum of $F_{B_1 B_2 \ldots B_h}(i)$'s, but we need to add also the number of page faults that are due to a 1-step expansion of $A_1 A_2 \ldots A_k$. If this number is f, then the expression for $F_{A_1 A_2 \ldots A_k}(i+1)$ contains an additional $f \cdot (\prod_{j=1}^{n} |R_j|)^i$ addend. Notice that the initial conditions this time are $F_{A_1 A_2 \ldots A_k}(0)$ for all configurations $A_1 A_2 \ldots A_k$.

Once $E_A(i)$ and $F_A(i)$ have been calculated, we readily find $P_A(i)$ and $R_A(i)$:

$$P_A(i) = \frac{F_A(i)}{E_A(i)}, \qquad R_A(i) = \frac{P_A(i)}{i}.$$

Recall that, as the recurrence equations defining $E_{A_1 A_2 \ldots A_k}(i)$ and $F_{A_1 A_2 \ldots A_k}(i)$ are linear with constant coefficients, it is easy to provide explicit expressions for them (assuming that one can find the eigenvalues of the matrix of coefficients, or at least good approximations of these eigenvalues). These expressions are combinations of exponentials (or exponential-polynomials if there are multiple eigenvalues). Hence their asymptotics is trivial to understand, and so is that of $R_A(i)$.

4   An Optimal Offline Algorithm: Full Execution Tree

In this section, we present a baseline for comparing online algorithms for scheduling multi-user concurrent distributed cache. This baseline is the optimal offline algorithm. This algorithm manages the cache in such a way that the average number of faults is minimal. Our first algorithm calculates the average accurately, for an arbitrary given distribution on the space of all request sequences, as long as this distribution results in an execution tree with a finite number of nonequivalent nodes. Usually, however, we will reduce the time this calculation requires by resorting to faster and less accurate algorithms. Our second and third algorithms will provide such simplifications.

In principle, to calculate #pf for the optimal algorithm, we need to run the algorithm for all possible request sequences, find the minimal number of page faults for each sequence, and then calculate the average over all sequences (under the assumed distribution over the space). This approach has indeed been taken in [2]. Below, we reduce the time required for the calculation by assigning some (unknown) number of future page faults to each state. We construct a tree, its nodes correspond to the possible states of the cache, and its edges correspond to the various possible requests at each state. Whenever we return to a state visited earlier, we do not need to continue from this state anymore. We simplify the calculation further by noticing that various pairs of nodes of the tree are equivalent.

Example 1: Suppose we have two servers S_1, S_2, with corresponding sets of possible requests $R_1 = \{r_1^1, r_2^1\}$, $R_2 = \{r_1^2, r_2^2\}$, assumed to be disjoint, a cache of size $K = 3$, and access latency time $t = 0$. The $\binom{4}{3} = 4$ singletons are

$$A = \{r_1^1, r_2^1, r_1^2\}, B = \{r_1^1, r_2^1, r_2^2\}, C = \{r_1^1, r_1^2, r_2^2\}, D = \{r_2^1, r_1^2, r_2^2\}.$$

At each time unit, there are 4 possibilities for the servers' requests, which we denote as follows:

$$1\text{-}1 = (r_1^1, r_1^2), 1\text{-}2 = (r_1^1, r_2^2), 2\text{-}1 = (r_2^1, r_1^2), 2\text{-}2 = (r_2^1, r_2^2).$$

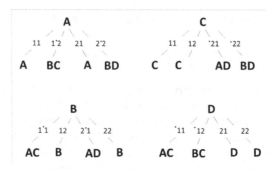

Fig. 1. A 1-step expansion of an execution tree for each singleton.

In Fig. 1, we depict the 1-step expansions of all possible execution trees started by singletons. Here, a '.' label to the left of a request signifies that it yields a page fault.

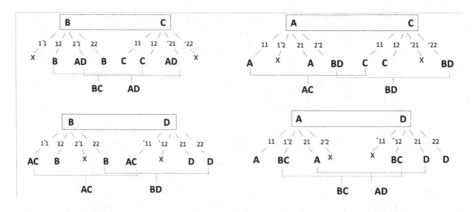

Fig. 2. A 1-step expansion of an execution tree for each generated pair of singletons.

Figure 2 provides 1-step expansions of the nodes comprising 2 singletons, obtained in Fig. 1. An 'x' means that the corresponding branch is crossed out.

We have expanded all the possible cache configurations. Since all singletons are equivalent, a two-step execution tree started from any singleton, say from A, is as in Fig. 3.

It is easy to verify in this case that all singleton nodes are equivalent to each other, and so are all nodes consisting of a pair of singletons. We will use A as a representative of the singletons, and AB as a representative pair. For the number of execution paths, we obtain the recursion:

$$E_A(i+1) \; = 2E_A(i) + 2E_{AB}(i),$$
$$E_{AB}(i+1) = 2E_A(i) + 2E_{AB}(i)$$

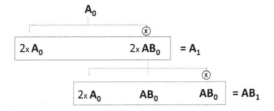

Fig. 3. A 2-steps expansion of an execution tree.

Along with the initial conditions $E_A(0) = E_{AB}(0) = 1$, this yields:

$$E_A(i) = E_{AB}(i) = 4^i, \qquad i \geq 0.$$

For the number of page faults, the recurrence is:

$$\begin{aligned}
F_A(i+1) &= 2F_A(i) + 2F_{AB}(i) + 2 \cdot 4^i, \\
F_{AB}(i+1) &= 2F_A(i) + 2F_{AB}(i) + 4^i
\end{aligned}$$

The initial conditions are $F_A(0) = F_{AB}(0) = 0$. We obtain

$$F_A(i) = (\frac{3}{8}i + \frac{1}{4}) \cdot 4^i, \quad F_{AB}(i) = \frac{3}{8}i \cdot 4^i, \qquad i \geq 0.$$

It follows that

$$P_A(i) = \frac{(\frac{3}{8}i + \frac{1}{4}) \cdot 4^i}{4^i} = \frac{3}{8}i + \frac{1}{4}, \qquad i \geq 0,$$

and finally:

$$R_A(i) = \frac{3}{8} + \frac{1}{4i} \xrightarrow[i \to \infty]{} \frac{3}{8}. \tag{1}$$

Thus, the expected #pf for the offline algorithm is 0.375, which is slightly more than one failure per 3 requests. Note that, by (1), the expected #pf per request reduces as we consider larger initial subtrees of the execution tree.

5   Heuristic Online Algorithm: Dynamic Machine Learning

A simple-minded approach to the question of optimizing the cache is to put in it those requests that occur most often. Namely, suppose we did not have a cache. At each stage, we would have n page faults. (Recall that, if several servers ask simultaneously for the same r, we count each of them as causing an additional fault). How much do we gain by placing some $r_j \in R$ in the cache? For each i such that $r_j \in R_i$, there is a probability of p_{ij} for S_i to ask for r_j (where $\sum_{j:r_j \in R_i} p_{ij} = 1$ for each i). Hence, by having r_j in the cache, we reduce #pf by

$v(r_j) = \sum_{i:r_j R_i} p_{ij}$. To reduce #pf as much as possible, we place in the cache those requests r for which the quantity $v(r)$ is among the K maximal ones (ties broken arbitrarily). Note, that this tends to give more cache lines to servers with fewer possible requests.

Lemma 1. *If the probabilities $p_{i,j}$ of each server S_i asking for each r_j do not change with time, and the servers are independent, then the algorithm proposed above is optimal.*

Proof. Denote the proposed algorithm by H, and let H' be some other algorithm. Denote by $C(H)$ the content of the cache when using H, and by $C(H')$ the analogous quantity for H' (which may change with time, depending on the way H' works). Then the expected number of page faults per time unit, when using H, is #pf$(H) = n - \sum_{r_j \in cache\ of\ H} v(r_j)$. The corresponding number for H' is #pf$(H') = n - \sum_{r_j \in cache\ of\ H'} v(r_j)$. Since the algorithm H chooses the j's with maximal $v(r_j)$, the number of page faults for H does not exceed the analogous number for H'.   □

6   Future Research Directions

The most challenging question is whether one can design an online algorithm with a bounded approximation ratio relative to the optimal offline algorithm. If so, how can we reach the best ratio?

References

1. Hassidim, A.: Cache replacement policies for multicore processors. In: Proceedings of 1st Symposium on Innovations in Computer Science (ICS), pp. 501–509 (2010)
2. Lopez-Ortiz, A., Salinger, A.: Paging for multi-core shared caches. In: Proceedings of the 3rd Innovations in Theoretical Computer Science Conference, pp. 113–127 (2012)
3. Awerbuch, B., Bartal, Y., Fiat, A.: Distributed paging for general networks. In: Proceedings of the 7th Annual ACMSIAM Symposium on Discrete Algorithms, pp. 574–583 (1996)
4. Borodin, A., El-Yaniv, R.: Online Computation and Competitive Analysis, vol. 53. Cambridge University Press, New York (1998)
5. Taylor, H.M., Karlin, S.: An Introduction to Stochastic Modeling, 3rd edn. Academic Press, San Diego (1998)
6. Dynkin, E.B.: Theory of Markov Processes, Pergamon (1960)
7. Sleator, D.D., Tarjan, R.E.: Amortized efficiency of list update and paging rules. Commun. ACM **28**(2), 202–208 (1985)

CryptoRNN - Privacy-Preserving Recurrent Neural Networks Using Homomorphic Encryption

Maya Bakshi and Mark Last[(✉)] [iD]

Ben-Gurion University of the Negev, 84105 Beer-Sheva, Israel
bakshim@gmail.com, mlast@bgu.ac.il

Abstract. Recurrent Neural Networks (RNNs) are used extensively for mining sequential datasets. However, performing inference over an RNN model requires the data owner to expose his or her raw data to the machine learning service provider. Homomorphic encryption allows calculations to be performed on ciphertexts, where the decrypted result is the same as if the calculation has been made directly on the plaintext. In this research, we suggest a Privacy-Preserving RNN–based inference system using homomorphic encryption. We preserve the functionality of RNN and its ability to make the same predictions on sequential data, within the limitations of homomorphic encryption, as those obtained for plaintext on the same RNN model. In order to achieve this goal, we need to address two main issues. First, the noise increase between successive calculations and second, the inability of homomorphic encryption to work with the most popular activation functions for neural networks (sigmoid, ReLU and tanh). In this paper, we suggest several methods to handle both issues and discuss the trade-offs between the proposed methods. We use several benchmark datasets to compare the encrypted and unencrypted versions of the same RNN in terms of accuracy, performance, and data traffic.

Keywords: Homomorphic encryption · Data privacy · Encrypted machine learning · Privacy preserving machine learning · Privacy preserving recurrent neural networks · Encrypted recurrent neural netwroks

1   Introduction

With the recent growth of cloud computing services and cloud cost reduction, machine learning as a service (MLaaS) has been in high demand. The main contribution of MLaaS is the ability of each data provider to consume machine learning services over the net using the cloud, with no need for machine learning

© Springer Nature Switzerland AG 2020
S. Dolev et al. (Eds.): CSCML 2020, LNCS 12161, pp. 245–253, 2020.
https://doi.org/10.1007/978-3-030-49785-9_16

skills. With the increasing spread of systems which are HIPAA (Health Insurance Portability and Accountability Act) and GDPR (General Data Protection Regulation) compliant, one of the most challenging issues for MLaaS is the need for security and privacy protection. Whether they are processing private medical records, sensitive security information, or confidential military data, data providers must trust the machine learning service provider. Privacy-preserving machine learning as a service allows such trust, if the data provider can send encrypted data to the service provider and get back an encrypted result.

Some of the privacy-preserving machine learning solutions are based on secure multiparty computation (SMPC), some are based on homomorphic encryption (which allows performing calculations directly on the encrypted data), and some combine both. Some of the solutions focus on the training phase, while others focus on the inference phase. In this research, we present a privacy-preserving machine learning inference system, based on a homomorphic encryption cryptosystem. The inference model is a recurrent neural network, which has not been studied in the context of privacy-preserving machine learning yet. RNN layer holds the previous layer's output as a context, which is then processed alongside the new input of the current iteration. Our main goal is to ensure that the prediction results of encrypted data will be as close as possible to the prediction results of plaintext in terms of performance and accuracy.

2   Methodology

2.1   Homomorphic Encryption Type

We implement privacy-preserving RNN inference with SHE (Somewhat Homomorphic Encryption) and handle the issue of noise increase by using a refresh mechanism which can be implemented using various suggested methodologies.

2.2   Homomorphic Encryption Tool

Our requirements of the HE framework were implementation of SHE, with the ability to encrypt and perform computations on both rational numbers and integers. We chose Microsoft SEAL (Simple Encrypted Arithmetic Library) developed by Microsoft Research [1], implementing the CKKS (Cheon-Kim-Kim-Song) [2] homomorphic encryption scheme, which is used for rational numbers.

2.3   Activation Functions

- Since we need to work with homomorphic encrypted data we can only perform multiplications and additions, thus any non-linear calculation on ciphertext is impossible. We propose three main methods to deal with the activation functions, each one resulting in a different classification accuracy.

2.4 Handling the Noise Increase

Due to the RNN structure we need to handle the noise increase of any ciphertext as well as the context. We implemented ciphertext refresh mechanism in three different methodologies and we discuss the trade-offs between them in this paper. The three suggested refresh methods are:

Client Performs Non-linear Calculations - For the use case of non-linear inference, the server sends ciphertexts to the client, which calculates the non-linear functions and returns the resulting ciphertext to the server.

Refresh After Each Multiplication - Using polynomial activation functions in the inference phase, this refresh mode requires a ciphertext refresh after each multiplication, resulting in faster inference and smaller ciphertexts, but more communication with the client.

Refresh After Each Record - Using polynomial activation functions in the inference phase, this refresh mode requires a ciphertext refresh after each record's classification, resulting in a slower inference and larger ciphertexts, but less communication with the client.

2.5 Security Level and Cryptographic Scheme Parameters

We ensure the security standard compliance as described in [3]. The parameter generation algorithm is used to instantiate various parameters used in the HE algorithms. We used security level of 128-bit and precision of 40-bit for all experiments. The rest of the parameters were selected as per the standard.

3 Experiments Design and Evaluation Methods

3.1 Datasets

Table 1 summarizes the parameters of the datasets we used.

Table 1. Dataset parameters

Dataset	Classes num	Features num	Feature types	Training records num	Testing records num	Majority rule accuracy
Wall-following robot navigation [6]	4	2	Real	3,890	1,565	0.406
Activity recognition with healthy older people [5]	4	8	Real	44,317	1,718	0.657
EEG eye state [7]	2	14	Real	11,234	3,746	0.275
Occupancy detection [4]	2	5	Real	8,143	1,000	0.210

3.2   Performance Metrics

All experiments implement classification. The following performance metrics are calculated for each experiment:

- **Classification Accuracy:**
  $$\frac{(TP+TN)}{(TP+TN+FP+FN)}$$
  We measure the accuracy of both encrypted inference and plaintext inference.
- **Inference time per record** - mean time in milliseconds for encrypted record inference.
- **Traffic per record** - total data traffic in bytes per record for both directions (client-server and server-client).
- **Number of communications** - number of communications from the server to the client during each record's inference. This communication is required for ciphertext refresh or for non-linear calculation on ciphertext.

3.3   Experiments Details

We performed five sets of experiments. Each set refers to one dataset from the list in 3.1 and an RNN architecture, which can be a simple RNN (with one RNN layer) or RNN with one RNN hidden layer and one feed forward layer. In addition, for each set we induced two models based on the selected architecture. One is non-linear model based on sigmoid activation function and the second is polynomial model with polynomial activation functions.

For each set, we defined five experimental configurations:

Exp1 - Non-linear Training, Non-linear Inference, No Refresh - the inference is based on the non-linear model, where the non-linear functions are calculated by the client. This calculation involves decryption and encryption of the ciphertext, thus an additional refresh is needed only for RNN with a hidden layer and the context needs to be refreshed as well. The ciphertext is small due to a low multiplicative depth.

Experiment Description :

- Non-linear model - training uses at least one non-linear activation function.
- Inference - based on the trained model, using sigmoid activation functions calculated by the client. For the RNN layer, the server sends the weights multiplication matrix to the client for refresh. For the feed-forward layer with non-linear activation function - for each unit, the classifier sends ciphertext to the client, which decrypts it, calculates sigmoid, encrypts it, and sends the ciphertext back to the server.
- Refresh mode - In addition to the calculation of the sigmoid by the client, for any layer with linear activation function the weights multiplication matrix is refreshed for each record.

Exp2 - Non-linear Training, Polynomial Inference, Refresh per Multiplication - the inference is based on the non-linear model, where the non-linear functions are replaced by a polynomial approximation to the non-linear activation functions. In this experiment, we refresh the ciphertext after each multiplication. The ciphertext is small due to a low multiplicative depth.
Experiment Description :

- Non-linear model - training uses at least one non-linear activation function.
- Inference – sigmoid activation function is replaced by sigmoid's approximation function of degree 2, or by square function. The polynomial activation functions are calculated by the server.
- Refresh mode – The ciphertext is refreshed after each multiplication on the ciphertext.

Exp3 - Non-linear Training, Polynomial Inference, Refresh per Record - the inference is based on the non-linear model, where the non-linear functions are replaced by a polynomial approximation to the non-linear activation functions. In this experiment, we refresh the ciphertext once per record. The ciphertext is large due a high multiplicative depth.
Experiment Description :

- Non-linear model - training uses at least one non-linear activation function.
- Inference – sigmoid activation function is replaced by sigmoid's approximation function of degree 2, or by square function. The polynomial activation functions are calculated by the server.
- Refresh mode – The context of the RNN layer is refreshed once per record.

Exp4 - Polynomial Training, Polynomial Inference, Refresh per Multiplication - the inference is based on the polynomial model. In this experiment, we refresh the ciphertext after each multiplication. The ciphertext is small due to a low multiplicative depth.
Experiment Description :

- Non-linear model - training uses at least one non-linear activation function.
- Inference – sigmoid activation functions are replaced by polynomial activation functions of degree 2, which are calculated by the server.
- Refresh mode – The context of the RNN layer is refreshed once per record.

Exp5 - Polynomial Training, Polynomial Inference, Refresh per Record - the inference is based on the polynomial model. In this experiment, we perform ciphertext refresh once per record. The ciphertext is large due to high multiplicative depth.
Experiment Description :

- Polynomial model - training uses sigmoid's approximation activation function of degree 2, or square function.

– Inference – based on the trained model, no change.
– Refresh mode – The context of the RNN layer is refreshed once per record.

Table 2 describes the dataset and the RNN architecture used in each experiment.

Table 2. Experiments description

Experiment set	Dataset	RNN description	RNN layer input dimension	RNN layer output dimension	Feed forward layer input dimension	Feed forward layer output dimension
Set1	Wall-following robot navigation	Simple RNN (no hidden layers)	2	4	–	–
Set2	Wall-following robot navigation	RNN with one hidden layer	2	6	6	4
Set3	Activity recognition with healthy older people	Simple RNN (no hidden layers)	8	4	–	–
Set4	EEG eye state	RNN with one hidden layer	14	10	10	2
Set5	Occupancy detection	RNN with one hidden layer	5	14	14	2

3.4 Summary of Results

As indicated above, the proposed CryptoRNN methodology was implemented in five different configurations:

– **Exp1 : Non-linear training, non-linear inference, no refresh** - This methodology is recommended for use when a model's confidentiality is low and we have trained a non-linear model, which we would like to continue using and we can expose the client to the non-linear units. In this case, we can use a low coefficient modulus and thus we get a short inference time, a moderate number of server-client communications, and a low data traffic size. The inference accuracy is close to the known accuracy of the trained model.
– **Exp2 - Non-linear training, polynomial inference, refresh per multiplication** - This methodology is recommended for use when the model's

confidentiality must be high, we have trained a non-linear model and we cannot expose the client to the non-linear units. Instead of using non-linear functions (which is not possible for encrypted data) in the inference phase, we replace them with polynomial approximation functions (using the same model). We can have as many communications as we need from the server to the client and we would like to achieve a shorter inference time. In this case, we can use a low coefficient modulus, send the ciphertext to the client for refresh after each multiplication, and thus get a short inference time, a high number of server-client communications and a low data traffic size. The inference accuracy may be lower than that of the trained model.

- **Exp3 - Non-linear training, polynomial inference, refresh per record**
  - This methodology is recommended for use when the model's confidentiality must be high, we have trained a non-linear model and we cannot expose the client to the non-linear units. Instead of using non-linear functions (which is not possible for encrypted data) in the inference phase, we replace them with polynomial approximation functions (using the same model). We would like to have minimum communications from the server to the client and we can accept a longer inference time. In this case, we can use a high coefficient modulus, the computational requirements become heavier, we send the ciphertext to the client for refresh once per record and thus we get longer inference time, low number of server-client communications and high data traffic size because the ciphertext size is larger. The accuracy of the inference may be lower then the accuracy of the trained model.

- **Exp4 - Polynomial training, polynomial inference, refresh per multiplication** - This methodology is recommended for use when the model's confidentiality must be high and we have trained a polynomial model, we can have as many communications as we need from the server to the client and we would like to achieve a shorter inference time. In this case, we can use a low coefficient modulus, send the ciphertext to the client for refresh after each multiplication, and thus get a short inference time, a high number of server-client communications and a low data traffic size. The inference accuracy is identical to that of the trained model, but in most cases is lower than that of the non-linear model.

- **Exp5 - Non-linear training, polynomial inference, refresh per record** - This methodology is recommended for use when the model's confidentiality must be high and we have trained a polynomial model. We would like to have minimum communications from the server to the client and we can accept a longer inference time. In this case, we can use a high coefficient modulus, the computational requirements become heavier, we send the ciphertext to the client for refresh once per record and thus we get a longer inference time, a low number of server-client communications and a high data traffic size because the ciphertext size is bigger. The inference accuracy is identical to that of the trained model, but in most cases is lower than that of the non-linear model.

Table 3 summarizes the trade-offs and compares the suggested methodologies. We referred to inference time as 'Moderate' when it was about 2 times higher

Table 3. CryptoRNN - Methodologies Comparison

Exp	Refresh mode	Training activation function	Inference activation function	Model confiden-tiality level	data traffic	Inference time	#Communi-cations	Coefficient modulo	Accuracy
Exp1	Once per linear layer	Non-linear	Non-linear (calculated by client)	Low	Low moderate	Low moderate	Moderate	Moderate	High
Exp2	Operation	Non-linear	Polynomial	High	Low moderate	Low moderate	High	High	Low
Exp3	Record	Non-linear	Polynomial	High	High	High	Low	Low	Low
Exp4	Operation	Polynomial	Polynomial	High	Low moderate	Low moderate	High	High	Moderate
Exp5	Record	Polynomial	Polynomial	High	High	High	Low	Low	Moderate

compared to 'Low', and as 'High' when it was at least 3 times higher than 'Low'. The data traffic was considered as 'Moderate' when it was less than 3 times larger than 'Low', and as 'High' when it was 3 times and above larger than 'Low'. We found that on average, the inference time of an encrypted record is longer than inference of unencrypted record by four orders of magnitude. Still, one should take into account that the encrypted inference times were between 100 to 3500 ms per record only.

4   Conclusions

In this research, we tested our hypothesis that RNN inference is feasible on encrypted data. We developed and evaluated a privacy-preserving machine learning system, CryptoRNN, which has the ability to train a Recurrent Neural Network based on unencrypted data and then use the induced model in order to perform inference on encrypted data. We proved that privacy-preserving inference for RNN is feasible under the limitations of homomorphic encryption by showing in all experiments that we obtain identical results for both encrypted and unencrypted inference using the same models.

Once we demonstrated successful inference on encrypted data, we suggested several methodologies to address the encrypted inference task while considering the trade-off between the issues of data traffic, inference time, server-client communications, accuracy, and the confidentiality of the model.

For future work, we suggest working with parallel computing. In this research, we executed the encrypted calculations of neurons in a layer one-by-one. With parallel computation, we could decrease the inference time. Polynomial approximations of higher order than two may also be considered.

References

1. Microsoft SEAL (release 3.3): Microsoft Research, Redmond, WA, June 2019
2. Cheon, J.H., Han, K., Kim, A., Kim, M., Song, Y.: A full RNS variant of approximate homomorphic encryption. In: Cid, C., Jacobson Jr., M. (eds.) SAC 2018. LNCS, vol. 11349, pp. 347–368. Springer, Cham (2019). https://doi.org/10.1007/978-3-030-10970-7_16
3. Melissa, C.: Security of homomorphic encryption. Technical report, HomomorphicEncryption.org, Redmond WA, USA (2017)
4. Occupancy detection data set. https://archive.ics.uci.edu/ml/datasets
5. Activity recognition with healthy older people using a batteryless wearable sensor data set. https://archive.ics.uci.edu/ml/datasets
6. Wall-following robot navigation data data set. https://archive.ics.uci.edu/ml/datasets
7. Eeg eye state data set. https://archive.ics.uci.edu/ml/datasets

Author Index

Printed in the United States
By Bookmasters